CHRISTIANS AND PAGANS

CHRISTIANS AND PAGANS

The Conversion of Britain from Alban to Bede

MALCOLM LAMBERT

YALE UNIVERSITY PRESS
NEW HAVEN AND LONDON

For information about this and other Yale University Press publications, please contact:
U.S. Office: sales.press@yale.edu   www.yalebooks.com
Europe Office: sales@yaleup.co.uk   www.yaleup.co.uk

Set in Minion and Columbus by IDSUK (DataConnection) Ltd
Printed in Great Britain by TJ International Ltd, Padstow Cornwall

Library of Congress Cataloging-in-Publication Data
Lambert, Malcolm (Malcolm D.)
   Christians and pagans : the conversion of Britain from Alban to Bede/Malcolm Lambert.
      p. cm.
   ISBN 978-0-300-11908-4 (cl : alk. paper)
   1. Great Britain—Church history—To 449. 2. Great Britain—Church history—
449-1066.   I. Title.
   BR748.L36 2010
   274.1'02—dc22
                                                                            2009052141

A catalogue record for this book is available from the British Library.

10 9 8 7 6 5 4 3 2 1

TO THE MEMORY OF
HUGH WILLIAMS
CHURCH HISTORIAN
1843–1911

Contents

	List of Illustrations	ix
	List of Maps	xi
	Acknowledgements	xii
	List of Abbreviations	xiii
	Introduction	xv
1	The Lost Church: Christianity in Roman Britain	1
2	British Christians and Germanic Pagans	44
3	The Fate of the British	79
4	The Irish Dimension: Palladius, Patrick and Columba	134
5	The Mission from Rome	164
6	Oswald and Oswiu	201
7	Conflict and Reconciliation: Wilfrid and Theodore	236
8	Christian Britain	277
	Index	302

Illustrations

Figures *page*

1 Drawing of Hinton St Mary floor mosaic. Courtesy of David Neal. 18
2 Plan of Roman temple and precinct, Lydney Park, Gloucestershire.
   Courtesy of the Society of Antiquaries of London. 33
3 The ogham alphabet. 85
4 Drawing of the Prittlewell burial chamber. Faith Vardy/Museum
   of London Archaeology. 184
5 Reconstruction drawing of royal palace complex, Yeavering,
   Northumberland, by Simon James. © The Trustees of the British
   Museum. 197
6 Genealogical table of the ruling houses of Northumbria. 202

Plates

1 Statue of Constantine, AD *c*.307–312, Palazzo dei Conservatori, Rome.
   German Archaeological Institute (photo: Koppermann, Neg. D-DAI-Rom
   1959.1716).
2 Hinton St Mary, detail of floor mosaic. © The Trustees of the British
   Museum.
3, 4 and 5 Water Newton treasure. © The Trustees of the British Museum.
6 Walesby lead tank, Lincolnshire. © The Collection: Art and Archaeology
   in Lincolnshire.
7 Reconstruction of frieze on the Walesby lead tank. Courtesy of Charles
   Thomas.
8 Vortipor stone. Carmarthenshire County Museum.
9 Latin-inscribed stone, Llanllywenfel. National Museum of Wales.
10 Standing stone from Fardel. © The Trustees of the British Museum.
11 Incised bone and bone pin, from Pool, Sanday. Orkney Library and
   Archive. © Orkney Islands Council.

12 Mains of Afforsk, near Kemnay, Aberdeenshire. © RCAHMS.

13 Reverse of cross-slab, Golspie, Sutherland. © RCAHMS.

14 Pictish cross-slab, Raasay House, Raasay. © RCAHMS.

15 Tailpiece illustration for Mark's gospel, from St Augustine's Gospels. The Masters and Fellows of Corpus Christi College, Cambridge (MS 286 f. 125r).

16 Finglesham man. Institute of Archaeology, University of Oxford.

17 Sutton Hoo helmet. © The Trustees of the British Museum.

18 Reverse of cross-slab, Aberlemno, Angus. © RCAHMS.

19 Front of cross-slab, Nigg, Ross & Cromarty. © RCAHMS.

20 and 21 St Andrews Sarcophagus. © Crown Copyright: RCAHMS.

22 Shrine of St Lachtin's Arm. National Museum of Ireland.

23 Symbol of St Matthew the Evangelist, introductory page to the Gospel of St Matthew in the Book of Durrow. © The Board of Trinity College Dublin (MS 57 f. 21v).

24 Lindisfarne Gospels, the Evangelist Matthew. © The British Library Board (MS Nero D.IV, f.25b).

25 Cross carpet page, Gospels of Chad, p.220. Used by permission of the Chapter of Lichfield Cathedral.

26 and 27 Franks Casket. © The Trustees of the British Museum.

28 Engraving of the Ruthwell Cross, by W. Penny after Henry Duncan, 'An account of the remarkable monument in the shape of a cross...', *Archaeologica Scotica* IV part 2, 1833, pl. XIII.

29 and 30 Ruthwell Cross, photographs of details from north and west sides. Copyright Department of Archaeology, Durham University, photographer T. Middlemass.

Maps

page

1 Anglo-Saxon cremations and burials (after H. Williams, 'Reminders of pagan Saxondom: the study of Anglo–Saxon cremation rites', S. Lucy, A. Reynolds eds *Burial in early medieval England and Wales* (London 2002), in Ch. 2; with special thanks to Howard Williams.   66

2 Solway Firth north shore (after P. Hill, *Whithorn and St Ninian* (Stroud 1997) fig. 1.7).   104

3 Irish settlements in Britain (after C. Thomas, *And shall these mute stones speak? Post-Roman inscriptions in western Britain* (Cardiff 1994) fig. 4.1).   112

4 Christian and secular power in northern Pictland (after M.O.H. Carver, 'An Iona of the east: the early medieval monastery at Portmahomack, Tarbat Ness', *MA* 48 (2004), fig. 3).   117

5 Ogham inscriptions in Scotland (after K. Forsyth, *The ogham inscriptions of Scotland: an edited corpus* (Harvard 1996), in ch. 3).   122

6 The kingdom of Dál Riata (after A. Woolf, 'Dál Riata', *KCC*, map 7).   151

7 Anglo-Saxon kingdoms (after N. Brooks, *Anglo-Saxon myths. State and Church 400–1066* (London, Rio Grande 2000) fig. 1).   219

8 Christian sites and foundations in Wales (after W. Davies, *Wales in the early middle ages* (Leicester 1982) fig. 49).   286

Acknowledgements

I am indebted to a number of scholars, to Dr C.E. Stancliffe for a survey of problems and the gift of her book on St Martin, Dr J.T. Koch for answering queries on Celtic Britain, Dr D. Petts for advice on fonts and votives in Roman Britain, Professor and Mrs Henderson for bibliography on hanging bowls, Dr J. Blair for information on Prittlewell, Dr M.C. Thomas re. Y chromosomes and ethnic survival, both Professor B. Yorke and Dr N.J. Higham for photocopies, Professor M.O.H. Carver for advice on Portmahomack, and Dr C. Lohmer for bibliographical help. I should also like to thank Mr Paul Webb for his invaluable technological help.

Many days were spent in the Reading Room of the National Library of Wales in Aberystwyth, unique among great libraries in its setting above the town, a view of Cardigan Bay below and a restaurant of quality in its basement. I am grateful to the library staff for their unfailing kindness. It has a copy of Hugh Williams's work on Christianity in early Britain dedicated to the Library by his widow, and to his memory I dedicate this book.

My greatest thanks are due to my wife. Together we have served more than the scriptural seven years on this book and it would never have been completed without her.

Abbreviations

Adomnán	R. Sharpe, *Adomnán of Iona: Life of St Columba* (Harmondsworth 1995); for translation, see below ch. 6 n. 29
AJ	*Antiquaries Journal*
Arch J	*Archaeological Journal*
ASAH	*Anglo-Saxon Studies in Archaeology and History*
ASE	*Anglo-Saxon England*
BAR	*British Archaeological Reports*
CA	*Church Archaeology*
CBA	*Council for British Archaeology*
CMCS	*Cambridge Medieval Celtic Studies*
ECMW	V.E. Nash-Williams, *Early Christian monuments of Wales* (Cardiff 1950)
EHR	*English Historical Review*
EME	*Early Medieval Europe*
FMS	*Frühmittelalterliche Studien*
Gildas	Gildas, *De excidio* in M. Winterbottom ed., *The Ruin of Britain and other works* (Chichester 2002)
HA	*Historia Abbatum* in D.H. Farmer, J.E. Webbs eds, *The Age of Bede* (Harmondsworth 1983); for translation see below ch. 6 n. 29
HB	*Historia Brittonum* in J. Morris ed. and trans., *Nennius. British history and the Welsh annals* (London, Chichester 1980)
HE	*Historia Ecclesiastica* in B. Colgrave, R.A.B. Mynors eds, *Bede's Ecclesiastical History of the English people* (Oxford 1969); for translation see below ch. 1 n. 10
IR	*Innes Review*

JBA	*Journal of the British Archaeological Association*
JEH	*Journal of Ecclesiastical History*
JMH	*Journal of Medieval History*
KCC	J.T. Koch ed., *Celtic culture: A historical encyclopaedia* (Santa Barbara, Denver, Oxford 2006)
LMA	*Lexikon des Mittelalters*
MA	*Medieval Archaeology*
NH	*Northern History*
NMS	*Nottingham Medieval Studies*
ODNB	*Oxford Dictionary of National Biography*
PBA	*Proceedings of the British Academy*
PP	*Past and Present*
SCH	*Studies in Church History*
SH	*Southern History*
SHR	*Scottish Historical Review*
TLS	*Times Literary Supplement*
TRHS	*Transactions of the Royal Historical Society*
VSC	*Vita Sancti Cuthberti*; for translation D.H. Farmer and J.E. Webb, *The age of Bede* (Harmondsworth 1983)
VW	*Vita Wilfridi* in B. Colgrave ed., *The Life of bishop Wilfrid by Eddius Stephanus* (Cambridge 1927); for translation see below ch. 6 n. 29
WHR	*Welsh History Review*

Introduction

Two personal experiences decided me to write this history. One was a conversation with a Bristol University student from Northumbria, who confessed that for years he had cycled past Jarrow knowing nothing of Bede and his monastic community. He knew of the hunger marches but nothing of Jarrow's importance in seventh- and eighth-century England. The melancholy light this conversation cast on the eccentricities and deficiencies of modern education made me think it was well worth while to write an up-to-date account of how Christianity came to the island of Britain, how it spread and developed until the death of Bede in 735.

I believe the primary task of an historian is to tell, as far as he possibly can, what happened. The development of research in recent decades has made a narrative more possible than ever before and enabled the story to be told of how Christianity fared in every part of our island, Wales and Scotland as well as England.

My starting point lies in two works of great calibre and readability, Charles Thomas's *Christianity in Roman Britain* and Martin Henig's *Religion in Roman Britain*. In his genial clubman's style, Thomas has taught us not to overlook the vitality and achievement of our earliest Christians. It was a pioneer work by a natural polemist and for decades was the subject of criticism in a series of articles and reviews, sometimes justified in detail, by W.H.C. Frend and my first preoccupation was to see how far these criticisms should prevail. I conclude that on the whole they should not. Christianity was indeed more of a minority religion than Thomas allows, a strand among others right down to the departure of the legions, but it had an undoubted vitality which, in ways now better understood, enabled the surviving Christians in face of the onslaught of the pagan Germanic invaders to transplant their faith to the west and north and adapt their Church to the needs of simple rural societies only lightly touched by Christianity in the years of Roman occupation.

Christianity in Roman Britain used to be treated as a separate subject, the theory prevailing that the Romano-British Church had suffered too much and had such internal weaknesses that it came very near to extinction and a fresh Gaulish missionising was necessary to renew the faith among the British who survived in what is now Wales. Such a hypothesis enabled historians to leave aside the history of the Romano-British Church as a specialist enclave and take the arrival of Augustine and his Roman mission in 597 as a natural starting point, with some reference to evidence from tombstones of a Christian presence in the west and its Gaulish connection.

New work makes it feasible to write an outline narrative right through from the martyrdom of Alban (with a reference as a *jeu d'esprit* to the legend of Joseph of Arimathea, still living in popular mythology) to the achievements of the Northumbrian Renaissance and of seventh- and eighth-century monasticism in Anglo-Saxon England, the survival of British Christianity and its traditions and the emergence of the Pictish Church with its remarkable memorial stones. Appreciation of the research on Christianity in Celtic Britain, not always conveyed as it should be to English readers, was stimulated in my case by the great Reading Room in the National Library of Wales, where the walls in my time were lined with periodicals on Celtic history and literature from Wales and Scotland and where that pillar of English history writing and reviewing, the *English Historical Review* by contrast had to be separately ordered from the stacks. Aberystwyth has been a salutary corrective and I remain deeply impressed by the high calibre of much writing on early Wales, Scotland and Cornwall, grappling with difficult evidence. As editor and prime contributor to *Celtic culture: a historical encyclopaedia*, J.T. Koch has recently presented Celtic scholarship over a very wide field, including Brittany, both in history and literature and has even added a dimension to the problem of Arthur. His publication will aid the dissemination of scholarship in Celtic studies, too often hidden in specialist periodicals.

Martin Henig's work has not quite the same instinctive feel for early Christianity as Charles Thomas's, but he understands paganism and, better than anyone else, conveys the appeal which it had in Britain. I closed his book with a grasp which I had never had before of the sway this often illogical, highly flexible blend of ancient Celtic religion and the classical gods long held in the areas of Roman occupation. In a tour de force he introduces Christianity in a chapter entitled 'Mithraism and the other Eastern Religions'. This is exactly how Christian belief began to secure its position, as part of a widespread reaction against conventional classical religion and a turn to the East in the fourth century. Henig also recalls how, in the disturbances of the fifth and sixth centuries, Christianity achieved a leading role in Celtic kingdoms in contrast to its minority status in late Roman Britain, a very ill-recorded process but traceable in linguistic history and the memorials and tombs of the Welsh chieftains. Richard Sharpe has demonstrated that, just like other contemporary Churches, the old Romano-British Church was influenced by the development of the cult of saints and martyrs. Our knowledge of them has been enfeebled by the catastrophic effect of the barbarian invasions on all records, but enough survives to hint at the veneration of saints other than Alban and the cultivation of their cults in the Churches of the west and north of post-Roman Britain. He and others have also shown that, though the Churches of the west mostly failed even to attempt to bring the faith to the barbarian conquerors, they were nevertheless active as missionaries and monastic founders both in southern Scotland and pagan Ireland.

Patrick is far from being the only personality from the British Church to have had an effect on Ireland. Its work there was handsomely repaid in the Irish foundation of Iona, which played so vital a role in the conversion and cultural life of Anglo-Saxon England. The chapters below on Oswald and Oswiu, Wilfrid and Theodore and Christian Britain recount this happening.

The history of Scotland and the Picts has been allocated as much space as possible. The Pictish language, known only in a very few fragments, has been demonstrated to be related to that of other Celtic peoples in Britain and Ireland and not to have been imported from the non-Indo-European family of languages. Through analysis and classification of Pictish stones, their symbols and inscriptions over many years, G. and I. Henderson and colleagues tell us about the impact of Christianity on Pictish art and the emergence and achievements of some of the finest sculptors of the British Isles, while Katharine Forsyth has illuminated the use of oghams on the stones. Even a flickering light has now been thrown on the downfall of Pictish power in the ninth and tenth centuries. An outline of Christian Pictish history is at last possible and is given below in the chapter on the fate of the British, the account of Columba and the last chapter.

My second experience was a reading of an eloquent passage in R.I. Moore's introduction to his classic *The origins of European dissent*, first published in 1977, where he expresses doubts about our knowledge of the response of the peasant to the preaching of Christianity. In Bede he sees a brilliant expounder of the way in which the faith was disseminated to kings 'who in turn commanded their people' and the way in which bishops made themselves useful in the councils of their patrons, offering Rome's techniques for organisation and government of stable societies to those in the course of transition from nomad warriors. But beyond that the deepest reasons for the rise of Christianity, he writes, 'are obscure' and he goes on to note that though we can have a good guess, so to say, about the numbers and organisation of the priests who carried the message to the peasants, we cannot answer more crucial questions.

> Why the peasant listened to them and what their message meant; when he disentangled his reverence for the new God from his observance to the old; when, how and even whether Christianity became the consolation of the simple in their misery, the source and frame of all their thoughts as the familiar picture of the age of faith would have us believe – these are questions which we scarcely dare ask, to which there is not a fragment of first hand evidence that permits the attempt to answer.[1]

These words echoed in my mind and led me to ask myself whether an examination both more detailed and more extended of the conversion process would lead me to the same conclusions.

'First hand evidence' from an illiterate mass of small farmers would admittedly not be available but, as I got into the subject, it seemed to me that the thoughts and aspirations of the many did leave an impress on the sources, especially archaeology, fruit of much extended research since 1977, and gave clues on reasons for the acceptance of Christianity more widely in society. A trail of evidence bears witness to the participation of the poor and shows at all levels a commitment to Christian belief. In Roman Britain there is the evidence in burial sites, as in the shabby old piece of Samian ware at Canterbury with a chi-rho scratched on its base. Water Newton's silver vessels, though product of a more well-to-do congregation, nonetheless show the

---

[1] R.I. Moore, *The origins of European dissent* (2nd edn Oxford 1983) 4–5

existence of a worshipping community, in being for a long time judging by the improvised repair to one of their vessels, its adherents taking the trouble to record their gifts on the face of the communion vessels, quite evidently not receiving the silver from some wealthy benefactor, but commissioning it themselves and burying it all in the expectation that it could one day be recovered and used again. This is grass-roots religion in action.

Burial goods, whether Christian or pagan, embracing the whole period from Roman Britain to Anglo-Saxon England, carry the marks of the hopes and aspirations for an afterlife for the beloved dead, whether these goods be hobnailed boots for the last journey in Celtic paganism, shoulders of meat for the Anglo-Saxon, toys for the children, amulets, crystal balls or girdlehangers for the housewife, or the cautious have-it-both-ways of the newly converted, combining the old and new symbols of Anglo-Saxon faith. The widespread diffusion of place-names incorporating heathen gods or worship sites – remarkably wide if one considers the massive erosion of Germanic place-names by subsequent changes of language and settlement – bears witness to the faith in his gods of many a small farmer as a means of achieving health, good harvests and an afterlife.

One system of belief in the supernatural confronted another. I concur with Moore's reference to 'the simple in their misery' and accept Bryan Ward-Perkins's strenuous rejection of the views of those who give an unduly bland account of life in an epoch given to warfare, tyranny and suffering under the precarious conditions of subsistence farming. But Christianity brought consolation to these troubled lives; shrines replaced temples and Michael Lapidge indicates the involvement of ordinary people in his description of the stench of sickness, the cries of pain and the screams of the mentally afflicted who sought healing through the intercession of saints and the veneration of their relics. Oswald's cult indeed began at grass roots with miracles first experienced by people of low status. It could be said that one form of folk magic had been replaced by another – but there is a difference. Christian folk magic was accompanied by prayer and associated with holy lives, the veneration of saints, who were examples to be imitated. It involved individual choice and commitment in contrast to the kin-based propitiation religion of Anglo-Saxon paganism and was, moreover, associated with the words of Jesus requiring compassion and aid for those in need, irrespective of rank.

When Wilfrid went to convert heathen Sussex, he taught his hearers about the place of humanity in the whole history of the world from the Creation to the Second Coming, the Judgment and the fate of the blessed and the damned. In this, all missionaries had a major advantage over the frail, shadowy picture of the pagan afterlife or the mead-hall Valhalla of dead warriors. The struggle between Christian monotheism and heathen polytheism indeed lasted over generations and was far from complete at the time of Theodore of Tarsus's Penitential, but the appeal of the scriptural vision of heaven and hell had a potency then which is commonly underestimated now and had its effect on the minds and hearts of the poor just as much as on the magnates.

CHAPTER 1

The Lost Church

CHRISTIANITY IN ROMAN BRITAIN

No one will ever know who first brought Christianity to the Roman colony of Britain. By contrast, a late medieval pilgrim would have had no doubt about it at all. He would without question have believed that St Philip sent twelve of his disciples to Britain, appointing as their leader 'his very dear friend Joseph of Arimathea'. They gained the goodwill of a barbarian king and were granted an island to live on in 'a place surrounded by woods, bramble bushes and marshes', subsequently building a church in honour of Mary, the lower part of its wall being made of twisted wattle. This was Glastonbury. The story emanated from the monks facing a long fundraising crisis and in the end made the fortunes of a monastery that had fallen on evil days, neglected by visitors after the Norman Conquest when Anglo-Saxons were out of favour. In 1129 the historian William of Malmesbury had been commissioned to write a life of their most famous abbot, St Dunstan, and to assert against detractors the antiquity of the monastery, which they believed to have been founded well before his time. William visited Glastonbury and saw there both an early wattle church and another dating back to Ine, a seventh-century Anglo-Saxon king of Wessex: the former was destroyed in the great fire of 1184 but traces of the other have been revealed by modern excavation within the precincts of Glastonbury. An ancient cemetery indicates there may well have been a Celtic monastery on the site before Ine's day: but there is no good evidence of a Roman or sub-Roman occupation. Behind the evidence of the wattle church and the archaeology, all is mist, romance and a monastic community seeking to recover prestige and pilgrims.[1] The Glastonbury monks embellished William's history in the

---

[1] J. Scott, *The early history of Glastonbury* (Woodbridge 1981) 45; A. Gransden, 'The growth of Glastonbury traditions and legends in the twelfth century', *JEH* 27 (1976) 337–58

thirteenth century by introducing the notion that Joseph of Arimathea was the true founder of their monastery, based on the general assumption that, as Christ sent out His apostles to preach, every national Church must have an apostle as its missionary: Joseph was, so to say, an honorary apostle. It was a medieval legend: in Denis Bethell's words, 'a resounding imposture'.[2]

All that one can say is that it is not impossible that the coast below Glastonbury was the point where the first Christian stepped ashore on British soil, because there were ancient trade links with the Mediterranean in this area. Who that first Christian was, missionary or trader, will always be hidden from us: a living tradition of the first coming of Christianity has gone beyond recall, lost in the harsh conditions of invasion by pagans in the fifth and sixth centuries, in which the old British Church of the Roman epoch under grave pressure lost its coherence and an understanding of the past. Documentary evidence for the Church's life and history is scanty and flawed and never likely to increase; the growth point is archaeology, where new and intriguing discoveries are made, to be incorporated in the outline reconstruction of early Christian history, still wavering and uncertain but nonetheless gaining in conviction as old theories are discarded and a better understanding is reached of the forces which played on the Romano-British and underpinned Christianity, emperor worship, indigenous Celtic paganism and imported Eastern cults.

When in AD 43 the emperor Claudius sent his legions to conquer Britain in pursuit of glory to bolster his initial precarious rule and to foster Roman belief in their god-given right to govern, his troops baulked at crossing the Channel. An inspired exhortation by a freed slave moved the troops; just as in the annual Saturnalia, the lowest in society taking command, the humour of the situation broke though their sullen fear and turned it to laughter. They crossed, attacked and prevailed.[3]

Though the legionaries' sentiment that Britain lay at the edge of the world lasted throughout the history of the colony, nevertheless it became a colony of some distinction. It had a strong military presence: indeed at one time as much as one-tenth of the professional forces of the Empire were stationed in Britain, and across the Solway–Tyne line the emperor Hadrian initiated the building of a frontier barrier more elaborate than anything to be found elsewhere in the Empire. London became a major port and the post of governor

---

[2] D. Bethell, 'The making of a twelfth century relic collection', *SCH* 8 (1972) 61–72 at 72
[3] T.W. Potter, 'The transformation of Britain: from 55 BC to AD 61', P. Salway ed., *The Roman era* (Oxford 2002) 11–36 at 25. The ex-slave was Narcissus, secretary to Claudius; see also ibid. 222

of the province carried prestige; at the temple of Sul-Minerva in Bath, Britain possessed one of the major healing centres this side of the Alps. In other words, although at the limits of the Empire, Britain was far from being a run-down, scarcely viable colony.

Despite the bitterness of the fighting in the course of conquest, the cruelty of some of the Roman leaders and the trauma of Boudicca's revolt, tribal notables soon came to be incorporated into the Roman way of life, encouraged by the development of towns, the building of temple, forum, basilica and bathhouse, notably under the Flavian emperors, and themselves building villas in the style of the Roman country house. Romans had a strong feeling for the guardian spirits of a locality and their easy polytheism enabled the indigenous inhabitants to blend the cult of their own gods with that of the Roman pantheon. The cult of the emperor, the ceremonies of classical religion and imperial rites practised in army installations acted as a cement to the Empire; loyalty to the state was widely accepted even when it was damaged by the follies of individual emperors.

A substantial number of British notables were aware of the advantages of Roman culture and formed a natural ground for the dissemination of Roman ideas, concepts of rule, language, art and literature. With their history of trading contacts with the continent, the tribes of the south accepted Romanisation more easily than those in the north and west, where the Roman military presence was much more manifest, and it is in the south that its outward signs, the temples and villas, were built.[4]

It has become clear that Britain should not be regarded as one of the less successful, more marginal provinces of the Empire. Admittedly, for many in the countryside, life was little changed – but this would have been the case in many parts of the Empire. In Britain, an elite culture evolved among the indigenous leadership which was genuinely Romano-British with an interaction between the local and provincial and the influences which came across the Channel. Christianity emerged openly into the light of day as a strand within that culture towards the end of the Roman occupation in the fourth century after Constantine's revolutionary decision to give it legitimacy. It had its supporters among both rich and poor and its own distinctive Romano-British characteristics.

[4] See line of argument in M. Henig, *The heirs of King Verica. Culture and politics in Roman Britain* (Stroud 2002) inc. imaginary conversations, reviewed by M. Millet, *Antiquity* 76 (2002) 1145–6; A. Sargent, 'The north–south divide revisited: thoughts on the character of Roman Britain', *Britannia* 33 (2002) 219–26

The indications are that Christianity came late to the province.[5] Clearly there was a Christian presence at some time in the third century, the time of the British martyrs, but all other details are lacking. The movement of merchants, the posting of soldiers and officers and their wives, the trade routes which opened paths to missionaries are likely to have brought in either families or individuals of the faith. However, in the earlier centuries no communities were founded which have left a datable imprint in our sources.

Irenaeus, Christian polemicist and bishop of Lyons from AD 178 to 200, joyfully listing the lands where Christian communities were to be found, fails to mention Britain; Gaul had its churches in his time, Britain probably not. Tertullian, the first major Latin theologian writing from Carthage c.200 in his *Adversus Judaeos*, rejoiced in a rhetorical phrase that Christianity had reached 'the haunts of the Britons – inaccessible to the Romans, but subjugated to Christ',[6] a reference which may not be based on any precise knowledge. A little later, the Alexandrian theologian Origen is no better witness when, celebrating the successful expansion of Christianity, he mentions Britain, seeing it, it appears, symbolically as an end point in the known world. There is no certainty to be gained from these authors about the beginnings of the Christian Church in Britain: no living tradition remained. Certainly, knowledge of the missionaries who brought Christianity and even of their own native saints disappeared. Nevertheless, like other Churches, the Romano-British Church had its martyrs, celebrated their memory, venerated their remains and revered the places where they suffered.

The unwillingness of Christians to participate in pagan worship and to accept, for example, that a pinch of incense for the imperial cult was no unreasonable requirement from authority, was widely misunderstood in the Empire and thought to be a sign of disloyalty, a refusal which could bring down the wrath of the gods on the heads of all and endanger the general welfare. Christians were a suspect minority in the centuries before Constantine, subject periodically to slanderous attacks, blamed for natural disasters and exposed to episodes of persecution initiated by emperors concerned for the unity and welfare of the

---

[5] C. Thomas, *Christianity in Roman Britain to AD 500* (London 1981) 42–4. The classic survey, idiosyncratic, grippingly written with the quality of the lecture course in Truro cathedral which sparked off the book; corrections in D. Watts (below n. 6) and F. Mawer (below n. 74)
[6] D. Petts, *Christianity in Roman Britain* (Stroud 2003) 30, concise, workmanlike assessment with some original hypotheses; D. Watts, *Christians and pagans in Roman Britain* (London 1991); id., *Religion in late Roman Britain. Forces of change* (London 1998). Both contain precise analysis and are underestimated

Empire. There is no more terrible cry than the words 'Salvum lotum', 'Did you enjoy your bath', shouted from the crowd at the presbyter Saturus, covered in blood as he was killed for his faith in Carthage in 203.[7] The persecutions of Decius in 250 led to the execution of another presbyter, Pionius of Smyrna; public opinion thought he was mad. Christians, however, circulated stories of the sufferings and courage of these men and women; persecution might split Churches and lead to apostasies but in the long run the fate of the martyrs confirmed faith and won adherents. This was especially true of the Diocletian persecution in 303 and subsequent years, the most determined effort ever launched to eliminate Christianity in the Empire, involving not only anti-Christian propaganda but destruction of churches and the Scriptures, wholesale penalising of believers and, in some regions, execution of those who refused to sacrifice when commanded to do so. Christians had shown endurance, and paganism in the long run lacked the vitality to defeat Christian belief.

In 311 persecution was halted by the emperor Galerius; in 313 Constantine and Licinius issued the Edict of Milan proclaiming a general religious tolera-tion and requiring the return of confiscated Church property and buildings.[8] Persecution was at an end, but the tradition of martyrdom and the veneration of those who died for the faith remained a source of vitality in the Church. Their burial places attracted pilgrims to venerate their remains, churches were built to house their shrines and cemeteries grew up round them, outside cities in accord with Roman health regulations. The blood of those who suffered was collected, cloths and sponges being used to soak it up at the execution of St Cyprian, bishop of Carthage under Valerian. Such cloths, fragments of martyrs' bodies, dust from their shrines, all became relics to be treasured and preserved to heal and to protect from the hazards of life and death. The stories of the martyrs' valour confirmed the faith of generations of Christians.

Only one Passion of a British martyr survives, that of St Alban, which has reached us after being subjected to extravagant accretions.[9] At the heart of the story is the arrival of a Christian priest at a time of persecution, whom Alban

---

[7] G. Clark, *Christianity and Roman society* (Cambridge 2004) 38–59 at 43; reviewed by W.H.C. Frend, *EHR* 120 (2005) 811–12
[8] Petts, *Christianity* 36
[9] R. Sharpe, 'The late antique Passion of St Alban', M. Henig ed., *Alban and St Albans. Roman and medieval art and archaeology* (Leeds 2001); M. Henig, 'Religion and art in St Alban's city', ibid. 13–29; Gildas, 19–20; Morris's hypothesis on dating, Thomas, *Christianity* 49–50

sheltered from his persecutors. Moved by this man's unbroken activity of prayer and vigil, Alban received instruction and renounced his paganism. When the hiding place became known, Alban put on the priest's long cloak and surrendered himself in his stead. The judge questioned him, he declared himself a Christian and declined to make the required sacrifice. He was condemned to be flogged but, still remaining resolute in defiance, was sentenced to death and taken out to a hill above the town. There on 22 June in an unknown year he was killed. His contact with the priest had been too short for him to receive baptism; his was what early Christians referred to as a baptism of blood.

There is nothing incredible in this story. It seems that Alban had no knowledge of Christianity before this meeting, which makes it more likely that his execution took place in one of the earlier persecutions in the Empire of the third century, before the reign of Diocletian. The early date of 209, which John Morris based on his reading of the Turin version of Alban's *Passio*, has been discredited; a more likely dating is during the persecutions of Decius, emperor from 249 to 251, or Valerian, 253–59/60.

Gildas, the sixth-century monastic writer and polemicist whose work *De excidio Britanniae* (On the Ruin of Britain), despite its grave omissions and inadequacies, is *faute de mieux* the major literary source for events and attitudes in the Britain of his day, knew very little about Roman Britain. His work demonstrates the degree to which a living tradition of Christian history in the island had crumbled in the century or so since the link with Rome was snapped in 410. For example, the *De excidio* conveys the extraordinary view that Christianity reached Britain in the last years of the emperor Tiberius and, most improbable of all, that Tiberius himself was a supporter of Christianity. Yet, little as Gildas knew of the Christian past of his own country, he had at least a fragmentary awareness of a Church's most precious possession at that epoch, its martyrs. It is generally agreed that he had in front of him a copy of the *Passio*, which he summarises with some of its accretions. He says that Alban was of Verulamium, the Roman *municipium* on Watling Street, a first staging post from London, from which medieval and modern St Albans developed, and tells a story of Alban opening a new way across the river Thames, a miracle like Moses at the Red Sea, which convinced Alban's first executioner to accept Christianity and himself suffer martyrdom.

More details from the *Passio* are found in the *Ecclesiastical history of the English people* by the Northumbrian monk of the eighth century, Bede, the finest of all early medieval historical works.[10] Bede's information on Christianity in Roman Britain was overwhelmingly derived from Gildas, sometimes verbatim. He gives a firm identification of Verulamium as the site of Alban's interrogation and execution and tells us that a beautiful church had been erected there, that pilgrims came to it, with miracles occurring at Alban's tomb. Little affected by pagan Germanic invasion, Verulamium long lay in a British enclave, a chance which preserved Alban's *martyrium* and provides a unique case of a Christian centre of worship lasting on from the Roman epoch into the Anglo-Saxon age.

More of the accretions in the *Passio* are retailed by Bede: when Alban crosses the river Ver and walks up the hill to his execution, a spring appears at his feet. When a second executioner was found to carry out the duties refused by the first one, he is punished by his eyes dropping out. The martyrdom story had been handed on over generations and these accretions might well be influenced by the preoccupation with the head in Celtic legend or by the curse tablets of Roman paganism begging a god to avenge the petitioner on his enemy by causing him to lose his eyes. However, topography confirms the authenticity of the core story; it all fits Verulamium, the river Ver, a tributary of the Thames, the hill outside the Roman town on whose slopes the medieval abbey now lies and the 'gay mantle of many kinds of flowers'[11] which Bede says decked the hill as Alban walked up, fits the June date.

It has been reasonably conjectured that the site of the church of which Bede writes now lies under the medieval abbey church. Excavations led by Martin Biddle have revealed a Romano-British cemetery lying under the south cloister, which is what one would expect.[12] A martyrdom takes place, the death is remembered and celebrated; there are visitors to the sacred site and the area nearby becomes a popular place for burial, where the benign influence of the saint remains. St Albans follows the customary continental pattern of cemetery churches commemorating a martyr and attracting Christian burials. It could well be that only the failure of transmission of

---

[10] *HE* I 7; C. Plummer ed., *Historia ecclesiastica gentis Anglorum* in *Baedae Venerabilis opera historica* 2 vols (Oxford 1896) I 18–22; B. Colgrave, R.A.B. Mynors eds, *Bede's ecclesiastical history of the English people* (Oxford 1969); L. Sherley-Price trans., *A History of the English Church and people* (2nd edn Harmondsworth 1968) 44–7; see also J.M. Wallace-Hadrill, *Bede's Ecclesiastical History of the English people: a historical commentary* (Oxford 1988); except where stated, quotations from Colgrave and Mynors

[11] *HE* I 7 Sherley-Price trans.

[12] M. Biddle and B. Kjolby, 'The origins of St Albans Abbey: Romano-British cemetery and Anglo-Saxon monastery', Henig, *Alban* 45–77

information from the Romano-British Church to its successors has obscured this process in Britain.[13] There are examples of cemeteries with apparent Christian burials, orientated west–east, ranged round central burial sites of some prominence: we have no names but they may well have been the last resting places of bishops, holy men and, perhaps, of influential men and women or of other martyrs whose names are lost to us.

By the fifth century, Alban had become a saint of international renown with continental churches dedicated to him. Germanus, bishop of Auxerre, made a major pilgrimage to venerate his relics and it is a good working hypothesis that the *Passio* of Alban which we have derives from placards set up by Germanus around his cathedral in Auxerre on his return from Britain, having carried back with him soil impregnated with the martyr's blood.[14]

Although the siting in Verulamium is put beyond reasonable doubt by its topography and the witness of Gildas and Bede, archaeological evidence for a Christian presence in the town is remarkably thin. Three possible sites for Christian churches have been suggested, none very convincing, and there are no small Christian finds. Outside the town on Oysterfield Hill stood a Romano-Celtic temple with a precinct, baths and a processional way leading to another temple within the town, while on its lower slopes lay votive pits with some evidence of a head or skull cult. The higher temple seems to have attracted visitors for centuries, only fading out in the first quarter of the fifth century, the lower one and a theatre seem to have been in use even longer. There is no sign that the old gods were dethroned by the cult of Alban in conservative Verulamium. Interestingly, however, house decorations show a certain concern with salvation, rebirth and the afterlife, which could have provided a fruitful background for Alban's cult.

Martin Henig speculates that the real Alban and his guest might have been victims of Constantius Chlorus's revenge on supporters of the usurpation of Allectus in the late third century and that a Christian cult was superimposed on what was initially a purely political event; there is no evidence to support

---

[13] Gildas, 105–30; R. Sharpe, 'Martyrs and local saints in late antique Britain', A. Thacker, R. Sharpe eds, *Local saints and local churches in the early medieval west* (Oxford 2002) 75–154, decisive for understanding the transition from Roman to post-Roman Britain and the contribution of the British Church: analysis of Thomas's and Frend's standpoints 94–102. Frend right to think Thomas overestimates the Church's strength but his long-held thesis that it was a 'failed' Church, unable to convert because of internal weakness, I believe to be mistaken; for an example of his work, below n. 64
[14] Sharpe, 'Martyrs' 114–17

this musing and no reason to think that, as Henig suggests, there was absence of persecution or shortage of martyrs in Britain.[15]

Gildas's introduction of the British martyrs follows on his description of Diocletian's persecution, and runs

> God therefore increased his pity for us . . . As a free gift to us, in the time (as I conjecture) of this same persecution, he acted to save Britain being plunged deep in the thick darkness of black night; for he lit for us the brilliant lamps of holy martyrs. Their graves and the places where they suffered would now have the greatest effect in instilling the blaze of divine charity in the minds of beholders, were it not that our citizens, thanks to our sins, have been deprived of many of them by the unhappy partition with the barbarians [i.e. the Germanic invaders]. I refer to St Alban of Verulam, Aaron and Julius, citizens of Caerleon and the others of both sexes who, in different places, displayed the highest spirit in the battle-line of Christ.[16]

Gildas's timing was faulty: terrible as the Diocletian persecution was in the Empire as a whole, it had little effect in Britain as Constantius Chlorus, Constantine's father, who was responsible for carrying it out in Britain, Gaul and Spain, seems to have done very little but close some churches.

Caerleon was a legionary fortress, occupied for many years by the Legio II Augusta; after a period of activity under Septimius Severus and Caracalla, the garrison diminished with most of the legion employed elsewhere till, in the time of Carausius and Allectus, the fortress was abandoned and the buildings demolished. Aaron and Julius is an odd combination of names: mention together implies they were executed together. There are several Juliuses on legionary epitaphs in Caerleon; it was a common name among soldiers, both because of family descent and because of the practice of enlisted men adopting the name of one of the greatest of all Roman commanders, perhaps in the hope that his military virtue might descend upon them. On the other hand, Aaron is very rare and an invented account would have been unlikely to associate a common military name with a very uncommon one; it might have been adopted at conversion, substituting for an unwanted pagan name that of the first high priest of Israel.

Although the martyrs could have been drawn from the supporting civilian population necessary for a legionary fortress, they are more likely to have been

---

[15] Henig, 'Religion and art', id., *Alban* 25; R.N. Niblett, 'Why Verulamium', ibid. 1–12
[16] Gildas, ch. 10 p. 19

soldier-martyrs, a category well known in the history of Roman Christianity. There were cases where, gripped by Christianity, soldiers repudiated their oath to the emperor, rejecting the classical gods and making an open act of defiance; they were sentenced to death not for their Christianity but for breach of discipline. So the centurion Marcellus at Leon in Spain in 298 at a banquet in honour of the emperor's birthday, jumped up from his seat, threw down his military belt and insignia and shouted out that he was a soldier of Jesus Christ and would no longer serve the emperors: his comrades, probably thinking he was drunk, carried him out of the room, but the case could not be hushed up and he was sentenced to death for breach of discipline and repudiation of his oath.

Aaron and Julius must have suffered their fate before the abandonment of the Caerleon fortress in the late third century; like Alban, they could have been victims of the empire-wide persecutions of Decius and Valerian in mid-century, or of a provincial governor or legionary commandant to whom he had delegated his powers. Usual procedure would have had the condemned taken out by the rear gate of the fortress and beheaded in the ditch outside, sympathisers being free to rescue the bodies and give them burial. How soon the development of a cult and the erection of a shrine would follow rested on local circumstances, the hostile pressure of anti-Christian elements, or, on the other side, the efficacy of prayers to the martyr, visions and miracles. Aaron and Julius had their *martyrium* above a Roman cemetery on the hillside opposite Caerleon; a ninth-century charter in the *Book of Llandaff* refers to the 'land of the holy martyrs Aaron and Julius'; a sculptured cross-slab from the same century probably emanated from this commemorative chapel, subsequently used as a barn and now vanished, on a site known as Mount St Alban. Both Caerleon and Verulamium in its British enclave lay outside the domination of the Germanic invaders of Gildas's day and traditions about martyrs there were not so readily lost; further to the east, where the Anglo-Saxons held sway, this was not the case.[17]

Nonetheless, two names from these regions can be added to Gildas's list: first, Augurius, bishop of London, plus eight others not named but alluded to in the same martyrology; it is reasonable to suppose they were his adherents from the same diocese, a group witnessed to in an awkward, corrupt text. London was the capital of Roman Britain; it would have been quite natural for it to have been the first see founded and its holder would have been a

---

[17] J.K. Knight, 'Britain's other martyrs: Julius, Aaron and Alban at Caerleon', Henig, *Alban* 38–44; W. Davies, *The Llandaff Charters* (Aberystwyth 1979) 121

natural target, very likely to have carried with him a heroic nucleus of non-compromisers. The second is St Sixtus, still venerated by a group of British Christians in the sixth century who came out of the shadows to seek advice about their lost saint from St Augustine in Canterbury. It is apparent from the text of Gregory the Great's reply to Augustine's questions that they did not know the circumstances of Sixtus's suffering or of miracles wrought by his intercession: they had evidently lost their records and probably their priests and clung only to the name of their martyr. Augustine assumed they were not venerating an authentic saint at all – he seems not to have considered that those Christians could have had a martyr saint of their own in the perse-cutions suffered by the Romano-British Church. Gregory agreed that they should be sent relics from the catacombs of the second-century martyr pope, Sixtus II. There was a pastoral concern for those British denied the benefits of the intercessions of a 'real' saint and a will to help them with an authentic one, but there was no understanding of their situation. Gregory advised Augustine to block access to the Romano-British cult site in any way he could and enshrine the 'true' relics elsewhere away from it. It is a vivid illustration of the way in which, under the harsh pressures of invasion and alien rule, the old British Church forfeited knowledge of its heroic past.[18]

One other documentary source for the Romano-British Church consists in the records of international councils at which British bishops were present. In 314, the year after the Edict of Milan, Constantine summoned a Council at Arles; to it came three bishops, one from York, one from London and a third from what is described as 'Colonia Londiniensium', either Colchester or Lincoln, most likely Lincoln, and two others described as 'Sacerdos presbyter' and 'Arminius diaconus'. The first three are clear enough – the bishops came from three of the four provinces into which Britain was now divided, London being the capital of Maxima Caesariensis, York, probably of Flavia Caesariensis, Lincoln of Britannia Secunda. This looks like a party of bishops occupying the role of metropolitans, overseeing the Christians in the four major divisions set up in the colony by the ruling administration. It does not preclude the existence of other bishops based in, or taking their titles from, some of the *civitates* of Britain, who were not sent to represent the British Church at the Council. We know that there were other bishops at some time

[18] Sharpe, 'Martyrs' 118–25; C.E. Stancliffe, 'The British Church and the mission of St Augustine', R.G. Gameson ed., *Augustine and the conversion of England* (Stroud 1999) 107–51 at 121–2

in British history – the Risley Park *lanx*, a silver dish discovered in the eighteenth century, has a text referring to a bishop Exuperius as donor and a lead salt pan from Cheshire has a reference to a bishop otherwise unknown.[19]

But there is no certainty here. On one interpretation, the named three led an episcopate which within the second half of the century may well have risen to double figures; on another, more cautious judgement, the British Church was still a small body with few bishops, which was emerging from the shadows of decades of semi-licit existence with a leadership both small and inexperienced in a Church newly organised, 'perhaps', it has been suggested, 'by imperial command'.[20]

The fourth element in the delegation is an oddity: are 'sacerdos' and 'presbyter' to be taken as synonyms? Is the text faulty? Or should we postulate that these non-episcopal representatives were stand-ins while their bishopric was temporarily vacant? To complete the pattern, they should be stand-ins for the bishop of the fourth province, Britannia Prima, whose capital is likely to have been Cirencester. One thing is certain – in 314, with its memories of its martyrs and its persecutions behind it, the British Church has an independent existence with its own representation at an international council. Sulpicius Severus, the biographer of St Martin of Tours and a passionate advocate of poverty, tells us of a British delegation at the Council of Rimini (Ariminium) in 359, where three bishops ('tres tantum ex Britannia') distinguished themselves as exceptions because they alone took up the emperor's offer of hospitality and use of the state postal system.[21]

Towards the end of the fourth century, the archbishop Victricius of Rouen was asked to come to Britain to settle a conflict among bishops. 'My brothers in the priesthood', he said, 'called on me to make peace there.'[22] A dispute which could not be reconciled within the British episcopate is not per se an advertisement for the Church, though it may show theological liveliness, but there is an implication that the number of bishops by the end of the fourth century was not so meagre.

These fragmentary stories of martyrs and statistical records about bishops are practically all the documentary evidence we have for the Romano-British Church. Beyond this lies the mute evidence uncovered over recent centuries

---

[19] Petts, *Christianity* 36, 38–9
[20] P. Salway, *The Oxford illustrated history of Roman Britain* (Oxford 1993) 517; see also his *Roman Britain* (Oxford 1981)
[21] Petts, *Christianity* 42
[22] Ibid. 46

by the spade, starting with the stray discoveries of antiquarians, gathering way with Victorian archaeologists, then in the twentieth century given impetus by the historical work of Hugh Williams. The arrival after his day of a fully scientific archaeology has scored striking successes in excavation and interpretation and has patiently examined a multitude of cemeteries and building foundations. This work is gradually illuminating the relationship between a rising Christianity and the paganism which obstinately refused to let itself be strangled by new beliefs, as well as lesser-known mystery cults from the East.[23]

The overwhelming body of datable materials evidencing Christianity comes from the fourth century onwards. The edict of toleration and the pattern of acceptance of Christianity under successive emperors created an atmosphere helpful to the spread of belief. Although there were hiatuses, notably the pagan revival sponsored by the short-lived emperor Julian the Apostate, the general trend was favourable. There is evidence of men in high authority in Britain being Christians and as numbers increased, effective pagan action grew less likely; by the end of the century the emperor Theodosius had forbidden the practice of paganism across the Empire. In contrast to the pre-Constantine epoch, imperial favour might well blur the position of Christianity and draw in self-seeking adherents; it also confused the relationship between Church and State in ways not always helpful to the former. The chi-rho, the first two Greek letters of 'Christ', was the emblem that Constantine in a vision was told his soldiers should carry on their shields before his crucial victory at Milvian Bridge and it became the emblem of the Empire as well as Christianity. Ingots from London carry it, a sign of imperial control of metal production; coins may carry it; a lead seal with a chi-rho cross from Silchester has the letters P C M for Provincia Maxima Caesariensis, the province in which Silchester lay, clearly implying a secular significance for the seal; belt-fittings, buckles and strap-ends manufactured in Britain, symbols of status in the field army or in the imperial administration, in some cases carried images of peacocks, Christian symbol of immortality.[24] The late Empire advertised Christianity. It also diluted it.

The ground for the expansion of Christianity was prepared by the popularity of imported Eastern cults which met a need for spiritual values

---

[23] H. Williams, *Christianity in early Britain* (Oxford 1912)
[24] F. Mawer, *Evidence for Christianity in Roman Britain. The small finds,* BAR Brit. ser. 243 (Oxford 1995) 59–65; Petts, *Christianity* 110–13

and care of the individual not adequately met by classical paganism. Mithraism attracted a select, high-calibre following in Britain through its mysterious, theatrical rites and the sense of rebirth it imparted, appealing especially to army officers and businessmen. At Carrawburgh, Housesteads and Rudchester on the northern frontier, the remains of mithraea bear witness to its appeal to disciplined men in the lonely circumstances of garrison duties, seeking salvation and companionship in a special society with a carefully guarded entry which required of its members exposure to ordeals and a long process of initiation marked by elaborate rituals. The remains of the mithraeum in Walbrook, London, indicate that wealthy men contributed generously to the temple and its sculptures. Adherents may well have originated in other parts of the Empire, officers posted there or businessmen attracted by trading opportunities, with native Romano-British participation somewhat limited. They were in any case a highly specialised group; numbers were small and women were denied entry altogether.[25]

The appeal of Mithraism is a straw in the wind. There are broad similarities to Christianity, the centre of Mithraist belief lying in the tauroctony, Mithras's sacrifice of the great bull created by Ormazd, from whose blood life sprang. Salvation through the sacrifice of a bull, salvation through the sacrifice of Christ on the cross – one may detect a broad affinity. On the other hand, in contrast to Mithraism, Christianity was not exclusive; it was open to all and consequently in the Empire at large had a special appeal to the poor and disadvantaged. Hostility between Mithraists and Christians was intense, dating back to the second-century work of Justin, who believed that demonic forces had created imitations of Christian rites to deceive mankind. All the Mithraic northern temples suffered attack at various times; at Carrawburgh there was a systematic attack on the sculptures of the shrine but altars were left undisturbed, perhaps because a commandant of Christian sympathies wished to eliminate obvious Mithraic imagery but was unwilling to destroy altars carrying dedications put up by officers in the past.[26]

The Walbrook mithraeum underwent a change of use. Cut off from the giant statue, the head of Mithras was buried and fragments of the sculpture scattered. This, it has been argued, was the iconoclastic work not of hostile Christians but of pagans of another allegiance, probably of Bacchus, who in the course of the

[25] M. Henig, *Religion in Roman Britain* (London 1984), sympathetic and imaginative reconstruction of appeal of paganism and change of outlook at coming of Eastern cults
[26] Petts, *Christianity* 168–9

fourth century took over, respectfully burying the statue's head. The old mithraeum was never destroyed; early in the fifth century the front, affected by shifting ground, came down and the temple area was modified, finally slipping into disrepair. Ruined walls and weed-grown spaces would have been all that confronted invading Anglo-Saxons in half-deserted Londinium.[27]

Though it sometimes may have amounted to no more than a convenient excuse for drinking parties, the cult of Bacchus nevertheless had a salvationist aspect and was another strand among the multifarious cults, often distinguished by a search for some inner spiritual reality and an escape from the discords and problems of the late Roman Empire. The cult of the mother goddesses Cybele and Atys, with their ecstatic rites and castration ceremonies, also had some following, to judge by the bronze castration clamp found in the Thames.[28]

Themes of death and resurrection, death of a god to save others, miraculous birth, ritual eating and drinking, moral codes, initiation rites and salvation through belief and ritual have resonances with Christianity and are likely to have prepared the way for its growth in the fourth century. In part at least, Christianity succeeded as a minority religion because it met needs the cults had once attempted to satisfy. It had the promise of salvation and the power of monotheism together with a firm administration and links via the episcopate to the continent in contrast to the disorderly individualism of both paganism and the mystery cults and their exclusivity. Christianity made no distinction of sex or wealth: entry was open to all and archaeological evidence, from expensive objects and mosaic floors to the evidence of poverty in cemeteries and churches, shows that it appealed to all classes. Paganism sought to protect and console its dead, with grave goods and aids for the journey to another world, but it was a shadowy, unsatisfactory place, a poor thing in comparison with earthly life; Christianity offered a much more confident and glorious afterlife to those who died in faith.

Some fourth-century villa owners, who had benefited from Diocletian's tax reforms favouring large-scale agricultural producers at the expense of small farmers,[29] demonstrated their Christian sympathies in the choice of themes for their mosaic pavements and, in the case of one house-church, murals. A

---

[27] J. Shepherd, *The Temple of Mithras* (London 1998) 227–9

[28] Henig, *Religion* 95–127

[29] Comment in P. Salway, 'Conclusion', id. ed., *The Roman era. The British Isles, 55 BC–AD 410* (Oxford 2002) 203–36 at 229–30; see also J. Hopkinson, 'Culture and social relations in the Roman province', ibid. 107–28

pavement on the site of a villa at Hinton St Mary in Dorset is the most remarkable of all. Short cross-walls divide a square, the largest of the sub-rooms,
from a rectangle, with an area of mosaic between. The rectangle is dominated
by a representation of Bellerophon on his horse slaying the Chimera, the
square by a roundel with a beardless man in tunica and pallium, flanked by
pomegranates, with a chi-rho behind his head and a hair style reminiscent of
that on the coinage of the emperor Constans (337–50). For some Christian
authorities, the Decalogue was still held to be a prohibition of human representation, yet, by general agreement, here we have a representation of Christ
and, moreover, Christ in a unique position, on a floor. It is one of the earliest
such representations with no hint of allegory, the key figure in the largest of
the mosaics: there are no imperial insignia, which makes identification with
Constantine unlikely. Pomegranates were symbols of immortality, the chi-rho
a major Christian symbol. It may be Christ as Pantocrator, with chi-rhos and
pomegranates together radiating out from his head like rays of the sun,
recalling the cult of Sol Invictus.[30]

Some have been inclined to see in the two rooms a house-church, catechumens being confined in the smaller area with the Bellerophon, perhaps
behind a curtain drawn back when the priest proceeded to celebrate the
sacred mysteries in the larger sub-room. On this interpretation initiates
would stand on the pavement on one side of the figure of Christ with priest
and altar on the other, the key cultural roundel exposed between them. But
the pavement forms part of the villa and appears to be the reception area for
visitors: a house-church would surely be in some way cut off from the main
building. The declaration of Christian adherence is nonetheless unmistakable.
Yet, although the Christ figure is central, the roundel itself is surrounded by
figures not overtly Christian, a tree, three scenes of a hound with stag or bird
and, in the quarter-circles, male busts, two with pomegranates, two with
rosettes, while in the surrounds of the Bellerophon are two lateral panels of
hunting scenes.

A pavement from a nearby villa at Frampton in west Dorset, known to us
only through drawings published in 1813, so resembles Hinton St Mary's as to
be undoubtedly a product of the same firm, also employed by a Christian

---

[30] For what follows, J.M.C. Toynbee, 'Pagan motifs and practices in Christian art and ritual
in Roman Britain', M. Barley, R.P.C. Hanson eds, *Christianity in Britain 300–700* (Leicester
1968) 177–92; J.M.C. Toynbee, *Art in Britain under the Romans* (Oxford 1964); comment in
Thomas, *Christianity* 104–6, 181–3; Sol Invictus, Petts, *Christianity* 36; but see the second-
century Neptune mosaic at Verulamium

owner. It would seem that he chose to place the chi-rho in a prominent position in the centre of a floral scroll at the entrance to the apse where he would stand to welcome his visitors. Within is a cantharus or chalice and around the central square of the mosaic from which the apse opens, dolphins. A mask of Neptune is at the square's edge with a Latin verse in his honour and a cupid is placed among the dolphins. In the centre of the smaller panel flanked by hunting scenes is Bacchus riding a panther. Its other pavements are adorned by various pagan figures, Oceanus, Neptune, Jupiter, Mars, Apollo and, again, hunting scenes.

In fact, although the prominence of the Christ figure with chi-rho and pomegranates at Hinton and the chi-rho at Frampton leaves no doubt of the Christian affiliation of both villa owners, the true significance of the great majority of the accompanying scenes, pagan or rustic, remains unclear. At Hinton St Mary, in addition to the Christ figure and the Bellerophon, there are a series of scenes not obviously connected to either. By the fourth century pagans had become accustomed to a non-literal interpretation of traditional myths and depictions of gods, seeing in the allegories and symbols real truths about life, morality and death, and, doubtless, so had Christians. Bellerophon could be taken as an allegory of the victory of good over evil or truth over error; Bacchus as a saviour god; Neptune and Oceanus with accompanying dolphins as symbolising the journey of the soul to paradise. More subtly, the intention may have been to convey to non-Christians that their own myths foreshadowed the great truths of Christianity, Bellerophon's courage, for example, being a foretaste of the heroism of Christ and His saints. On the other hand it could be that these wealthy men, imbued with the literature of the Roman world, enjoyed displaying their knowledge to visitors and took pleasure in commissioning a miscellany of myths, probably chosen from a pattern book with an eye to colour and ornamentation and no thought of particular religious significance.

A more far-reaching Christian interpretation has recently been propounded by Martin Henig, arguing that this whole mosaic area, including the Bellerophon roundel, forms a sustained visual commentary on Psalm 22 with the title, 'To the leader: according to the Deer of the Dawn. A Psalm of David'.[31] On this view, the title which in fact refers to the melody for the psalm, was taken

[31] M. Henig, 'Central roundel of floor mosaic, Hinton St Mary', E. Hartley *et al.* eds, *Constantine the Great. York's Roman emperor* (York 2006) 204–6 for Psalm 22 theory; R. Ling, 'Mosaics in Roman Britain: discoveries and research since 1945', *Britannia* 28 (1997) 259–95; for Gnostic interpretation of certain mosaics, D. Perring, *The Roman house in Britain* (London 2002)

Fig. 1 The mosaic at Hinton St Mary.

up by the mosaic's designer. Here, indeed, are stags or deer; here too, echoing verse 16, are dogs, 'For many dogs are come about me', and verse 20, 'Deliver my soul from the sword: my darling from the power of the dog'. In the hunting scene flanking the Bellerophon, the dogs run through trees; below the Christ figure is a panel, wholly occupied by a huge, spreading tree. Christians, it is said, would be reminded of the cross by the woodland trees, and of the Tree of Life by the great tree below. The interpretation of the psalm, it is stated, remains 'oblique' in the smaller mosaic dominated by Bellerophon and more explicit in the larger one dominated by the Christ roundel, culminating in the representation of the Tree of Life. The figure of Christ as ruler of all commands the eye; the male busts, with pomegranates or rosettes in the four corners, replace the representation of the seasons or the winds of a pagan mosaic and recall humanity subject to the power of Christ, as in the triumphant verse 28, 'For the kingdom is the Lord's; and he is governor among the people.'

In the Passion according to Mark and Matthew, Christ on the cross used the first verse of Psalm 22 when He cried out 'My God, my God, why hast Thou forsaken me?' There could be no more potent scriptural allusion for the mosaic designer than this psalm, which rises from despair to triumph. But did he intend through the roundels and lunettes to convey – to the initiate – both the suffering and triumph implicit in the psalm? The whole design is indeed a masterpiece of mosaic art in the quality of the scenes represented, but the arguments put forward for allusions to the psalm are ingenious rather than compelling. It attributes to the villa owner a 'highly sophisticated knowledge of the Bible';[32] yet he allowed his mosaicist to put an image of Christ on the floor of his villa where it could be trodden on, a very odd decision. The older view, a casual combination of the Christ roundel with a miscellany of allusions, myths and rustic scenes, still holds the field.

Mosaics touched by Christianity all have in common an attachment to the literature and mythology of the Mediterranean rather than to the gods and stories of the Celtic background of Britain: Romanisation within these households ran deep. A certain geographical concentration can be observed. Hinton St Mary and Frampton are in Dorset, as is the site of a villa in Fifield Neville where two gold rings with chi-rhos have been found. Not far away there was a substantially Christian cemetery at Poundbury. The mosaics may be dated c.325–c.340; the impression given is of a small nucleus of rich

[32] Henig, 'Central roundel' 206

families with Christian sympathies, who may well have given patronage and
aid to local families.

Further to the east at Lullingstone in the Darenth valley in Kent another
villa site has yielded an unambiguous Christian presence in the fourth century
with the one clear-cut case of a house-church.[33] The villa had a long history;
it was the centre of a substantial estate and was repeatedly renewed and
extended. Paganism had left its mark: a cult chamber had a triad of nymphs,
perhaps water sprites from the Darenth river. Two marble portrait busts of
the Hadrianic period from the east Mediterranean were placed on steps with
beakers in front of them, one holding a sheep's rib in his nymphaeum.
Circumstances would suggest that the pair, once centre points of an ancestral
cult, had been transferred to an obscure position below ground when a new
family took over, unwilling simply to destroy images of the dead who might
sustain the fortunes of the house or, if harshly used, damage it. Veneration
might, of course, have continued in some secrecy after the Constantinian
acceptance of Christianity.

In mid or late fourth century, a Christian was in charge and commissioned
wall paintings including a frieze of *orantes* with arms in the customary attitude of prayer, arrayed in richly coloured clothing. One stands in front of a
curtain or screen, often used as a symbol of death: here we may well have a
dead member of the family, not venerated as were those of an earlier generation represented by the busts in the cellar, but commemorated with other
members of the family in a Christian context. On the east side of the villa in
a complex of rooms which constituted the house-church blocked off from the
rest, the chi-rho sign of Christ's victory was depicted with an alpha and omega
on either flank. These letters of the beginning and end of the Greek alphabet
were well-established Christian symbols, recalling the verse from the Book of
Revelation I 8: 'I am Alpha and Omega, the beginning and the ending, saith
the Lord.' Impressive chi-rhos with surrounding wreaths, the Roman victory
symbol, were to be found on other walls.

The narthex, or entrance area, and the sanctuary seem to have been constituted by two main rooms, entered, after alterations had been made, only from
an outside door. Trouble had been taken in creating the place of worship from
a basement at the north end, which had formerly been used for the drying,
airing and bleaching of cloth. The villa fell on evil days but, even when it

---

[33] G.W. Meates, *The Roman villa at Lullingstone* (Maidstone I 1984, II 1987); review of II by
K.S. Painter, *Britannia* 21 (1990) 420–1

ceased to be inhabited, the use of the church went on for a time longer. The religious significance may well have outlived the catastrophic intervention of Germanic invaders in Kent: it is probably not chance that an Anglo-Saxon church was built athwart the early fourth-century pagan mausoleum which lay behind the villa.[34] On this site we have both the most unequivocal signs of Christian commitment together with classical scenes depicted in the mosaic of the main reception room – Europa the bull, Bellerophon and the Chimera. Clearly such classical myths were not felt to be incompatible with Christianity in the minds of this cultivated villa-owning class.

At one of the finest of Romano-British country houses, Chedworth in the Cotswolds, a Christian hand set about rededicating the nymphaeum, a reservoir in an octagonal basin fed by a natural spring on the hillside clearly once devoted to a water sprite, by putting Christian symbols on its stones. A chi-rho was carved on one stone supporting the nymphaeum; another, probably once part of the octagon, has no less than four Christian symbols. It looks as if that owner's Christianisation was not allowed to last, for a subsequent owner, doubtless a pagan who had no respect for his predecessor's beliefs, carelessly reused these stones.[35]

That the Church also had supporters who were not well off is shown by the simplicity and poverty of certain of the graves: some could not afford coffins. Although some of the examples cited by Charles Thomas as the work of poor or uneducated Christians, such as the roof tile at Wickford, supposedly incised with a Christian inscription for good fortune before firing, or the broken portion of a glass bottle from Catterick on which a chi-rho was alleged to have been scratched in such a manner that it could be seen by looking down the bottle, have not survived scrutiny, others remain. The chi-rho on a storage jar from Colchester is clearly authentic, as is another lightly incised on the base of a bowl of Oxfordshire ware from Kelvedon in Essex, a rho cross on a cooking jar from Exeter, and at Canterbury an old piece of chipped and repaired second-century Samian ware with a chi-rho scratched on it, which had been put into the grave of a poor Christian. Alpha and omega were used in some cases without understanding, omega being written upside down and the sequence of letters reversed. The Vyne ring from Silchester or its environs

---

[34] Tyler Bell, 'Churches on Roman buildings: Christian associations and Roman masonry in Anglo-Saxon England', *MA* 42 (1998) 1–18; on the working of cloth, W.H.C. Frend, *The archaeology of early Christianity. A history* (London 1996) 350
[35] Thomas, *Christianity* 219–20

was intended to be inscribed to a certain Senicianus, 'Senicianus vivas in Deo' ('Senicianus may you live in God'), but because the craftsman, no Latinist, put in an extra 'i' he was forced to leave out the final 'o' and the actual version reads 'Senicianus vivas iin De'. This is a long way from the high skills of Hinton St Mary and Frampton.[36]

Still, the Church was more than a fringe mission. It had the marks of a fully developed ecclesiastical organisation: it had an episcopate and remained in contact with the continent, as is shown by the call to Victricius, archbishop of Rouen, to adjudicate in an inner dispute. It is likely that the Church had an indigenous liturgy; certainly it possessed some of the earliest eucharistic vessels so far discovered in the epoch of Roman Christianity. Church plate buried in a field at Water Newton which in the late fourth or early fifth century lay within the walls of the Roman town, Durobrivae, a centre of the pottery industry near the modern town of Chesterton in Huntingdonshire and also close by a main Roman artery to the north, shows the existence of a Church with fine eucharistic vessels.[37] This congregation had an ornamented bowl in sheet silver that may have served as a hanging lamp, perhaps by the altar, and a set of seventeen votive plaques, with remains of others, all in silver plus one in gold, inscribed to a high standard with chi-rhos, alphas and omegas, names, dedications and – most interesting of all – a likely fragment of the text of the mass. A chalice carries the name Publianus, surely the donor, and together with two sets of chi-rho, alpha and omega, the words 'sanctum altare tuum domine subnixus honoro', a dactylic hexameter which can be translated, 'I, Publianus, humbly honour Thy holy altar, O Lord'.[38] 'Subnixus' is an uncommon word, with a sense of dependence on God, of humility or prostration before the altar – perhaps simply 'on bended knee' – all reminiscent of the celebrant at mass. 'Altare' is sometimes translated as 'church' or 'sanctuary' but in the Confession of Patrick, himself a child of the Romano-British Church, it obviously means altar, on which the Irish convert women throw their jewels, and that is likely to be the meaning here.

The implications are of the existence of a settled Church with its own building and liturgy, regularly used sacramental vessels and donors with both

[36] Mawer, *Evidence* 11 (Wickford) 32 (Catterick) 37 (Colchester) 38–9 (Kelvedon); Thomas, *Christianity* 89 (Exeter) 172 (Canterbury but see Mawer 36–7); Mawer, *Evidence* 10 (alpha and omega), 70–1 (Vyne ring)

[37] Ibid. 18, 87–9; K.S. Painter ed., *The Water Newton early Christian silver* (London 1977); id., 'The Water Newton treasure', Hartley *et al.*, *Constantine* 210–22

[38] Mawer, *Evidence* 18

wealth and commitment. A second bowl of silver has an incomplete inscription recording its offering or dedication by two women, Innocentia and Viventia. The range of silverware and the absence of any family connections running across the collection make plain that it represents the eucharistic equipment of a church and not simply of a private chapel. Within the hoard there is also a beautiful two-handled silver cup without inscription, probably a chalice, a silver bowl readily identifiable as a paten, a strainer for the eucharistic wine and a silver jug, probably for the water to mix with the wine at the mass. In other words, a full and rich communion apparatus was in existence accompanied by triangular silver or silver-gilt votive plaques adorned in nine cases with chi-rho, flanked in all bar one by alpha and omega and clearly part of the treasures of this Church, which, though unequivocally Christian, closely resemble the votive plaques of pagan temples.[39]

The point is reinforced by one inscription above a chi-rho and alpha and omega, 'Iamcilla votum quod promisit conplevit' ('Iamcilla fulfilled the vow she promised'),[40] which corresponds precisely to the wording 'votum quod promisit' on a pagan plaque of the fourth century from the temple of the Celtic god Nodens at Lydney. Some plaques were designed for rivets to fix to walls or other backing of wood or leather. The bargaining of pagan religion has been carried over into Christianity in a Church that is fully up to date in its liturgy and equipment but not yet fully emancipated from its pagan habits. These donors were making substantial gifts, the first known Christian plaques of this kind, though comparable ones of later date have been found in other areas.

Some of the plate was worn. The handle of the strainer had been broken and mended with three rivets, a jug handle was loose, so the vessels could have been long in use before being carefully packed together around one silver dish and buried, perhaps in the garden of a supporter, at a time of great crisis. Durobrivae was surrounded by fertile farmland, a possible base for wealthy benefactors who could donate the plate for the benefit of the industrial workers of the town, a class quite often attracted to early Christianity, who could have made up the majority of the congregation. On the other hand, we might infer from its position close by a main route that the treasure was buried by the leaders of a Church community in flight, who aimed to recover it when the danger was over.

[39] Ibid. 87–9
[40] Ibid. 88

The vessels for a less well-known rite, the Agape or love feast, which in early centuries provided an occasion for convivial informal meeting of Church members, have been detected by George Boon in a corner of a room in a Roman town house at Caerwent, where household items, a pewter plate and bowl, two cooking pots and three bowls, a knife and a double swivel-hook had all been buried together in a large urn. In 1961 he noticed that the pewter bowl had a chi-rho on the underside, concluded that these had been a Christian household's possessions and asked himself why such ordinary domestic equipment should have been thus segregated and buried. He concluded that they had been reserved for the Agape and set apart so that no contaminated food such as meat that had once been offered to idols should reach them.[41]

The converts became full members of the Church through baptism, a solemn rite customarily administered by the bishop after a period in the cate-chumenate.[42] Until baptised, they would remain apart from the main body along with the penitents. Adult baptism was the norm and its timing was tightly controlled: Easter, Pentecost and sometimes Epiphany were the feasts held to be the suitable occasions. Although immersion of the whole body under water was the primitive rite, for practical reasons affusion, where the candidate, called a *competens*, stood naked in the font while a jug of water was poured over the head and trickled down over the body, was widely used in these early centuries. A stark symbolism of the casting off of the old self was conveyed by the removal of all clothing, the cleansing by the sanctified water and the entry into new life by the stepping out of the font. That affusion was practised in Britain is demonstrated by the existence of several stone purpose-built fonts in close proximity to churches, low-standing for ease of access, the poured water reaching probably up to the calves.

At Witham in Essex, on a slight hill by the main London to Chester road, a church was built about mid-fourth century on a site once dominated by a pagan complex which included a temple, possibly devoted to a horse cult, and an artificial pond fed by a spring which may have had religious significance. The Christian takeover would have purified the site to eliminate any demonic influences from the pagan past. A font was built near the pond and trouble was taken over its construction; it was octagonal, tiled on both base and sides,

---

[41] G.C. Boon, 'The early Church in Gwent I: the Romano-British Church', *The Monmouthshire Antiquary* 8 (1992) 11–24 at 15–18; Mawer, *Evidence* 19
[42] The best introduction remains Thomas, *Christianity* 202–27

just over a foot deep and some four feet wide, giving easy access, subsequently to be replaced first by a timber-walled version and then by a rectangular wooden box no longer projecting above ground, representing more significantly the descent into death to the old life and the rising into the new.[43]

At Icklingham in Suffolk a font was placed on another pagan site neutralised by the Christians placing a layer of chalk over the earlier structures and remains, which included six human skulls, one of them showing signs of decapitation. It is a good working hypothesis that this was the site of a pagan sanctuary. The font is another small masonry structure with some evidence nearby of the kind of wooden boarding that would be a natural accompaniment in the British climate. It had been coated with white plaster and lay to the east of a building commonly identified as a church. A third example comes from the Roman fortress of Richborough in Kent, where an elongated hexagonal tank was placed within a rough circular base of stone and cobbles originally covered in pink plaster, and lying north of a building identified as a church.[44] Another fort, Housesteads on Hadrian's Wall, has a stone-lined tank which could have been a font; it is of the right character and accords with the developing evidence of a Christian presence within the Roman army.[45] Close by the site of a cemetery which includes Christians at Butt Road, Colchester, a low tiled structure has also been identified as a font despite evidence of burning, which may well be secondary. There is evidence of a wooden housing having surrounded the supposed font which is accessible from the substantial building some have identified as a cemetery church.[46] A recent discovery at Bradford-on-Avon reveals the presence of a baptistery inside a private dwelling, placed by a fifth-century villa owner in the centre of his best room.

Just over two yards away from the west wall of a two-aisled basilica close to the forum at Silchester is a free-standing, rectangular flint platform with a tiled base of the kind identified as open-air fonts, with a small pit at hand readily identifiable as a soakaway. There are no apparent traces of supports for

---

[43] R. Turner, *Excavations of an Iron Age settlement and Roman religious complex at Ivy Chimneys, Witham, Essex 1978–83*, Essex County Council Archaeology Section (Chelmsford 1999)

[44] Thomas, *Christianity* 218; Petts, *Christianity* 67–9; summary, A. Woodward, P. Leach, *The Uley Shrines* (London 1993) 322–4

[45] Petts, *Christianity* 90–1 (Richborough), reflections 166–8 (inc. Housesteads); Mithras at Housesteads, Henig, *Religion* 102

[46] D. Watts discusses Christianity on Butt Road site in N. Crummy *et al.*, *Excavations of Roman and later cemeteries in Colchester* (Colchester 1993) 192–201; reviewed by M. Struck, *Britannia* 28 (1997) 496–8

boarding erected for the privacy of the candidates, but these could have been put up ad hoc at the baptismal seasons.[47]

Churches may have had baptisteries directly attached to them. At a remarkably long-lived sacral site, Uley near Dursley in Gloucestershire, where Iron Age timber shrines were succeeded by a stone Romano-Celtic temple to Mercury, it is argued that a timber Christian church with an annexed baptistery was built in the early fifth century; the purpose of the annexe is nonetheless hypothetical and, as in other cases of alleged church sites, the absence of inscriptions or any other archaeological evidence makes it hard to be decisive in assuming that the buildings were Christian.[48]

The other class of evidence for the practice of baptism in the Romano-British Church are mobile lead tanks, wholly unknown on the continent, a category unique to Britain, still puzzling historians.[49] Like the surviving outdoor stone fonts, they appear to presuppose the practice of affusion and the custom of administering the sacrament in the open air, even if behind temporary screens. Most informative is the relief on the tank from Walesby near Market Rasen in Lincolnshire; only a portion was uncovered in a fragmentary state, but in its original condition it was evidently about three feet wide and eighteen inches deep, certainly not big enough for submersion or immersion, but suitable for affusion. Part of a frieze on one side of the tank has a unique representation of a candidate coming for baptism, set above a chi-rho and divided into three panels within the conventional pillars, each with three figures. The centre panel is the crucial one; as reconstructed by Jocelyn Toynbee it shows a naked woman, her robe slipping off her right shoulder, supported by two fully clothed women. It is a stylised representation of a Romano-British baptism: aided by her supporters, the *competens* approaches the rite, removing her clothing to receive the pouring of the consecrated water over her head. The other two panels represent the rest of the congregation come together at this supreme moment in a contemporary Christian's life, the acceptance to full membership of the Church after penitence and instruction.

---

[47] G.C. Boon, *Silchester: the Roman town of Calleva* (2nd edn Newton Abbot 1974); S.R. Cosh, 'A possible date for the Silchester Roman "church"', *Britannia* 35 (2004) 229–33
[48] Woodward and Leach, *Shrines,* with general synthesis on churches and baptisteries; reviewed by A. King, *Britannia* 25 (1994) 347–9 (with doubts on the church); P. Rahtz, *EME* 4 (1995) 246–8
[49] Thomas, *Christianity* 220–5; Petts, *Christianity* 96–9; Watts, *Christians* 138–73, *Religion* 147–53 (tank from Brough, Notts); for Walesby see, M. Henig, Hartley *et al., Constantine* 208, Flawborough, R.J.A. Wilson, 'Front part of tank' ibid. 208–9; 'Tank' reconstruction of Walesby, J.M.C. Toynbee, *Art in Britain under the Romans* (Oxford 1964)

Some nineteen other tanks have survived in a scattering generally corresponding to areas of Christian strength. All are of broadly comparable size, all of lead and decorated with symbols, some of universally accepted Christian provenance, such as the chi-rho, others likely to be so. There are recurring motifs and the same sort of construction. At Flawborough, four figures stand in the *orans* posture, as at Lullingstone. However, there is no sign of any industrial link or central point of manufacture of these tanks: although not all have Christian symbols, they are sufficiently alike to be taken as part of the baptismal liturgical apparatus of the Romano-British Church, devised for the same purpose and made where they were commissioned.

But there are oddities. The tanks are small, hardly of size readily to accommodate both candidate and bishop; they are also heavy and would take four men to carry. Charles Thomas has suggested they were mobile fonts designed to facilitate baptisms in rural areas, perhaps carried in a cart accompanying the bishop on his journey to the church of the entrant. This raises the objection that, if so, one would hardly expect more than one to be extant on a given site, yet there are several instances where more have been found on the same site – two at Bourton-on-the-Water, two or more at Ashton. At the Icklingham complex which has a building often identified as a church with a font close by and an inhumation cemetery likely to be Christian, there are three lead tanks. Why three and why were they buried? Was it at a time when Christians feared pagan reaction? If we survey the whole body of tanks, we have to note that many have been damaged: were they deliberately attacked by hostile pagans? David Petts reminds us of the importance of the burial of sacred objects in the Roman epoch. Associated with the supreme Christian rite of baptism, a tank is a vessel of great sacral power; unused, superseded, buried, even ritually damaged by Christians, the tank may be honoured, not humiliated; a ritual killing does not imply dishonour. He also draws attention to a remarkable concentration in the Icklingham area of burials of pewter coins, masks and statuettes.

Icklingham has an unusually powerful Christian character; it is also a central point for a remarkable volume of buried objects and raises major questions about Romano-British Christianity which lived and grew in a society where the majority remained pagan and where deep-rooted pagan sentiments would play on individual Christians. The Water Newton votives are one symptom of this; the burials in the Icklingham area may point in the same direction. The pagan instinct to bury lasted a long time: there are interesting parallels in the practice of burying superseded fonts, perhaps below a new one, in certain places in the Middle Ages.[50] There seems to have been a will to bury rather than destroy.

Dorothy Watts is uneasy with Thomas's hypothesis of the mobile fonts and prefers to see the tanks as serving the purpose of *pedilavium*, a ceremonial washing of the feet current in some countries as an adjunct to baptism itself.[51] Petts speculates on the possibility that the tanks were intended to retain holy water for sprinkling the faithful as they entered church or baptismal water valued for its curative properties. And yet – in what was still a young Church – it seems a remarkable investment in metalwork and expense to provide these tanks simply for the sprinkling of holy water or for the minor rite of *pedilavium*. Perhaps, after all, Thomas is right and, heavy as they were, these were mobile fonts designed to bring baptism to more distant areas, sent out, it may be, from specific centres. Around them still hangs an air of mystery.

The Romano-British Church was no exception to the custom of including scriptural representations on its artefacts. In a child's grave in an Anglo-Saxon cemetery at Long Wittenham in Oxfordshire, a wooden beaker covered in a bronze sheet with three scenes, showing the baptism of Christ, the marriage at Cana and Zacchaeus, had, it seems, been preserved by the Christian community there as an heirloom from a British past, probably the property of a church in Dorchester-on-Thames. However, it has a cross flanked by the alpha and omega and, as the cross came late into Christian usage, this raises doubts about its dating.[52] Another artefact was discovered on the site of the temple of Mercury at Uley, evidently part of the sheeting from a casket of copper alloy, depicting four scenes: two from the Old Testament, Jonah under his gourd and Abraham about to sacrifice Isaac, and two from the New, where Jesus is shown healing the centurion and the man blind from birth. Curiously the sheet was folded tightly into four as though to 'kill it' to give it reverential burial, or alternatively, it is possible that a pagan was trying to neutralise a Christian object. So tightly was it folded that it had to be opened by British Museum staff. The workmanship and choice of subject ally it to continental work and there would doubtless be other scenes on the missing portions of the casket.[53]

---

[50] D. Stocker, 'Fons et origo. The symbolic death, burial and resurrection of English font stones', *CA* I (1997) 17–25. I owe this ref. to Dr Petts; see D. Petts, 'Votive deposits and Christian practice in late Roman Britain, M.O.H. Carver ed., *The Cross goes north* (Woodbridge 2003) 109–18

[51] Watts, *Christians* 171–3

[52] M. Henig, P. Booth, *Roman Oxfordshire* (Stroud 2000) 45–6, 85–7; Henig, *Verica* 134

[53] M. Henig, 'Votive objects: images and inscriptions', Woodward and Leach, *Shrines* 88–112; M. Henig, 'Sheeting from casket', Hartley *et al.*, *Constantine* 225; illus. 224

Though not numerous, the Christian artefacts which survive from Roman Britain – the Constantinian sign of victory, the alpha and omega from the Book of Revelation, the peacock as a sign of immortality, the olive branch, the Tree of Life, customary figures and allegories – are sufficient to show a Church with a ritual and vessels to serve it and a membership willing to devote wealth and skill to its cause. The inscriptions show confidence in salvation and belief in Christian hope, joy, perseverance and holiness.

Cemeteries also provide evidence of the slow, patchy but definite influence of Christianity in the fourth century. Neonatal and infant burials within a cemetery are sure signs of Christian influence. It is apparent that Roman tradition did not place sufficient value on an infant life to believe it warranted formal burial; infant remains were got rid of casually, some within dwellings. Some tradition of ritual burials survived from pre-Roman times. There were, for example, first-century infant burials at Uley in a position which suggested a specific religious purpose: an infant was buried by the entrance to the Iron Age shrine at Maiden Castle; at Gatcombe remains of infants were found under the foundations of one building dating from the fourth century. At Hambledon, ninety-seven infant corpses by a Romano-British house must be the result of infanticide.

By contrast, in cemeteries which other indications suggest are Christian, infants and neonates are buried with care – at Icklingham, for example, among the forty burials in the third and Christian phase, three were of infants; at Colchester, the infants were buried with the same care as adults, never superimposed untidily or carelessly on other burials and at Cannington, an unusually long-lasting site, there were some sixty or seventy infants and neonates among 574 burials excavated. The emperor Julian the Apostate commented on the care taken by Christians over the disposal of their dead and believed it was one reason for the popularity of their beliefs. But there is no body of direction for Christians on what they should do with their dead. Augustine condemned the *refrigerium*, the ceremonial meal by the grave, and noted that the survivors' expenditure on funerals and commemorations benefited them rather than the deceased. There was no explicit condemnation of the practice of burying grave goods with the dead, though there would be pressure to abandon the crudest practices of paganism, like the insertion of joints of meat as a kind of substitute for sacrifices for the dead, or the inclusion of boots or hobnails of boots for the last journey, an ancient Celtic practice; the custom just faded out.[54]

---

[54] R. Philpott, *Burial practices in Roman Britain. A survey of grave treatment and furnishing AD 43–410*, BAR Brit. ser. 219 (Oxford 1991) with modifications in Sparey-Green (below n. 55); A. Taylor, *Burial practice in early England* (Stroud 2001); diagrams, Watts, *Christians* 91–7

Another type of cemetery, which, though not ordered overall, includes disciplined rows of graves and organised clusters, probably family groupings, will more often have grave goods and a greater variety of positions for corpses, whether on the side, prone or crouched. Burial with the head to the west is a common, though not exclusive, feature of Christian graves because it was traditionally believed that with the whole body facing east, the dead would be ready to rise at the Last Judgment. Not all authorities accept this and it is clear that many factors, not just questions of religious belief, affect burial practice. In the case of mixed cemeteries, archaeologists have to weigh carefully the indications of paganism or Christianity.

There are examples, however, where Christians gained the confidence and authority to develop their own cemeteries or to claim sections for themselves. This happened at Poundbury between early and mid-fourth century, where graves were laid out in an orderly fashion, the corpses placed west–east and children treated in death with the same respect as adults. In some cases gypsum, a drying agent, was applied by the kin to leave the dead well prepared for a bodily resurrection. A series of stone mausolea was integrated into the whole plan. One of them had painted plaster depicting stately, brightly dressed figures facing east, some carrying black wands with a line of light along the edges as if they represented ebony gleaming in light from the east. They were evidently part of a much larger ensemble of figures, which have been identified as ancestors of the Poundbury settlement, a chi-rho on the plaster confirming their Christian identity. An alternative view suggests they were apostles, and even identifies a heavily built bearded figure in a purple tunica as St Peter. The site also contained a coin of the usurping emperor Magnentius, 350–3, with chi-rho and alpha and omega on the reverse, pierced so that it could be attached to the wall. Even here, within the ordered and presumably Christian cemetery, there are cases where kindred have placed the coins of Charon's fee in the mouth. Around the edges are other groups of graves with grave goods or prone burial and the Celtic practice of decapitation. Funerary arrangements are notoriously conservative and old habits died hard.[55]

Burials at Ilchester in Somerset correspond to the managed cemetery pattern with west–east graves and a general absence of grave goods, while

[55] D.E. Farwell, T.I. Morrison, *Excavations at Poundbury 1966–80 II* (Dorchester 1993); rev. G.C. Boon, *Britannia* 26 (1995) 400–2; comment C. Sparey-Green, 'Where are the Christians? Late Roman cemeteries in Britain', Carver, *cross* 93–107; K. Davey, R. Ling, *Wall painting in Roman Britain* (London 1987)

stray burials along roads have grave goods and include decapitation and a variety of corpse positions, crouched or prone; in the Little Spittles area nearby, burials were in enclosures by houses. At Ashton in Northamptonshire, the small managed cemetery has practically no grave goods, the burials are aligned west–east and there is a number of burials of young children, infants and neonates. Outside in various sites in the town are burials with grave goods and sometimes decapitated corpses. It looks as if the post-Constantinian managed cemetery had the effect of banishing pagans to odd burial points.[56]

Within a major burial site at Butt Road, Colchester, we find a cemetery datable to the early fourth century and clearly pagan in character for it has north–south alignments and grave goods in fifty per cent of the cases. Then between 320 and 340 a major reorganisation resulted in burials orientated west–east, placed in orderly rows – in other words, the emergence of the managed cemetery, generally without grave goods. Uncertainty surrounds the reason for the stone building at the north-west edge of the cemetery. It appears to be orientated to a single grave lying in front of what could have been an apse, suggesting the remains of a *martyrium*, a focus for Christian burials: on the other hand, remains of animal and bird bones suggest a hall for pagan funerary feasting. The probability is that the building at different times had both pagan and Christian use.[57]

The evidence from cemeteries confirms that from other spheres: in the fourth century Christianity existed side by side with paganism and, despite the impetus given by Constantine and Christian emperors, did not establish a dominant position for itself. Advances and converts there were, as archaeology demonstrates, but the absence of literary sources for the period means that the work of bishops, priests and leading laymen in preaching, baptising and evangelising, confirming, protecting and expanding the faith have gone wholly unrecorded. Heroic determination may well have existed, but the age of martyrdom was over and no descriptions of the Romano-British leadership in this century have come down to us. That some pressure was felt by the pagans is a possible conclusion from the plethora of cases of decapitation, hobnails and hobnail boots, extensive grave goods, prone burial and the like which are found generally on less favoured sites and outside the contemporaneous, ordered cemeteries of the fourth century. Petts has suggested that this represents, at least in part, a conscious defiance on the part of the pagans, a

[56] Petts, *Christianity* 141
[57] Watts in Crummy *et al.*, *Colchester* 192–201

means of asserting their independence of the novel claims of Christianity.[58]
Certainly paganism was not put down by Christianity and retained vitality
through the first half of the fourth century: below all the religious currents,
classical paganism, Christianity or mystery cults, lay the ancient practice of
burying dogs and other animals in the foundations of buildings.

The healing shrine of Nodens-Mars at Lydney in Gloucestershire consisted
of a substantial set of buildings within an Iron Age fort developed in the
second half of the third century – probably not later than 286. It consisted of
a temple to Nodens and a long building to its east, an *abaton*, containing a set
of cubicles interpreted as bedrooms in which pilgrims slept, hoping to receive
from the god dreams and visions from which a resident interpreter could give
healing and encouragement. There was a bathhouse and a guest house with
fine views as far as the heathen shrine at Uley. It attracted wealthy devotees,
including women, who left behind many pins used to affix votive plaques, and
it remained fully in business well into the first half of the fourth century, when
a refurbishment included the laying down of a mosaic and an extension of the
abaton.

It was an impressive site; the pilgrims had to climb a hill before passing
through a gate guarded by sea beasts into the compound where the mosaic
laid by the priest Titus Flavius Senilis in association with Victorinus the interpreter of dreams marked the limit of access to the ordinary worshipper:
beyond lay the most sacred area with images of the gods. Here, as Christianity
spread, Lydney continued to attract its worshippers. There were fifteen figures
of dogs in stone or copper alloy, reminiscent of the dogs kept on Greek sites
to aid the healing process by licking patients' limbs. Nodens, it seems, had
multiple functions both as a nature god and a god of healing and Lydney had
the characteristics of adaptability and multifunction together with a bedrock
of Celtic belief common in Romano-British religion, as well as the potent
appeal of a healing shrine. Nevertheless, it fell on evil days. There was a
serious deterioration in the buildings in the second half of the fourth century:
coin evidence suggests an abandonment at a time comparable to that of the
pagan temple at Harlow.[59]

[58] Petts, *Christianity* 149

[59] M.G. Fulford, 'Links with the past: pervasive "ritual" behaviour in Roman Britain',
Britannia 32 (2001) 199–218; R.E.M. and T.V. Wheeler, *Report on the excavations on the site
in Lydney Park, Gloucs* (London 1932) modified by P.J. Casey, B. Hoffman, 'Excavations in
the Roman temple in Lydney Park Gloucestershire in 1980 and 1981', *AJ* 79 (1999) 81–143

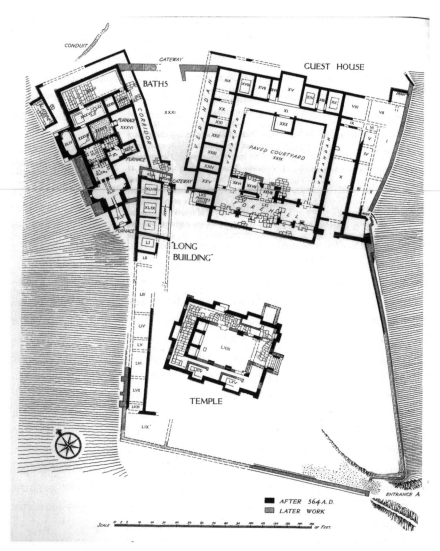

Fig. 2 The pagan shrine, Lydney. A spacious *temenos* or precinct holds a temple, shown in the foreground, with an ambulatory floored with mosaics and three niches in the back wall, possibly for statues, a long building most plausibly explained as an *abaton* with small bedrooms for the receiving of messages from gods in dreams, a substantial bathhouse and a guesthouse with a courtyard. Interpretation of the site follows the classic report of R.F.M. and T.V. Wheeler; their dating of phases of building has been superseded.

The Uley temple lasted longer. A collection of curse tablets summoning the aid of the god to recover stolen property and prevent harm from enemies shows how the pilgrims valued the shrine. Over time votives tended to change character but not to diminish. It seems that Mercury took over from a Celtic warrior cult, attracted the characteristic sacrifices of goat and cockerel and the votives, consisting most of all of coins, rings and bracelets, suitable for the patron of trade, but did not wholly displace the spears of the shrine's earliest phase, which in the fourth century tended to be miniature, though there was an ever increasing trend towards simplicity of items and more personal offerings. In other words, fourth-century Uley still had vitality and adaptability: like Lydney it had multiple functions. Votive legs and a plaque with a foot are reminders that Mercury was a god not only of trade but of travellers, with an interest in healing diseases which inhibited movement. At some time towards the end of the fourth century, the front of the stone temple gave way and there was a rapid, improvised building operation designed to keep the religious complex alive and to continue to attract pilgrims. There were not sufficient resources for full replacement but still enough to justify building adaptation. Eventually, it is believed, a Christian timber church was built within the Uley complex.[60]

For all the richness of its sanctuary and the degree of official support, the temple of Aquae Sulis at Bath was not of a kind fundamentally distinct from the simpler rural shrine at Uley: it continued for a long time in vitality, with resources sufficient to pay for excellent buildings and progressive repair. It resembled Uley in that the Romano-British temple was heir to a sacred site of pre-Roman date, as the hot springs, the foundation of the temple's success, had been a source of healing and the object of veneration before the occupation. The flow of pilgrims did not dry up in the course of the fourth century, but it did diminish. The shrine became meaner and less public, able to receive only a proportion of those who had once passed through its doors.[61]

The imperial cult, veneration of the deities Fortuna and Disciplina, together with the respectful care of legionary standards and the setting up of altars to Jupiter Best and Greatest, formed bonds holding together the army in Britain, whether defenders of the frontier, *limitatenses*, or members of the field army, *comitatenses*. Such official devotions in no way inhibited the dedication of altars to other deities, native Celtic or Germanic; the frontier area was also fruitful for the worship of Mithras. A native Celtic cult could flourish, as at

[60] Woodward and Leach, *Shrines* 318–21
[61] Summary, ibid. 317

Coventina's Well near Carrawburgh where, even after the altar was no longer on view, offerings were still made. With the Constantinian revolution the way was open for change and perhaps it should not be surprising that excavations at both the key port of Richborough and the forts along Hadrian's Wall and its hinterland have revealed evidence of a Christian presence associated with army personnel and dependants.[62]

Buried at a time when central authority was acting more decisively against paganism at the end of the fourth or possibly early fifth century, the Thetford treasure gives a glimpse of the attractions the old religion could still exert. A fine collection of gold jewellery and silver ladles, strainers and spoons was deposited, antiquarian in dedications to Faunus, a Latin rustic god known in Horace and Virgil, equivalent to Pan and Silvanus; its high value, together with the nature of the inscriptions, make plain that we are dealing with a wealthy pagan circle with intellectual and literary interests. Some of the spoons carry a member's name; others invoke Faunus, with his epithets 'guardian of treasure', 'mead-begotten', 'prick-eared'. The impression given is of a genial dining club under the protection of Faunus, in close touch with the natural world but taking an impetus from ancient Rome. The strainers and the Bacchic decorated spoons suggest a parallel to the Christian liturgy, perhaps a case of pagan borrowing from Christian. At any rate, it is a reminder that, even in the age of the Christian disciplinarian, the emperor Theodosius, paganism had not lost its force or power of innovation.[63]

Examples of old cults continuing and even of new temples being built have led Dorothy Watts to argue for a pagan revival, albeit at a low level, in late Roman Britain in the aftermath of the reign of Julian the Apostate. Part of her case rested on what is now seen to have been the Wheelers' faulty dating of Lydney based on coin evidence.[64] 'Revival' is a little strong. Nevertheless, the balance of fourth-century evidence across Britain shows that, though now more rural than urban, paganism continued to show strength, was still able to defy Christianity and survive official disapprobation, but was clearly fading and weakening on some sites during the later part of the century. The situation is complicated by the fate of the towns; the local elite tended to desert

---

[62] J.C. Mann, 'Hadrian's Wall: the last phase', P.J. Casey ed., *The end of Roman Britain* (Oxford 1979) 144–51

[63] T.W. Potter, C. Johns, *The Thetford treasure. Roman jewellery and silver* (British Museum, London 1983); Watts, *Christians* 158 with apostasy theory

[64] Watts, *Religion*, see esp. 66; W.H.C. Frend, 'Roman Britain, a failed promise', Carver, *Cross* 79–91 with comments on sites and discoveries

them, and temples along with other public buildings became neglected, not
necessarily due to Christian competition or a decline in belief and practice,
whereas in the countryside villa owners continued to support pagan cults.

What is noteworthy about the British situation was the comparative absence
of religious repression and violence. The cults, classic pagan, Celtic, Germanic,
the mystery religions, and Christianity existed side by side without major
iconoclastic episodes such as occurred in other parts of the Empire. Of course
there were episodes of deliberate, even ostentatious, destruction as in the case
of the pagan cult objects piled up in a well constructed in the fourth century
at Lower Slaughter in Gloucestershire, where two seated deities had been
beheaded and there were remains of altars and votive slabs. It all looks like the
methodical destruction of a pagan rural shrine. It is clear also that consistent
moves were made against mithraea in the military zone of Roman Britain,
at Carrawburgh, Rudchester and Housesteads on Hadrian's Wall and, somewhat later, Caernarvon. Doubts and ambiguities exist about damage done
to Christian baptismal tanks, as we have seen, but they do not exclude the
possibility that pagans were responsible for their destruction. It also needs to
be taken into account that there was deliberate fragmentation of their own stat-
uary by pagans themselves, wishing to diffuse among their colleagues the god's
protective power, to provide amulets and objects of private devotion, especially
in dark times of economic decline and loss of order in society. Not all apparent
iconoclasm is necessarily hostile and not all is necessarily of Christian origin:
in the majority of cases, paganism faded and its constructions collapsed.[65]

No record has reached us of any prophetic figure in Britain comparable
to the former Illyrian soldier, St Martin of Tours, bishop from 372, who
conducted assaults on pagan temples and sacred trees, evangelising the countryside with his preaching, thaumaturgic powers and confrontation with
heathen peasants and their practices, not only in his own diocese but making
forays into the dioceses of Bourges and Autun. His biographer Sulpicius
Severus describes him as persuading pagan country dwellers by his preaching
so that they themselves destroyed their temples. But sometimes there was
resistance and divine power had to be called upon: at Leroux, two armed angels
protected him in his work of destruction. There were also more mundane aids,
monks or perhaps soldiers. He had the passive support of sections of the

[65] E. Sauer, *The archaeology of religious hatred in the Roman and early medieval world* (Stroud
2003) Lower Slaughter 59; reviewed by W.H.C. Frend, *Antiquity* 78 (2004) 471–2, C. Clay, *AJ*
84 (2004) 447–8; comment in B. Croxford, 'Iconoclasm in Roman Britain?', *Britannia* 34
(2003) 81–95

Gaulish aristocracy and of officials who appear to have winked at the illegality of his attacks on buildings. He was concerned to put Christian structures in place of the demolished temples: wherever he had destroyed pagan shrines, he instantly built either churches or monasteries, Severus says.[66]

Martin succeeded in part because of his direct emotional challenge to the powers of the old gods. Country pagans waited to see what would happen as he set about demolishing what was sacred in their religion and were ready to hear about the new beliefs when they found that the god under assault did not strike Martin down. We have a glimpse of this when one set of villagers accepted Martin's demolition of their temple but played safe when it came to cutting down their sacred pine. They insisted that Martin stand beneath it as it came down and the situation was turned into a demonstration of the superior power of Christianity when Martin, by making the sign of the cross, deflected its fall. He lost no time in following up his advantage and ceremonially laid hands on the villagers as the preliminary to securing them for baptism. In Britain, Martin would not have had sufficient support from the powerful to set about such forcible campaigning and in fact no comparable hammer of the pagans has emerged from the sources.

A curse tablet in Bath implicitly sums up the situation as it evolved in Britain in the aftermath of the Constantinian revolution. For the very first time the word Christian was used on this tablet: the donor wished to secure the return of his money, stolen probably while he took the waters and venerated Sul Minerva. 'Whether pagan or Christian, whosoever whether man or woman, whether boy or girl, whether slave or free has stolen from me, Annianus, in the morning six silver pieces from my purse, you, Lady Goddess, are to exact them from him.' 'Gentilis' is the word used for pagan – both that and Christian are misspelt – and it seems an odd term for a pagan to use if he is a practising one, yet the tablet implies belief in the powers of the goddess Sulis. Christianity had arrived and made its place as an alternative to paganism, but it was still a minority cult; sometimes paganism won, sometimes Christianity.[67]

At Icklingham, the Christian takeover was not superseded; at Witham, despite the suppression of temple worship and the progressive reworking of the font, the Christian presence faded out and then after a phase of demolition and filling in ditches, the site reverted to farmland. At Cirencester a

---

[66] C.E. Stancliffe, *St Martin and his hagiographer* (Oxford 1983). I am indebted to Dr Stancliffe
[67] Mawer, *Evidence* 85

column was re-erected to a governor of the old religion, the *prisca religio*, perhaps under Julian the Apostate. At two Somerset sites, Lamyatt Beacon and Brean Down, churches may have succeeded temples. The former has an east–west aligned stone building with remains of stone benches, identified as a church on the analogy of two ancient stone-bench churches, one on Ardwall Island and one on St Helens in the Scilly Isles. As it stood close by a small temple, it is reasonable to assume that the one superseded the other. At Brean Down a temple was demolished and a rectangular building like that at Lamyatt Beacon was erected. At Water Newton, as we have seen, Christians used pagan-style votive plaques in their church life; at Thetford there is a strong suspicion that a pagan liturgy had emerged in reaction to the Christian one. In a word, there was a relatively free market in much of fourth-century Britain, with a two-way influence between paganism and Christianity.[68]

Romano-British church buildings have proved elusive. They were abandoned and in many cases fell down in the harsh centuries when strongly pagan Germanic invaders from areas little touched by Roman influence took power in eastern and southern areas of the island, and their sites were often lost to knowledge, whereas on the continent late Roman churches did not suffer this fate, having continuity of use as places of worship. Moreover, British churches tended generally to be bare of corroborative evidence of a Christian presence in contrast to the profusion of statues, chippings of statues, votives, tablets and remains of sacrifices which make it so much easier to identify pagan temples and the gods worshipped in them. In Christian practice, the earliest churches of all were house-churches, unobtrusive, inexpensive and secluded from persecution; an early centre for worship was often a room in a bishop's house or a villa. As we have seen in the case of Lullingstone, the Christian owner created a place of worship within the building; at Icklingham, the small rectangular building near a structure identified as a font and with a set of west–east burials almost all without grave goods close by may well be a free-standing house-church designed for a Christian family and its immediate connections. With the end of persecution, the faithful built places of worship and assembly adopting the basilica format, a familiar feature of town life serving as a meeting hall and magistrates' court

---

[68] See interesting chapter 'Links with pagan religions and practices', Watts, *Christians*; on Cirencester, Watts, *Religion* 37; on Ardwall, Thomas, *Christianity* 151; on St Helens, Petts, *Christianity* 71–2; on late Roman Britain, T.W. Potter, C. Johns, *Roman Britain* (London 1992, 2nd edn 2002), a sensitive survey; see also M. Henig, 'Religious diversity in Constantine's empire', Hartley *et al.*, *Constantine* 85–95

in contradistinction to the classical form of the pagan temple. The Christian church was essentially an assembly room; the pagan temple a *cella* reserved for its cult statue, its priests and a few attendants, with perhaps an ambulatory for the individual pilgrim or worshipper.

The martyrial churches, the *memoriae* commemorating the heroic dead, acted either as a focus for veneration of their remains, holy places where healing and the prayers of saints were sought, or functioned simply as memorials of leading Christian men and women of holy life. They were always and necessarily placed outside town walls because of the Roman prohibition of burials within inhabited places. Across the Empire they were potent forces in the rise of Christianity. A *memoria* for St Alban can reasonably be assumed to lie beneath the modern abbey church. Shrines of this type can also be assumed to have existed outside Canterbury, Roman Durovernum, where, with her chaplain, Queen Bertha of Kent took over an old church outside the walls and, it is highly probable, dedicated it to St Martin of Tours. A church of St Pancras, also outside the walls of Canterbury, fits the pattern. We have the witness of Bede that Augustine took over a church from the Roman period inside Canterbury which became the nucleus of his cathedral.[69]

There were also fortress chapels for soldiers serving along the frontiers. A church for legionaries at Richborough in Kent, a major military centre of late Roman times, was identified in 1923 in an excavation by Bushe-Fox at a time when archaeological techniques were less advanced than now; nevertheless the conclusion that a rectangular structure with an apse in the north-east corner in proximity to an hexagonal font was indeed a church for the soldiers is certainly arguable. More recent investigations have provided evidence for a Christian presence in the forts of Hadrian's Wall – a building of *c.*400 with an apse in the praetorian courtyard at Vindolanda; a rectangular structure on the site of the headquarters at South Shields with an unusual stone altar, unlike a pagan one and possibly Christian; at Housesteads another, similar structure with an apse at the west end. These four sites suggest that the influence of Christianity on serving members of the Roman army and their dependants has been underestimated and that this influence may well have been a factor in the development of missions and monasteries in the north of England and in Scotland in the post-Roman era.[70]

---

[69] Below, 171

[70] Bushe-Fox and Richborough, Petts, *Christianity* 75, 90–1; A. Birley, *Garrison life in Vindolanda* (Stroud 2002) 15; P.T. Bidwell, S. Speak, *Excavations at South Shields Roman fort* I (1994) 45–6, 103–4; J. Crow, *A fort and garrison on Hadrian's Wall* (Stroud 1995) 124–7

The site of St Paul in the Bail, Lincoln, is an intriguing example of two churches being built one after the other athwart the old forum after it had been abandoned. Lincoln has also yielded evidence of a fourth-century basilica of substantial size, with signs of high-quality decoration in marble and wall plaster. At Colchester House in London, excavation in 1992–3 uncovered part of the foundations of a large, west–east orientated, aisled building from the middle of the fourth century, 150 feet wide and almost twice as long, built over the south-eastern side of the shrunken Londinium. Its resemblance to the cathedral of St Tecla in Milan has suggested that it was the cathedral of Roman London, an exciting piece of evidence when so little is known about Christianity there. Major changes, including the razing of the old centre with its forum and basilica, make the south-eastern siting credible, yet there is no evidence of Christian usage of this great structure for worship and it may equally well have been an imperial granary or treasury.[71]

Other identifications are precarious. The small buildings at Lamyatt Beacon and Brean Down are more like the oratories of the post-Roman Celtic West and may, indeed, be post-Roman and not strictly Romano-British at all. It may simply be an inference that there was a church built within the pagan complex at Uley: the one Christian item on the site, the fragment of a casket with biblical scenes, was found in an unquestionably pagan section. It is sometimes argued that a temple at Nettleton Shrubs in Wiltshire was altered with the aim of creating a cruciform-shaped space within it to act as a church; it is not impossible, but there is no positive evidence of it and no other comparable example in Britain. One of Silchester's buildings has long been cited as very likely a Christian church because of its basilica form, the quality of its stonework and tessellation and its proximity to the font site; yet closer analysis of a piece of mosaic design has undermined existing dating and placed it well down the list of possible churches: an alternative view that it was the *schola* of a guild now becomes the most convincing hypothesis.[72] Given the doubts and uncertainties attached to many of the sites that have been put forward as Romano-British churches, it is not easy to see what general inferences can be drawn from them about the Church in Britain which they served, but in any case the total number is small.

---

[71] D. Sanky, 'Cathedrals, granaries and urban vitality in late Roman London', B. Watson ed., *Roman London, recent archaeological work* (Portsmouth and Rhode Island 1998) 70–82
[72] Above n. 47; Watts, *Christians* 221 is unable to support Thomas on church sizes; summary, Woodward and Leach, *Shrines* 318

In a most determined attempt to recover a good working list, Dorothy Watts, in her *Christians and Pagans in Roman Britain* of 1991, gave a total of twenty-six sites and selected seventeen (assuming two in both Verulamium and Uley) as 'almost certain' and 'probable'. Three more should be added from Hadrian's Wall and the Colchester House site in London; Silchester must be removed and there are still other very insecure identifications. Fresh excavations and the discovery of Christian symbols, inscribed stones or eucharistic vessels in association with the foundations of buildings yet unknown could change the picture; in the meantime, a provisional conclusion must be that the evidence of the supposed church sites coheres with the general conclusion that the Romano-British Church was a minority religious organisation with a limited number of adherents.[73]

Caution is the keynote of Frances Mawer's disciplined analysis of small finds associated with Christianity. She omits tombs, sarcophagi, gravestones or coffins and examines small portable items – structural material, ritual objects and furniture, vessels and utensils, personal ornaments and amuletic and utilitarian items. From the 260 examined, she rejects half and leaves sixty in limbo as possibly Christian but requiring more analysis. Failures in information and the over-zealousness of antiquarians and archaeologists result in significant casualties among their assertions. Iota-chi, sometimes thought to be a newly discovered Christian symbol, is dismissed; simple greetings such as 'Long life to you, Desiderius' remain just that ('vivas' without added words is neutral); spoons in the fourth century had no special and provable link to baptism such as they came to acquire later; neither a palm nor a fish, nor a combination of them, can be classed as Christian symbol per se; a stray bird at the cemetery site of Holme Pierrepoint in Nottinghamshire cannot be identified as a peacock, the symbol of immortality – it struck the author as resembling a parrot; the set of alleged Christian burials in Lankhills 6 (Winchester), identified by an assumed iota-chi and filleted fish on a black-burnished oval dish in a grave, cannot be accepted; a spoon, perhaps attributable to a Canterbury hoard, does not have the misread injunction 'Live dutifully', but is an amorous slogan freely translatable as 'Be mine for ever'; a villa at Rockbourne, Hampshire, was not only wrongfully classified as a Christian site after a volunteer forged a fish on a slab – in itself not necessarily a Christian sign at all – but was also the setting in which two other authorities found (erroneously) other signs of a Christian presence; known now only from a photograph, a lead

---

[73] Watts, *Christians* 134–5

casket found at Aquae Sulis, carrying an exchange between a supposedly Christian man and woman, turns out to be a complaint about a theft.[74] Musing at the end of the most rigorous analysis yet applied to small Roman remains in Britain, Frances Mawer notes that expectations in the past have been unduly high and that Christianity was 'far less prevalent' than once supposed.[75] She provides a map of the portable items she accepts as Christian and those she regards as possible, but notes that their geographical spread can be misleading as an index of the places where Christianity was strongest; hoarding, looting, casual losses can distort the picture.

This is emphatically true of the Traprain Law hoard, consisting of 152 pieces of silver buried in, perhaps, the middle of the fifth century and found east of Edinburgh at a hill fort of the Votadini, an indigenous tribe of the Lowlands in constant contact with Roman occupying forces, although well north; it has been thought to originate either as loot from raiding or tribute from the Romans to a client tribe or the savings of a veteran officer, a Goth preparing for his retirement, the hacked silver dating from an epoch when soldiers would be rewarded by such cut-up plate.[76] Amongst the silver are fragments of a gilded jug without its handle having scenes from the Old and New Testaments, the Fall, Moses striking the rock in the desert, and the Magi; it has no necessary connection at all with Traprain Law, though it may be Romano-British. The same must be said of another silver jug or bottle with a chi-rho and alpha and omega, two chi-rho ornamented spoons and a strainer with the inscription 'Jesus Christ' and a monogram chi-rho. Though these hoards show large on the map, they naturally do not indicate a substantial Christian presence at the places indicated. A slighter hoard was found near Mildenhall in Suffolk consisting of silver spoons with chi-rho and alpha and omega among thirty-four silver items otherwise pagan or neutral.[77] Apart from certain distortions of the kind noted, the broad pattern of Frances Mawer's small finds, however, fits the geographical pattern of other evidence: the strength of the Church lay to the south and east of England, with some extension to the south-west, considering, for example, Poundbury, Hinton

[74] F. Mawer, *Evidence for Christianity in Roman Britain. The small finds*, BAR Brit. Ser. 243 (Oxford 1995) 138; ibid. 23 (Desiderius) 43 (spoons) 30, 137, 142 (palm, fish) 33 (Holme Pierrepoint) 41–2 (Winchester) 51 (amorous slogan) 141 (Rockbourne) 85 (Aquae Sulis)
[75] Ibid. 140
[76] K. Painter, 'The Traprain Law treasure', Hartley *et al.*, *Constantine* 229–46; Mawer, *Evidence* 15, 16, 22, 28, 50, 60
[77] Ibid. 142

St Mary, Fifield Neville and with a northern representation especially associated with the military zone.

There is nonetheless one significant gap in this pattern of geographical distribution – London, which in the fourth century was a nodal point for trade, wealthy enough to spend substantially on its defence and surely an attraction for foreign visitors, including Christians. Yet out of thirty-five items claimed in various sources as 'possibly Christian', the author rescued only three. No doubt London is a difficult archaeological site, but Mawer's small finds gap remains puzzling.[78]

For all the idiosyncrasies of recording small finds, a broad similarity emerges between Mawer's map and those made in 1981 for Charles Thomas's *Christianity in Roman Britain* and in 1991 and 1998 for Dorothy Watts's books,[79] and shows that, with the exception of the military zone sites in northern England, Christianity was a phenomenon of the lowlands of Britain – in sum, one aspect of Romanisation. Imported from elsewhere in the Empire, most probably Gaul, it had taken on a distinctive character of its own. It was not a strong force in the larger towns but was most of all a country movement, with strength in country towns and a certain body of patronage among the villa-owning elite and a capacity for establishing itself among the *limitatenses* on Hadrian's Wall. But compared with the immense non-Christian heritage from the Roman past, the whole body of Christian remains is quite small. It was a minority religion. Yet, when the Church was faced with the catastrophe of pagan Germanic invasion, it showed itself capable of winning new ground in the west to compensate for its losses to the invaders in the east.

[78] Ibid.
[79] Thomas, *Christianity* 138; Watts, *Christians* 216–17, 219; Watts, *Religion* 14

CHAPTER 2

British Christians and Germanic Pagans

On the last day of 406 the Rhine froze.[1] A mixed force of German barbarians crossed into Gaul and thereby initiated a crisis which led Britain into snapping the threads which linked her to the Empire. The emperor Honorius III, preoccupied with defence against his enemies in Italy and the East, could send no troops to aid Britain, which feared the barbarians would take control of the Channel and threaten the island. The army chose self-help and elected usurpers; when the third of these, Constantine III, despite initial success in Gaul, was besieged in his capital at Arles and killed by the agency of Honorius in 411, the British leadership decided not to renew the connection with the Empire. They had had enough of the fighting, the taxation and the draining of resources through usurpers. No doubt Honorius envisaged that Britain would one day be recovered to the Empire. The opportunity never came and Britain ceased to be subject to the structure of imperial command for peace and war, no longer paid taxes or received money to pay troops.[2]

The loss of links to the Empire after 411 did not, however, preclude contacts with the continental Church. There was clearly communication over the teaching of Pelagius, a native of Britain, educated there to a high standard, who for decades after *c.*380 lived in Rome in close contact with the aristocracy to whom he acted as spiritual director; it was here that he developed his views on the doctrines of original sin, predestination and grace in contradistinction

---

[1] Conventional date. M. Kulikowski, 'Barbarians in Gaul, usurpers in Britain', *Britannia* 31 (2000) 325–45 argues for December 405

[2] P.J. Casey, 'The fourth century and beyond', P. Salway ed., *The Roman era. The British Isles, 55 BC–AD 410* (Oxford 2002) 75–104, pungent and realistic; A.S. Esmonde Cleary, *The ending of Roman Britain* (London 1989), reviewed by I.N. Wood, 'Internal crisis in fourth century Britain', *Britannia* 22 (1991) 313–15

to those of St Augustine of Hippo. In effect, Pelagius had become a Roman: he moved in those aristocratic Roman circles just as Jerome did, where a yearning for the ascetic life developed – what has been described as a kind of do-it-yourself monasticism in which, for example, the matron Albina and her daughter Marcella turned their house into a kind of nunnery. Often misrepresented by his enemies, Pelagius believed that man's God-given nature permitted, indeed obliged, him to reach perfection. His views aroused sympathy among theologians who reacted against Augustine's harshly predestinarian views, especially in the writings of his last years. St John Cassian was the most distinguished thinker to oppose a rigid predestinarianism; he in turn was attacked and misrepresented by a passionate supporter of Augustine, Prosper of Aquitaine whose *Carmen de ingratis* of 428 referred to the 'British serpent' who 'vomits' a doctrine 'steeped in the venom of the ancient serpent'.[3]

Prosper formed part of a group of churchmen concerned by the influence of Pelagianism. Agitation had led the emperor Honorius, ineffective in dealing with barbarian incursions but the son and successor of Theodosius the Great who so firmly committed the Empire to Christianity, to condemn Pelagianism as heresy in 418, to require those who disseminated the heresy to appear before a civil court and, if found guilty, to be condemned to exile. His measures affected the continent but not the island of Britain, now independent of imperial orders, and attracted Pelagians to Britain which, they now believed, would be a safe refuge for them from orthodox repression. A certain Agricola, son of a pro-Pelagian bishop, was said to have come to Britain to spread his father's views. Pelagian treatises which went on circulating in Britain during the fifth century indicated that the internal disorder and long-standing problems of barbarian attack that afflicted the independent British leadership were not so overwhelming as to snuff out the intellectual life of the British Church, the background of Pelagius's own upbringing.

An impression of a residual survival of Roman-style government, of a Church capable of debate and of an aristocracy which still had some prosperity, is given by the description of St Germanus's journey to Britain in 429 to repress Pelagianism. His Life was written some forty years after his death

[3] G. Bonner, 'The Pelagian controversy in Britain and Ireland', *Peritia* 16 (2002) 144–55 at 149; G.A. Markus, 'Pelagianism in Britain and the continent', *JEH* 37 (1986) 191–204

by the priest Constantius as a model life of a heroic bishop, a pattern of saintly power, who confuted supporters of Pelagius by argument and miracle.[4] The Life says that he was asked to come by the British, Prosper of Aquitaine that he was sent by Pope Celestine on the advice of Germanus's Gaulish deacon Palladius. The accounts are not necessarily in conflict; the request and the papal mission may well have interlocked.

Germanus was well chosen as a representative of the orthodox Church seeking to put down heresy. He was a naturally authoritative figure, part of a new breed of Gallic bishops, capable and experienced, summoned from a secular career to take up the episcopate, a response to the development in Gaul which made the bishop a leader in all affairs, from welfare and government to defence. Born in Auxerre, Germanus was a successful son of his city, who went to study law in Rome and had been both an advocate and military commander before being called to be its bishop in 418. To the British, he would appear just like a high official from the central imperial administration and the more persuasive because of it. Constantius's account is shot through with the conventions of hagiography, with the need to assimilate his hero to the great figures of the Bible and, not least, to provide good stories for audiences who would have such lives read out to them.

So when Germanus with his companions, including another bishop, Lupus of Troyes, a monk from the crack monastery of Lérins, probably taken as theological adviser to a secular-trained bishop, crossed the Channel and a great storm arose, it was Germanus who calmed it. Constantius's hearers would pick up the echo of Jesus stilling the storm on Lake Galilee, and, behind that, the equating of the sea with the evil forces with which a bishop must contend. Germanus and Lupus preached. There was a debate with the Pelagians, who 'flaunted their wealth . . . in dazzling robes';[5] their support evidently was aristocratic, just as in Rome. Germanus prevailed. Conventionally, heretics were men of substance and influence in the world but readily brought down by God's power. In an episode echoing Jesus's healing of a Roman centurion's daughter, a man of 'tribunician power' is described as

[4] I.N. Wood, 'The end of Roman Britain: continental evidence and parallels', M. Lapidge, D.N. Dumville eds, Gildas. New approaches (Woodbridge 1984) 1–25 illuminates Germanus's Vita; B. Yorke, The conversion of Britain. Religion, politics and society in Britain c.600–800 (Harlow 2006) analytic account, concise, wide-ranging, excellent bibliography, cautious judgements
[5] Vita 14 trans. C. Thomas, Christianity in Roman Britain to AD 500 (London 1981) 55

bringing forward his daughter, blind for ten years, who is then healed by Germanus putting a bag of relics on her eyes. The daughter is Britannia, cured of the blindness of heresy and, significantly, it is a blindness of ten years' standing, dating back close on the 418 decision of Honorius to condemn Pelagianism.

Germanus and his party set out for St Alban's tomb at Verulamium to give thanks for their victory over error. On the way a fire broke out in a building where Germanus was staying after injuring his ankle; he did not flee but trusted in the power of God to save him and the fire duly leapt over the building, leaving the saint unscathed and free to travel on to Verulamium, where he found soil stained with the blood of Alban, which he gathered up to take back with him as a relic for his church at Auxerre. The surviving Passion of St Alban, as we have seen, was most probably based on placards set up by Germanus outside the church, which betray his preoccupation with the power of God, faith, confession and grace; in other words, the *Passio* is a facet of the campaign against Pelagianism. Germanus put relics collected from elsewhere into Alban's tomb, thus both strengthening and internationalising the cult.

During his stay in Britain Germanus again shows his mettle and the power of God in defeating barbarians, whom Constantius describes as 'Picts and Saxons'. The encounter has heavy religious overtones. British bishops preach and many are baptised and the enemy decides to attack, but Germanus, who becomes leader in the manner of Moses or Joshua, prepares an ambush. The Christian troops shout Alleluia three times; taken unawares, the barbarians flee and many are drowned. God's authority is displayed, the religious leader turns out to be an effective general and a Christian slogan wins the battle. The timing of the battle, with its echoes of Joshua's triumph before the walls of Jericho, is Lent – clearly leading to the Easter baptisms. What may in reality have been a skirmish is so overlaid with symbolism that it is hard to tell what happened.

The 'Picts and Saxons' have long puzzled historians. It is not known that these two ancient enemies of Britain had ever combined before. Resident in the north-east of modern Scotland beyond the Antonine Wall running across the Forth–Clyde isthmus, the Picts were made Rome's bitter enemies by the emperor Septimius Severus, who, making a prolonged stay in Britain in order to renew Roman defences, led an unusually ferocious punitive expedition against them in 210 in which the heavy slaughter was probably designed to be a preliminary to a full-scale occupation of the far north. Severus died and his successor abandoned these intentions but an enemy was left, embittered yet unsubdued. This heavy-handed repression opened a new phase in the history of the northern peoples: separate groupings coalesced into two major alliances, the Caledonii and the Maeatae and threw up a line of warlike leaders. By the end of the century, Romans were naming them 'Picti', the painted people, in allusion to their habit of tattooing. With the security of the highland fastnesses at their back, a restless will to attack and a capacity for naval warfare made them dangerous and expensive enemies in the fourth and fifth centuries as they raided over generations down to the south.[6]

Once, in a strange episode of 367 described by the historian Ammianus Marcellinus as a 'barbarian conspiracy', they were said to have combined with two groups of Irish raiders, the Scotti and the Attacotti, in a coordinated assault. Doubts have been expressed about the reality of this; it is not clear that either of these groupings was sufficiently organised to be able to exchange information and mount an assault. Rather, aware of attacks of Picts and Scots and grappling with internal unrest, hard-pressed commanders came to believe in a planned, conspiratorial move against them. However, it was never suggested that any of these barbarians had combined with the Saxons, a generic term for raiders from the coastlands of modern Netherlands and Germany who afflicted late Roman Britain.

A survey of Roman writers demonstrates that, for rhetorical effect, they were prone to fling in indiscriminately names of barbarians attacking parts of the Empire. So, for example, Claudian, praising the work of Count Theodosius, father of Emperor Theodosius the Great, who was mainly responsible for ending the crisis of 367 particularly through campaigning in the south and near London, said that 'the Orkneys ran red with Saxon blood, Thule was wet with the blood of Picts, ice-bound Ireland wept for the heap of slain Scots'. It would be a bold historian indeed who would argue from this that Saxons ever set foot in the Orkneys and certainly they were not on hand when Ireland was ice-bound.[7]

What we may infer from Constantius's Life is that barbarians, of whatever ilk, had continued their attacks on post-Roman Britain and were able to

[6] T.O. Clancy, B.E. Crawford, 'The formation of the Scottish kingdom', R.A. Houston, W.W.J. Knox eds, *The new Penguin history of Scotland* (New York 2001) 28–95 broad synthesis

[7] J.K. Knight, *The end of Antiquity: archaeology, society and religion AD 235–700* (Stroud 1999) 59–62 reviewed by D. Whitehouse, *Antiquity* 76 (2002) 998; ethnic labels, G. Ausenda ed., *Towards an ethnology of Europe's barbarians* (Woodbridge 1995)

penetrate inland, but they had not taken over the country. Germanus was able to travel freely, St Alban's shrine was open to pilgrimage and continued to be a cult centre, Church life had continued after the breach with the Empire, though the bishops had evidently not taken the general leadership roles which Gallic bishops had and conditions were such that an intellectual debate could take place. As a former advocate, Germanus was ideally suited for a polemic characteristic of the Roman world and we have no reason to doubt that he scored a victory. He returned in about 435 and, again showing that restoration to orthodoxy went hand in hand with physical healing, cured the son of a certain Elafius, a local leader. In the interim, though Pelagianism had not been eliminated, the position of orthodoxy had strengthened: where in 429 Germanus had merely overpowered his opponents in debate, on his second visit with his companion Severus, he was able to condemn them to exile. On both missions there are signs of some post-Roman authority being in existence, as is shown by the appearance in 429 of the 'man of tribunician power' and in 435 the leading man Elafius. Both pope and Gaulish bishop are treating Britain as if it was still part of the Empire. A British leadership had, in fact, held on to power and prevented a collapse in the face of external enemies for about half a century after the events of 406–11.

St Patrick, most remarkable of all British Christians, lived as a child on the west coast of Britain where he was a member of a clerical family, his father Calpornius being a deacon and his grandfather Potitus a priest. Calpornius was a decurion, a man of substance, possessing both male and female slaves to work his estate and combining service to the Church with civic duties as part of the governing body of the local *civitas*, a regional centre. Ordination was sometimes seen as a means of avoiding the heavy financial obligations of a decurion, the married state implying no decadence at this time as celibacy had yet to be seen as the ideal for clergy. The implication of Patrick's account of his father's activities is that in this region the skeleton of a Roman-style administration was still in being.

Patrick's secure childhood ended abruptly just short of his sixteenth birthday, when he fell victim to Irish raiders who snatched him up and carried him off to Ireland to be sold into slavery. His mother tongue was the indigenous Brittonic, and, but for this dramatic cutting short of his education, he would have gone on to the higher stage of rhetor and developed a surer grasp of Latin than he later managed to reach, a traditional Roman education being still available to men of his class. His Latin always lacked fluency and elegance but he used the Vulgate as well as the pre-Jerome Old Latin Bible and his knowledge of the Scriptures was profound, constantly and skilfully adapted and quoted in his writings.[8]

The Irish raid, no rarity, shows up a prime weakness of both late and post-Roman Britain: its inability to keep its citizens secure from barbarian attack and harassment. Irish sea power had grown in the fourth century: there is some evidence that trading between Irish merchants and Britain in more secure days had been regulated by mutual agreement with set emporia, which in 310 broke down, an increase in raiding being the consequence. One merchant confederation which turned into a bandit association, led, it may be, by the kings of Leinster, was known in Roman sources as the 'Scotti'; another, the Attacotti, may well have been led by the kings of Ulster. Late Roman Britain had the classic features of an attractive target for pirates and raiders: it was still prosperous and was no longer able to defend itself effectively. Slaves were an attraction: snatched from western coastal regions, they had but scant opportunity for escape. They contributed to the build-up of Irish agriculture and aided competition in wealth production among aristocrats. Loot or black-mail by Irish raiders will have been the source of the deposited coins gained from Britain placed as offerings to a pagan Irish god at the foot of stones at the prehistoric site of New Grange.[9]

The kidnapping was the major event in Patrick's early life, a traumatic experience whose aftermath led him into a life of prayer and the sense of a God-given mission to evangelise the pagan Irish, who had taken not only Patrick but also his father's slaves back to Ireland and sold them on. Patrick's master put him to herding sheep. He took to prayer: 'My spirit was quickened,' he wrote, 'so that in a day I prayed up to a hundred times and almost as many in the night. Indeed I even remained in the wood and on the mountains to pray. And – come hail, rain or snow – I was up before dawn to pray.'[10] Years after the kidnapping, he heard a voice in the night telling him he would travel 'very soon' to his homeland and then a 'revelation', 'Behold! Your ship is prepared.'[11]

[8] Comment in Casey, 'Fourth century' 100–1; K.R. Dark, 'St Patrick's *villula* and the fifth century occupation of Romano-British villas', D.N. Dumville ed., St *Patrick* AD *493–1993* (Woodbridge 1993) 1–12; comment N.J. Higham, *Britannia* 25 (1994) 229–32
[9] T.M. Charles-Edwards, *Early Christian Ireland* (Cambridge 2000) magisterial, full account of Irish missions; D.J. Breeze, 'The edge of the world: the imperial frontier and beyond', Salway, *Roman era* 173–200 at 195; P. Rance, 'Attacotti, Déisi and Magnus Maximus: the case for Irish *federates* in late Roman Britain', *Britannia* 31 (2001) 243–76
[10] T. O'Loughlin, *Discovering St Patrick* (London 2005) 149
[11] Ibid.

Trust in providence and the authenticity of the revelations he received gave him the strength to escape and persevere in flight; the same trust which gave the nineteenth-century slave in antebellum America, Harriet Tubman, the strength to leave her master and then become the resilient leader of a series of her fellow slaves fleeing across the Mason–Dixon Line. When Patrick eventually arrived home, he found his father's estate still flourishing and his parents wished him to stay and run it. But he refused because he felt an overriding call to go back to evangelise the Irish.

No governing authority in Britain, no naval or military force was able to choke off Irishmen in search of loot, slaves or, ultimately, land; in Ireland there was no authority to check slaving, or to appeal to for the return of slaves. It does not seem that Calpornius had been able to do anything to recover his son; Patrick was resourceful, felt God's hand on him and was able to escape, but many others would not have been able to do so.

In the *Confessio*, Patrick was writing a spiritual odyssey, a narrative of God's treatment of him: he gives no dates and few details. He refers to his former home as a 'villula', a word characteristic of Patrick's love of diminutives: there is reason to believe that his family lived in a full-scale villa comparable to those which existed in lowland Britain in the fourth century. His village he named as Bannavem Taburniae, no knowledge of which has come down to us. It has been conjectured that the name originated in Banna, that is Birdoswald, the village lying close to the western side of Hadrian's Wall, and that the *civitas* where Calpornius carried out his duties was Carlisle, the raiders coming in through the river system. They had only to slip across the Wall and draw in victims from the Irthing valley. But archaeology has given scant evidence generally of villas in this area. A more likely site, equally on the western coast and accessible to raiders but further south, would be by the Severn estuary where Roman influence was still strong and villas more frequent.[12] Research has tended to place Patrick's career as missionary and bishop within the second half of the fifth century. If this is so, then the picture given of the state of affairs near the coast of a part of western Britain in his childhood relates to the post-Roman interlude of British independence.

The impression given by both the Life of Germanus and Patrick's *Confessio* of a continuing, residual, albeit tattered post-Roman state authority and of a

---

[12] Thomas, *Christianity* 310–14 argues for site near Hadrian's Wall; arguments for Severn estuary I believe stronger

society where Church life had not been seriously disrupted by barbarian
raiding and looting begins to dissolve during the second half of the fifth
century. The Gallic Chronicle of 452 says in its annal for the year 441: 'the
Britons, having hitherto been overrun by various calamities and events, are
subjected to Saxon authority'.[13] This cannot be taken literally. The fragmentation of authority within Britain will have removed the possibility of any one
source being able to give an overall summary of events and there is no support
for the notion of a wholesale takeover by the Germanic invaders at this stage.
Nor need the date be taken literally. It may well, however, mark broadly the
point in time at which raiders who had harassed eastern and southern Britain
for generations began to settle. Another indication of crucial change comes
from the account of Gildas: writing some seventy years later, he describes the
vain appeal by the British for continental help. 'To Aetius, thrice consul: the
groans of the British . . . The barbarians push us back to the sea, the sea
pushes us back to the barbarians; between the two kinds of death we are either
drowned or slaughtered.'[14] Aetius was one of the last strong men of the
Empire, the victor of the battle of the Catalaunian Plains over Attila the Hun
in 451, whose third consulship was in 446. Beset by problems himself, he
refused help. The story is not incredible and, if true, demonstrates how far the
situation had deteriorated since the British had asserted their independence
after Constantine III's death in 411.

The events of mid-fifth century form the prelude to a long, confused period
of infiltration, fighting and conquest by a mixed body of Germanic peoples
generally from coastal lands. Influenced by the weakened state of Britain's
defences, they invaded across the North Sea and English Channel, impelled
sometimes by drowning land and shortage of territory or by the impulse for
betterment. Fourth-century Saxon raiders had been met by a centralised system,
underpinned, like all Romano-British defences, by taxation and central leadership; the approach of raiders was registered by signal stations; camouflaged crews
and vessels were deployed to cut off pirate ships while still at sea, while on land
the Forts of the Saxon Shore acted as strongpoints to deny free use of land to

[13] Quoted N.J. Higham, *The English conquest: Gildas and Britain in the fifth century*
(Manchester New York 1994) 120, reviewed by P. Bartholomew, *Britannia* 27 (1996) 486–7,
P.J. Casey, *EME* 167–9, P. Sims-Williams, *TLS* 26 May 1995; Patrick's dates, D.N. Dumville,
'The floruit of St Patrick: common and less common ground', id., *Patrick* 13–18
[14] Gildas 20. I have not been able to accept Higham's reassessment of the Aetius appeal;
whole context, B. Ward-Perkins, *The fall of Rome and the end of civilisation* (Oxford 2005)
128, 130

raiders and to support authority against rebels and mutineers within Britain. With the departure of the legions, the British decision to act independently, the end of taxation and the coin economy ruled out of court such high-calibre mechanisms. Weak, more localised defences opened the way to increased raiding and finally invasion. The rising sea level and consequent loss of territory on the North Sea coastline was one precipitating factor for migration; more important were the effects of a decline in the economy of the Western Empire which had negative results on the peoples beyond the *limes* who had grown accustomed to reaping benefits from contacts across the frontier.[15]

Evidently a wide range of Germanic peoples drawn from the long coastline from the Channel to southern Scandinavia participated in a piecemeal, haphazard and individual migration lasting many years. Most, including Franks (albeit on a small scale), Frisians, Saxons and Danes, were maritime people accustomed to voyaging – although Thuringians, who had no contact with the sea, were also participants. Piracy is a common prelude to migration. Young men will have been the pioneers, stimulating movement by knowledge of the British coastline and rivers acquired through raids. Warrior elites will have sought new fields of action and conquest. Once inaugurated, migration will have had a knock-on effect as established settlers exchanged information with relatives: we should imagine continuing passages to and from the continent. Ships of the time, having no masts or sails, did not make the passage of family or goods easy as places for rowers greatly reduced passenger space.[16] Weather conditions would have made winter crossings hazardous and put a premium on the narrow seas of the Channel and adjacent areas. Those who lived furthest north, in Jutland and beyond, had to face the challenges of wind and tide across the North Sea or a substantial journey down the coast or overland to find easier crossing points. Such difficulties would have worked to select the hardiest, most enterprising and most motivated from among the

[15] I. Wood, 'Before and after the migration to Britain', J. Hines ed., *The Anglo-Saxons from the migration period to the eighth century* (Woodbridge, 1997) 41–54; unrehearsed discussion, often illuminating, 55–64; see also W. Pohl, 'Ethnic names and identities in the British Isles: a comparative perspective', Hines ed., *Anglo-Saxons* 7–32, discussion 32–40; H. Vollrath, 'Die Landnahme der Angelsachsen nach dem Zeugnis der erzählenden Quellen', M. Müller-Wille *et al.* eds, *Vorträge und Forschungen* 41 (1993) 518–57; did Bede's list of origins *HE* I 15 come from lost lit. source? J. Campbell, 'Bede', *ODNB*

[16] M.E. Jones, *The end of Roman Britain* (Ithaca, NY 1996) reviewed by P. Salway, *WHR* 19 (1998–9) 143–6; G. Halsall, 'Review article: movers and shakers: the barbarians and the fall of Rome', *EME* 8 (1999) 131–45; N.J. Higham, *Rome, Britain and the Anglo-Saxons* (London 1992) argues for small numbers; reviewed by H. Hamerow, *EME* 2 (1993) 172–3

tribes involved. Shipping space and travel hazards would have been a check on numbers in any one year, though sails were beginning to come into use by *c.*500; on the other hand, migrations extended over many years from *c.*450 well into the following century, perhaps up to *c.*650, allowing for the possibility of substantial immigration.[17] No chronicle of these complicated – yet crucial – events has survived. Gildas was writing a moral treatise showing how God's hand sent barbarian raiders and settlers against the British in punishment for their sins. As Hanna Vollrath observes,[18] it was immaterial to him whether these instruments of punishment were Picts, Scots or Saxons. He gives scant detail on how this all happened and no time scale. Bede is almost wholly dependent on Gildas: he was the descendant of one of the Germanic groups, the victors in the invasions, and might, therefore, have written from their perspective. He does not – he takes up Gildas's text and views the events from the point of view of the victims, not the victors; all he adds to Gildas are a few names.

The invaders were illiterate. Their memories could only be committed to writing after Christian missionaries brought literacy to their descendants in the late seventh century. At an unknown date, churchmen jotted fragments of oral tradition under dates in tables for the finding of Easter. These fragments of information were subsequently incorporated into the early part of the *Anglo-Saxon Chronicle* which, in its extant form, is a compilation made at the West Saxon court in the late ninth or early tenth century. Unless encased in a poetic or ritual format, oral tradition cannot maintain its accuracy. At a high point in Victorian popular historical writing, J.R. Green, using the *Chronicle*, described the Anglo-Saxon invasions, it has been said, as if he were standing on the shore watching them come in. This is no longer possible. Recent study of the place of oral tradition in both African and early medieval Germanic societies has further undermined the value of these fragments, once used as the basis for an outline chronology and geography of the invasions.[19]

---

[17] I owe comment to Dr J. Wooding of University College, Lampeter

[18] H. Vollrath, 'Landnahme' 41

[19] D.N. Dumville, 'Sub-Roman Britain: history and legend', *History* N.S. 62 (1977) 173–92, reflecting on L. Alcock, *Arthur's Britain. History and archaeology AD 367–634* (London 1971) combining excavation at South Cadbury, Somerset, with a broader narrative, and J.R. Morris, *The age of Arthur: a history of the British Isles from 350–650* (London 1973), marked by deep learning and failure to assess unreliability of lit. sources, esp. Celtic hagiographies, rev. D.P. Kirby, J.E.C. Williams, *Studia Celtica* 10–11 (1975–6) 454–86, J. Campbell, *Studia Hibernica* 15 (1975) 177–85; comment, R.A. Fletcher, *Who's who in Roman Britain and Anglo-Saxon England 55 BC–AD 1066* (London 1989, repr. Mechanicsburg 2002) 18

The historian is left with archaeology, place-name study and linguistic history in the attempt to recover some outline of the course of events, the long-term effects of the attacks and conquests, and the impact on Romanised Britons and Christians. This is based overwhelmingly on evidence from burial sites, crema-tion pots or grave goods, from inhumations, with jewellery and metalwork and the decoration of handmade pots being deployed to establish the continental origins of the settlers and to attempt to provide an overall scheme of the pattern of migration and subsequent development of Anglo-Saxon societies.

Writing many years after the invasions, Bede himself, in a passage of Book I of his *Ecclesiastical History*, attempted to rationalise this confusion and told his readers that the invaders were divided into three main groupings, Angles, Saxons and Jutes, and attempted to reconstruct their places of both origin and settlement in Britain. It was an oversimplified solution. However, in Book V, recording the attempt by the monk Egbert to go to the lands of the still-pagan ancestors of the Anglo-Saxons and convert them to Christianity, he inciden-tally threw up a list of the continental peoples to which mission was to be directed, a list not coterminous with, but almost certainly including, those who came to Britain. Nevertheless, it is clear that this list of miscellaneous peoples is much nearer the truth than his reconstruction in Book I.[20] The invaders came over in varied, often quite small, groups, with differing polit-ical backgrounds, speaking different dialects and with a variety of customs and artefacts. Here were no organised armies, but a mixture of peasants and fighting men, adventurers seeking their fortune. For their part, the British also lacked an effective overarching organisation for political action or defence.

Self-help had long been a keynote and, just as even before the end of Roman Britain magnates had hired *bucellarii*, mercenary soldiers, to defend them, so during the phase of independence under British leadership the *civi-tates* would have done the same. A defensive weakness is implied in the choice of a visiting bishop as an army commander. The Germanic migration fell most heavily in the lowland east of Britain and Gildas's account of what led up to this speaks of a 'proud tyrant', named by Bede as Vortigern, and his council making a treaty with *federati*, that is, barbarian troops operating under their own commanders but receiving pay collectively from their employers, a Germanic force 'let in' in settlements, to beat off attacks from enemies of Britain, not now Picts and Scots but enemies of the same race as the

---

[20] *HE* I 15, V 9; Hines, *Anglo-Saxons* 55–64; C. Hills, *Origins of the English* (London 2003); H. Härke, 'The debate on migration and identity in Europe', *Antiquity* 78 (2004) 453–6

federati. A dispute arose over provisioning and the *federati* rose in revolt and began to take over. In a manner characteristic of such stories, the key point is betrayal, the stab in the back which destroys a state; but it is certainly possible that the abuse of the *federati* system was a factor leading to a British defeat and an inflow of invaders.[21]

Lowland history now enters on a prolonged phase of 'micro-communities', a balkanisation of authority, in which a multitude of small-scale successes and failures marks the relationship between the indigenous British defenders and the Germanic invaders.[22] The invaders were not necessarily united; nor necessarily were the British defenders. There is no reason to suppose that tensions which existed between population strata in late Romano-British society had somehow dissipated in the fifth century. A variety of responses to events can be expected, from peaceful coexistence to fierce resistance or submission to the invaders. Literary sources tend to stress fighting and though this will not always have been the prevailing activity, there was nevertheless enough military action to give a strong edge of hostility to the relationship between the two sides. Gildas paints the invasion events in sombre colours and describes wholesale slaughter and destruction, as rams battered down defences, swords glinted, flames crackled and fragments of corpses lay covered with congealed blood. Burnt debris which would substantiate all this has not been found: it derives from literary models dear to Gildas, the fall of Troy in Virgil's *Aeneid*, the Psalms, the Book of Kings, the Prophets.[23] The towns of Roman Britain were in decline before the Anglo-Saxon invasions: they were not burned, but decayed and their decline was sharply hastened by the invasions. The attacks were mounted by peoples from beyond the Roman *limes* who had been little touched by Romanisation and the long time scale of the invasions militated against the survival of Roman ideas, language, structure and institutions. In some respects the slate was wiped clean by the immigrations of the fifth and sixth centuries and the history of Britain diverged sharply from that of Gaul, which was conquered by the Franks, barbarians who succeeded much more rapidly, taking over the country by 480. They had been more touched by Roman influence than the peoples who came over to Britain and they entered

[21] Gildas 23

[22] R. Sharpe, 'Martyrs and local saints in late antique Britain', A. Thacker, R. Sharpe eds, *Local saints and local churches in the early medieval west* (Oxford 2002) 75–154 crucial for following reconstruction

[23] M. Lapidge, 'Gildas's education and the Latin culture of sub-Roman Britain', Lapidge and Dumville, *Gildas* 27–50

into a symbiosis with the Gallo-Romans, the heirs to the Empire, in which much of the past was retained and Gaulish came to be replaced by a Romance language based on Latin.

In the lowland zone of Britain, Brittonic suffered a remarkable decline; it was eclipsed by a Germanic tongue, the basis of modern English. It is remarkable how little was carried over from Brittonic to Old English, which developed almost as if the indigenous British had never existed. The number of Brittonic words taken over into the tongue of the invaders is pathetically low: it stands at probably no more than thirty, including stray words for animals, tools and some natural features. This argues for a high degree of apartheid between the two and, given the normal influence of a mother's tongue on her children, an absence of marriages between the British and the invaders. The appearance of British names in some early genealogies, such as that of Cerdic, ancestor of the royal house of Wessex, suggests that there was no absolute barrier to intermarriage but, nonetheless, that such high-level pairings were very much the exception and that the immigration was an immigration of families. An overwhelming dominance of the language of the incomers over that of the existing inhabitants was established and maintained. Brittonic became profoundly unfashionable.[24]

A similar picture has been confirmed by Kenneth Jackson in his classic analysis of river names. In the areas of prime Anglo-Saxon settlement east of a line from Southampton up to the coast north of Flamborough Head only the Celtic names for the longest rivers were taken over by the incomers; lesser waterways were renamed. It is another proof of the overwhelming superiority established for their language by the invaders.[25] As with language, so with religion. The incomers were pagan and in the long years of immigration they established their beliefs at the expense of the Christianity of the British, whose religion had no prestige within the lands of prime conquest: it was the religion of the defeated. Germanic paganism was the religion of the conquerors.

The seventh-century laws of Ine, Anglo-Saxon king of Wessex, open a window on the fate of the vanquished, setting the *wergild* (blood price) for them consistently lower than for his Anglo-Saxon subjects: the Old English *wealas* means both slave and Briton. Opportunities certainly existed to rise

---

[24] H.R. Loyn, *Anglo-Saxon England and the Norman Conquest* (2nd edn Harlow 1991) ch. 1; D. Kastovsky, 'Semantics and vocabulary', R.M. Hogg ed., *The Cambridge history of English language* I (Cambridge 1992) 290–408 at 316–20
[25] K. Jackson, *Language and history in early Britain* (2nd edn Dublin 1994) 221–2

under his rule and the records show that British cavalrymen were in his service: language rather than descent may have been critical, but given incentives, assimilation is likely to have taken place on a very large scale over the years. A cogent analogy lies in the fate of Christian subjects in ancient Byzantine lands in Egypt and Palestine conquered by the Muslims: they were not maltreated but were taxed with Jews as People of the Book and, with both social and financial incentives to convert, they did. It would seem that the British responded similarly.[26]

The number of Germanic immigrants in the key centuries continues to be debated, with an increasing and valuable input from genetic studies based on contemporary populations both on the continent and in the British Isles. Sampling has grown more sophisticated, with more attention paid to genetic analysis from a range of small towns, one startling result of which has been to show a level of Y chromosomes among men in central England today corresponding to those in modern Friesland. This is far higher than is compatible with any level of immigration that can reasonably be presupposed under the historical conditions of the fifth and sixth centuries. This genetic analysis certainly argues against some modern views that would restrict Germanic immigration to a small, determined elite who by force of arms imposed their will on a much larger indigenous population. Even though these figures might be to a limited extent affected by the further immigration of the Viking age, they are still too high to support a 'small elite' hypothesis.[27] The problem seems to have been solved by analogy with modern studies of social isolation of ethnic groups and the effects of wealth and status producing greater fertility among richer and more privileged groups than among the poorer and disadvantaged. This was emphatically the case in post-Roman Britain, and the British population declined.

In sum, the immigrants quite evidently were aware of the distinction between themselves and those they had conquered or wished to conquer, did not accept their religious beliefs and were disinclined to accept literacy from them or to marry with them. These emphatic refusals were an aspect of the social isolation which the immigrants imposed. There is an analogy here with

---

[26] T. Charles-Edwards, 'Language and society among the insular Celts', M. Green ed., *The Celtic world* (London 1995) 703–36 at 733 (Ine); B. Ward-Perkins, 'Why did the Anglo-Saxons not become more British?', *EHR* 115 (2000) 513–33 at 525 (Islamic analogy)

[27] M.E. Weale, *et al.*, 'Y chromosome evidence for Anglo-Saxon mass immigration', *Molecular Biology and Evolution* 19 (2002) 1008–21; C. Capelli *et al.*, 'A Y chromosome census of the British Isles', *Current Biology* 13 (2003) 979–84

the imposition of restriction of marriage in the fifth century by the Visigoth king Euric who wished his people in southern France and Spain to reject marriage with those they conquered, which they did. Moreover, marriage barriers do not spring solely from the decisions of rulers: the remarkably low incidence of marriage in modern times in Pembrokeshire between English and Welsh speakers has sprung spontaneously from the inclinations of the local population. An apartheid separated the peoples and over time the Anglo-Saxons outbred the British they dominated.[28]

The fate of Christianity was bound up with the severe economic decline of post-Roman Britain, the loss of central mechanisms for trade and distribution, the disappearance of the money economy, the decline of towns and disappearance of villas. Christianity had been to a considerable degree an aspect of Romanisation; the Romanised classes and their dependants who had accepted Christian belief were displaced and the economic basis of their lives weakened or destroyed. There is a reversion to subsistence agriculture. Nothing could be more striking than the events in the south-west at Poundbury where the Christian cemetery came to be overlaid by a farming settlement with simple timber structures, grain driers, a threshing floor, pottery, some facilities for weaving and metalworking – almost as if the cemetery had never been – and this was an area not affected by the Germanic invasions.[29] In the south and east where they did strike home we must with all probability reckon with a flight of the wealthier and more civilised to more secure lands further west; over time, the British lost cohesion, British churches in the lands heavily affected may well have lost their clergy and the ability to transmit their culture and beliefs to the incomers.

Being illiterate, the invaders leave us no direct account of their beliefs. Churchmen who in the seventh century laboured to put down paganism and draw the former invaders to the worship of Christ wrote very little about the subject and they certainly did not write in the manner of a modern historian or anthropologist. Paganism was the enemy, tenacious and treacherous, its practices and beliefs the work of devils: acceding to them was a sin to be

---

[28] M.G. Thomas, 'Evidence for an apartheid-like social structure in early Anglo-Saxon England', *Proceedings of the Royal Society* B (2006) 273, 2651–7. I am indebted to Dr M.G. Thomas, Dept of Biology, University College, London, for sending copies of this article and those in n. 27 above; examples and discussion, Ward-Perkins, *Fall of Rome*; survey, H. Härke, 'Kings and warriors. Population and landscape from post-Roman to Norman Britain', P. Slack, R. Ward eds, *The peopling of Britain* (Oxford 2002) 145–75

[29] D.E. Farwell, T.I. Morrison, *Excavations at Poundbury 1966–80* II (Dorchester 1993) xi; Esmonde Cleary, *Ending* 178–9

expiated by penance. Expedients for tackling it, tempering the wind to the shorn lamb, appear in the letters of Church leaders, the narratives of Bede's *Ecclesiastical History* and of saints' lives, which describe confrontations with the enemy and episodes where missionary effort overcame, sometimes slowly, the antagonists of the Christian faith. The enemy had behind him the power of Satan and could never be taken lightly.

Bede was well equipped to inform about Germanic paganism; his native Northumbria's conversion was only a generation away and the Anglo-Saxon kingdom of Sussex was still in heathen hands at the time of his birth. Much information, folklore and memory would have lingered on into his lifetime, but he chose not to expound it. His purpose was to confirm faith through narrating the lives and achievements of Christian missionaries and the kings and aristocrats who aided them; paganism was sin and the less said about it the better. So we have from him little more than some fragments of information about the pagan deities whose names were attached to days of the week, some inferences about the residual force of paganism, a staged pair of speeches on the occasion of the first acceptance of Christianity in Northumbria contrasting pagan materialism with the Christian promise of the understanding of the meaning of life and some references to feasts and animal sacrifices.[30]

The invaders carried with them ideas and practices comparable to those outlined for the Germanic homelands by Tacitus in the first century, no doubt with differences due to the passage of time. He describes processes of divination – writing runes on strips from a fruit tree branch, selecting from them with prayer and reading from them messages, positive or negative, for some chosen enterprise, or drawing conclusions from the flight of birds or the actions of horses. Sacred groves played a special role. Tacitus describes priests who officiated in them taking horses, 'pure white and undefiled by work for man', led by priest, king or 'chief of state' who secured them to a sacred chariot and went along with them, noting their 'neighings and snortings'. He saw the horse ceremony as the highest, most valued form of divination of his day; though this particular ceremony is not detectable in the conversion age either in England or on the continent, there are indications that there may well have been a cult of the horse. Whether the Germanic pagans used birds, horses, tree branches or entrails in the manner of the Romans is not, however, the key point. Ceremonies based on natural phenomena were used both in Tacitus's

---

[30] Bede is inaccurate in attributing Easter to pagan goddess Eostre instead of O.E. *eastan*, the east

time and later in England and on the continent for the purpose of forecasting events and understanding the will of the gods.[31]

Divination and taboo went side by side. Together they created a structure of security for a people or tribe: observe the ceremonies of divination and act on the result, avoid forbidden actions, perform the requisite sacrifices, maintain the ceremonies appropriate to the seasons, wear rings and equipment for battle that will bring a god's support and success, and health and fertility of crops will be enjoyed by all. How much tension surrounded the divination process can be observed in the seventh century, in the actions of Radbod, ruler of the Frisians, responding in anger to the actions of the missionary Willibrord who had gone to an island, usually identified as Heligoland, where the heathen god Fosite had temples. It seems that the whole island was a sacred place. Inhabitants took water from a spring there with awe: they drew from it in complete silence. There were sacred cows left strictly alone. This did not daunt Willibrord, who with his companions bluntly challenged the god by baptising three candidates in the spring and slaughtering some of the cattle for food. Radbod wished to apply the death penalty for this blasphemy. For three whole days he cast lots three times a day 'to find out who should die'. The law evidently did not operate in a straightforward way; for all his anger, Radbod had to consult the gods before acting. In the end one person was executed and Willibrord's life was saved.[32] But the episode shows the strength of heathenism: if rites were correctly performed, the gods gave secure guidance. Conversely, actions which disrupted the structure of observance and affronted the gods could be dangerous and destructive to a whole people. The same applied to taboo. Bede gives us a glimpse of taboo in action in his story of the pagan high priest, Coifi, who, opting for Christianity after Paulinus's campaigning, defied taboo by choosing to ride a stallion, forbidden to priests, and carry arms, as with sword and spear he set off to profane a heathen temple.[33] This defiance so impressed the people they thought he had gone mad.

Sacrifices to gods in England are well attested. Gregory the Great was concerned about them and recommended replacing the pagan festivals,

---

[31] D.M. Wilson, *Anglo-Saxon paganism* (London, New York 1992) 26

[32] Ibid. 40, using Alcuin's Life of Willibrord; wide-ranging reflections on paganism in I.N. Wood, 'Pagans and holy men 600–800', P. Ni Chatháin and M. Richter eds, *Ireland and Christendom* (Stuttgart, 1987) 347–61, id., 'Pagan religions and superstitions east of the Rhine from the fifth to the eighth century', Ausenda, *Ethnology* 253–79; J.D. Niles, 'Pagan survivals and popular belief', M. Godden, M. Lapidge eds, *The Cambridge companion to Old English literature* (Cambridge 1991) 126–41; comment, C. Hills, *Antiquity* 56 (1982) 146–8

[33] *HE* II 13

assimilated to the immemorial rhythms of the agricultural year, by Christian feast days. Bede refers to the 'blood month' roughly approximating to November, a festival at which oxen were sacrificed: this combined religious observance with the practicalities of slaughtering to avoid pressing too hard on limited stocks of winter fodder for the beasts and providing stores for the populace. Days of the week were named after deities, Tuesday after Tiw, the god of war, Wednesday after Woden, Thursday Thunor and Friday Frig, the goddess of fertility: the eve of 25 December was called *Modranect*, the night of the mothers. In other words, pagans had a timetable mapped out for them with repeated reminiscences of gods and patterns of observance into which they would be born and which was their inheritance from parents and more distant ancestors.[34]

It was hard for converts to throw off the example and practice of this inheritance. In a story usually regarded as *ben trovato*, but undoubtedly corresponding to the realities of the German mission field, Radbod had one foot in the font when he drew back, unwilling to break with his ancestors, who, he had been informed, would be in hell because of their heathenism.[35] This was the direct consequence of the churchmen's conviction that heathenism meant the worship of devils, that there could be no compromise with evil and that baptism was a necessity if a candidate was to hope for heaven. Though Radbod did later accept baptism, this stark contrast made for hard decisions for pagans in authority, given the immense importance of family and descent.

The fact that the sacred sites which focused belief were natural ones – springs, trees, hills and the like – made for an easy adaptation when Anglo-Saxon settlers made their landfall in Britain and began carving out their own lands and spheres of authority. Natural features were adopted as in their homelands and gained a sacral authority as they became points of focus for pagan rites. The place-names with *hearg* and *weoh* or *wig* imply open-air sanctuaries. Harrow on the Hill in Middlesex is a classic pagan site, a steep hill rising three hundred feet from the plain, a natural feature visible for miles, the *hearg* element demonstrating that it was a sanctuary. Harrow Hill in Sussex is a hill south of the Downs where animal teeth and bone fragments have been found, remains primarily of Iron Age ritual sacrifice but since the connotation in Anglo-Saxon is a shrine, it may be a case where a Celtic site was taken over. The original name was Gumeninga-hergae, i.e. the sanctuary of the

---

[34] Hines, *Anglo-Saxons* 375–401, discussion 401–10
[35] Wood, 'Pagan religions', 263, using *Vita Vulframni*; W. Levison, *England and the continent in the eighth century* (Oxford 1946) 56

Gumenings, some tribal sub-group. *Wig* or *weoh* was sometimes combined with *leah*, wood or grove, implying a holy place centred on woodland, as in the description by Tacitus. A major event in the mission to Hesse-Thuringia of the eighth-century Anglo-Saxon evangelist, Boniface, was his felling of the great oak at Geismar sacred to the god Woden – an open challenge to the deity to do his worst. Nothing happened and Boniface's courageous example encouraged conversions. The point is that paganism's focus was on natural features.[36]

Sometimes place-names which include animal heads, as at Swineshead, which has been interpreted as a 'hill with a projecting snout of land', may be playful, casual allusions with no pagan implications. But some archaeological evidence suggests a special role for animals in pagan cults. A single burial of an ox skull at Soham in Cambridgeshire took place in circumstances suggesting some cultic significance and there is a similar example involving a pig's skull at Frilford in Berkshire.[37] Aldhelm, Anglo-Saxon scholar and abbot of Malmesbury, denounced worship of 'crude pillars of the foul snake and stag', still occurring decades after the arrival of Christian missionaries. Bladbean in Kent, meaning 'blood-beam', could carry an allusion to heathen sacrifice; Bampton in Oxfordshire, 'tun by a beam', is another intriguing example – animal heads on posts are a likely part of the apparatus of heathen worship.[38]

There are also inferences to be drawn from place-names in England linked to the gods Woden, Thunor or Tiw, and in one instance, Frig, associating them with groves and mounds or, as in the case of Tyesmere in Worcestershire, with a pool. In two or three cases the names translate as Woden's open country, implying a dedication to the god of their land by pagan farmers. Reference to Woden's or Thunor's mounds sometimes indicates man-made barrows including burial sites of the past; reverence for the dead or simply an assumption that a prominent earthwork must be the work of a god would have led to the naming. Some are likely to have been cult centres for the deity; others to have been dedications in honour of a favoured member of the pagan pantheon in gratitude or hope. In summary, a survey of place-names reveals the presence of two kinds of sanctuary or holy place and a scattering of references to gods, reinforcing the impression that as Anglo-Saxon custom and speech prevailed in the age of migration, so the dedication of sites and making of sanctuaries to the heathen gods multiplied, creating in time a network of reminders of their

[36] Wilson, *Paganism* 41–2 (Boniface)
[37] Ibid. 100 (Soham, Frilford)
[38] J. Blair, 'Anglo-Saxon pagan shrines and their prototypes', *ASAH* 8 (1995) 1–28 at 2–3; id., *The Church in Anglo-Saxon society* (Oxford 2008) 186

presence and influence, a living heathen landscape. We can fairly assume that in some areas the net was much tighter, as names may have been lost in time, and in certain areas, especially in East Anglia, subsequent Scandinavian immigration has overlaid the Anglo-Saxon name pattern.[39]

Woden mattered. The immigrants had to build up a kingship of their own. Individuals won power by their swords, then sought with the help of their scops to build genealogies with great names from the continent, mythic heroes generally with Woden at the head. The notion of a royal family, a *stirps regia*, grew up: it was a means of fending off outsiders. Within the *stirps* a man who wanted to be king had to show his calibre by success in war and shrewd deal-making or he would be pushed aside. But, first, royal descent had to be there. He and his followers evidently felt the need for Woden at their back, the god of war and the master of *fortuna*, the good luck so necessary to a warrior-king. Occasionally other names came in, such as Saxneat, but Woden was the usual choice. We owe knowledge of these genealogies to the churchmen who wrote them down, Bede being one of them. They kept Woden but reduced him in stature by linking him to the Old Testament, so we have the curious situation in which Alfred of Wessex has a genealogy which includes Woden as a descendant of Noah.[40]

The immigrants brought with them their customary burial practices of cremation and inhumation, and with such factors as the decorative styles of cinerary urns and the typology of grave goods, the incidence of such burials has been used to provide clues to their origins, status, daily life and beliefs. Cremation, especially strong in East Anglia and the East Midlands, was a primitive rite which had generally faded out before the conversion epoch; it was also one burial custom which was rejected by the Christian Church, though grave goods were not per se rejected as incompatible with belief; the Christian Frankish lands continued to provide grave goods for their dead and were not censured for doing so. Nevertheless, the ceremonies accompanying the disposal of the immigrant dead, now obscure to us, included some grave goods which are clearly indicative of pagan beliefs. Funeral customs are notoriously conservative and they formed part of the skein of custom broadly resistant to the new religion.

From both cremations and inhumations, the evidence points to rituals important to mourners, relatives and their communities, with implications for their understanding of the world and their place in it. More commonly than

[39] Wilson, *Paganism* 15 (Tyesmere) 11, 14–15, 19–20 (Woden)
[40] E. John, 'The point of Woden', *ASAH* 5 (1992) 127–34; K. Sisam, 'Anglo-Saxon genealogies', *PBA* 39 (1953) 287–348; C. Behr, 'The origins of kingship in early medieval Kent', *EME* 9 (2000) 25–52

inhumations, cremations were accompanied by animal sacrifices, and though both had grave goods, those cremated were necessarily of a specialised character. We can infer from remains of jewellery found in the ashes that bodies would have been festively dressed before being laid on the pyre: sometimes grave goods would be included then and exposed to the flames, others put with the ashes in the cinerary urn and then buried. It was not unusual to find animal bones mixed with the human ones in a strange intimacy; it appears that specially killed animals were placed on the pyre with the body and then incorporated into the urn, or, less commonly, buried separately but still in association with the dead. In the great cremation cemetery at Spong Hill, Norfolk, forty-six per cent of two thousand cremations included animal bones.[41]

Prominent among grave goods are combs, tweezers, shears, occasionally razors; items, it has been observed, all linked with hair care. Why toilet implements, especially combs, played such a significant part on cremation sites remains obscure, the more so since some are evidently not those actually used by the dead, some bone or antler combs being too blunt or too small for use, or sometimes the equipment consists of purpose-made miniatures, only symbolising those in real life. It would seem some equipment was made, and badly or hurriedly made, solely for the final ceremony. Hair can be used in sympathetic magic: did relatives wish to prevent any abuse by evil forces, if not of the hair itself, of the implements used to care for it? Or, as Howard Williams argues, were the combs, tweezers and the rest designed to aid the rebuilding of a new body after the destruction of the old, 'a necessary or auspicious means of ensuring the proper transformation of the dead'?[42]

Cremation was expensive and demanding. The cost of pyre-building is likely to have been a factor in its demise. Everywhere there is evidence of a careful ritual and of trouble taken to commemorate the dead: the ceramic urns in which remains were usually deposited were often elaborately decorated.[43] There are glimpses of the supernatural and awareness of an afterlife. Serpents or dragons were in Anglo-Saxon myth the guardians of treasure and

---

[41] H. Williams, 'Material culture as memory: combs and cremation in early medieval Britain', *EME* 12 (2005) 89–128; whole context, S. Lucy, *The Anglo-Saxon way of death* (Stroud 2000) finely comprehensive, 937 sites, stresses fashion, family and individual taste; see also S. Lucy, A. Reynolds, 'Burial in early medieval England and Wales: past, present and future', id. ed., *Burial in early medieval England and Wales* (London 2002) 1–23; survey, A. Taylor, *Burial practice in early England* (Stroud 2001)

[42] Williams, 'Material culture' 127; see J.D. Richards, 'Anglo-Saxon symbolism. The early Anglo-Saxons', M. Carver ed., *The age of Sutton Hoo* (Woodbridge 1992) 131–47

[43] Wilson, *Paganism* 156–8

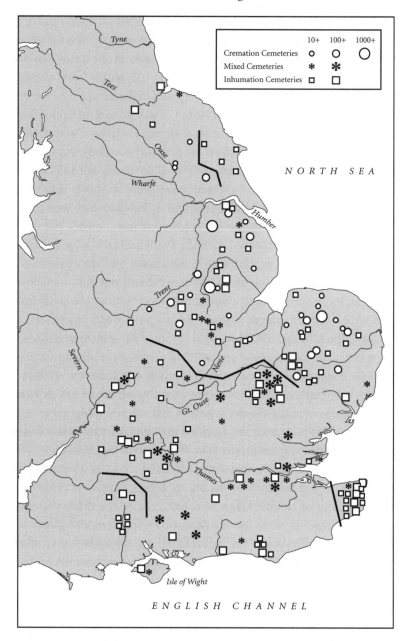

Map 1 Anglo-Saxon cremations and burials. Principal sites are plotted for the age of earliest immigration, the fifth and sixth centuries. Lines fence off regions to show certain prevailing patterns. Inhumation cemeteries are shown in the heartland of Deira in the Yorkshire wolds, in the south west, and clustered in Kent where Frankish customs prevailed. Cremation sites are in substantial numbers in East Anglia and Lincolnshire. Research indicates that local influences played a larger part in the choice of funerary rites than was once supposed.

this will have been the function of the *wyrm* figures stamped on cinerary urns: they were there to guard the last remains of the dead. A small proportion of cinerary urns have windows inserted, usually at the base; they have no practical significance that archaeologists can think of. Were they apertures for the escape of the spirit of the dead?[44]

Inhumation graves carry a wide variety of grave goods surrounding the corpse or forming part of their clothing, making in the first instance an open display within the grave to be viewed before the earth closed it up. Both the display itself and its enclosure under the earth were of high importance, to judge by the number and value of the goods put into many Anglo-Saxon graves. The 'cunning woman' of the Germanic tradition may have led ceremonies, supervising the display which preceded both cremation and inhumation, receiving from the relatives the artefacts to be burned or buried in urns or placed beside the body. Her presence, consulting with and advising the kin, may help to account for the spread and vitality of fashions in the disposal and commemoration of the dead, the selection of possessions to be included and in inhumation the placing of the body in the grave, prone, supine, with legs drawn up and the like.[45] A remarkably miscellaneous collection of items in a woman's grave at Cassington in Oxfordshire would suggest its being that of just such a 'cunning woman'. An amulet bag contained a loop of bronze wire threaded with a cast iron ring, a fourth-century bronze strap-end, three discs, one of bone, one of lead and one of iron; also two boar's teeth, a bronze rivet and a rolled-up piece of iron wire. Animal materials may have decayed away. There is a resemblance to the contents of a stone cist of the Bronze Age in Denmark, which included a leather bag, the tail of an adder, a conch from the Mediterranean, a piece of wood sliced through, part of an amber bead, a piece of red stone, pyrites, a falcon's claw and the lower jaw of a squirrel. A guess would suggest that this strange collection was not designed primarily to protect the owner but to work magic and that in life this woman was following an age-old scenario, which links Anglo-Saxon grave goods to the prehistoric society behind Germanic paganism.[46]

Tania Dickinson has argued that the choice of grave goods in the earliest phase of immigration reflects the immense disturbances created in the society

[44] Ibid. 150

[45] H. Geake, 'The control of burial practice in Anglo-Saxon England', M.O.H Carver ed., *The cross goes north* (Woodbridge 2003) 259–69

[46] A.L. Meaney, *Anglo-Saxon amulets and curing stones, BAR* Brit. ser. 96 (Oxford 1981) 249; Theodore's *Penitential* 255

of the invaders by socio-economic processes undermining family and household relationships. Kinship ties were weakened inevitably by dispersal through the chances of sea-crossing and settlement in new lands; displays at death and the depositing of grave goods were a means of stabilising a new reality within the lands of settlement, firmly setting out the roles of man and woman, reflecting the military necessities of an invading people, and recalling the cultural patterns of the homeland in new settings.[47] Heinrich Härke has emphasised the attachment of the Anglo-Saxon male to his weapons, especially spear and shield, reflected over and over again in his grave goods.[48] The role of the woman of the household may be reflected in the mourners' choice of grave goods for her: keys, girdle-hangers and spindle whorls as well as jewellery, some examples worn and old, others of high calibre, perhaps sacrificed by the relatives out of love for their dead. Generally the woman was arrayed in her best clothes with jewellery, beads and pendants, illustrating her role within the family. Tania Dickinson goes on to stress the role of women in the sixth century as wives and mothers, forming a nucleus, she argues, in 'newly established kindreds', as the Germanic society in a new land settled and achieved some stabilisation.[49]

For all the significance of wealth, status, gender and family links in the choice of grave goods and the importance of display to be witnessed by both family and community, there are also indications of the presence and importance of pagan beliefs, the role of the gods and the afterlife. The swastika is commonly assumed to be a sign of the god Thunor, appearing occasionally on military equipment, on a spearhead, for example, in a grave at Buckland near Dover and on a sword pommel at Bifrons in Kent, where it is incised on one side, with zigzagged lines on the other, recalling the god of lightning. Its use is not confined to male graves. There is a pair of swastika brooches from the early immigration epoch at Alfriston, Sussex, and in an intriguing case from Sleaford, Lincolnshire, a crucifix brooch has undergone modification after its original casting to incorporate an incised swastika, which suggests that the motive behind the action was a religious one, a will to incorporate the symbol of Thunor rather than a simple modification of design for decorative purposes. A rune on a spear blade in a seventh-century grave at Holborough

[47] T.M. Dickinson, 'What's new in early medieval burial archaeology?', *EME* 11 (2001) 71–87

[48] 'Changing symbols in a changing society: the Anglo-Saxon weapon burial rite in the seventh century', Carver, *Sutton Hoo* 149–65

[49] Dickinson, 'What's new?' 84; Lucy, *Way* 45–7

in Kent is best interpreted as a symbol of the god Tiw: its very small size indicates it was intended to give encouragement and protection in battle to the warrior, who alone knew it was there, bringing down the god's protection rather than intimidating an opponent.[50]

It was evidently hoped that the qualities of animals would somehow be made to benefit the user or wearer. The boar was an ancient symbol of courage and strength. At Stowting in Kent, boar tusks as well as spears were buried as grave goods and two high-calibre graves gave prominence to the boar. At Benty Grange, the richest grave in the Peak District, a man of high rank was commemorated by a helmet surmounted by the bronze figure of a boar with garnet eyes and gilded silver studs sunk into the body, presumably to represent bristles. The helmet dates from the conversion age, having a cross placed on the boar's nose, and one has the impression that the relatives who created the grave gave weight to both the boar and the cross as powerful, magical symbols, to guard the wearer; the cross had not displaced the boar. At the richest of all Anglo-Saxon graves, at Sutton Hoo, a magnificent parade-ground helmet was decorated along the eyebrows with garnets culminating in boars' heads and at each end of the shoulder-clasps was a design created from garnets and millefiori glass of two entwined boars. A bronze boar at Guilden Morden in Cambridgeshire may once have been attached to a helmet; a boar decorating a shield boss at Bidford-on-Avon in Warwickshire was clearly placed there to protect its warrior owner.[51] In the seventh century, beavers' teeth make an occasional appearance in graves of women and children, sometimes mounted in copper alloy, even in gold. The beaver has a powerful bite and it is natural to see here presents given to the child to ensure he or she grew up to have a powerful bite and, perhaps, a charming smile. Clearly the notion that association with animal assets would impart something of their strength was in full vitality in the conversion age.[52]

In the seventh century, cowrie shells may be found in Christian cemeteries: they were expensive items obtained from the Red Sea and beyond. On the basis of their resemblance to female genital organs, the case has been made that these were amulets designed to aid fertility: certainly they come generally from the graves of women and girls, bestowed on the latter in life, it has been

---

[50] Meaney, *Amulets* 242–3 (swastika); Wilson, *Paganism* 115 (Buckland, Bifrons) 118 (Alfriston) 115, 119 (Sleaford) 117 (Holborough)
[51] Ibid. 110 (Stowting, Bidford) 109–110 (Benty Grange)
[52] Meaney, *Amulets* 264; Blair, *Church* 173

suggested, to aid their sexual development. A pathetic example of their use is to be found in two graves at Camelton and Shudy Camps, Cambridgeshire, where in the first a woman was buried with a twenty-eight-week-old foetus and in the second a woman with an infant at her left shoulder.[53] Overall more common with women than men, amulets continued to play a significant role well into the conversion era. Sometimes they are touched by heathenism proper, sometimes they are best classified simply as lucky charms. The pervasiveness of these items is so great as to make plain how much they mattered in life, and perhaps in death, to the Anglo-Saxon community.

The line distinguishing a beautiful object, valued for decorative purposes – or a piece of beloved life-furniture – from one designed to win health, warrior strength or prosperity is a fine one: in the last resort, as Helen Geake has observed, judgement rests on an assessment of the state of mind of the dead and the mourners. However, some indications assist the archaeologist in coming to a decision: amber had a lasting reputation for its medicinal properties and was well known in Europe from the time of Pliny. No doubt it could be included in necklaces for decorative purposes, but a bead on its own, or in a box or bag where it could not be seen, can be presumed to have been placed there as an amulet. So also can a bead when attached to a sword. A single bead at the neck of a skeleton is there as a protection rather than a decoration and some beads may have been intended to ward off the Evil Eye in life. Rock crystal is repeatedly found in women's graves and has been linked to the prophetic power traditionally attributed to Germanic women. Stray talismans make their appearance, as in the case of a warrior at Faversham in Kent, who had a whetstone, a bivalve shell and a piece of glass buried with his sword-guard.[54]

Behind the attachment to a miscellaneous array of objects buried with the dead lay the fear and uncertainty of humanity in face of the whims of the gods and the unpredictable chances of life, war, agricultural failure, illness, infertility; propitiatory rites in life and in death were means of defence in a world whose mechanisms were so little understood. A belief in gods, spirits, benign

[53] Meaney, *Amulets* 123–4 (cowrie shells); doubts in Blair, *Church* 171 n. 158; Wilson, *Paganism* 104–7 (shells, Camelton, Shudy Camps)

[54] H. Geake, *The use of grave-goods in conversion-period England c.600–c.800*, BAR Brit. ser. 261 (Oxford 1997), reviewed by E. O'Brien, *Peritia* 16 (2002) 507–10, Blair, *EME* 9 (2000) 261–2; E. O'Brien, *Post-Roman Britain to Anglo-Saxon England: burial practices reviewed* BAR Brit. ser. 289 (Oxford 1999) stresses afterlife; Meaney, *Amulets* 127 (evil eye) 28, 240 (Faversham)

or hostile, helped to make life more comprehensible and manageable: belief in an afterlife is a motive power behind the placing of food in graves to sustain the dead on their last journey. A number of burials include joints of meat; in one at Little Wilbraham, Cambridgeshire, a young man was put in his grave with a shoulder and foreleg of either a sheep or a goat lying on his chest. At Garton Slack in Yorkshire, thirteen burials out of a total of sixty included similar meat deposits. These substantial portions of meat carry a clear implication that the dead are to be given food on their way to another world. If the remains of a whole animal are in the grave, the presumption is that a well-loved pet has not been left behind; so in a rich grave at Minster Lovell, Oxfordshire, the bones of a small lapdog were mingled with those of the female owner, while at Foulden in Norfolk the remains of a dog lay with its head on the knees of the man buried there.[55]

Sometimes the quantity of food is very small and has a symbolic or totemic significance now lost to us, or represents simply a snack for the dead; cups and horns may have contained drink to comfort them. In a barrow at Ford Laverstock in Wiltshire, a male was left with a bronze hanging bowl containing two bulbs identified with probability as onions, and four small crab apples. A child's grave at Holywell Row, Norfolk, contained a pot with two duck eggs. Food residues have also sometimes been detected, suggesting the remains of a common meal held at the graveside before closure.[56]

The nature and purpose of the various grave offerings are made more difficult to establish by lack of evidence on the pagan afterlife, not elucidated by our written sources, so heavily dominated by the pens of Christian clerics. The actual circumstances of the burial itself may give clues. Stones placed over bodies may have been put down to prevent spirit walking: revenantism, a widespread European belief, repeatedly stresses the dangers of infants returning.[57] At Soham in Cambridgeshire charcoal and stone slabs were laid over the body of an old woman, possibly because of the fear of her magic powers, but there is an undoubted preponderance in juvenile cases. Much about burial customs necessarily remains obscure: what, for example, is the role of charcoal on grave sites? How are we to interpret the pyrite balls placed

---

[55] T.C. Lethbridge, 'Recent excavations in Anglo-Saxon cemeteries in Cambridgeshire and Suffolk', *Cambridge Antiquarian Society* Quarter Pubns New ser. 3 (Cambridge 1931–2) 73 (Little Wilbraham); Wilson, *Paganism* 92 (Garton Slack) 100 (Minster Lovell, Foulden)

[56] Wilson, *Paganism* 99 (Ford, Holywell Row); Lucy, *Way* 93; Lethbridge, 'Recent excarations', 33–4 (food residues)

[57] S. Crawford, *Childhood in Anglo-Saxon England* (Stroud 1999) 80–1, 84–5

at the hips of four men in Cambridgeshire – as light for the last journey? Is the placing at the hips significant? We have no means of knowing.[58] An unscientific excavation in 1847 at Cuddesdon in Oxfordshire resulted in a case susceptible to a sinister explanation. Skeletons were uncovered arranged like spokes of a wheel, heads outwards, legs crossed, all lying prone and without grave goods, though within the area some rich artefacts have been found. It looks uncommonly like a princely burial accompanied by human sacrifice, perhaps slaves to support their lord.

Although a number of Anglo-Saxon sites carry no evidence of grave goods and no clues about the beliefs of those who carried out the last rites for their dead, there remains a mass of material drawn from many years of archaeological investigation reinforcing and illuminating limited literary and linguistic evidence showing that there was an active paganism in continuing vitality from the age of immigration onwards. An animistic religion that focused on natural features, springs, trees and hills, endowed certain animals with special powers and practised divination, sacrificing to gods for health, fertility and victory in war, gave its adherents an infinitely flexible means for persuading, bribing or coercing higher powers to provide desired human objectives. These practices, inherited from the customs of their continental homelands, developed with continuing life in Britain and carried with them the mute force of ancient custom. Children born in many Anglo-Saxon settlements in Britain grew up accustomed to shrines and sacrifices, the wearing of amulets and to immemorial burial or cremation practices. No experience in the early years of invasion gave the newcomers reason to jettison an apparatus of worship, divination and sacrifice which had long served them and was readily adapted to their life in a new land.[59]

A structure of sanctuaries, sites for worship and pillars with animal heads built up as invaders moved deeper into the country, the practices of heathenism being reinforced as other groups and families came over from the continent. It proved impossible for indigenous Christians to break into this heathen world and impart their own beliefs. It was natural also, in the context

[58] Wilson, *Paganism* 123–30; comment in Meaney, *Amulets* 240
[59] T.M. Dickinson, *Cuddesdon and Dorchester-on-Thames: two early Saxon princely sites in Wessex, BAR* 1 (Oxford 1974); reflections in D. Bullough, 'Burial, community and belief in the early medieval west', P. Wormald *et al.* eds, *Ideal and reality in Frankish and Anglo-Saxon society* (Oxford 1983); magic, R.A. Fletcher, *The conversion of Europe* (London 1977) 245; theme illuminated, V. Flint, *The rise of magic in early medieval Europe* (Oxford 1991), with A. Murray, 'Missionaries and magic in Dark Age Europe', *PP* 136 (1992) 186–205

of loss, disruption, isolation and fighting, not to wish to bring salvation to their enemies. Gildas's *De excidio Britanniae* was a work modelled on the Hebrew prophets: like them, Gildas recalled the sins of his nation and the temporal punishments which fell on them in order to summon them, their leaders and lax bishops and clergy to repentance and so ward off further disasters. In fact he wrote very little history, as opposed to polemic, at all; he was heavily dependent on literary sources such as Orosius, probably basing his work on a collection of notes and extracts. But on his own age and its immediate antecedents he is a first-hand authority.

He wrote in a period of relative calm after a revival of British arms under Ambrosius Aurelianus, a man of high descent whose parents are described as having 'worn the purple',[60] who emerged after the long period of British defeats and began to reverse the tide. 'Under him, our people regained their strength,' Gildas wrote and warfare became more balanced, with victory going first to one side, then to the other, 'so that in this people the Lord could make trial . . . of his latter day Israel to see whether it loves him or not'. This phase lasted till the British won a major victory at the unknown site of Mount Badon. An oddity in Mommsen's edition of Gildas has led to the assumption that Ambrosius Aurelianus was not leading the resurgent British at this time, but a simple modification of his layout may well restore a more authentic version, confirming Ambrosius as the leader at Mount Badon as well as in the earlier, lesser engagements. The victory of Mount Badon has a critical role in Gildas's polemic. While it did not bring a complete end to warfare, it nonetheless provided a respite in which the British could, if they wished, turn from their evil ways and ward off the wrath of God which had fallen on them earlier because of their moral failures.[61]

Ambrosius had been a man of virtue and valour, in Gildas's eyes a Constantine who combined Roman virtue and Christian belief: his descendants were greatly inferior to their grandfather and Gildas lamented the absence of such leaders in his own day. The book would have made no sense had there not been a battle of Mount Badon and a check in the Germanic advance which had continued into Gildas's own time. Inferences from the *De excidio* enable us to give the battle an approximate dating. Had the great plague which afflicted Britain *c*.549 occurred before he wrote, he would

---

[60] Gildas 25
[61] Ibid. 26; O. Padel, 'The nature of Arthur', *CMCS* 27 (1994) 1–31 at 16–17

undoubtedly have used it as another example of God punishing His people for their sins. His errors on the defensive system of Roman Britain and his lack of accurate information about the province make it clear also that he had passed out of range of the oral tradition which would still have been there had he been composing his book a generation earlier, when his grandparents would have been alive and able to give accurate information. He tells us that Mount Badon took place in the year of his birth and that he was forty-three years old when he wrote the *De excidio*; the *Annals of Ulster* give his death date as 570; viewing all the circumstances, a dating of the *De excidio* to the 540s and consequently of Mount Badon to *c.*500 is a fair conclusion.[62]

The danger Gildas saw in his own day lay in the evil deeds of British leaders and the effects of civil war which could so easily open the way to renewed Anglo-Saxon advance. These sorry events provide the stimulus for his passionate writing. In Gildas's work, the only function of the Germanic invaders was to act as an instrument of God's wrath: he describes them as 'the ferocious Saxons . . . hated by man and God', 'the sprig of iniquity, the root of bitterness'.[63] There is no word here of the possibility of converting these enemies to Christian belief.

A British synod, the Synod of the Grove of Victory, whose proceedings are listed in two manuscripts, supposedly of Welsh origin and dating from the early sixth century, imposed heavy penalties on those who gave military assistance to the Anglo-Saxons. The clauses run as follows: 'They who afford guidance to the barbarians, thirteen years, provided there be no slaughter of Christians or effusion of blood or dire captivity. If, however, such things do take place, the offenders shall perform penance, laying down their arms for the rest of life. But if one plan to conduct the barbarians to the Christians and did so according to his will, he should do penance for the remainder of his life.'[64] It is significant that the British are being defined as Christians. The barbarians can only be the Germanic invaders. The context, albeit military, is by implication one of hostility to contact and to conversion.

Gildas became known to the Anglo-Saxons, attractive to them because of the evidence he provided of the deficiencies of the British Church. There is a reference in the text we have of the *De excidio* to the Anglo-Saxon legend that they first came in three 'cyuls', the Anglo-Saxon word for ships, and the

[62] C.E. Stancliffe, 'The thirteen sermons attributed to Columbanus', M. Lapidge ed., *Studies in the Latin writings of Columbanus* (Woodbridge 1997) 93–202 at 177–81
[63] Gildas 23; Vollrath, 'Landnahme' 41
[64] L. Bieler ed., *The Irish Penitentials* (Dublin 1963) 69; corruptions 242

prophecy that they would live for three hundred years in the land to which their ships had been directed and would lay it waste for 150 years, that is, in effect, until the coming of Augustine's mission.[65] It was an Anglo-Saxon Christian comment, probably originally a marginal gloss, referring, firstly, to the coming of Augustine in 597 and, secondly, to the consolidation of the Church during and after the archiepiscopate of Theodore of Tarsus in the late seventh century. One can infer that some student of Theodore inserted the legend in the margin of the text as he read the *De excidio*, a remarkable case of a British text coming into use among Anglo-Saxon scholars for reasons which need no explanation. A text from the British side which excoriated their sins and follies would not be uncongenial to churchmen sprung from the Germanic conquerors of the fifth and sixth centuries. Gildas had seen his people as favoured by God, as the children of Israel in the Old Testament had been, and the main purpose of his work was to urge them not to fall away and in consequence be subjected to more temporal punishment. In his turn, Bede felt deeply the failure of the British to convert his heathen ancestors and believed therefore that they had forfeited the position once assigned to them and been rightly conquered. In broad terms this was not unfair. In general, the British did indeed fail to convert their invading enemies: the shock and pain of the Germanic attack had been too great.[66]

And yet there are indications that there were exceptions and that some British churchmen did succeed in passing on the faith: the refusal was not total. There is evidence that British Christians carried the faith to two outlying groups of Anglo-Saxon settlers in the West Midlands, the Magonsaetan of what is now Worcester diocese and the Hwicce of Hereford diocese, the former farming a frontier region lying at the point of division of the highland and lowland zones of Britain and the latter occupying an area of low-lying fertile territory in the west.[67] The British were settled in force in these lands and the level of immigration was low. Wenlock is a place-name deriving from the defeated people, meaning a white or holy monastery. Major British churches, quite possibly the site of bishoprics, lie thickly on the map, at Letocetum (Wall),

---

[65] Gildas 23

[66] A. Woolf, 'An interpolation in the text of Gildas's *De excidio Britanniae*', *Peritia* 16 (2002) 161–7; M. Miller, 'Bede's use of Gildas', *EHR* 90 (1975) 241–61

[67] P. Sims-Williams, *Religion and literature in western England 600–800* (Cambridge 1990); gen. context, H.R. Loyn, 'The conversion of the English to Christianity: some comments on the Celtic contribution', id., *Society and peoples. Studies in the history of England and Wales, c.600–1200* (London 1992) 20–44, outpaced on St Dyfrig, 42

at a substantial late Romano-British settlement at Wroxeter, at Worcester and perhaps Gloucester; evidence of a surviving British paganism has not come to light. Stretton-on-the-Fosse is a site where, before Christianisation, a Romano-British cemetery appears to overlap with an Anglo-Saxon one, and has evidence of cross-posting in grave goods, Anglo-Saxon graves containing some British-style studded boots and in some women's graves remains of material woven by traditional Romano-British methods. Such cultural interpenetration would have made it easier for British Christian priests to be in contact with potential Anglo-Saxon converts. The conditions were right for a quiet overspill of Christianity to the enemy camp, feasible at grass-roots level despite a more general hostility between the peoples. British Christian influence may well account for the speed with which the Anglo-Saxons of this region gave up their burial practices and abandoned grave goods. Christianisation at the hands of the British is the most likely explanation of the case of the princess Eaba from the Hwicce who became queen in the pagan kingdom of Sussex and was Christian when she married. Eventually, such independent people as the Magonsaetan became part of the expanding Anglo-Saxon kingdom of Mercia and in the process Anglo-Saxon bishoprics replaced British churches. But in a violent society this move was, notably, a comparatively bloodless affair.

Reflecting on the faults of his people in the Roman past in the preamble to the *De excidio*, Gildas let drop in his declamatory way a remarkable comment on the state of belief among the British of his own day, a century or so after the beginnings of the Germanic settlements.

> I shall not speak of the ancient errors, common to all races, that bound the whole of humanity fast before the coming of Christ in the flesh. I shall not enumerate the devilish monstrosities of my land, numerous almost as those that plagued Egypt, some of which we can see today, stark as ever, inside or outside deserted city walls: outlines still ugly, faces still grim. I shall not name the mountains and hills and rivers, once so pernicious, now useful for human needs, on which, in those days, a blind people heaped divine honours.[68]

We must accept what Gildas says. He knew the British Church in the lands where the immigrants had not penetrated and he is telling us that the paganism of his people which, we have seen, was far from extinct in the last

[68] Gildas 4

century of Roman rule had died out in his time. The temples, once so much part of the landscape, had gone. There had been a major shift in the direction of Christianity. This is borne out by the main body of Gildas's text, in which he picks out five rulers to stigmatise for their wickednesses. 'Britain has kings,' he wrote, 'but they are tyrants.'[69] They were the chieftains who took power as Roman authority collapsed in the least Romanised parts of Britain, generally in the highland zone where the indigenous peoples had not been demilitarised as they had been in the lowlands. Iron Age strongpoints were refortified: power passed to those who could exert effective force. It may be that one of these highland chieftains exercising power far over in the eastern side of Britain at the request of the *civitates* is the 'proud tyrant' described by Gildas as betraying his country by inviting in Germanic federate troops.

Gildas's list of the five 'lascivious horses' whom he denounced were rulers of kingdoms in the west stretching from Cornwall to the lower Severn, through Wales and on, probably, to Cumbria. The point of his acid criticism is that they were, officially at least, Christian: Constantine, ruler of Dumnonia embracing Cornwall, Devon and part of Somerset, was targeted as such for the slaughter of two royal princes. He is attacking with scorn hypocritical, ruthless members of his own Church. There is never any suggestion that they are pagans. Leslie Alcock tabulated their failings in a quarter-page of his masterly work on the craftsmanship and ideas of the heroic age in northern Britain.[70] As well as failings which might be attributed to only too many early medieval rulers, such as ungodly rage, haughtiness, trust in riches, preferring lying praise-poetry to praise of God, they include such evil deeds as patricide, the murder of a wife and a husband of a desired second wife, the torture of royal youths, the rape of a daughter and the desecration of an altar. These men are, in Gildas's description, terrifying, plundering, military men, profiting from anarchy and the need for an internal security in the aftermath of the breakdown of Roman rule. Yet they act within a Christian framework. One of the most powerful of these rulers and a multiple murderer, Maelgwn of Gwynedd, had once been a monk: he was a man of education who had received instruction 'from the refined master of almost all Britain'.[71]

---

[69] Ibid. 27
[70] L. Alcock, *Kings and warriors, craftsmen and priests in northern Britain AD 550–850* (Edinburgh 2003) 32; for Constantine, see Gildas 28
[71] Ibid. 36

For all the attacks which Gildas launches on unworthy rulers and lazy and corrupt bishops and clergy, it is plain that Christianity has moved into areas where no trace of its presence had existed under Roman rule. The river Exe had marked an end point in the effective rule by Romans and no discernible Christian presence can be traced further west in Roman times. Yet Tintagel, site of a promontory fortress and an entrepôt for trade in tin from Cornwall in return for imports of wine from the Mediterranean, had an early Christian graveyard on the mainland opposite the fortress in the post-Roman period, when Christian-inscribed stones begin to appear on the coasts of west Britain, including Cornwall. In the north there is evidence that the Christianity which had emerged within some forts of Hadrian's Wall and the settlements supporting it had begun to act as a springboard for missionary endeavours towards people living north of the Wall. Amongst the British a monastic movement, with its transforming power, had begun to exert influence within the Church. For all the weaknesses of individual churchmen, it is plain that, though the British Church was very different from that which functioned in the villas and towns of Roman Britain, it was nevertheless active in the far west, in the old Roman highland zone and beyond Hadrian's Wall and was winning new converts.

CHAPTER 3

The Fate of the British

Events in the fifth and sixth centuries had ushered in a period of major change in which Britain was sharply divided between the lands dominated by the Germanic immigrants where the surviving Christianity of the old Romano-British Church was being stifled to death and those of the independent British where that same Christianity had won a wide, if superficial, victory. In the south and east Christianity lost; in the south-west, west and north Christianity gained. This victory is extraordinarily ill-documented: we can see the long-term results in literature and archaeology and can trace the missions which this Church sent out from its heartland in the west but because of the obscurities of these centuries we have scant evidence as to how the original victory was won.

The pressure of alien immigration in the east and south from the coast and river systems will certainly have led to the exiling of wealthier Christians and, probably, their priests to safer territory in the west. Analysis of Brittonic shows how Latin, especially a correctly pronounced and grammatical Grade I Latin, came into the indigenous language, transmitted in the first instance no doubt by the Romano-British squirearchy and its priesthood: from the fourth century onwards a range of ecclesiastical Latin loan-words were current and survived in Old Welsh. The experiences of the upper classes of Roman Britain in the face of economic deterioration and Germanic attack would have been profoundly disturbing: a way of life in town and villa was destroyed. This is likely to have fostered a turn to Christianity as a support in hard times. Martin Henig argues that the key factor lay in the 'organisation, power and security' offered by the Church 'in a collapsing world', as Roman power ebbed away and the Germanic invaders arrived.[1] Perhaps, too, it was being seen as a last pillar

[1] M. Henig, review of Watts, *Christians*, *Britannia* 23 (1992) 377–8

of *Romanitas*. Because of Constantine, Christianity had become the religion of the Empire: when the legions had gone, the coins of the emperor had ceased to reach Britain and the more sophisticated infrastructure of the island had been eroded, the Church was the last remnant of a Roman way of life. Patrick, a child of Roman Britain in its last phase, recalling in older age the 'Christian Roman Empire'; uses the term 'cives' (citizens) of marauders under the direction of a British king whom he denounces, implying by his scornful phrase that these men had betrayed the ideals of a Christian empire, for which he still had a residual respect.[2]

There would have been informal evangelists – men of substance who backed their priests and sustained the economy of the Church in difficult days – and the priests who carried belief over into highland regions where the Christians had had no strong presence. They have for the most part remained anonymous, and we can only surmise that their faith and determination form part of the story. Holy men and their shrines were sources of spiritual power in times of disorder and fear: their veneration and the cult of relics gave protection against evil, supernatural forces, disease, infertility and the hazards of famine and battle. The development of the cult of saints was an international phenomenon and although, because of the hazards of survival of evidence in Britain, we know little of such saints apart from St Alban, there is no reason to suppose that they were not also present in the Christian parts of the island and played a role in the remarkable changes in belief that were taking place in the post Romano-British world.

Gildas's work reflects the continuing link surviving in the sixth century between Christianity and *Romanitas*. The language of the *De excidio* reveals that he was making use of a living Latin and not simply relying on glossaries, was aware of Latin literature, echoing Virgil and other poets, and assembling his treatise within the conventions of classical rhetoric. It is as if he is making a speech for the prosecution in a courtroom against the five tyrants he denounces; much of his phraseology is in fact better suited to an oral delivery. The implication is important: in childhood and youth Gildas had obtained in Britain – there is no evidence that he trained elsewhere – a full classical education in grammar and rhetoric, of the kind desired across the Empire in its heyday by men of substance. By this time, a training in rhetoric would have had to be obtained by private instruction, which in turn implies the existence

---

[2] D.R. Howlett, *The book of letters of Saint Patrick the bishop* (Dublin 1994) 26–7; comment, B. Ward-Perkins *EHR* 115 (2000) 515 n. 1

still in one part of Britain of rhetors able to provide this and of parents able to afford the fees for it. It may not imply that the opportunity to use rhetorical skills in courts still existed, but it shows that a Roman-style education and Christian belief coexisted in a part of sixth-century Britain and that they supported each other.[3]

Gildas's life also reflects the great changes which affected the British Church in the sixth century. Though it values the monastic life and praises those who follow it, the *De excidio* has in mind but a small-scale movement as a corrective to laxity within the Church, but when we turn to his later Epistolary Fragments we find a much deeper involvement in more narrowly monastic issues and duties of abbots and bishops alongside judgements on excommunication, fasting and abstinence. It is apparent that the monastic movement has grown and that divisions have appeared between stricter and more relaxed abbots. In Gildas's own lifetime monasticism had come of age and Gildas, whose zeal for reform had helped it to burgeon, became one of the authorities who gave advice on monastic life and whose decisions – often humane and balanced – came to be regarded as normative.[4] They influenced both the great pilgrim and monastic reformer, St Columbanus, and Uinniau, the mysterious British churchman and missionary to south-west Scotland who had a second career as a monk in Ireland, where he was known as St Finnian of Moville.[5] It is most likely that Gildas became a monk. Monasticism was the great force sweeping across the Church and it gave birth to missionaries and reformers who link together Britain, Ireland and the Breton Church, a refuge for Britons fleeing from the Anglo-Saxons. But it never displaced bishops; an episcopal structure stemming from the old Romano-British Church still remained in place.

Where did Gildas write? His reticence about names and dates leaves this in obscurity. It seems reasonable that he cannot have been in range of the five tyrants or they would have made an end of him; Devon and Cornwall, though Christianised, had been little touched by Romanisation. A case has been made for the north of Britain but the most likely siting is west of the lands of the Anglo-Saxon conqueror but well short of the highland tyrants he stigmatises. A suitable area would be Gloucester, Cirencester and Bath, with possibilities further south into Somerset or north towards Worcester, prosperous areas

---

[3] Lapidge, 'Gildas's education', M. Lapidge, D.N. Dumville eds, *Gildas. New approaches* (Woodbridge 1984) 27–50; R. Sharpe, 'Gildas as a Father of the Church', Lapidge, Dumville eds, *Gildas. New approaches* 193–203
[4] M.W. Herren, 'Gildas and early British monasticism', A. Bammesberger, A. Wollmann eds, *Britain 400–600. Language and history* (Heidelberg 1990) 67–78
[5] Below, 108–9, 160.

where there were still landed estates capable of supporting a leisured class, a level of education appropriate for a writer of Gildas's calibre and sufficient lines of communication for him to receive information about the doings of his tyrants and be aware of the commemorations of martyrs at St Albans and Caerleon.[6] As a writer he was not alone: the *De excidio* refers to two other British authors whose works have not survived. Roman Britain seems to have produced no writer of note at all: post-Roman Britain has Gildas, Pelagius and Faustus, bishop of Riez in Brittany, who is known to be British and is recorded as sending one of his works via an intermediary to contacts in Britain in about 471. Up to the death of Gildas in 570, there was a surviving Late Antique literary civilisation within Britain, albeit probably by this time lying solely in the hands of a small social class, fast diminishing under the pressures of the weakening economy and of the barbarians. Gildas himself was in one respect an innovator. He is not greatly interested in the Empire: his work is concerned with one former province only, Britain.[7]

He did not have a successor. The torch passed to the monks and, completing the division from the Gaulish Church where Latin was still commonly spoken, in Celtic Britain Latin survived only as the language of the Church and of learning. If Gildas wrote within the area of Gloucester, Cirencester and Bath, then the Anglo-Saxon advance of the last quarter of the sixth century eroded one important base for this Latin culture, submerging it under the weight of heathen warriors and peasants taking over the land.

The independent British were now pinned back more firmly to the highland zone and to the west generally, where Romanisation had been weakest. Within these lands a pattern of Church life developed which has been broadly described as Celtic; it derived from the passion for monasticism – often with a strong eremitic strand, adapted to the circumstances of highland areas focusing on the shrines of saints – the spur to the erection of churches and to missionary activity. However, one support point for this lay in the surviving Romano-British Christianity of the lowland zone. The Roman way of life, for example, lingered on in modern Monmouth and parts of Glamorgan where there were a number of villas and Christian owners to aid and encourage the new monasticism. One at Llantwit Major, lying a little over a mile from the

---

[6] Placing, Sharpe in A. Thacker, R. Sharpe eds, *Local saints and local churches in the early medieval West* (Oxford 2002) 108; N.J. Higham, *The kingdom of Northumbria AD 350–1100* (Stroud 1993) 61–2 rejects case for north

[7] P. Sims-Williams, 'Gildas and the Anglo-Saxons', *CMCS* 6 (1983) 1–30

church of St Illtud with a post-Roman cemetery beside it, was the probable springboard for what has been described as 'a gentleman's monastery' on a similar pattern to the community in Gaul of Sidonius Apollinarius. Here in the early sixth century St Illtud presided over and created a centre of ecclesiastical learning. A possible villa site lies close by. Another case is that of Llandough in Glamorgan, St Docco's *llan*, or settlement, on a site which includes in close proximity an abandoned villa, a seventh-century monastery and an early burial ground. Bassaleg, also in Glamorgan, west of Caerleon is intriguing because its name is unique amongst place-names derived from Brittonic in that it incorporates the Latin 'basilica', used in Gaul and Ireland for churches which housed important relics. The patron saint was St Gwladys; nothing is known of her, but her relics lay in a grave chapel, an *eglwys y bedd*, church of the dead.[8]

On a ridge above Caerleon close by the Roman road to Caerwent and lying on the edge of an extra-mural cemetery, the *martyrium* identified as the burial place of the Romano-British martyrs, Aaron and Julius will have been a focus for an expanding Christianity along the central border of Wales. Not far away lay the Christian community of Caerwent, whose existence was suggested by a pewter bowl with a chi-rho on its base and associated domestic ware, and further north, Wroxeter, a *civitas* of considerable population, where a town life of some vitality continued well after the end of Roman Britain, and which is conjectured to have been the seat of a British bishopric and can probably be numbered among the sites which carried Christianity deeper into Wales.[9]

Generally where the Brittonic-based place name *merthyr* is to be found, paralleled by the Cornish *merther* and the Breton *merzer*, there will once have been a *martyrium*, a centre for veneration, pilgrimage, petitions and Christian burials, with other place-names for church sites and monasteries, *ecclesia, locus, monasterium, podum, llog, llan*; in Cornwall *eglos, lan* – from the same root as the Welsh *llan*. Aaron and Julius are well-authenticated cases of native martyrs on what became Welsh soil and there may well have been others of whom we now know nothing. At a further stage, men and women of heroic virtue, known as confessors, might also be commemorated without suffering

---

[8] J.K. Knight, *The end of Antiquity: archaeology, society and religion* AD 235–700 (Stroud 1999) 144 (Llantwit Major) 139, 144, 165, 173 (Llandough) 144 (Bassaleg); id., 'Basilicas and barrows. Christian origins in Wales and western Britain', M.O.H. Carver ed., *The Cross goes north* (Woodbridge 2003) 119–26; re-evaluation of age of saints, B. Yorke, *The conversion of Britain. Religion, politics and society in Britain c.600–800* (Harlow 2006) 25
[9] Above, 24

martyrdom such as bishops of saintly life, founders of monastic settlements or individual monks of local fame. The British Church disliked the practice of breaking up saints' bodies and preferred where necessary to make use of secondary relics of internationally significant saints to form the basis for a shrine. As Romano-British Christianity faded in the lowland zone, its heirs carried the faith into the highlands and created a landscape of saints typical of the movement of the veneration of saints which prevailed across the Western Christian world and is recorded fully in the literary evidence for Gaul, Spain and Italy. In varied forms, monasticism was the major feature. The episcopate, once based on *civitates* in Roman Britain, now shifted to courts and royal households. The chieftain ruled in the independent British lands and power lay with him.

The Christianity of the British and the influences which played on their Church are illuminated by the epitaphs on the western coasts which also show the impact of Irish immigration. For some reason, the indigenous British of the Roman occupation never took up with any enthusiasm the practice of inscribing stones to the memory of their dead; extant examples tend to come most frequently from outsiders, especially soldiers, government officials and visitors. Given this restriction, the incidence of funerary inscriptions in the island generally follows the pattern for the whole of Western Europe outlined in 1973 by the Polish scholar S. Mrozek, revealing a steep rise from AD 1 to 200, followed by a fall to a low point at *c*.300 and a small-scale continuance thereafter.[10] Within these fourth-century inscriptions there are a few which suggest the commemoration of a Christian.

There were evidently fashions influenced by geography; funerary stones tend to be found in the north and west. It has been pointed out that there is very little epigraphy to be found in eastern England from Claudius's invasion to the coming of William the Conqueror. Some Christian sites have no inscriptions at all; the cemeteries at Poundbury and Cannington are cases in point and neither Lincoln, Canterbury nor St Albans with its martyr has produced any. In summary, although the number of probable Christian

---

[10] Above, 80; M.A. Handley, 'The origins of Christian commemoration in late antique Britain', *EME* 10 (2001) 177–99 supersedes all other work; classic, V. Nash-Williams, *The early Christian monuments of Wales* (Cardiff 1950) (*ECMW*), complemented and superseded by M. Redknap, J.M. Lewis eds, *A corpus of early medieval inscribed stones and stone sculpture in Wales* I and N. Edwards ed., II (forthcoming); dating and history of language, P. Sims-Williams, *The Celtic inscriptions of Britain. Phonology and chronology* (Oxford, Malden 2003), reviewed by F.R. Eska, *Speculum* 80 (2005) 978–80

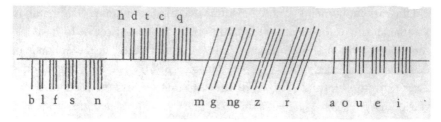

Fig. 3 The ogham alphabet.

epitaphs from the period of Roman occupation is very small and confined to a limited geographical area, this is in itself no proof that the Christian Church was weak, and arguments put forward based on their absence should be dismissed.

For some reason the commemoration of the dead in stone rose in popularity after the end of the Roman occupation in lands held by the British in the west and though in all likelihood pagans are also included, there are some 250 Christian epitaphs in either Latin or ogham, the script developed in fourth-century Ireland – or conceivably south-west Wales – probably from tally sticks, in effect a kind of semaphore, an alphabet based on groups of long and short strokes set in relation to a line, most commonly on the sharp edge or arris of a stone. Based on the Latin alphabet, it was developed by an Irish speaker from the works of Roman grammarians and was suitable for simple messages such as bare information on a memorial stone, providing the name and descent of the dead. Though never conquered by Rome, Ireland was not immune to Roman influences via trade and the army, in which Irishmen served as auxiliaries. Ogham appears on the memorial stones of Irish immigrants to Dyfed in Wales and lasted there for two generations before Latin took over. Its use was pre-eminently an assertion of the dignity of the Irish vernacular: Latin, it implies, is not the only language worthy of use in inscriptions in stone for the honoured dead.[11]

---

[11] C. Thomas, *And shall these mute stones speak? Post-Roman inscriptions in western Britain* (Cardiff 1994) 47 (intro. to ogham) pioneer work, finely illustrated, engaging style and sense of topography, some inferences unacceptable, reviewed by K. Forsyth, *Peritia* 9 (1995) 439–42 sympathetic but qualified; C. Thomas 'Ogam inscriptions and primitive Irish', *KCC* rich biblio., access to Celtic lit.; D. McManus, *A guide to ogam* (Maynooth 1991); dating, M. Fulford *et al.*, 'An early date for ogham: the Silchester ogham stone rehabilitated', *MA* 44 (2000) 1–2; Sims-Williams's doubts, Bammesberger and Wollmann, *Britain* 226

Funerary monuments tend to be dominated by stock phrases. 'Dis manibus' (To the spirits of the departed) is traditionally pagan but seems to have lost something of its original meaning as it is certainly used in the epitaphs of Christians. 'Hic iacet', or in late Roman vulgar spelling 'Hic iacit', 'Here lies', is a very common formula known in Late Antiquity across the Mediterranean world, in Spain, Italy, Dalmatia and North Africa as well as Gaul. It appears amongst the Welsh stones analysed in the classic compendium of Nash-Williams and can fairly be noted as diagnostically Christian.

Nash-Williams compared the 'Hic iacit' stones in Wales with two inscriptions in Lyons dated respectively to 447 and 449 and believed the correspondences between the west British epitaphs and these two gave both a dateline for the beginnings of the remarkable series of Christian-inscribed stones and revealed where the inspiration and pattern for them came from – i.e. Gaul. It is a remarkably narrow basis for the hypotheses which run through his work. Along with his contemporaries, he believed that Christianity in Roman Britain was comparatively frail, and especially so in the highland zone comprising much of Wales, and further, arguing from the Gaulish funerary formulas, that some kind of re-conversion, or fresh Christianising, of western Britain and especially his native Wales had been successfully undertaken by Gaulish Christians after the severing of links with Rome. Nash-Williams put too much weight on the Lyons inscriptions and his 'Gaulish missionary' hypothesis has not prevailed in the light of modern research. He and his contemporaries had underestimated the capacity of the small Romano-British Church to respond to the catastrophe of Anglo-Saxon invasion by conquering fresh fields over to the west and beyond Hadrian's Wall, and overemphasised the Gaulish factor in post-Roman Britain; there is no longer ground for believing either in a complete dearth of native Christian epitaphs in the fourth century, or that Christianity in the fifth had to be rescued by some fresh missionary enterprise from the continent.[12]

This new class of vertical, free-standing stones, monoliths, appears especially in north, central and west Wales which had been little touched by Romanisation. The explanation lies, at least in part, in the power of a new elite over in the west, successors to the authorities of Roman Britain, highland chieftains who seized power by military might and developed a new fashion in the memorialising of their dead. They were imitating Rome, but from a distance. Their memorial stones were, in Charles Thomas's memorable

---

[12] *ECMW* no. 55

phrase, 'blackboards on which to chalk up Latinity',[13] but they were handicapped by the lack of craftsmen equipped to Rome's standard. In fact, those who commissioned the stones were content enough with a low-level lettering characteristic of the Roman army and do not seem to have been offended by eclectic mixtures of styles. Whereas classical epitaphs used marble or other forms of limestone with smooth, shaped slabs and regular horizontal lines of text, their craftsmen had to make do with existing pillars and any type of stone available, even occasionally putting boulders into service. They may not have been literate and there are sometimes oddities and grammatical errors; lines straggle and there are rough finishes due to the effect of pocking. The stones are necessarily the memorials of a wealthier leading class, including clergy; the poorer inhabitants would not have been able to afford them. The presence of pottery sherds attests to a trade with the Mediterranean and then south-west France, so it could well be that funerary epigraphy was brought in as much through casual commercial contacts as missionary enterprise, though the precise channel through which the conti-nental formulas reached the stones cannot now be ascertained. Another possible source for the fashion lies in the Roman milestones with their Latin inscriptions recording the emperor of the day. Thus an inscribed stone made use of the language of the Empire to proclaim a cultured elite and the status of the dead. The fact that Brittonic, developing into Welsh, is not normally in evidence gives a clue to the motives of those who commissioned the stones.

Most of the stones are Christian, discernibly so when the formulas are of an established type or include references implying belief: sometimes on early stones chi-rhos and alphas and omegas are carved, supplanted later by crosses when the cross became the major Christian symbol. They develop and continue as an assertion of Britishness over against the heathen Anglo-Saxons, conveying *Romanitas* by using the language of both the Empire and the Christian Church rather than their own vernacular, an implicit declara-tion of belief in opposition to the heathen enemy. Some names are Roman, preserving continuity with the past, others Celtic, but Celtic in an archaic orthography made to consort with the Latin text: Cadfan of Gwynedd, for

---

[13] C. Thomas, *Christian Celts. Messages and images* (Stroud 1998) 71, hidden messages hypothesised from Bible and numerology unacceptable, reviewed by M. Handley, *Britannia* 31 (2000) 463–4, T.O. Clancy, *IR* 51 (2000) 85–8, but substratum of real value, 23–6, 33–42, 56–71, 123–9, 198–9

example, in the seventh century becomes Catumanus.[14] Once established, the genre lasted for centuries, spread to Cornwall and appeared in Scotland on the Whithorn peninsula. There is some association with coastal areas, especially in Wales, where such stones are strongly in evidence in the northern and southern peninsulas of Cardigan Bay.

The stone of Votepor at Castelldwyran in Dyfed expresses a Christianity that appears to be linked to the memory of the Empire.[15] A ring-cross has been awkwardly jammed down on top of the inscription 'Memoria Voteporigis Protictoris' ('the memorial of Voteporix Protector') in Roman capitals laying claim to what was once a high Roman rank, the title of protector deriving from membership of an elite corps of bodyguards to the emperor and entitling whoever lay buried here, in a traditional phrase, 'to adore the sacred purple'. This was not likely to have been a meaningful title any more but those who commissioned the inscription 'wanted him to look very important and very Roman',[16] which reveals the continuing allure the ideas and practices of the Empire had over these kinglets. To satisfy his Irish subjects it was thought important to have an Irish element on his stone, for this man ruled the Demetae, i.e. the people of Dyfed, the principal area of Irish settlement. Consequently there is an ogham inscription up the side of the stone with the Irish version of his name, Votecorigas. Some have identified the man as Vortipor, one of the wicked rulers, the 'five lascivious horses', the tyrant of the Demetae, accused by Gildas of sitting on a throne stained with murders and adulteries and of raping his own daughter. But the identification of this stone as that of Gildas's Vortipor rests on the assumption that the carver made a slip and missed out the letter R and that he made the same slip when carving the ogham version of the name. Alternatively, given the habit of these dynasties of choosing very similar names for their rulers in family descent over genera- tions, it could be that the stone commemorates not the evil ruler of Gildas's treatise but an earlier member of his line who lived when Roman influence was strong.[17] The stones do not only claim status and record descent. A memorial,

---

[14] P. Sims-Williams, 'The uses of writing in early medieval Wales', H. Pryce ed., *Literacy in medieval Celtic societies* (Cambridge 1998) 15–33 at 29; milestones, C. Thomas, *Christianity in Roman Britain to AD 500* (London 1981) 274; Knight, *Antiquity* 136
[15] *ECMW* no.138; R.C. Stacey, 'Text and society', T. Charles-Edwards ed., *After Rome* (Oxford 2003) 221–57 at 243–5; compare Thomas, *Mute stones* 82
[16] Thomas, *Mute stones* 108
[17] A. Orchard, 'Latin and the vernacular languages', Charles-Edwards, *After Rome* 192–219 at 200

now in the churchyard at Llanerfyl in western Montgomeryshire, takes consolation from belief in the afterlife. It mourns a young daughter: 'Here in the tomb lies Rosteece, daughter of Paterninus, aged 13. In Peace'.[18]

It is possible that they were originally inspired by pillar stones of the distant past, prehistoric menhirs, and that the mere spectacle of these mute monuments led to the setting up of new ones. Or did it go further, with the assumption that such stones had a sacredness: did relatives hark back to past ages as Roman control ebbed away? Although the menhirs were not being reused, as is sometimes alleged, there is evidence that some of the new pillar stones were placed on or near the sites of Bronze Age barrows. In a recent analysis David Petts cites ten such cases from Nash-Williams and believes that there may have been more that were originally so placed, then subsequently moved to graveyards.[19] Or was the motivation territorial? Did heirs and supporters place stones close by alleged ancestors in order to buttress their claims to the land? Two post-Roman stones, one inscribed, the other not, lay close by the mounds near Clocaenog in Denbighshire on the west edge of a ridge called today Bryn y Beddau, the hill of the graves. There is not, or should not be, any sacredness attached to these mounds, since they are natural features and not graves at all: Jeremy Knight argues that the erectors of the stones in this case wished their dead to be associated with the mounds which they took to be the graves of the notables of yesteryear. They were seeking what he calls 'fictive ancestors'[20] to justify entitlement to land. Tania Dickinson and her colleagues have reminded us of the extent to which Anglo-Saxon burial practices were influenced by secular factors, family considerations and fashions and this is a reminder to be applied also to the grave and memorial stones of western Britain generally.

Nevertheless, Church influences do make themselves felt among the other forces playing on the Celtic elite. There is, for example, a moving inscription from Llanllywenfel in Brecon commemorating a king of Brycheiniog, Riuallaun or Riuallon, and his son Ioruerth, probably killed together in battle about mid-seventh century. With this monument Welsh memorial stones have made a major advance from the simple commemoration of death and descent: here we have a dignified bookhand inscription in regular lines, 'a fragment of contemporary manuscript cut into rock',[21] as Charles Thomas

---

[18] *ECMW* no. 294; Knight, *Antiquity* 137
[19] D. Petts, 'Cemeteries and boundaries in Western Britain', S. Lucy, A. Reynolds eds, *Burial in early England and Wales* (London 2002) 24–46
[20] Knight, *Antiquity* 141; *ECMW* no.176
[21] Thomas, *Mute stones 322; ECMW* no. 62

puts it. Probably a composition by Riuallaun's bishop, it runs: 'Here in the shroud, silent – Ioruert and Ruallaun in the graves, await in peace the dreadful coming of the Judgement'. Riuallaun's daughter, Keindrech (Fair of Face), was subsequently married to a son of the king of Dyfed and thereafter the small kingdom of Brycheiniog in South Wales became subordinate to Dyfed.

We have a number of names for priests and can use Patrick's letters and Gildas's writings to elucidate titles, presbyter for priest, diaconus for deacon, while sacerdos should mean a man consecrated as bishop but, in Charles Thomas's interpretation, not necessarily acting as a diocesan. A stone at Capel Anelog, near Aberdaron on the Llyn peninsula in Caernarvonshire, gives evidence of a community of priests, where Senacus presbiter is commemorated in ungrammatical Latin 'cum multitudinem fratrum', 'with a multitude of the brethren'.[22] A stone at Capel Bronwen near Llantrisant in Anglesey is a reminder that clerical marriage was the norm: Bivatisus sacerdos, described as a 'famulus Dei', 'servant of God', commemorates his wife Audiva. He could well have been a court bishop to rulers of Gwynedd.[23]

The stones mirror the advances of the Christian Church. At first when there was no network of churches in the countryside and the faith had not wholly won over the elite, individual stones were erected in places with no specific Christian links. As churches were built, stones came to be put inside them or in the churchyard. A saint's body might be housed in a chapel at the west end of a church or in a free-standing chapel close by, an *eglwys y bedd*.[24] Here the relatives sought comfort, prayers and aid for their dead from association with the burial places of holy men and women and their relics. In remote areas, we may surmise that individual stones with Christian symbols acted as assembly points where Christians could meet their priest. Two likely examples of this are a pair of sculptured stones representing Christ, in one case in mass vestments dating from the eighth or ninth century in Gelli Onen, Pontardawe and Cefn Hrfynydd in the parish of Llangyfelach in Glamorgan.[25]

A stone found in the churchyard at Llansadawrn in Anglesey introduces us to 'beatus Saturninus', i.e. Sadawrn, evidently a man commemorated for his holy life and likely to be a patron or founder of a church on the site, which

[22] *ECMW* no.78; Knight, *Antiquity* 135
[23] *ECMW* no. 33; Knight, *Antiquity* 135
[24] Knight, *Antiquity* 139
[25] Ibid. 177; *ECMW* nos. 256, 269

might well have contained his body or his relics.[26] We know nothing about Saturninus: he will probably have had no *Vita*, nor have attracted veneration from other places, but will have had only local fame. The analogy of place-names in other Celtic lands – Cornwall, Ireland, Brittany – suggests that there will have been other founders, patrons, holy men and women known only to their own locality or a little beyond: these were the infantry of the post-Roman conversion.

In Wales many of these names have been lost, victims of changes of sentiment by patrons and benefactors and battles for power among rulers and secular authorities through the centuries of Welsh Church life. Dedications might assert the new authority of a successful over-king taking control of a territory and its churches and do honour to his favourite saint: this was especially true in the great age of political consolidation in the ninth and tenth centuries, up to the death of Hywel Dda. Major saints displaced minor ones. Bishops might seek to justify gains for their estates and their authority by attributing dedications to acquired churches to do honour to their supposed founder and confirm their rights. So a twelfth-century bishop of Llandaff, in Reuben Davies's phrase, 'cooked up' a cult of St Dyfrig from the conversion age and attributed a group of churches to him and a disciple in Ergyng or Archenfield in what is now Herefordshire: there is no evidence that Dyfrig and his followers ever went there.[27]

Greater understanding of the evolution of church dedications and the way in which saints were used as battle standards by competing authorities has put paid to attempts to use dedications found in later sources to reconstruct the movements and responsibilities of the founder saints of the age of conversion. Emrys Bowen believed the evidence of the bishop's propagandising compilation of the twelfth-century *Book of Llandaff*, and put down Dyfrig and his following as the sixth-century evangelists of this part of Herefordshire: when he plotted the dedications to St David on a map of modern Wales, he understood that he was recovering the outline of the sphere of the saint's activity in his lifetime. He was mistaken on both counts. Modern research has diminished rather than enlarged knowledge of the conversion age, the Age of Saints. We have to accept that we are unlikely ever to have more than broad outline

---

[26] *ECMW* no. 32; see J. Blair, *Church* (Oxford 2008) for fundamental reassessment of development of churches and settlements, concise, fruitful summaries on Roman and post-Roman eras 8–78, round churchyards 21

[27] J. Reuben Davies, 'The saints of South Wales and the Welsh Church', Thacker and Sharpe, *Local saints* 361–95

knowledge of this period of Welsh history, viewed, as Reuben Davies observes, 'as from an aeroplane, with glimpses of clearly defined features in a vista that is otherwise obscured by cloud'.[28]

Contemporary or near-contemporary saints' Lives pertaining to this region were either not written or have not survived. What we have are tendentious compilations full of hagiographical conventions and imaginative fantasies put together in the interest of some objective far removed from the world of the early evangelists. We know a little about St David – enough to accept that he was a major figure in the sixth century, regarded with veneration in Ireland, with a cult spanning centuries. Author of an influential Penitential, his Rule was austere, eschewing meat-eating, with hard manual labour and a commitment to common property, a regime in accord with the asceticism of Cassian and the Desert Fathers. The soubriquet 'Aquaticus' probably refers to his daily custom of standing up to his neck in cold water in order to subdue fleshly appetites. His exact dates and his effect on the conversion of Wales all remain obscure.[29]

The Life which the High Middle Ages read was compiled at the end of the eleventh century by Rhigyfarch of Llanbadarn, son of Sulien, bishop of St David's: its aim was to restore the reputation of the saint after the Norman invasion of Dyfed and use the opportunity provided by the Life to assert the claim of Mynyw/St David's to be one of the leading bishoprics of Wales. It served its purpose, but provides no new historical information. Rhigyfarch's David is the son of Sant, king of Ceredigion, born in a thunderstorm on the cliffs at St Davids, of a beautiful nun whom Sant had raped. The rape fitted hagiographical preconceptions for it allowed a birth in circumstances where carnal desire on the mother's part was wholly precluded; it was the nearest the author could get to a virgin birth. David was described as the founder of twelve monasteries, including Bath and Glastonbury, and as a man who not only performed miracles but was also transported by an angel to Jerusalem where the patriarch made him an archbishop; on his return he appeared triumphantly at the Synod of Llandewi Brefi and preached against Pelagianism, whereupon he was recognised as archbishop and St David's as the metropolitan see of all Britain, before dying at the age of 147, that is, at the

---

[28] Thacker and Sharpe, *Local saints*, 395; E.G. Bowen, *Saints, seaways and settlements in the Celtic lands* (Cardiff 1969)

[29] J. Wyn Evans, 'Dewi Sant', *ODNB*; D.N. Dumville, *St David of Wales*, Kathleen Hughes memorial lecture (Cambridge 2001); fasting, D. Jenkins, *CMCS* 45 (2003) 88

age of an Old Testament patriarch. Bar the description of his dedicated life in his monastery, there is little to be made of all this: most such Lives, written long after the death of their subjects, are to be dismissed.

Tall stories abound in the tradition of St Bueno, the seventh-century holy man, probably originally from Powys, who occupied the same position of reverence in North Wales as St David did in the South; he is said to have revived St Winifred after her decapitation, to have performed a miracle of resurrection on Digiwg, daughter of Ynyre Gwent, and to have raised the Irishman Lorcan from the dead. He was not to be cowed: he cursed the sons of Salyf ap Cynan when they drove him from the land he had been given and did exactly the same to Cadwallon, king of Gwynedd, when he attempted to endow him with stolen land. The geographical placing of the stories about him, the tradition about the lands given to him, his burial place in an *eglwys y bedd* at Clynnog, Gwynedd, and the picture of an independent-minded, charismatic British abbot capable of standing up to princes are all that can safely be inferred from such legendary material. In general, the Welsh saints of the *Vitae* are figures of power, sometimes indeed healing, but more often cursing, punishing those who crossed them and demonstrating the authority given to them from on high by their control not only of people but of animals and the elements.[30]

We are, however, fortunate to have one, perhaps two, Lives of saints written closer to the events they describe and not overwhelmed by anachronistic, contemporary needs. The Life of St Samson, a genuinely peripatetic monastic founder with a likeness to St Martin of Tours, is a source which brings to life the common Celtic field of mission. Although written by a seventh- or eighth-century Breton admirer, the time lag is not such as to destroy the veracity of the main lines of this account. It has also the great advantage of throwing light on the birth of Christianity in Cornwall.[31]

A child of the aristocracy of western Britain, Samson was brought as a boy to Llantwit Major, was ordained by St Dubricius and went to Ynys Byr, recently established as a smaller daughter-house of Llantwit Major, and ruled by a priest called Piro – Caldey Island, in fact. One night, coming back drunk to his hut, Piro fell into a well and was drowned and Samson succeeded him as abbot. On a visit to his family, his passion for asceticism so influenced his

[30] P. Sims-Williams, 'St Bueno', *ODNB*; E.R. Henken, *The Welsh saints. A study in patterned lives* (Cambridge 1991); id., 'Hagiography in the Celtic countries', *KCC*

[31] Thomas, *Mute stones* ch. 14 (Cornish context)

relatives that he persuaded his mother, father, brothers, aunt and an uncle and his family to join him in monastic life. The family's wealth was devoted to the cause and to the building of churches, which Samson, having become a bishop, consecrated.[32]

His restless search for a perfect way of life led him, with his father and two companions, to go to a Roman fort near the Severn's bank on the Welsh side, where they lived for a time. There followed a journey to Ireland – a passage which may well be an interpolation into the original manuscript – and then, in consequence of a vision, a further journey which took them overseas to Cornwall, to Padstow at the mouth of the river Camel. They sailed up the estuary, disembarked and went two miles inland to a monastery at what is now St Kew but was earlier known as Landocco, i.e. the church settlement of Docco, probably a daughter-house of the monastery at Llandough in Glamorgan. The party was met by a spokesman who explained that the standard of the monastery was not adequate for a bishop's visitation since the monks had lapsed from their original ideals. Samson and his party accepted the explanation and travelled on with a cart and larger wagon along the traditional route south to Fowey, carrying books and liturgical vessels suitable for the founding of a monastery. En route, or perhaps on another occasion, Samson's group chanced on a party of the inhabitants engaged in the ritual worshipping of an idol, and attempted to dissuade them, without success.[33] A horse race was taking place, possibly part of the pagan celebration, and a boy was thrown and apparently killed. Samson challenged them: their idol could not heal the boy and restore him to life, his God could. He struck a bargain. The boy would be brought back to life if they would destroy their idol and abandon its worship. They accepted and when, after two hours of prayer by Samson, the boy revived, they kept their side of the bargain and destroyed the idol. It was a dramatic confrontation reminiscent of Elisha's cure of the boy with sunstroke, and characteristic of the great saints and missionaries of this era. In the sequel Samson insisted on the people accepting baptism followed by confirmation at his hands and scratched the sign of the cross on a standing stone in the vicinity.

Samson went on to found another monastery near Fowey, leaving his father there as abbot, and for a time lived as a hermit in a cave at Golant, ridding the

---

[32] E. Rees, *Celtic saints, passionate wanderers* (London 2000) surveys sites; T. Taylor trans., *The life of St Sampson of Dol* (London 1925); A. Minard, 'St Samson', *KCC*

[33] Pagans, not apostates, as M. Dunn, *The emergence of monasticism* (Oxford 2000) 140

local inhabitants of a serpent, after which he went on to Brittany where he founded other monasteries, which he later handed over to an Irish cousin, and became bishop of Dol. He is likely to have been the Samson 'bishop and sinner' who was witness to the acts of Councils held at Paris in 553 and 557. The sentence containing his witness was written, surely not by accident, in a leonine hexameter, a stray piece of evidence of his learning on which his biographer had little to say.

Although the Life is encased within the conventions and fantasies of Celtic hagiography – his conception despite his mother's barrenness, his precocious learning, his escape from poisoning by a herbal drink, his cure of his dying father, the fire from his mouth when ordained, his miraculous healings and exorcisms – it nonetheless conveys much about the presuppositions of the conversion age.[34] Monasticism had potency and variety, with very different levels of observance. Samson could hold his drink; abbot Piro drank to excess and lost his life. Samson repeatedly seeks higher standards for himself: early in his career, he is apparently not satisfied with the quondam gentleman's monastery of Llantwit Major and goes over to Caldey Island. The ideals of Cassian and the Egyptian monks living in austere solitude or near-solitude clearly have entered the reading of monks and monastic aspirants: in the Celtic west, the islands form 'the desert' to which the most devoted may flee. The eremitical life is interchangeable with the cenobitic: wandering monks, alone or accompanied, still go round evangelising pagan societies, employing Old Testament methods of dismissing pagan gods through confrontational contests, with mass baptisms as the sequel. Brittany, originally settled by former mercenaries and then by a limited number of leading British families whose presence created a milieu in which the ideals of Celtic monks could flourish, had common links with Cornwall and Wales and water travel ensured they stayed in close touch. Kinship mattered. The faith spread through families, and informal monastic federations were held together by continuing family links.

Another monk, St Paul Aurelian, whose career is recorded in a ninth-century Life, also by a Breton, had a similar lifestyle to Samson and, like him, after having some impact in Cornwall went over to Brittany where he was a monastic founder.[35] The Lives of these two saints are part of the evidence for

[34] Henken, *Welsh saints*, B. Merdrignac in J. Carey *et al.*, *Studies in Irish hagiography* (Dublin 2001); Thomas, *Christian Celts* 58–9
[35] Thomas, *Mute stones* 280, 310

the problems of the Cornish mission field. On the one hand, Paul Aurelian had to wrestle with the ruler of Dumnonia, who was evidently not a committed Christian, on the other, Samson was implored by inhabitants of Fowey to stay as their bishop. Plainly there was no one there to exert discipline or give pastoral leadership; instead there was a series of missionaries and founders of churches who worked on their own.

The British kingdom of Dumnonia included some of the least Romanised territory in Roman Britain, so when Samson made his journey across Cornwall he was travelling through lands where there were no villas, no temples, only a few classical altars and some milestones. Tin mining mattered to the Romans but beyond the river Exe the impact of their civilisation was minimal and no evidence of Christianity in these far western regions under Roman rule has been found. In other words, with one possible exception, here, as opposed to Wales, there were no pre-existing bases for later missions to build on. Paganism occupied the field.

The current of evangelisation flowed from Wales into Cornwall. Both Samson and Aurelian were monastic founders but were quite ready to confront paganism and grapple with the problems of local society. Inscribed stones in Cornwall and Devon, though reticent sources awkward to interpret, are independent witnesses to the likely origins of Christian mission in the far south-west and confirm the implication of the Lives of Samson and Aurelian that the source of mission lay predominantly in Wales.[36]

The stones are much less numerous than in Wales: they extend over parts of western Devon, with four outliers on Lundy Island and an isolated group at Wareham in Dorset but are concentrated overwhelmingly in Cornwall. Sixty-nine stones are extant; ten more have either vanished or become so worn by weather that their inscriptions have become indecipherable, but have been recovered from transcriptions by antiquarians. The total includes altar-slabs and sculptured crosses dating from the ninth century and later, and one remarkable stone with an English inscription put up by an immigrant family, which cannot be earlier than the eleventh century. The crucial ones are the pillar stones. Some will certainly have stemmed from the conversion age but Cornwall was a conservative region and others may have been erected in later centuries in the old style.

---

[36] E. Okasha, *Corpus of early inscribed stones of south-west Britain* (London 1993); id., 'The early Christian carved and inscribed stones of south-west Britain', B.E. Crawford ed., *Scotland in Dark Age Britain* (St Andrews 1996)

The layout differs from that prevalent on the continent although some formulas in the inscriptions do correspond: only eight of the total have a version of the Gaulish 'hic iacit', a small proportion compared with its preponderance in Gaul. Gaul has spaced inscriptions running horizontally across the front of the stones, sometimes with margins; the south-west stones are usually unspaced, lack margins and have letters running vertically down the surface. A common south-western formula is that of the simple memorial, giving only the name and descent of the deceased with no indication of religious adherence: this is unknown in Gaul.

Latin is the staple language of the epitaphs. Six of the pillar stones add to the Latin a version of ogham, obviously by and for the Irish who had migrated to the south-west either directly from Ireland or from their settlements in Dyfed. There is a distinction of usage from that prevalent in Wales which has some stones exclusively in ogham. This never happens in the south-west, where ogham is found only on bilingual stones. The Latin is sometimes shaky: standards tended to be lower in a society with fewer resources and less literacy. Instead of 'hic iacit' we may find 'ic iacit' or 'fili' for 'filii'. What is wholly missing is native Cornish, the child of Brittonic, which developed separately over time as Germanic invasion broke the landward communication between the territories of the independent British, and the vernacular of Roman Britain broke up into Cornish, Old Welsh, Cumbric and Breton (the fruit of British immigration into Gaul). Those who erected stones for their distinguished dead in Wales hardly ever thought their own vernacular suitable to be included on an epitaph – a stone at Tywyn is the unique exception – and the elite of the south-west took the same view.

The pillar stones make use of granite outcrops, often only roughly shaped or not dressed at all. In a society of very limited literacy, writing conferred prestige on the dead and their kin. Perhaps, as Elizabeth Okasha has suggested, the Christian epitaphs were an appeal to the saints in heaven for their prayers for the dead: a priest might read the inscriptions aloud.[37] Those which give no other information than name and descent are an indication of the vital importance of kinship ties in this society. The family may well have been Christian but have felt no necessity to carve any statement of adherence whether via symbol or word.

Though there are some points of difference, the pillar stones resemble the Welsh memorial stones most closely. Some Gaulish influence on masons and

[37] Crawford, *Scotland*

patrons cannot be ruled out given the strong commercial link between Cornwall and the continent but the likeliest hypothesis is that we are here confronted with a Dumnonian funerary style which developed in its own way from the Welsh model after it was taken up by local clergy and the elite of the area.

That there was some Mediterranean influence can be inferred from evidence at Tintagel, the rocky promontory on the north Cornish coast inhabited and developed from c.300 to c.700, thus spanning the late Roman epoch and its aftermath.[38] It gained economic vitality from its trade in tin, which drew in high-calibre pottery and glass, including red-slipped fine ware and amphorae manufactured in the Christian eastern Mediterranean. An intriguing theory suggests that under Justinian's government Byzantine merchants were given subsidies to trade further west than would normally have been economic in the interest of winning hearts and minds for a planned expansion of the Empire into western lands.[39] It was an unusually far-flung enterprise to bypass the Romanised lowlands and sail to the most peripheral regions of the island, but it may well have carried seeds of Christian influence with it. Tintagel was unique in Dumnonia, a fully developed Late Antique settlement with industrial storage sites scattered across the Head, a massive artificial terrace, a reception area for distinguished visitors and for ceremonial, perhaps including an initiation ritual in which a new ruler put his foot in a carved footprint as he entered office. Carved slates, one recording a construction under the auspices of a certain Artognou, are reminiscent of Roman building dedications: memories of Rome and Roman techniques may also have provided fertile ground for a transfer from paganism to the late Roman official religion for a ruler who inherited Tintagel.

On the cliffs opposite the promontory there is an early Christian burial ground, overspilling the modern graveyard of St Metheriana, with evidence suggesting the practice of feasting at the graveside on east Mediterranean lines, and in west Cornwall a curious dedication of a church to St Ia, a Byzantine saint whose church stood outside the Golden Gate at Constantinople. We have no direct evidence about the circumstances in which kings of Dumnonia accepted Christianity, only a scathing reference in Gildas to Constantine of Dumnonia as one of the hypocritical Christian rulers of his day, 'the tyrannical whelp of the unclean Dumnonian lioness' whom he

[38] C. Thomas, *Tintagel, Arthur and archaeology* (London 1993)
[39] K.R. Dark, *Civitas to kingdom* (Leicester 1994) 210–11, reviewed by J.L. Davies, D.P. Kirby, *CMCS* 29 (1995) 70–2

accused of killing two royal princes and their guardians in church while disguised as an abbot.

With its peerless natural defensive position, reinforced by an earthwork bank and ditch to fence off access from the land and a secure harbour, Tintagel will necessarily have been the strongpoint for the early kings of Dumnonia, who alone would have the authority and command structure necessary to secure the raw material from tin mining and control far-ranging commerce. Like their fellow Celtic potentates, they would have been peripatetic rulers, eating as they went, doing justice and liaising with their leading men; but there is no doubt that Tintagel would have been their main palace and long-term residence. A Christian influence on them through commerce is not to be ruled out.

Cornish place-names often betray the presence of founders, patrons, holy men and women who were the pioneers of conversion. The county is remarkable for the number of names it still has with an ecclesiastical significance, consisting either of a saint's name pure and simple or a place-name equivalent, most commonly *lan, signifying an enclosed cemetery or church and its associated settlement combined with a personal name, usually that of a saint.[40] It is likely that the formation of the ecclesiastical landscape of Cornwall was a slower and longer process than once thought, the formation of such place-names being continued over centuries. There are, in addition, place-names in west Cornwall, all but one in the county's westernmost hundreds, mostly associated with purely local saints incorporating or reflecting the place-name element *merther*, a saint's shrine, and some thirty-five instances of the prefix *eglos*, church. At Altarnun, altar, no doubt in effect meaning shrine, was combined with the name of the female saint Non. A few of the saints belong to a category which can be called inter-Celtic, that is, they have a cult in more than one of the churches of the Celtic fringe, including Ireland; other dedications are to the great international saints.

This leaves a pool of names of purely local significance, patrons of one place only or of one or two more, otherwise unknown and with no surviving authentic information on their lives. We can fairly assume that in these cases

[40] O. Padel, 'Local saints and place-names in Cornwall', Thacker and Sharpe, *Local saints* 303–53 at 306; discussion of C. Thomas's hypothesis of churches' development from enclosed cemeteries, Blair, *Church* 21; D. Brook, 'The early Christian Church east and west of Offa's Dyke', N. Edwards, A. Lane eds, *The early Church in Wales and the West* (Oxford 1992) 77–89

we are getting back to the pioneers of conversion. That we are on the right track in assuming an early origin for these saints is demonstrated by the inclusion of some of the names in a vernacular list contained in a tenth-century manuscript whose immediate provenance was Brittany, possibly the work of a Cornishman there compiling a list of the saints he knew.[41] Their names lie thickly indeed across the landscape: it has been estimated that out of some 196 ancient parishes, 147 have names of ecclesiastical origin or significance, often involving these saints: in west Cornwall, the proportions are even higher, standing at ninety-seven out of 105.

In the adjacent county of Devon, the situation is very different: out of 454 parish names only twenty-nine can be said to have a religious significance. Devon was anglicised and the pattern of place-names, so much more secular than in Celtic Church lands, corresponds to that which prevailed generally in Anglo-Saxon England. Dumnonia's territories crumbled slowly in face of Anglo-Saxon infiltration. For reasons still not fully clarified, the kings of Wessex over time had the upper hand; their warriors, albeit no longer reinforced by fresh settlers from overseas, cut away Dumnonian territories. In 658 the Anglo-Saxons entered Somerset; there was a see-sawing of power over Devon but in the 680s the monastery of Exeter, to which the young Wynfrith, the future St Boniface, missionary and martyr, came as a child, was presided over by an English abbot, an indication of the extent of the Anglo-Saxon takeover by late seventh century. Cornwall, however, did not succumb.[42]

Only in the ninth century at the battle of Hingston Down in 838 did Wessex finally succeed in taking over Cornwall. It remained a conservative region, Cornish went on being spoken and the Anglo-Saxon takeover did not extinguish the local saints. They mattered to the Cornish and were sustained by them in later times despite some incomprehension and puzzlement by ecclesiastical authority and possible attempts in the late Middle Ages to supplant them by better-known ones as patrons for their churches. Saints' days were feast days of importance in these localities. The long-lived recusant Cornish hagiographer, Nicholas Roscarrock, writing in the early seventeenth century, remembered such festivals being celebrated in his childhood.[43] The saints

[41] Padel, 'Local saints', 316–18
[42] B. Yorke, *Wessex in the early Middle Ages* (London 1995) 53, 60; reviewed by H. Loyn, *SH* 18 (1990) 152–3
[43] N. Orme ed., *Nicholas Roscarrock's lives of saints*, Devon and Cornwall Record Soc. new ser. 35 (1972)

generally have no *Vitae*; we have only names as mementos of the pioneers who founded settlements in the far south-west or perhaps served as the first priests of their churches. The scale is likely to have been small – one or two men, a church building and a farm, perhaps monastic in the loose style of the time, perhaps not. The defining and embanking of churchyards was a feature of the conversion process; but it may have become more frequent in the ninth century and beyond when the Cornish came to feel that it was appropriate for burials to take place in Christian churchyards rather than in traditional burial grounds which sometimes reached back before Christianity.

It is not always easy to decide which were the earliest Christian sites: Lynette Olson has distinguished early monasteries at St Kew, St Keverne, Padstow, Crantock and St Neot, and Charles Thomas has made a good case for Phillack in west Cornwall, with the Constantinian chi-rho on a stone discovered in 1856 embedded in the south wall of the church. Here the evidence of early burials suggests a monastic settlement of some calibre, like Llandough in Glamorgan, as early as the fifth century.[44]

For all the necessary caveats and problems about dating, the broad lines of Christianisation in Cornwall are nonetheless clear. Place-names with their strongly ecclesiastical cast and their saints' names reflect the incoming of priests and monks. It has often been noticed how isolated many Cornish churches are from habitation, by the sea or by farms with no more than a hamlet nearby, unlike churches of so much of the English landscape, which lie within the villages they serve. It is a consequence of an ancient, piecemeal pattern of Christian settlement, often by very small groups requiring limited housing with adjacent farmland, which they worked. Sam Turner has recently added another dimension to the analysis by making the case for a major reorganisation of land-holding following a fall in population, diminution of cultivated land and the ending of the ancient system of cultivation known as rounds in the sixth and seventh centuries.[45] Subsequently, gifts of land for Christian purposes helped to transform the landscape, he argues. Endowment brought to ecclesiastical sites contiguous blocks of land, open farmsteads with access to arable land and water meadows. The donation of good-quality land

[44] L. Olson, *Early monasteries in Cornwall* (Woodbridge 1989) reviewed by P. Sims-Williams, *EHR* 107 (1992) 978–9; A. Preston-Jones, 'Decoding Cornish churchyards', Edwards and Lane, *Early Church* 104–24; Thomas, *Mute stones* 200 (Phillack); Okasha, *Corpus* 205–7 (Phillack)

[45] S. Turner, *Making a Christian landscape. The countryside in early medieval Cornwall, Devon and Wessex* (Exeter 2006)

and evidence for freedom from taxation leads him to suspect that the rulers of Dumnonia came to play a major part in the provision of resources for the ecclesiastical communities vital for the evangelisation of the area. The founder saints, still commemorated in Cornish place-names, may well have needed longer than has sometimes been assumed for their work in the mission field in the face of a tenacious paganism and an adherence to old ways in a conservative society.

Parts of what became the kingdom of Dumnonia on the eastern side of the Exe had been Romanised and show evidence of a Romano-British Christianity continuing peacefully into the sub-Roman age. As elsewhere, with the decline of central authority chieftains seized power and ruled by military might. One striking example is the reoccupation of the Iron Age hill fort of South Cadbury, whose defences were extensively remodelled at some time within the period c.475–c.550, providing a strongpoint for its owner and a hall for feasting on a scale and in a luxury demonstrable from the expensive glass vessels and red slipware remaining on the site. It became one of the five or six impregnable sites in early medieval Britain.[46] A sister strongpoint at Congresbury overlooked and perhaps acted as guardian to the nearby cemetery of Cannington, which was in use from c.300 to 700. It included Christian burials and what may well have been two shrines. A grave marked out from the rest, with imported stone being used for a tomb, is perhaps the burial place of an early seventh-century saint. It was a cemetery evidently available for use by everyone and incorporated some Anglo-Saxon graves with corpses equipped with knives. Here a Romano-British cemetery had durability and traditional funerary practices continued, absorbing Anglo-Saxons: it is at the opposite end of the spectrum from the massive pagan Anglo-Saxon cemeteries of East Anglia, where Germanic invaders overwhelmed the indigenous population.[47]

At Wareham in Dorset there is evidence of a Christian nucleus wealthy enough to commission five memorial stones recording names and using the Latin 'filius'.[48] Nothing shows what links they may have had with Christians outside Dorset. Had there been a geographical sequence of memorial stones with Christian symbols or allusions, the case might have been made for a

---

[46] L. Alcock, *Cadbury Castle, Somerset. The early medieval archaeology* (Cardiff 1995)
[47] P.A. Rahtz, *Cadbury-Congresbury 1968–73. A late post-Roman hilltop settlement in Somerset* (Stroud 1992)
[48] Yorke, *Wessex* 69–71

landward Christianisation stretching down the south-western peninsula of Britain; as it is, the working hypothesis of missionary endeavour and the founding of monasteries by men passing over sea routes from Wales must stand.

There are other scattered indications of a Christian presence east of the Exe dating back to Romano-British times. At the Roman garrison town of Shepton Mallet, the evidence suggests a small Christian enclave. One of the cemeteries has seventeen burials facing east within a ditched enclosure and a silver alloy pendant cross with a chi-rho dating to c.400 was recovered from one of the graves. On the Tor at Glastonbury, excavations by P.A. Rahtz uncovered a number of postholes for small timber buildings, which he concluded were housing for hermits, evidence of metalworking, some amphora shells and a curious grave-shaped cairn which may have been a saint's shrine. He believes that here on this wild and deserted site was a sixth-century Celtic monastic settlement, which appealed to men seeking seclusion from the world, earning a living from their metalwork. Had it been a stronghold for a chieftain of the post-Roman Age, signs of defensive works would be expected. There is none. There are signs that the hermits were meat eaters, which by no means excludes the identification of the site as a monastic settlement: Celtic monasteries were not necessarily vegetarian.[49]

How the Christians of these lands fared in the political and military developments of the centuries following the end of Roman Britain is obscure. The rulers of Dumnonia, it would seem, took power from the chieftains, then gradually lost ground to the Anglo-Saxon rulers of the kingdom of Wessex as they advanced into the peninsula, till by the early eighth century Dumnonia was more or less confined to Cornwall. A straw in the wind is the letter sent by St Aldhelm from his Wessex bishopric to Geraint, king of Dumnonia, which, for all the differences between their Churches, is sympathetic in tone. As the Wessex kings accepted Christianity, the possession of a common faith may have done something to mitigate the hostility between the British and the people of Wessex.[50]

The spread of Christianity in northern Britain in the years after the ending of the Roman occupation is hardly less obscure than its history in the south-west. In contrast to Wales, even to Cornwall, there is but a thin scattering of

[49] P.A. Rahtz, 'Excavations at Glastonbury Tor', *Arch J* 127 (1971) 1–81
[50] Yorke, *Wessex* 179; id., *Conversion* 121

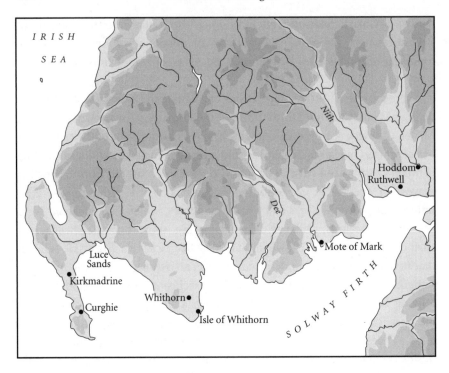

Map 2 The north shore of the Solway Firth showing early Christian sites, trading points and fortresses in Galloway. On the west Kirkmadrine and Curghie with their Christian memorials look across the water to the Isle of Whithorn and the monastery inland. Mote of Mark is a metal-working centre inside fortress walls. Further east lies Ruthwell with its outstanding eighth-century high cross and, north and east the Northumbrian monastery of Hoddom.

memorial stones in the earliest category, Class I in Nash-Williams's classification, in the coastal lands north of Wales. There are two on the Isle of Man and ten in all on the west coast between Hadrian's Wall and the Forth–Clyde line, once defended by the Antonine Wall; of those ten, five discovered in Galloway are important for our understanding of the evangelisation of Scotland.

The oldest comes from Whithorn in Wigtonshire near the tip of Burrow Head on the northern shore of the Solway Firth. A rectangular stone was discovered late in the nineteenth century near the north transept of its medieval cathedral, explicitly Christian and of an early date. Surmounted by a Constantinian chi-rho, the inscription reads: 'Te Dominum laudamus Latinus annorum XXXV et filia sua annorum IV ic sinum fecerunt nipus Barrovadi' ('We praise thee O Lord. Latinus of years thirty-five and his daughter of years four here a "sinus" made. Descendant of Barrovadus'). In the first line we have a quotation from Psalm 146 and perhaps a fragment of the lost Romano-British liturgy: there follows what appears to be a commemoration of the dead, a Christian dying at what might have been the average age of death in the fifth century and his young daughter. It has been suggested that the last two lines were added later, to do honour to Barrovadus, who, had he been a pagan, is unlikely to have been named on a Christian stone: 'nipus' can be translated as grandson or nephew. The implication is that we are dealing with a settled Christian family, and perhaps community, lying north of Hadrian's Wall, two, possibly three generations strong. The term 'sinus' is crucial. It originally meant a fold in a garment, a gown or a toga and then, metaphorically, a refuge, a place of security and thus, perhaps, a church. If Latinus and daughter have found a last resting place here, then this is a memorial stone: if the meaning is 'church', then the stone commemorates its founding, Latinus including his daughter in a kindly paternal way, and can be interpreted as a foundation stone, early because it was inscribed before the chi-rho had given way to the cross.[51]

Across the water from the Burrow peninsula at Kirkmadrine in the Rinns, the extreme south-western peninsula of Galloway lapped by the Irish Sea, lie three more early inscribed stones: a little way off, at Curghie, a fourth of apparently the same age and type carried the name Ventidius, described as 'diaconus'. The most interesting of the three is early, carrying the remains of an alpha and omega and records the names of two 'sancti et praecipui sacerdotes', 'holy and outstanding bishops', Viventius and Mavorrus. Another stone has two names, no longer legible, and the third has a chi-rho and the words 'Initium et finis', Latinising alpha and omega. These stones together point to a strong, early and substantial Christian presence in Galloway beyond the Wall and bear witness to the will of its leading class to make use of the Latin script and Roman style of monument in their post-Roman world.[52]

It has come to be realised that the Wall did not represent a watertight barrier to Roman influence further to the north; trade and the need for Roman authorities to influence British tribes by treaties and gifts as well as by intimidation mitigated the traditional division between the peoples of the Empire and the barbarians outside. Frontier garrisons were drawn widely from the provinces and would not necessarily have felt a profound difference between themselves and the British tribes around them. With Roman

---

[51] Thomas, *Christianity* 283–4; id., *Christian Celts* 101–14 (temple of Solomon); P.H. Hill, *Whithorn and St Ninian* (Stroud 1997)
[52] Thomas, *Christianity* 284–5; id., *Christian Celts* 114–23

influence came Christianity, through routes that are not made clear by the frail sources for the period. One possible route lies around the Wall itself through links established by commerce, family ties or missionary work.

One striking result of twentieth-century excavations has been the uncovering of a Christian presence amongst the military personnel of late Roman Britain. Not all the frontier troops were marched off in support of would-be usurpers; some, including Christians, remained with their families and manned the fortresses. At Piercebridge in County Durham fresh defensive ditches were dug round the fortress some time after 400; work was done at South Shields and at Malton in Yorkshire and on the Wall around this time. There is evidence of continued occupation at the strongpoints of Housesteads and Vindolanda. Birdoswald is especially interesting as there are signs there that the fort was taken over by one of the self-made chieftains, as observed in the south-west, the Roman granary being replaced by timber-framed halls. A chieftain with his warriors could maintain a local taxation system, an echo of the Roman past, in return for the protection of his 'subjects'. The cutting of the ties between the province and the Empire did not eliminate the Christian presence amongst the former *limitanei* of the years of Roman occupation and though the civilian settlements to the south of the Wall, the supply points for the garrison, were hard hit by the ending of the formal occupation, they remained in existence and included Christian families.[53]

The Romans had been at pains to secure the south bank of the Solway Firth against marauders and block off its crossing points: there were, for example, three forts in proximity to Burgh, site of the southern end of the shortest and easiest crossing points, and contacts from these may also have carried Christian influence across the Firth. The stones' major sites, both Whithorn and Kirkmadrine, lie a little inland in quiet places but not far from the water. There was once an island of Whithorn, which had a citadel dominating the natural harbour, possibly the seat of a post-Roman chieftain profiting from trade and piracy. It attracted distant trade, as is witnessed by B-amphorae from the Mediterranean. In both places we have evidence that Christianity had arrived, either by stepping over the Wall or through contact with the Mediterranean via the channels of commerce. Much depends on dating. A consensus would place the Latinus stone in the immediate post-Roman age, the first half of the fifth century; the Kirkmadrine stones have been placed

---

[53] P.J. Casey, 'The fourth century', P. Salway ed., *The Roman era. The British Isles, 55 BC–AD 410* (Oxford 2002) 75–104 at 102–4

later and so the presence of an Irish-influenced mission cannot be ruled out there.[54]

Whithorn has resonance for the early history of Christianity. Bede, relying probably on the witness of Pecthelm, the Northumbrian bishop imposed on Whithorn in 731 after the defeat of the British, and using what contemporary information he had, believed it once to have been the seat of a British bishop, 'a most reverend and holy man', Ninian, who brought Christianity to the southern Picts. It was a story that had reached him from hearsay and he recorded it with his usual prudent phrase, 'ut perhibent' (as they say). He called the site Hwitaern, the name current in his own time, linking it to the nature of the church which he believed Ninian had built there, the Candida Casa, the White Building, so named 'because he built the church of stone, which was unusual among the Britons'.[55] Excavation has confirmed part of Bede's story, uncovering lumps of lime, more likely to be remains of a timber structure coated with a white lime plaster than to be mortar from a limestone building, as there is no positive evidence of such a building of the requisite date. White is the colour of theological purity and *candida* can also mean shining, radiant; stone recalls for Bede the Petrine rock of Christ's response to Peter. So, although the tradition of the White Church stands independently of Bede, from his ecclesiastical view-point it was peculiarly appropriate for such a church to appear in what he believed to have been a cradle of Christianity in northern Britain.

The Latinus stone occupied a position within the enclosure of an early monastery on the mainland beyond Whithorn harbour; the earliest site plan from the record of the excavation shows a sub-circular bank and ditch with small timber buildings outside; in a second phase the space enclosed by the vallum has been extended with an additional enclosure likely to have been a shrine with a cemetery. The earliest buildings and Christian burials are orientated south-west/north-east, the orientation, as Ian Smith has pointed out, of the midsummer solstice sunrise and midwinter solstice sunset: a fact which may suggest the Christianising of pagan practices usual in the earliest stages of conversion. It was a British monastery which was succeeded by an Anglian one on the same site and Bede records that it became a place of pilgrimage.[56]

---

[54] C. Thomas, *Whithorn's Christian beginnings*, First Whithorn Lecture (1992)

[55] *HE* III 4; J.E. Fraser, 'Northumbrian Whithorn and the making of St Ninian', *IR* 53 (2002) 40–59

[56] I. Smith, 'The origins and development of Christianity in North Britain and Southern Pictland', J. Blair, C. Pyrah eds, *Church archaeology. Research directions for the future, CBA research report* 104 (York 1996) 19–37 at 26; *HE* III 4

On Ninian's achievement Bede was less well informed. He forms part of the little-known contribution of the Romano-British Church and its heirs to the faith and learning of Christian Ireland, the last, it may well be, of the major figures who assisted in the growth of monasteries and spread of learning after Patrick. The form of his name is based on scribal and historical errors, the most common scribal one of confusing a 'u' with an 'n'. Bede's Latin transmuted the original Brittonic Uinniau into Nynia, in the ablative, which the author of the twelfth-century Life, Ailred of Rievaulx, wrote as Ninian. In fact, Uinniau was a saint from Britain, most likely from south-west Scotland or possibly a descendant of Irish immigrants into Wales; he had an early career in Scotland, then passed over to Ireland where he founded the monastery of Moville and was the teacher of the young Columba, being known in Ireland as St Finnian of Moville, where he had a distinguished career and was the author of a Penitential and a correspondent of Gildas.

The loss of a first Life of Uinniau, Pecthelm's information to Bede and Bede's own passionate adherence to the cause of the Roman Easter have contrived to confuse the truth. When Bede incorporated his brief reference to Ninian in his chapter on the conversion of the Picts, he was concerned to show that Ninian had been entirely orthodox over the Easter question and said that 'he had been regularly instructed in the mysteries of the Christian faith in Rome'. It is very unlikely that Uinniau ever went to Rome: the passage of time from Uinniau's *floruit* in the sixth century and Pecthelm's arrival as bishop of Whithorn in 731, together with a prejudice in Bede, have misplaced an early British missionary, teacher and monastic founder and claimed him for Whithorn. P. Hill's excavations have shown that the traces of a Celtic monastery there go back to c.500, whereas Uinniau/Finnian died c.579. If he had been the founder of the Candida Casa one would have expected to find more early dedications to him in its immediate vicinity. He may well have had an importance in south-western Scotland more generally, as is witnessed by the number of dedications in early place-names elsewhere in Galloway, Dumfriesshire, Renfrewshire and Ayrshire and the adoption of his name for use as a personal name. There is no evidence that he ever went to the southern Picts. Bede knew very little about the conversion of Scotland and incorporated a few fragments of information about Whithorn, its white church and its dedication to St Martin in a chapter mainly devoted to Columba. Some have argued that in putting in Ninian and his supposed mission to the southern Picts, he wanted to produce a kind of 'proto-Columba', who was also a missionary but, unlike Columba, had sound views on the dating of Easter. His account is anachronistic.[57]

Whithorn has a long Christian history involving four distinct layers: firstly, a tombstone or a church's foundation stone from the immediate post-Roman age; secondly, a British monastery from *c*.500 onwards; thirdly, a British monk who is likely to have been an evangelist in south-western Scotland, was certainly a monastic authority known to Gildas and was a teacher and monastic founder in Ireland; fourthly, a pilgrimage site of the twelfth century, popularised by Ailred's Life of Ninian.

The stones at Whithorn and Kirkmadrine represent the major archaeological evidence for the existence of early Christianity in Scotland: this has led historians to suggest that Galloway was the springboard for mission further north. There are other stray stones: one from Overkirkhope in Selkirkshire has the distinction of being the earliest vernacular figure carving in northern Britain. In its crudity it is a far cry from any late Roman Christian carving, with its massive head, curious short tunic and badly modelled feet. Yet the carver portrays the traditional Roman *orans* position of prayer, and the devotional feeling behind it is unmistakable.[58] Stray finds further to the north and east in Tweeddale bring us echoes of the presence of Christians and the activities of clergy: a stone at Manor Water in Peebleshire has an early, equal-armed cross; a boulder at Peebles the inscription, 'Neitano sacerdos' (the priest Neitano); another there, now lost, is said to have referred to a bishop Nicholas. The Catstane in East Lothian with a Latin inscription on a great boulder, possibly a prehistoric standing stone, and the Carantus stone in Liddesdale indicate an early presence of Christianity in these areas and show that the faith had reached the Forth by the late fifth or early sixth century. Little else, however, is to be gleaned from them.[59]

Despite its composition so many centuries after his *floruit* in the late sixth and early seventh centuries something more can be made of the twelfth-century Jocelyn of Furness's Life of St Kentigern, the patron saint of Glasgow, also known by his hypocoristic name of Mungo. Jocelyn has a strange and obviously incorrect description of bishop Kentigern dying at a great age in a warm bath prepared for him by his followers, who then go after him into a

---

[57] T.O. Clancy, 'The real St Ninian', *IR* 22 (2001) 1–28; id., 'Scottish saints and national identities in the early Middle Ages', Thacker and Sharpe, *Local saints* 397–423
[58] Smith, 'Origins' 22 (Over Kirkhope)
[59] Ibid. 20 (Catstane)

happy death by bathing in the same water themselves. The traditional obit for the saint is 612; Jocelyn gives the day as the octave of the feast of the Epiphany on 13 January and this has alerted Charles Thomas to a bedrock of fact behind this mythical excursion. Baptism in Kentigern's day was administered by a bishop and only took place at a limited number of seasons of the Church's year, including Epiphany. Jocelyn would have known nothing of this: the bishop's instructions to the catechumens have been transmuted into a farewell address and the baptism by immersion, long superseded by Jocelyn's day, into a warm bath. No doubt in Glasgow's January, the water would have needed heating for an old man, but it was still too much for Kentigern, who died dramatically and fittingly exercising a bishop's duty. Whispers conveying the strength of the paganism against which Kentigern and his converts had to struggle can also be heard in Jocelyn's account: there is a herdsman who is 'secretly a Christian', obviously for fear of the consequences, and a record of Kentigern denouncing paganism at Hoddom in Dumfriesshire on the shore of the Solway Firth. Excavation at Hoddom has uncovered the remains of a building of about 600, part above and part below ground, predating the Northumbrian monastery. The sunken chamber is of Roman masonry packed with clay, with a soakaway near at hand: the care taken to make it waterproof makes it possible that this was a baptistery of Kentigern's time. Washed with lime, the clay and timber superstructure would have looked like Whithorn's Candida Casa, white symbolising the purification offered by baptism.[60]

The kingdom of Dál Riata, literally the gift of Riata, so called from an eponymous prehistoric hero who may not actually have existed, emerged as a result of long-term infiltration by the Irish across the narrow sea from Antrim. Bede, who probably got his information from Pictish sources, speaks of a migration from Ireland under their chieftain Reuda, who, 'by a combination of force and treaty', obtained from the Picts 'the settlements they now hold'. In historic times, Dál Riata embraced modern Argyll and Bute with contiguous islands. With characteristic fairy-tale simplicity, an origin-legend in the *Annals of Ulster* under the year 501 attributes the making of the kingdom to one man, Fergus Mor mac Eirc. A dynastic takeover by princely kindred from Antrim was spurred into action by pressures against them from

[60] Thomas, *Christianity* 209–11; C. Lowe, *Angels, fools and tyrants. Britons and Angles in Southern Scotland AD 450–750* (Edinburgh 1999) up-to-date summaries by excavator of Hoddom; S. Driscoll, 'Kentigern', *KCC*; A.D. Macquarrie, 'The career of St Kentigern of Glasgow: *vitae, lectiones* and glimpses of fact', *IR* 37 (1986) 3–24

the rival house of the Uí Néill and compensated for a weakening of their position in Ireland by establishing new claims across the North Channel. The distance between Ireland and western Britain is very short; a bare twelve miles at the closest point between Antrim and the Mull of Kintyre and casual, largely peaceful immigration may well date back as far as AD 300.[61]

Among all their settlements along the western seaboard of Britain, from Cornwall up as far as the Pictish lands of northern Scotland, only once did the Irish establish a kingdom of their own – in Dál Riata. One kindred, the Cenél nGabráin, contrived with scanty exceptions to exclude rivals and prevent anything approximating to the anarchic competition of the many petty kingdoms, *túatha*, which prevailed so long in Ireland. Families came over to settle, bringing the culture of their homeland with them: Adomnán's Life of Columba makes it clear that in his time they were Gaelic speaking, using Irish names and staying in constant contact with Ireland. Families are the natural, unheralded and unrecorded transmitters of the faith and as Christianisation proceeded within Ireland, so it did also in Dál Riata. The Gaelic tradition tended to settle on minimal apparatus for the practice of Christianity – small gospels, croziers, bells, portable reliquaries – and roving monks and priests would have sustained faith by services at shrines or in front of prayer crosses in the open air.

Argyll and Bute were not naturally well endowed territories: a living had to be eked out through agriculture and stock breeding with the aid of the riches of the sea. There was a limit to the population which could be supported, and the struggle to sustain economic life, to bring in subjects' tribute to defended centres and maintain people and monarchy under the constraints of the exploitable terrain seems to have focused the energies of the kingdom's leaders. The *Senchus fer nAlban* of the tenth century, based on a seventh-century core text, combined the genealogy of the great kindreds of Dál Riata with an analysis of the strength, civil, military and naval, of the kingdom; a precocious document, it no doubt had overtones of propaganda and may not have had as much practical utility as some commentators have assumed, but it bears witness to a kingdom with an unusual level of organisation and assessment and its rulers' concern to maintain their war fleet, crucial for the security and welfare of a kingdom where transport by sea was of overriding importance.[62]

[61] *HE* I i.; R. Sharpe, 'The thriving of Dalriada', S. Taylor ed., *Kings, clerics and chronicles in Scotland 500–1297* (Dublin 2000) 47–61 stresses monarchy; T.M. Charles-Edwards, *Early Christian Ireland* (Cambridge 2000) 293; D. Broun, 'Dál Riata', M. Lynch ed., *The Oxford companion to Scottish history* (Oxford 2001)
[62] Yorke, *Conversion* 51–5, 67, 75, 271

Map 3 Irish settlements in Britain from the late fourth century.

At Dunadd, the most important of the sites where rulers established bases for defence and the exaction of tribute, a substantial fortress was built on a rock above the plain of the river Add with an upper citadel reserved for ruler and entourage and a series of natural terraces below, which, among other buildings, included metal workshops. A footprint cut into a rock with a natural rock chair formation and an ogham inscription in Old Irish recall the king-making ceremonies of old Ireland; in the seventeenth century, no doubt also under Irish influence, a footprint in stone formed part of the inauguration of the Lord of the Isles, accompanied by an exhortation to new rulers that they 'should walk in the footsteps and uprightness of [their] predecessors'. Like other aristocratic sites on the western seaboard, it reveals the far-flung contacts, commercial and diplomatic, of the Dál Riatan rulers: they drank imported wine, used Merovingian and German glass vessels and Mediterranean amphorae and were generous patrons of metalworkers. The Dunadd site has the largest and most diverse range of pottery from the continent of any of the sites in the Celtic west and a great variety of raw materials, gold, silver, bronze, lead, iron, glass and jet, even including a piece of sulphide of arsenic used in manuscript illumination, which may have been in transit to Iona. Rulers seem to have had an intense interest in craftsmanship in metal and in some way to have controlled the making and distribution of brooches which acted as status symbols. There is a Christian presence – a quern with a cross on it and a slate disc with an invocation to God.[63]

Columba's decision in 563 to found his monastery on the island of Iona off the coast of Dál Riata and in its territory lent distinction to the kingdom and reinforced Christianity as it became one of the most notable of all early medieval monasteries. He came into a territory already Christian because of immigration across the sea from Ireland and had indeed not come as a missionary, but out of the desire to lead a more perfect monastic life: but he was a statesman-saint of the highest calibre with many connections and his developing association of dependent monasteries spread the faith and aided the converting of the Picts in proximity to Dál Riata. His presence, his travels and the abbots who succeeded him helped to pull Dál Riata out of obscurity: without Iona, the kingdom might well have become a backwater.[64]

---

[63] A. Lane, E. Campbell eds, *Dunadd. An early Dalriadic capital* (Oxford 2000), appendix, K. Forsyth, ogham inscription 264–72

[64] M. Herbert, 'The legacy of Columba', T.M. Devine *et al.*, *Celebrating Columba* (Edinburgh 1995) 1–14

To the north and east of Dál Riata lay the Picts. They were a formidable people. The mountainous barrier of the Mounth dividing northern and southern Picts, the Druim Alban range at Dál Riata's eastern border, the sheer size of their territory – Adomnán refers to a sub-king of the Orkneys subject to the great Bruide visited by Columba at Inverness – militated against speedy Christianisation.

No Rosetta Stone has been found to crack the language, so effectively suppressed and driven out of use by the victory of Gaelic and the supersession of the Pictish elite in the ninth century. No manuscripts survive from the Pictish era, although a painstaking investigation by Katherine Forsyth has shown that a lost Pictish chronicle lies behind the twelfth-century text of Simeon of Durham and a fourteenth-century manuscript contains Pictish king-lists. There is no surviving book-art from their Christian Church and no liturgical vessels. There was no Bede to write up the history of the coming of Christianity to Pictland – or indeed to any of the kingdoms which emerged among the British beyond the Wall after the fall of the Empire. It is an important story, but only a hazy outline of the conversion and Christian life of the Picts can now emerge.[65]

What research has uncovered, however, is a picture of a prosperous people, their wealth based on an efficient, settled agriculture. Excavations at Easter Kinnear in Fife revealed that where there was fertile land, there was intense cultivation. Pictish stones feature well-nourished horses, modelled from life, not manuscripts, with grooms to care for them, trained thoroughbreds relying on specialist attention and an abundant supply of oats: only an economy with surpluses could have afforded the cost of these animals, horses fourteen hands high, trained for cavalry and hunting. The stones also reveal their owners as a confident well-equipped aristocracy able to commission and pay skilled craftsmen to memorialise themselves and their families with scenes of the hunting so beloved of the upper classes of the day. The mounted warriors on the stones are vivid symbols of the authority of the ruling elite. There are wisps of evidence from the seventh century that in the aftermath of the Pictish victory over the Northumbrians in 685 at the battle of Nechtanesmere, the region of Fortriu, the south of modern Perthshire, emerged as the core of the kingdom, and steps were taken towards greater unity. Nechtanesmere showed

---

[65] K. Forsyth, 'Evidence of a lost Pictish source in the *Historia Regum* of Symeon of Durham', Taylor, *Kings* 19–34; K. Forsyth, *Language in Pictland. The case against Indo-European Pictish*, *Studia Hameliana* 2 (Utrecht 1997); S.M. Foster, *Picts, Gaels and Scots* (London 1996) ch. 5 strength of belief

that the Picts were now a force to be reckoned with. All in all they were no longer the wild marauders of late Romano-British history, the 'foul hordes' of Gildas's *De excidio*, but a settled, prosperous, dynamic people.[66]

The Church became established during the seventh century in Pictland, but the number of monks, missionaries and secular clergy in the mission field is likely to have been small and the terrain was vast; there would have been a long process of Christianisation. One gleam of light comes from excavation at the site of the monastery of Portmahomack on Tarbat Ness, which juts out into the Moray Firth and lies in the heart of northern Pictland. This has revealed grave markers of an Ionan style, radiocarbon evidence of burials as early as *c*.560, signs of the zoning of activities typical of a major monastic site as at Iona or Whitby – in other words, a full monastic settlement whose origins may even date back to Columba's lifetime. The Tarbat peninsula at the far eastern end of the Great Glen along which Columba travelled to meet the Pictish king would have been, as Martin Carver observes, 'the nearest thing he could find to an island' and was a natural site for a monastery on fertile land with access to the sea. The earliest monks established a water supply and a burial ground. There was substantial development from *c*.650 with evidence of cattle herding, hide processing and the making of vellum for the scriptorium. Many fragments of carved stone have been found, deriving from grave markers, a sarcophagus and vertical cross-slabs; there is likely to have been a single-cell church capable of holding some thirty worshippers, whose remains lie beneath a later structure. From *c*.650 there was a development of skilled artisan work: it is a good conjecture that an early monastery was catching the tide of the development of monastic life in the later seventh and into the eighth century, providing the books and vessels for the mass, the study of Scripture and the daily office for use on other sites still unknown to us.[67]

Close by are massive stone monuments, commissioned well after Columba's day, perhaps designed to act as visual markers for ships at sea or to commemorate holy men or women of the locality now lost to history. There are stones showing awareness of subtle interpretations of Scripture, with

[66] T. Clancy and B. Crawford, 'The formation', R.A. Houston, W.W.J. Knox eds, *The new Penguin history of Scotland* (New York 2001) 40 (Easter Kinnear); I. Hughson, 'Horses in the early historic period: evidence from the Pictish sculptured stones', S. Davies, N.A. Jones eds, *The horse in Celtic culture* (Cardiff 1977) 23–42; A. Woolf, 'The Verturian hegemony: a mirror in the north', M.P. Brown, C.A. Farr eds, *Mercia. An Anglo-Saxon kingdom in Europe* (London, New York 2001) 106–12

[67] M. Carver, *Portmahomack. Monastery of the Picts* (Edinburgh 2008) excavation and provisional results, engaging

probable representations of the apostles. One, which has echoes of book decoration, is datable to the late eighth century and bears an inscription of eight lines of Latin sculptured in relief in Insular majuscule invoking Christ and the cross. It is remarkable how many of the finest Pictish stones – Nigg, Hilton of Cadboll, Shandwick – lie along the Tarbat peninsula. An ancient foundation evidently maintained its recruitment over the years and acted as a beacon of light and culture in the far north into the Viking age.[68]

Burghead on a headland of the Moray Firth gives a glimpse of the wealth and power of Pictish leadership. An ancient site, with a form of multiple ramparts across the headland characteristic of the pre-Roman era, its carbon datings from the bank round the headland stretch from the third to the tenth century AD: that is to say, it was a key defensive site, constantly worked on and improved to ensure its security. Though it ranks in size below the greatest of the Dark Age fortresses in the south, Cadbury Castle and Tintagel, it is no less than eight times larger than the Dál Riatan fortress of Dunadd and exceeds by one-third the Northumbrian strongpoint of Bamburgh. In the early nineteenth century, demand for building stone at the expense of the ancient site caused the destruction of a whole sequence of carved stones with images of bulls, assessed at twenty-five to thirty strong, probably forming a procession along the entrance passage to the fortress. Only three survive, one of a bull at rest, one aroused and one about to charge. Such a sequence is unlikely to have been created simply as an impressive piece of decoration to overawe distinguished visitors: it surely had an inner spiritual significance for the Pictish leadership. Perhaps bulls played a major role in their pagan rites, or perhaps, like the pagan Anglo-Saxons, they believed in the efficacy of animal symbols for the transference of qualities, especially fighting abilities, to those who depicted and venerated them. It may well be significant that the Sculptor's Cave at Covesea, only three miles from Burghead, has no fewer than fifteen varied symbols, conjectured to have been carved in pre-Christian days within the fifth and sixth centuries. The cave may have been a ritual site of Pictish paganism.[69]

[68] I. and G. Henderson, *The art of the Picts* (London 2008) no. 201 (Tarbat) nos 202, 203 (Nigg) no. 50 (Hilton of Cadboll), classic work, art history but with historical implications, finest photographs, European comparisons, sensitive to biblical allusions; new ground on Pictish jewellery and Old Scatness bear, Shetland, demonstrated to be a source for certain illuminations rather than vice versa

[69] L. Alcock, *Kings and warriors, craftsmen and priests in northern Britain AD 550–850* (Edinburgh 2003) vividly illustrates many years of archaeological investigation 192–7 (Burghead); S. Driscoll, 'Burghead', Lynch, *Companion*; Foster, *Picts, Gaels and Scots* 44 (Covesea)

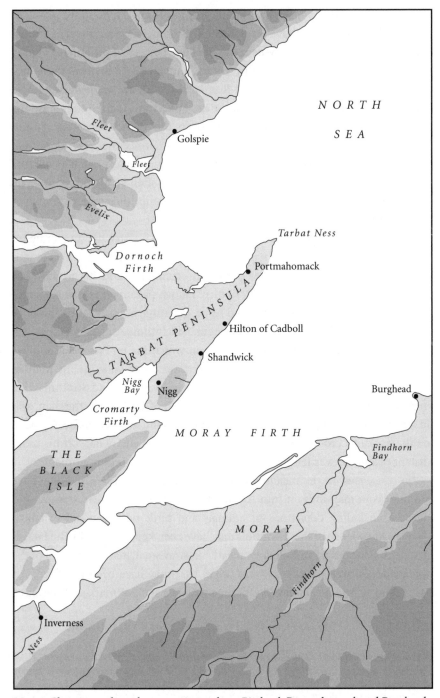

Map 4 Christian and secular power in northern Pictland: Portmahomack and Burghead.

The nature of this paganism remains elusive. There are no grave goods to provide the evidence we have for the Anglo-Saxons; there are signs of animal sacrifices on Iron Age sites, evidence of the head cult, most prominent among the Celts of Gaul but also present in Britain, and of ritual activity at pools and wells. Votive deposits, sometimes of Roman objects, were made in honour of the gods. Apart perhaps from the king-lists, carved and incised stones are the only evidence that reaches us directly from the Picts themselves. Stones incised with symbols peculiar to the Picts are numerous: there are more than fifty of them, some abstract, some of objects in everyday use, such as mirrors and combs, and there are many showing animals, often vivid and naturalistic but also including mythical beasts and a strange composite creature known as the 'Pictish beast'.[70]

One human representation surely has links to the pagans: the sinister figure on a boulder at Barflat near Rhynie in Aberdeenshire is impossible to put into relation with the evil powers of Christian cosmology and it certainly has nothing to do with the saints or Scripture. Pictish paganism remains its likeliest point of origin. A man in a belted tunic, grinning, holds over his shoulder an axe-hammer. The Hendersons comment: 'His intimidating appearance will be his function, a ritual prophylactic one in which his tool or weapon plays some part.' He does not stand alone; there are other versions, in Mail in Shetland, again at Rhynie, at Kilmorach west of Inverness and Strathmartine in Angus. In the representation at Kirkton, north of Loch Fleet, the man, still in a belted tunic but gripping a knife and holding out an axe, has been placed on the back of a cross-slab, demonstrating that in the end, whatever his more distant origin, he was felt to be compatible with a Christian monument.[71]

No consensus on the meaning of the symbols has yet emerged. Some have affinities with markings on Iron Age military equipment, armlets, harness and the like, including depictions of animals and birds on the metal of shield plaques: knowledge of these symbols may have been kept in being by the Pictish practice of tattooing. Symbols appear early on stray small items and in out of the way places on walls of caves where pagan rites may have been practised. An excavation at Pool on Sanday in Orkney revealed a symbol-marked stone and a

[70] Foster, *Picts* ch. 5; I. Henderson, *Pictish monsters: symbol, text and image*, H.M. Chadwick lecture (Cambridge 1997); G. Markus, 'Christianity, conversion to', Lynch, *Companion*

[71] Henderson, *Art of the Picts* no. 180 (Barflat, near Rhynie) no. 181 (Mail) no. 24 (Kilmorach, Strathmartine, a second Rhynie) no. 84 (Kirkton near Golspie); quotation 123

bone pin in association with the building of a courtyard, carbon-dated to the sixth century, giving a starting line for the use of symbols, which on the bone pin look very much like a good luck sign. They came to be incised on field monuments and sometimes on prehistoric standing stones and their use spread across Pictland. For reasons that are still obscure, they grew in popularity and passed through a stage in which the symbols were to a degree standardised and new ones added. So far from dying away as Christianity edged in, they were used often and with emphasis and became a regular feature, right up to and including the ninth century. They are never to be found in Dál Riata and are exclusively Pictish. Ross Samson has argued that the symbols, which often appear in pairs, are in fact names and what we witness on the stones is a passion for recording names and descent with the same interest in ancestors we have seen in Cornwall and in Wales. Katherine Forsyth argues that we are dealing with a writing system comparable to Irish oghams and Anglo-Saxon runes, both invented by peoples on the margin of the Empire.[72]

Cross-marked stones begin to appear in Pictland on a variety of sites, on boulders, in caves, on slabs and in the form of high crosses, at first, one would surmise, on their own and in no way combined with pre-existing Pictish stones. They originate without doubt in missionary work by the Irish – or Scots, Scotti as they are confusingly known in contemporary sources – from Dál Riata, the Western Isles and western Scotland generally. They recall the famous scene in Adomnán's Life of Columba in which the saint has his way barred at the gates of the fortress of King Bruide and then promptly marks the sign of the cross on the gates, which fly open to receive him. The cross invoked Christ's guardianship; it was used in a variety of ways, to establish Christian territory, to mark a grave, to protect a mountain pass or a harbour, to act as a focus for private prayer or to mark a site for public worship. Crosses would have been of central importance before churches were built.[73]

Iona is the natural starting point with its varied collection of crosses and especially the Irish style with hollowed armpits. A cross-slab in Raasay on Skye, with a curiously narrow stem and arms spreading out like petals, is likely

---

[72] Origins, Thomas, *Mute stones* 19–25; Henderson, *Art of the Picts* 118–21 (jewellery) no. 251 (Pool) 167–74 (role of symbols); R. Samson, 'The reinterpretation of the Pictish symbols', *JBA* 145 (1992) 29–65; K. Forsyth, 'Some thoughts on Pictish symbols as a formal writing system', D. Henry ed., *The worm, the germ and the thorn* (Balgavies 1997) 85–98
[73] Henderson, *Art of the Picts* 159–66; *Adomnán* II 35; I. Henderson, 'Early Christian monuments of Scotland displaying crosses, but with no other ornament', A. Small ed., *The Picts: a new look at old problems* (Dundee 1987 repr. 1996) 45–68

to be an early stage of development before an established style had been worked out. Then representations of the cross and the pre-Christian art of the stones come together and a convention builds up in which the cross is often represented on one side of the stone and the signs and symbols of the past on the other. Symbols and animals, however, are never allowed to spill over and obscure the cross, which always stands pre-eminent.

The Pictish elite converted to Christianity evidently felt no difficulty in commissioning their masons to continue carving these symbols, which perhaps were by this time quite fossilised and any pagan associations lost. Or it may be that Picts came to regard their past paganism in a softer light than Anglo-Saxon Christians did, just as in Ireland where paganism and Christianity were forced to live side by side for a time and the Christians were inclined to view the paganism of the past as a stage in the development towards the true religion, imperfect but not a demoniac creation. Because the meaning of the symbol stones has yet to be deciphered, there has to be a strong element of informed guesswork. As they are conspicuous field monuments in an unmapped landscape, they would readily have been a natural focus for communal transactions and ceremonies, where authority could be exercised. They continued, the Hendersons argue, to be 'numinous tokens'. Certainly they sometimes acted as boundary stones or memorialised the dead, but the latter function, on present knowledge, was much less in evidence among the Picts than in Wales. The symbol stones stand out: they are meant to have a visual impact and this gives weight to the belief that in addition to being boundary stones they may have had ceremonial functions.[74]

The Hendersons have reflected that, with their past military associations, pre-Christian symbols and stones and the Christian cross have an object in common: both sought guardianship and protection from all ills, thus facilitating the coming together of the old Pictish style of stone and the cross as a symbol of the new religion. There are some 160 stones with symbols only, Class I in traditional categorisation, and in Class II, another fifty-seven or so crossslabs with symbols. Some of the symbol stones will certainly be pre-Christian; cross-slabs are the fruit of the coming of Christianity, but it is significant that they have symbols as well. Though in some cases the old symbols are squeezed in with the cross, they are not being marginalised but, on the contrary, are felt

[74] Henderson, *Art of the Picts* no. 253 (Raasay) 27–8, 172 (symbols and cross) 172 (numinous tokens) 167 no. 246 (funerary stone, Dunrobin)

to be too important to be left out and must be included even when they look awkward and detract from the aesthetic appeal of the whole.[75]

Inscriptions mattered less than the symbols and were more frequently in ogham than in Latin. Katherine Forsyth's analysis lists thirty-seven ogham inscriptions or their illegible remains on thirty-four objects in thirty sites scattered through Pictland, including one in the Western Isles and a number in the Northern Isles. There are in addition perhaps a dozen inscriptions in the Roman alphabet and they tend to be in ecclesiastical contexts; Pictish churchmen were applying the language of the Church to their stones. This is in major contrast to Wales, where Latin had pride of place because of its association with the Empire. In Pictland, the elite used ogham rather than Latin, having lived outside the Empire and been its determined enemies. Because of the happy chance of the association of an ogham text with carbon-dated material at Pool, we know that the use of ogham on Scottish territory reaches back to the sixth century and predates Christianity. It was used in a greater variety of contexts than in its native Ireland, from small domestic objects to great monumental crosses, such as the Dupplin Cross and the pillar at Altyre. Though it is not Columban – no ogham at all is found on Iona or on Columban monastic sites – it reflects Irish influence, immigration and, sometimes, mission. It also throws a flickering light on the early history of Christianity and on settlement generally in the Northern Isles. The recognition that the inscription on a spindle whorl at Buckquoy on Orkney is an ogham in Old Irish asking for a blessing on someone known only as L is a reminder of a little-known track of pilgrimage and mission from south-west Ireland up as far as Shetland, an element in Christianisation of the Northern Isles we can postulate in addition to better-known missions stemming from Northumbria. The evidence is that the little Christian message, in form not unlike the amatory phrases sometimes put on spindle whorls by men for sweethearts, was a local carving composed and put on the white stone of the spindle whorl by a resident of Buckquoy.

At Burrian on North Ronaldsay, inside a ruined broch on one of the bleakest sites on Orkney, there is a simple, delicately incised cross which could be as early as the seventh century. It has an ogham inscription in Pictish, including a unique record of the verb 'to make', and is so small that it could only be read by a close observer. Now illegible, it records in all probability the name of its maker, who by implication asks for prayers for his soul. This obscure site points to a Pictish population, not simply Irish immigrants, who

[75] Ibid. 171–2; K. Forsyth, 'Literacy in Pictland', Pryce, *Literacy* 39–61, nos of stones at 57

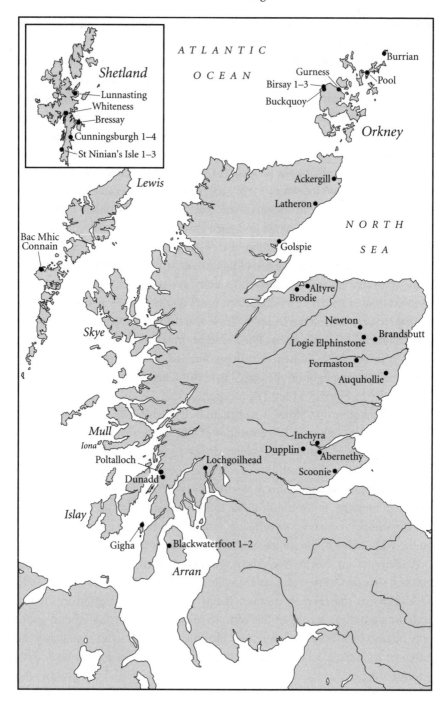

Map 5 The ogham inscriptions of Scotland.

were sufficiently influenced by the Irish to use oghams as a vehicle for their own vernacular.[76]

South of Dál Riata and Pictland lay turbulent British kingdoms, successor states to the collapsed Roman Empire, where kings struggled for supremacy or survival and stimulated a heroic, panegyric or lamenting verse, which passed down into Wales, forming the earliest level of its poetry. Amongst the kingdoms were men of authority and combative power who could match the Anglo-Saxon invaders; they, and the war bands on which their strength rested, together with those who tilled the land and by rendering food made their display, feasting and campaigning possible, were known as *Yr Hen Ogledd*, the Old North. They straddled the former frontier of Hadrian's Wall and fought over the roads and strongpoints with which the Romans had held down the highland zone of their colony. They had not been Romanised as the indigenous southern British had been, and had retained their fighting capacity. From the time of the severing of British links with the Empire to the victories of Aethelfrith, king of Bernicia, in the early seventh century, their deeds, victories and tragedies are the dominant theme of the history of northern Britain, from Cumbria into southern Scotland.

The kingdom of Dumbarton, or Alt Clut, sometimes known as Strathclyde, which extended over much of modern Dumbartonshire and Renfrewshire, had its political centre on a volcanic plug, a great rock 243 feet high at the confluence of the Clyde and the Leven, a natural fortress dominating river trade and a quondam supply base for Roman troops at the western end of the Antonine Wall. A rampart of massive oak beams on the eastern side up the Clyde valley to Loch Lomond and Lennox may have been constructed by a ruling chieftain in the late sixth century. Amphorae, shreds of E-ware from Gaul and remains of glass vessels bear witness to the wealth of its rulers; like the kings of Dál Riata, they participated in the luxury trade along the western seaboard of Britain, albeit at a lower level; crucibles on sites are signs of the manufacture of fine jewellery.[77]

---

[76] K. Forsyth, 'The ogham inscriptions of Scotland: an edited corpus' (Ph.D. thesis Harvard 1996) definitive analysis, catalogue of sites, intro. L, doubtful cases 503; intro. summarises research in Ireland and Scotland and rationale of readings, 456–66 (Pool) 243–60 (Dupplin) 23–40 (Altyre) 60–86 (Buckquoy) 187–205 (Burrian); id., 'The inscriptions on the Dupplin cross', C. Bourke, ed. *From the isles of the north* (Belfast 1995) 23744; E. Okasha, 'The non-ogam inscriptions of Pictland', *CMCS* 9 (1985) 43–69
[77] Dumbarton, *Alt Clut* Alcock, *Kings* 39, 42–3, 205, 212; S. Driscoll, 'Dumbarton', Lynch, *Companion*

The Rock stood close to the capital of Dál Riata and, in the many conflicts between the kingdoms, its defensive power alongside the kingdom's economic strength preserved it from destruction or assimilation. Of all the British successor kingdoms of northern Britain, Dumbarton proved to be the most durable and, though at one time it had to submit to the Picts, kept itself in being into the Viking age when it fell to Scandinavian attack in 870; even then, though the Rock ceased to be its major fortress, the kingdom revived, moving its centre of power upstream to Govan. Its survival makes it the most likely channel for the transmission of the poetry of the bardic traditions of the Old North to Wales, where the near-unique evidence for the doings of these vanished British kingdoms in the fifth and sixth centuries was preserved from oblivion.[78]

The successor kingdom to the tribal lands of the Votadini of Roman times, which stretched from Edinburgh to the Tees, was Gododdin, famous for the longest surviving poem of the Old North, *Y Gododdin*, elegies in over a thousand lines for men of the kingdom who set out for war far to the south and suffered defeat in a battle at Catraeth, usually identified as Catterick by the river Swale in north Yorkshire. The poem is imbued with the heroic ethos. In what is obviously a literary convention, its heroes are feasted for a year at the table of their lord, the king Mynyddog the Wealthy, at Edinburgh before going into battle. The attraction of a rich court and the reputation of a vigorous war band had brought together warriors from other kingdoms with the Gododdin elite to form what is best reconstructed as a raiding party penetrating far into enemy territory, possibly aiming at the Roman strongpoint of Catterick or being brought to bay there. The result was the loss of a celebrated body of young men trained to form the spearhead of a full army.[79]

Had a major campaign seeking the destruction rather than the discomfiture of an enemy been intended, winning booty and glory, Mynyddog would have

[78] Outline M. Löffler, 'Ystrad Clud (Strathclyde)', *KCC*; A. Woolf, 'Britons and Angles', Lynch, *Companion*

[79] J.T. Koch, *The Gododdin of Aneirin. Text and context from Dark Age Britain* (Cardiff 1997) reviewed by O. Padel, *CMCS* 35 (1998) 45–55, comment G.R. Isaac, *CMCS* 37 (1999) 55–78; see C. Cessford, 'Where are the Anglo-Saxons in the Gododdin poem?', *ASAH* 8 (1995) 95–8; earlier views, D.N. Dumville, 'Early Welsh poetry: problems of historicity', B.F. Roberts ed., *Early Welsh poetry. Studies in the Book of Aneirin* (Aberystwyth 1988) 1–16, debate, Koch, *Gododdin* lxxxix n. 1; T.M. Charles-Edwards, 'The authenticity of the Gododdin: an historian's view', R. Bromwich, R. Brinley Jones eds, *Astudiaethau ar yr Hungered* (Cardiff 1978) 44–71; Old North, J.T. Koch, 'Yr Hen Ogledd', *KCC*; id., 'Gododdin', *KCC*; T.M. Charles-Edwards, 'Mynyddog Mwynfawr', *ODNB*

been expected to lead in person, with infantry included. That this was the exuberance of young warriors on horseback is supported by the stuff of the verse; personal tragedies are recorded, many names otherwise unknown are the subject of the bard's lament and this fact has buttressed the credibility of the source as a broadly authentic account of one historical event. The convention of saga tends to exaggerate disaster: of the three texts, B2, distinguished by its latest editor, J.T. Koch as the most archaic, does not even admit that the battle was a defeat. At the heart of all three lies the stark contrast between the pleasures of life and the end of young heroes on the battlefield.[80]

The B2 text has no Christian allusions. That, Koch argues, does not imply that Gododdin at the time of the battle was not a Christian kingdom but rather that it took time for Christian references to penetrate the conventions of the bards. The other texts include Christianity as the assumed background of the warrior life. Warriors give alms, go to confession, are shriven and do penance; they are part of the *bedydd*, the baptised, and to the contrast between the mead-drinking in the lord's hall and their end in death is added their hope of heaven.

The *Gododdin* is only known to us in one thirteenth-century manuscript from which all inferences made by historians and literary analysts have to be drawn. A presumed oral phase, the sovereign power of the bards to compose their verse, to subtract and add stories and allusions, the reality of interpolations which can be demonstrated and the justified fear of others which cannot, all militate against the drawing out from this moving, often beautiful collection of verse much reliable and datable historical information – a conclusion which is all the more to be regretted when we are dealing with a time that Koch typifies as 'a-historical'. The text contains stray pieces of material, a lullaby sung by a woman to her son, an address to the ruler of Dumbarton/Strathclyde referring to the death at his hands of Domnall Brec, ruler of Dál Riata, who was killed in 642 at the battle of Strathcarron and a reference, perhaps the oldest of all, to Arthur in a panegyric to Gorddur, praised because 'he used to bring black crows down in front of the wall of the fortified town – though he was not Arthur – amongst men mighty in feats . . .'[81]

Analysis leaves us with a core of seventh-century verse and a real event, the killing at Catterick. Most of all, the verse leaves us with an impression of Gododdin's elite society, the delight in warfare, the gold torques of the leading warriors, the mead-hall, the transience of life in a violent society.

[80] J. Rowland, 'Warfare and horses in the Gododdin and the problem of Catraeth', *CMCS* 30 (1995) 13–40; Koch, *Gododdin* [XIII]–[XXXIV]
[81] Ibid. [23]

Men went to Catterick fighting and raising the battle cry,
A force of stallions and dark armour and shields,
upturned lances and sharp spears
gleaming mailcoats and swords
was accustomed to forcing breaches through hosts.
Five times fifty used to fall before their blades.
Rhufawn used to give much gold to the altar
and gifts and fine offerings to the singer.[82]

Though a British kingdom and at least loosely Christianised ('casually' Christian, in the phrase of Clancy and Crawford), Gododdin differed little from the assumptions and lifestyle of the warrior class of the still pagan Anglo-Saxons. Amongst the majority of the successor states of the old Roman Empire, there was too little infrastructure of state and too little continuity of succession to avoid an extreme fluidity of military and political life in which one leading warrior ruler could achieve much for himself and his followers but could rarely succeed in creating a lasting supremacy. Such a fluidity was also characteristic of early Anglo-Saxon society. Yet the future lay with them rather than with the surviving British.[83]

The winning kingdom, Bernicia, whose ruler ended the glory days of the British rulers of the Old North, emerged from what is believed to have been a late foray by Anglo-Saxon warriors from a comparatively secure base in Deira, a firmly settled Germanic area based on the well-tilled lands of Yorkshire and extending from the Humber to the Tees. These warriors aimed to seize new lands for themselves from the British of the kingdom of Gododdin on the north-east coast above the Tees: they were not immigrants from the continent, but, it seems, men restive with life in Deira and desirous of both land and glory at the expense of British kingdoms.

The move was no easy option, for the rulers of Gododdin had been blooded in battle with the Picts and, as we have glimpsed from the poetic elegies after Catterick, had powerful forces at their disposal. According to the *Historia Brittonum* it was in 547 that Ida, traditionally regarded as founder of the new Bernician dynasty, first made landfall, but whatever progress he may have made, it was his successors who faced the crucial test when they found themselves up against the most forceful leader of the British kingdoms of the Old

[82] J.T. Koch, J. Carey eds, *Celtic heroic poetry* (Andover, Mass. 1997) (A2 version)
[83] Clancy and Crawford, 'The formation', 35

North, Urien of Rheged, who came nearest of all the British of the sixth century to fulfilling the dream of later generations, that of pushing the invaders back into the sea.[84]

Rheged, a name linked to the Brittonic for gift, alluding to the generosity of its rulers to their bards, lay on the western side of Britain, its history so ill recorded that the extent of its territory is still a matter of debate, but the achievements of Urien are so impressive that it seems reasonable to suppose that he had behind him resources drawn not just from lands south of Hadrian's Wall, as some allege, but from a great swathe across the Wall and the Solway Firth, embracing both its shores and extending as far as Stranraer in Galloway to the north and reaching across the Pennines to the south, including not only the old Roman centre at Carlisle but the rich agricultural area of the Eden valley, all providing sinews of war for the most notable war band of its day.[85]

Urien's career is marked quite as much by victory against other British leaders and warriors as against the Anglo-Saxons. In the *Book of Taliesin*, possibly a sixth-century contemporary, a poem on the battle of the White Valley describes him as the lord of Catraeth (Catterick) and 'the battle-victorious cattle-rich sovereign' and this has raised the disquieting possibility that his lands at their maximum reached down as far south as Catterick and that the battle was not one of a Gododdin raiding party against enemy Angles, but of Gododdin and allies against the fellow British kingdom of Rheged. Panegyrics to Urien in the *Book of Taliesin* twice allude to him fighting against an arrogant warrior nicknamed Flamddwyn, flame bearer, possibly a pseudonym for one of the Bernician leaders. These poems in the panegyric tradition see no blemish in Urien, celebrate his victories over both British and Anglians and scatter references to many places, probably names of minor British kingdoms which he had subjected to his rule, but say nothing of his death.[86]

---

[84] Rests on queried interpretation of passage in *HB*; D.N. Dumville, 'The origins of Northumbria: some aspects of the British background', S. Bassett ed., *The Origins of Anglo-Saxon Kingdoms* (London 1989) 213–22; A. Woolf, 'Bernicia', Lynch, *Companion*; J.T. Koch, 'Brynaich (Bernicia)', *KCC*; id., 'Ida' *KCC*; story accepted, D.P. Kirby, *The earliest English Kings* (2nd edn London, New York 2000) 56–7; N.J. Higham, 'Britons in northern England in the early Middle Ages: through a thick glass darkly', *NH* 38 (2001) 5–25

[85] J.T. Koch, 'Urien (fab Cynfarch) of Rheged', *KCC*; id., 'Rheged', *KCC*; C. Phythian-Adams, *Land of the Cumbrians. A study in British provincial origins AD 400–1120* (Aldershot 1996); D.E. Thornton, 'Urien Rheged', *ODNB*

[86] On Flamddwyn, Koch, 'Urien'; T.M. Charles-Edwards, 'Taliesin', *ODNB*; interpretations Lowe, *Angels* 12–13

By contrast, mourning over Urien's death is a theme in englynion, known to us in compositions in three-line metre, dating from the ninth century but believed to be based on lost saga narratives, a genre giving greater scope for reflections and more subtle emotions than panegyric which concentrates on the great deeds of patrons and their ancestors. Llywarch Hen, for example, is described as an old warrior who had seen his sons killed in battle and in his englyn looked with a sceptical eye on the heroic ideals of the past which he himself had once supported – impossible in the praise-poetry of the *Gododdin* or Taliesin.[87]

Probably including fragments from more than one saga, the englyn on Urien recalls his bravery, generosity and success in war but stresses the loss and ruin brought about by his death. One of the most remarkable poems, the 'Pen Urien' is narrated by a former supporter and follower who is carrying Urien's head, by implication from the battlefield. In the reconstruction by the editor and translator Jenny Rowland, he is prey to conflicting emotions of guilt and sorrow, the product of a clash of loyalties. Urien was once his lord but he had been compelled to fight against him and so had a complicity in bringing about his death. Verse after verse begins with the words 'I carry a head'.

I carry a head on my shoulder
Shame did not use to receive me
Alas, my hand, (for) the striking of my lord.

I carry a head which cared for . . . (?)
I know it is not for my good.
Alas, my hand, it performed harshly.

I carry a head from the side of the hill
and on his lips is a fine foam
of blood. Woe to Rheged because of this day.

It has wrenched my arm,
it has crushed my ribs,

---

[87] J. Rowland, *Early Welsh saga poetry. A study and edition of the englynion* (Cambridge 1990) definitive; reviewed by R. Geraint Gruffydd, *WHR* 15 (1991) 599–601, P. Sims-Williams, *CMCS* 27 (1994) 88–91

it has broken my heart.
I carry a head which cared for me.[88]

Elsewhere in the englynion, several named British leaders are described as conspiring against Urien. This has support in the historical section of the *Historia Brittonum*, where the author describes the attacks of the British on the Bernician kings:

> Against them four kings fought: Urien, and Rhydderch the old, and Gwallwg, and Morgant. Theodric used to fight bravely against that Urien with his sons, yet at that time sometimes the enemies, sometimes the citizens, used to be vanquished. And he [Urien] shut them [the enemies] up for three days and three nights in the island of Lindisfarne and while he was on [this?] campaign, he was slain at the instigation of Morgant out of jealousy, because beyond all other kings he [Urien] had the greatest skill in renewing war.[89]

The history has been skewed by literary distortions. It is not an accident that the *Historia* in the sentence 'Sometimes the enemies, sometimes the citizens, used to be vanquished' echoes Gildas in the *De excidio* describing the years before the British victory of Mount Badon: 'from then on victory went now to our countrymen, now to their enemies'. The author means to point a parallel. Wavering British fortunes before Badon ended 'by God's aid' in victory; in the case of Urien and his contemporaries the process is reversed and ends in defeat. He means also to point a parallel with the actions recounted earlier in the *Historia* of the 'proud tyrant', Bede's Vortigern, who at the beginning of the Anglo-Saxon invasions invited in mercenaries and gave them the island of Thanet as a reward. When they rebelled, Vortigern fought them, and his son Vortimer after him, pressing them hard in Thanet 'and there three times shut them up and attacked them'. Only when Vortimer died and his followers failed to follow his commands about his burial did the invaders prevail. Lindisfarne – Thanet, 'three days and three nights', 'three times', betrayal of Urien – disregard of Vortimer's commands: the echoes are

---

[88] Rowland edn 478
[89] P. Sims-Williams, 'The death of Urien', *CMCS* 32 (1996) 25–56 subtle and wide-ranging; this trans., ibid. 33, correcting Mommsen's 'contra illum' to 'contra illos' (i.e. Bernician kings); Mommsen edn discussed, I. Wood, *Britannia* 18 (1987) 385–6

obvious and the message is plain.[90] Just as folly, treachery and the disregard of the dying Vortimer's command brought about the loss of southern Britain, so disunity and treachery leading to the murder of the greatest leader of the British led to a successful takeover of British lands in the north. The conscious parallel with the Vortigern/Vortimer story and the deployment of Lindisfarne as an echo of Thanet renders it uncertain whether Urien's forces really had pressed the Bernicians right back to the island, although a reference in the englyn to Urien's death at Aber Lleu suggests a site at an estuary near the fortress of Bamburgh and thus not far from Lindisfarne. All the same, the mention of Lindisfarne is suspect. There is a long transmission history of this text and the later awareness of Lindisfarne as a great ecclesiastical centre may have contaminated the story. Sufficient to say that Urien was the greatest warrior of his day in this region and that he pressed hard both British rulers in the struggle for power and Anglo-Saxons as well. He was the one man who might have eliminated the Germanic kingdom of Bernicia in the north-east but, in the literary source, he was victim of both jealousy and treachery by his fellow British. Doubt has been expressed about the motive of our informant, the author of the *Historia Brittonum*, a Welsh antiquarian and would-be historian at the court of Merfyn Frych, ruler of Gwynedd in the ninth century, when he attributes to Morgant, the killer of Urien, an impulse of jealousy for his greater prowess as a warrior. Not so. In this passionately competitive fighting society crude personal jealousy is an entirely convincing motive.[91]

Some adjustment of time scale may be needed. The compiler of the *Historia* was inclined arbitrarily to synchronise differing traditions and sources. The enemy against whom Urien fought may indeed have been Theodric or his son and successor Hussa, so placing Urien's death either between 572 and 579 or 585 to 592; conceivably it was later still. Whatever the dating, we can infer from the poetry and the *Historia* that Urien's end marked a critical point in the history of the northern British kingdoms. Long after the death, verses giving a lament for their loss tell of a mourning journey, perhaps by Llywarch Hen himself, where the narrator views with sorrow the ruins of the seat of Rheged's rulers, its sad condition ultimately the fruit of Urien's assassination. The poem concludes:

---

[90] Gildas 26; *HB* 43 trans. P. Sims-Williams; parallels, id., 'Gildas and the Anglo-Saxons', *CMCS* 6 (1983) 1–30

[91] J.T. Koch, 'Gwrtheyrn (Vortigern)', *KCC*; Aber Lleu in Sims-Williams, 'Death of Urien' 38–41; context of *HB*, N.J. Higham, *King Arthur. Myth-making and history* (London, New York 2002) 116–28

This hearth – a wild pig digs in it.
It would have been more accustomed to the rejoicing
of warriors and carousal around drinking horns.

This hearth – a chick digs in it.
Need did not use to trouble it
In the lifetime of Owain and Urien.

This pillar and the one yonder –
around it the merry-making of the host
And a path for gift-giving would have been more customary.[92]

It was the misfortune of the North British that between c.592 and 617
the ruling house of Bernicia chanced to produce one of the greatest of all
Anglo-Saxon warriors, still a pagan, Ida's grandson Aethelfrith. Bede
compared him to Saul and quoted with approval Jacob's blessing of Benjamin,
looking forward to him ravaging like a wolf. He had a threefold achievement,
all, as far as we can see, based on military prowess. He took over the more
powerful northern kingdom, Deira, displaced its rulers and married
Acha, sister of Edwin, heir to Deira. He damaged Rheged and laid the foundations for the combined kingdom of Northumbria, the leading kingdom of
the Anglo-Saxon world for much of the seventh century, a platform for
Christian missionary work and the cradle of a renaissance which produced
some of the finest works of art ever produced in Britain. A Germanic kingdom
based in the north-east had every interest in penetrating over the Pennines
deeper into Rheged, weakening what had hitherto been a major force in
dangerous coalitions of the British, to reach fertile farmland on the west side
and gain access to lucrative trade on the western seaboard. Aethelfrith's
victory over the British at Chester in 615 or 616, recorded in Irish and Welsh
sources as well as Bede, was a decisive stage in this weakening of Rheged. Two
British kings were killed. A party of monks from Bangor-is-Coed, praying for
a British success, was massacred. Aethelfrith still did not totally command
the land between Chester and his homeland; he had to bypass the small
British kingdom of Elmet in the area of what is now Leeds. Nevertheless

---

[92] Rowland edn 482; W. Davies, *Wales in the early Middle Ages* (Leicester 1982) standard
work; emergence of kingdoms 90–102; reviewed by G.C. Boon, *Britannia* 15 (1984) 366–7,
M. Richter, *Studia Hibernica* (1975) 164–5

his advance to Chester was a major move which altered the balance of power.[93]

Although the problems of the terrain made a full and immediate takeover of Rheged impossible, the victory began the process of cutting the landward links between the British of the north and their counterparts in Wales and taking Cumbria into Anglo-Saxon territory. Over decades, all independence was taken from Rheged, its final absorption being marked by the marriage of Aethelfrith's son Oswiu to Rhieinfellt, descendant of Urien and the last princess of the kingdom. As Northumbrian power prevailed over the lost British kingdoms of the north, so British Churches and churchmen forfeited military protection and patronage. A glimpse of their fate emerges from an incidental allusion in the life of the Anglo-Saxon abbot and ecclesiastical prince, St Wilfrid, which describes how in the 670s King Ecgfrith of Northumbria endowed Wilfrid's monastery of Ripon with 'holy places' left vacant by British clergy 'fleeing from the hostile sword in the hand of our race'. Such scenes must have been repeated over the years of British decline, undermining the authority of their churchmen and leaving their flocks open to takeover by Anglo-Saxon clerical leadership.[94]

Aethelfrith's third success had come in 603 or 604 when he defeated Áedán mac Gabráin, ruler of Dál Riata, at Degsastan. Alarmed at the threat which the rise of Bernicia-Deira and Aethelfrith's personal success in battle represented for the balance of power in the north, Áedán intervened. He had support from a disappointed member of the Bernician royal house, Hering son of Hussa, as well as his own powerful army. It proved a hard-fought encounter in which Aethelfrith lost his brother but still was victorious – a major event. Bede commented on the sequel, 'From that day until the present, no king of the Scots in Britain has dared to do battle with the English'.[95] Aethelfrith thus stabilised frontiers in the north and destroyed the hopes of British rulers; he brought into existence the kingdom of Northumbria and sired two of the greatest Anglo-Saxon kings, Oswald and Oswiu. If he was author of some of the remarkable timber buildings at the royal site of Yeavering in Bernicia, then he also had gifts outside the military field.

It took an Anglo-Saxon ruler from the south, Redwald of East Anglia, to put an end to Aethelfrith's career by battle at the river Idle in 617; the

---

[93] *HE* II 3; R. Cramp, *Whithorn and the Northumbrian expansion westwards*, Third Whithorn Lecture (1994)
[94] J.T. Koch, 'Rhieinfellt', *KCC*; Wilfrid, below, 241
[95] *HE* I 34

achievement did not destroy Northumbria, for it passed into the hands of Redwald's protégé, Edwin, as effective a leader against the British as Aethelfrith had been. The British had lost; for reasons that are not quite clear the balance of power had shifted against them and never for long moved back in their favour. Barbara Yorke has surmised that the ability to tax and provide the sinews of war eluded the British leaders. One disastrous episode shook the Anglo-Saxons[96] but the pattern of events through the bulk of the seventh century is one of British defeat and loss and Anglo-Saxon advance. Their warriors did not lack courage and their traditions, like those of their opponents, were those of heroic warfare but from an early stage the Anglo-Saxons appear to have had a greater capacity to underpin their war bands and mobilise wealth for war. The hopes of Urien's time were falsified.[97]

During the decades in which the British kingdoms in the north flourished and fought amongst themselves and against the Anglo-Saxons, it had looked as if the political map of the island was going to turn out to be one in which the midlands and south would be dominated by the Anglo-Saxons while the British held sway in the lands of the north around and beyond Hadrian's Wall, in Cumbria, the lowlands of Scotland and in Wales. It was not to be. Urien's end and the terrifying career of Aethelfrith proved to be pivotal. The era of the northern British princes, the Men of the North of early Welsh literature, was at an end.

---

[96] *HE* III 1
[97] Yorke, *Conversion* 270; clue in H. Pryce, 'Ecclesiastical wealth in early medieval Wales', Edwards and Lane, *Early Church* 22–33; W. Davies, *Patterns of power in early Wales* (Oxford 1990) notes vulnerability to Anglo-Saxons from mid-seventh century; battle of Chester 63, see below, 181

CHAPTER 4

The Irish Dimension
PALLADIUS, PATRICK AND COLUMBA

Preaching in Rome on the feast day of Peter and Paul in 441, Pope Leo the Great called it 'a priestly and royal city' and rejoiced that through the see of Peter it had come to rule over 'a wider territory through the worship of God than by earthly dominion' – in other words, that papal authority had now extended beyond the bounds of the secular Roman Empire. It had indeed. Ten years earlier Pope Celestine, in his care for orthodoxy, had sent Palladius to Ireland, in the words of the chronicler Prosper of Aquitaine 'as their first bishop to the Irish who believe in Christ', as there was an assumption that British Pelagianism would infect Irish Christians if they did not have a bishop. In his polemical thesis *Contra collatorem* directed against the Pelagians, Prosper, a reliable witness and close to Leo, praised Pope Celestine for his action against the heretics. 'He has been, however, no less energetic in freeing the British provinces from this same disease: he removed from that hiding-place certain enemies of grace who had occupied the land of their origin; also, having obtained a bishop for the Irish, while he labours to keep the Roman island Catholic, he also made the barbarian island Christian.'[1] Although this latter claim is rhetorical and wildly optimistic, it was true that Pelagian refugees had fled to Britain, profiting from the severance of links with the Empire which rendered Honorius's legislation against Pelagianism void. It was, as we have seen, the reason for Bishop Germanus's visit in 429 and his biographer believed him to have been successful; nonetheless, determined Pelagians could still find refuge beyond the bounds of the Empire where the

---

[1] Quoted in T.M. Charles-Edwards, 'Palladius, Prosper and Leo the Great: mission and primatial authority', D.N. Dumville *et al.* eds, *Saint Patrick AD 493–1993* (Woodbridge 1993) 1–12

writ of the British Church did not run. Determination to stop up this ultimate refuge in Ireland seems to have been Germanus's motive in sending his deacon Palladius to seek the pope's authority for his mission there. Returning to his see, Germanus would have reflected on the implications of what he had seen in Britain and so turned his mind to the potential problem of Ireland. His second visit to Britain in c.435 may well have brought reinforcements to this Gaulish and papal mission.

Palladius left no cult centres and no dedications. He had been sent primarily to repress heresy, to administer, to give the sacraments to what was in all probability a small and perhaps scattered flock; still, Prosper's language and papal thinking about the duty to move across the Roman frontier to bring the faith to the barbarians show that side by side with the caretaking task was an aspiration to mission. Palladius remains a mystery. He may well have had successes, but we know nothing of them; the mission of Patrick and the great fame he came to acquire obliterated Palladius's memory. He has nonetheless a symbolic importance as the first to be sent by the papacy in aid of Catholicism beyond the frontiers of the Empire.[2]

Patrick was the major innovator. Snatched by raiders from his secure home and a hereditary Christianity, he describes his conversion as developing in years of suffering and isolation through his prayers and the answers he received from God, uninfluenced by any Christian layman or churchman on the spot. Thereafter his life and the decisions he made were based on a series of visions and revelations. He was, in effect, a self-appointed missionary obeying God's call, with not only a vocation to care for existing Irish Christians but the positive call to convert the Irish pagans. In the context of the assumptions of the time and the surviving attitude to barbarians of Christians within the old Empire, this was a considerable innovation. In the *Confessio*, the letter he wrote to defend himself against his enemies and accusers, he describes himself 'like a stone that lies in deep mud' raised by God and placed by Him 'on the highest wall'.[3]

---

[2] T.M. Charles-Edwards, *Early Christian Ireland* 202–14; D.N. Dumville, 'Some British aspects of earliest Irish Christianity', P. Ni Chatháin, M. Richter eds, *Ireland and Europe* (Stuttgart 1984) 16–24; M.W. Herren, S.A. Brown, *Christ in Celtic Christianity: Britain and Ireland from the fifth to the tenth century* (Woodbridge 2002) unconvinced reviewers G. Bonner, *Peritia* 16 (2002) 510–43, T.M. Charles-Edwards, *EME* 13 (2005) 428–31; see also T.M. Charles-Edwards, 'Britons in Ireland c.550–800', J. Carey *et al.* eds, *Ildánach Ildirech* (Dublin 1999) 15–26

[3] D.R. Howlett, *The book of letters of Saint Patrick the Bishop* (Dublin 1994) transforms understanding of letters; Patrick's mind, id., 'Ex saliva scripturae meae', D.Ó. Córrain ed., *Sages, saints and storytellers* (Maynooth 1989) 86–100

It was indeed an improbable start for one of the greatest apostles, to be made a slave as an adolescent and develop his prayer life entirely unaided as he looked after sheep. After years of labour and devoted prayer, he obeyed the revelation he was given in a dream: 'I heard a voice saying to me, "It is well that you are fasting, bound soon to go to your fatherland"', and again, 'after a very little time I heard the answer saying to me, "Behold! Your ship is prepared".'[4] Inspired by the dream, he set off from the place of his enslavement, the wood of Foclut by the Western Sea, usually identified as a site near Killala in Co. Mayo, significantly close to the Atlantic coast, the furthest point of habitation in the known world, and 'after some two hundred miles of travel' reached a ship. The two hundred miles need not be taken literally; in Patrick's mind it may simply have represented a great distance, probably based on the sixteen hundred stadia of Revelation XIV 20.[5] A decurion's son would have no difficulty in understanding the Roman measurement but walking to the east coast without knowledge of the terrain would indeed have been a long and harsh journey.

Perceiving that Patrick was a runaway slave, the captain at first refused to take him aboard, then changed his mind, probably reflecting that he could make a profit by selling him after the voyage. After three days at sea, they landed and made a strange twenty-eight-day journey through a desert where there was no food. The captain appealed to Patrick and the Christian God to appease their hunger – an appeal answered by the opportune appearance of a herd of pigs, so ending the crisis and establishing both Patrick's authority and the prestige of Christianity. 'After this,' Patrick says, 'they gave the highest thanks to God, and I was made honourable in their eyes.'[6] The apparent necessity of these men to travel through a desert has baffled historians: was there such a site in Gaul or Britain where there was such destitution and lack of food? We should postulate a blurring of historical fact by Patrick, writing in old age, despite the differences in time scale comparing his own escape from slavery in Ireland to the scriptural precedent of the children of Israel's escape from slavery in Egypt, their journey through the wilderness and their miraculous feeding.[7]

---

[4] Howlett, *Letters* 63
[5] T. O'Loughlin, *Discovering Saint Patrick* (London 2005), esp. ch. 3 on space and time; trans. *Confessio* 141–72, *Epistola* 173–83; id, *Saint Patrick. The man and his works* (London 1999)
[6] Howlett, *Letters* 65
[7] E. McLuhan, '*Ministerium servitutis meae*: the metaphor and reality of slavery in Saint Patrick's *Epistola* and *Confessio*', J. Carey *et al*. eds, *Studies in Irish hagiography* (Dublin 2001) 13–71. I accept a spiritualising interpretation of Patrick's desert journey: see O'Loughlin, *Discovering* 54–6 and C.E. Stancliffe, review of E.A. Thompson, *Who was Saint Patrick?* (Woodbridge 1985), *NMS* 31 (1987) 125–32; Charles-Edwards, *Ireland* 217

Patrick came home to the welcome of his family, but the Latin in which he describes his return to his parents' home has led to controversy. 'Et iterum post paucos annos in Brittanniis eram cum parentibus meis' has commonly been translated, 'And again after a few years in the Britains I was with my parents', sparking debate on what he had been doing in these apparently missing years and why he should delay before reuniting with his parents, when the revelation he received in the wood of Foclut promised that he would soon go to his fatherland. An alternative translation banishes these difficulties: 'And (so) after (these) few years (in captivity) I was again with my parents in Britain',[8] the 'paucos annos' then referring to his six years in slavery. His parents asked him after such tribulations to stay and not depart again from them, but a revelation not only prevented this, but gave a direction to the whole of the rest of his life. 'I saw', he says,

> in a vision of the night a man coming as if from Ireland, whose name (was) Victoricius, with innumerable epistles, and he gave me one of them, and I read the beginning of the epistle containing 'the Voice of the Irish' and while I was reciting the beginning of the epistle I kept imagining hearing at that very moment the voice of those very men who were beside the Forest of Foclut, which is near the Western Sea, and thus they shouted out as if from one mouth, 'We request you, holy boy, that you come and walk farther among us'. And I was especially stabbed at heart, and I could not read further.[9]

It was a decisive intervention.

Patrick was about sixteen when he was kidnapped, spent six years in captivity and so would have been about twenty-one or two when he fled from his slave master and returned to Britain. The message of the dream led him to follow his father and grandfather in seeking ordination and to train via apprenticeship and study in the manner customary in that age: it has been suggested that he went to Gaul for this purpose. Certainly, in his letter of appeal against a tyrant called Coroticus, he refers approvingly to the Gaulish practice of ransoming Christians enslaved by pagans; and in the *Confessio* he notes that he cast aside his personal wish to go to Gaul 'to visit the brothers' so as not to interrupt his call to convert the Irish. He evidently had an

---

[8] Howlett, *Letters* 66 (Latin text); O'Loughlin, *Discovering* 153
[9] Howlett, *Letters* 67

affection for the Gaulish churchmen and he had spent some time in Gaul but this is not a decisive argument for a Gaulish training. It is at least as likely that he trained in his homeland, where, as we have seen, the Church had retained its cohesion and its culture despite the loss of order and the effects of the barbarian invasions. He never tells us about his training: he was not writing an autobiography and the historical details he provides are incidental to his purpose of defending his ministry against his critics.[10]

He may well not have responded immediately to the message of his dream.[11] He knew only too well the dangers of Ireland. He had to face going back to minister to those who had snatched him from his home, through whose agency he had had to endure the harsh life of a herdsman in all weathers. Nor would it have been easy or straightforward to find a bishop within the British Church to ordain him as a priest with a mission to Ireland.

The lack of support he found for his Irish vocation reinforced his natural reluctance to go there, as he wrote, 'the Lord has shown pity to me up to thousands of thousands of times, because He saw in me that I was ready, but that I did not know for myself for these circumstances, what I should do about my own condition, because many were hindering this embassy. They were even talking among themselves behind my back and saying, "Why does this man dispatch himself in peril among enemies who do not know God?"'[12] The British had suffered much from Irish raids. Like their counterparts elsewhere in the Roman Empire, their churchmen had inherited Eusebius's understanding of the intimate connection between Constantine's Empire and Christianity, in which his empire was the providential instrument for building the kingdom of God on earth, Empire and Church moving towards identity. It followed from such a view that the proper place for spreading the Gospel lay among the peoples within the Empire rather than outside. This implicit hostility was reinforced by the long-standing contempt of educated Roman society for the barbarian, which originated in pagan society but remained potent among Christians, and in Britain was no doubt the more acute because of the damage done by barbarian raiding. Amongst some churchmen, the Augustinian stress on grace

---

[10] I accept late dating of Patrick in D.N. Dumville, 'St Patrick's missing years', id., *Saint Patrick AD* 493–1993 (Woodbridge 1993) 25–8 and 'The floruit of St Patrick: common and less common ground' 13–18 in preference to Howlett. See S. Young, 'St Patrick and Clovis', *Peritia* 16 (2002) 478–9, Charles-Edwards, *Ireland* 239; comment, D. Ó'Cróinin, 'Patrick', *LMA*

[11] C.E. Stancliffe, 'Patrick', *ODNB*; O'Loughlin, *Discovering* 153

[12] Howlett, *Letters* 83

may well also have acted unconsciously as a barrier against missionising. It was these inhibitions of emotion and ideology which Patrick had to break down, both in his own mind and among the Church members whom he wished to make his supporters, before he could set off on his odyssey.

The circumstances in Ireland made it impossible for him as a missionary priest simply to live off his hearers and although he somehow persuaded authority in Britain to support him and give him financial backing, it is likely that at some stage he sold the family estate in order to continue his mission. He was a stranger, with no lord and without kin, *cú glas*, the grey wolf in Irish law, in a land which had no central authority. He had to pay bribes to kings because they were technically responsible for him and there was a multitude of them, perhaps between eighty and 180 *túatha*, grouped in a kaleidoscopic way under kings who were overlords and lesser kings loosely subject to them, though the over-kings had no powers of intervention; their authority was only a personal one. Dynasties struggled to enlarge their power, but the basic, primary unit of authority in Patrick's lifetime remained the individual *túath* and thus to carry out his mission he had to offer inducements in order to obtain personal security, to be able to move to and fro between *túatha* to meet his flock and win recruits.[13]

The payments to kings and princes were part of the allegations of wrongful conduct made against him late in his career. He wrote about this in his *Confessio*, explaining the chronic insecurity within Ireland and pointing out the degree to which his life remained under threat despite these payments. 'Meanwhile,' the passage runs, 'I kept giving rewards to kings, besides which I kept giving a fee to their sons, who walk with me, and nonetheless they apprehended me with my companions, and on that day they wanted most eagerly to kill me, but the time had not yet come.'[14] He spent fourteen days in irons as a result of this episode. Payments to kings were necessary if the mission was to continue; his security was facilitated if he could acquire and pay for a bodyguard of princes, whom he had persuaded and recruited and would expect to be a bulwark against other hostile kings or the representatives of paganism, the brehons, judges who were guardians of an immemorial Irish law which they administered and interpreted. He evidently had a roving commission, for he

---

[13] C.E. Stancliffe, 'Kings and conversion: some comparisons between the Roman mission to England and Patrick's to Ireland', *FMS* 14 (1980) 59–94 illuminating, not sufficiently known, at 78
[14] Howlett, *Letters* 87

rehearses the payments to kings of different *túatha* and when he writes of payments to the brehons, he refers to the amount he paid out 'through all the regions which I kept visiting quite often'.

His own emphasis is on his work among the Irish who had no contact with Christianity. He writes of his actions in 'remote parts, where there was no man beyond, and where no one had ever come through, who would baptise or ordain clerics or bring the people to the highest perfection'.[15] This was no accident but a crucial part of the vocation which he believed he had received from God. His slavery near the Western Ocean was, in the geography of Late Antiquity, on the edge of the world and he understood the words of Scripture about the Gospel being taken to the ends of the earth before the Second Coming to apply especially to him and his missionary work.[16] Here, at the rim of the world, lived those who had never heard the message of Christ. He believed it was pre-eminently his task to bring it to them and so complete the work of preaching and hasten the End. He cites a series of texts from Acts and the Gospels in which the Lord's command to preach to all nations is given, with the promise of divine aid and the association between its fulfilment and the end of the age, then goes on to speak of the change taking place among the Irish, who had become a 'folk of the Lord' and of the Irish men and women who had been converted and taken up the ascetic life. He had longed to go to Britain, his homeland where his family was, and to Gaul 'to visit the brethren' but felt that he would then be guilty of not doing the work he had undertaken. He believed that it was the Lord's command that he should go to Ireland and be with the people there for the rest of his life.[17] Patrick's references to the Irish as a 'folk of the Lord', or, in Thomas O'Loughlin's translation, 'a prepared people', does not imply that the task of conversion was fully completed: he does not write of the conversion of kings.

Druids and brehons formed part of the *nemed*, a sacred class not appointed or controlled by kings. They had functions in pre-Christian religion and formed a body of interests opposed to Patrick and his fellow priests, and their influence could not be swept away by royal diktat as were Germanic pagan powers, where the conversion process revolved round the attitude of kings and leading aristocrats and where the missionary's task was to proceed through royal courts and gain protection and aid from rulers. Decisions about

[15] Ibid.
[16] O'Loughlin, *Discovering* 72–8
[17] Ibid. 163

the relationship between traditional law and the new religion were made after Patrick's time and the body of Irish law only slowly received the imprint of Christianity.

The missionary in Ireland had a harder and more dangerous task: he had to proceed by persuasion from individual to individual, had to continue to live with pagans and was vulnerable to personal attacks and imprisonment or even threat of execution. He could not count on royal power either to protect him or his converts or to suppress his religious rivals, the pagans and their druids. Patrick refers to many persecutions 'up to the point of chains' and of a further enslavement which lasted for months, from which 'the Lord freed me', he wrote.

The root of his problem lay in the position of the kinless man in Irish law. In Britain, he was of the decurion class, in Ireland he did not even have the status of a freeman. Though Patrick saw his early enslavement as a punishment from God for a serious sin of his youth and the means of bringing him to an active faith through his life of prayer as a herdsman, he interpreted his missionary life in Ireland as a second but voluntary slavery, in the same way that Paul understood himself to be a slave to God.

The sin of his youth dogged him. It was committed, probably before he was fifteen, 'in one hour' when, he wrote, 'I was not a believer in the true God'. In an unwise moment before he was ordained deacon, 'when I was anxious and worried' he revealed to his most intimate friend what he had done. Much later on – thirty years later, he writes, but it is not clear whether he means thirty years after his sin or after he made his admission – his confidence was betrayed without his knowledge or permission and this contributed to accusations made against him after he had become bishop and had long been serving in Ireland. The friend did not reveal this sin at the time when there would have been a formal examination of Patrick's suitability for the episcopate; indeed, Patrick implies, he supported him then. The disclosure was the more damaging because of the Church's uncertain attitude at this time to serious sins committed after baptism and because of the barriers set in canon law against the ordination or consecration of men who had committed such sins. There were other allegations made against him of such a kind as to suggest that the authorities in Britain did not understand the conditions of ministry and evangelisation in Ireland and, probably, were still at heart unsympathetic to the Gospel being taken to these barbarians.

The *Confessio* is a passionate defence of his ministry, an open letter, in effect, addressed to the 'seniors' who had made and received accusations against him, most probably a synod of British bishops. He sometimes addresses and subtly denounces them and at other times veers away to address his supporters in Ireland, both British and Irish, relying on the Latin-trained clergy to interpret his case. The accusations related to his management of finance, the impropriety of receiving gifts, making profits and distributing bribes; he relied on the situation of a kinless missionary in Ireland to explain the gifts he had made to kings, princes and brehons and utterly denied simony. When priests were ordained, he took nothing: 'Did I even charge them the cost of my shoes?' he asked. 'Tell it against me and I will all the more return it to you.' He refused the little gifts from Christian converts, the virgins of Christ and the religious women even when 'they kept hurling some of their own ornaments over the altar, and I kept giving them back again to them'. Patrick's great care not to receive the smallest gift was due not only to the fear of occasions of profit-making and accusations of greed, but also to a care not to be drawn into any of the implications of gift-giving in Irish society.[18]

The heart of the case against the 'seniors' was the revelation to him of the will of God through a series of visions and interventions, tabulated in the manner of the time as three calls by God to this mission, twelve perils surmounted with His help and seven visions of increasing force and importance; God was his defender. His claim against the formal structure of synod, hierarchy and accusation is that he was exercising the role of prophet directly under the power and inspiration of God.

The claims are immense. He said he had been victim of a visitation from Satan, who 'fell over' him like a 'huge rock' while he was asleep. He felt paralysed. He called on Elias, 'Elia, Elia', then in a word-play on Helios, the sun, he saw the sunrise. He was rescued. 'I believe that I was come to the aid of by Christ my Lord, and His Spirit was already then shouting for me', he wrote. In another vision he felt the presence of God with him: 'He who has given His own soul for you He it is Who speaks in you'; and in an even more remarkable piece of reporting, he says of another night vision at a time of great stress after a hostile hearing that he understood God to speak to him rejecting the accusations as if 'He had joined me to Himself, just as He has said, "He who touches you (is) as he who touches the pupil of my eye"'.[19]

---

[18] Ibid. 155 (sin) 166 (shoes, citing 1 Sam. XII 3); Howlett, *Letters* 85 (ornaments); on dating and (rightful) assumption that Patrick was priest in Ireland before he became bishop, C.E. Stancliffe, 'Patrick', *ODNB*

[19] Howlett, *Letters* 65, 67, 69, 71

From these descriptions, we may glimpse both the power which Patrick exercised in the mission field through his utter conviction of God's presence and aid, and the unease which conventional churchmen are likely to have felt in dealing with a prophet of this calibre. In the end the accusations failed: he was not removed from his bishop's dignity but it is likely that tensions were unresolved and a shadow remained on his relations with his Church of origin.

Patrick was kidnapped before he had reached the stage of rhetoric in his Latin education and he may also, as he implies, have been neglectful of his studies. He depicted himself as 'unlearned' and a 'rustic'. Nonetheless he knew how to use the rhythms of the Latin cursus and, though Patrick's work is influenced overwhelmingly by an immersion over many years in Scripture, Peter Dronke has given grounds for detecting some traces of memory of other sources, Augustine's *Confessions*, Cyprian and Pastor Hermas.[20] He was not quite the man of one book he is sometimes taken to be. There was, moreover, a sting in the tail of his rusticity. David Howlett has taught us to see in both the *Confessio* and the *Epistola contra Coroticum* a mastery of the rhythms of the Bible, above all the techniques of chiasmus.

Patrick refers with distaste to the clever rhetoricians – 'vos domini cati rhetorici' – who were able to make use of all the skills of Roman rhetoric and polemic, that is, the techniques of the secular advocate, and contrasts them with the great and small who fear God – 'magni et pusilli qui timetis Deum'. The clergy who knew their Latin Bible would be aware that the 'magni et pusilli' were the faithful of the Book of Revelation XIX, enjoined by a voice from the throne to praise God. As they are mentioned in contrast to the Harlot of Babylon and her adherents described in chapters XVII and XVIII, it would be obvious to them where Patrick was placing the clever rhetoricians. In another passage interpreted by Howlett, Patrick apologises for his lack of knowledge and 'slow tongue' – 'tardiori lingua' – the exact phrase used by Moses in Exodus IV of his weakness that is cancelled out by God's power in just the same way that Patrick's weakness in the conventions of secular Latin writing is cancelled out by the words of Scripture which he deploys with skill and the adoption of the rhetoric of the Bible.[21]

Despite obscurities, despite changes of addressee, despite the loose structure, at the heart of the *Confessio* lies a sophisticated mosaic of scriptural texts and references deployed with great skill. Just as the first fifteen verses of Mark's

[20] P. Dronke, 'St Patrick's reading', *CMCS* I (1981) 21–38
[21] Howlett, *Letters* 58–9; Rev. XIX 5, Exodus IV 10; chiasmus, Charles-Edwards, *Ireland* 231

Gospel appear at first reading to be a simple narrative yet on examination prove to carry a set of cogent allusions to the Hebrew Scriptures familiar to a Jewish audience soaked in knowledge of them, setting up powerful echoes in the mind, so Patrick, who had closely read the Scriptures over decades, uses implicit allusions to Old and New Testaments to give emotional force to the case he makes for himself and his mission. Charles-Edwards summarises Patrick's case in the following words: 'True, I was a slave by the Wood of Foclut when I should have been in the rhetor's school, but God was my teacher in the midst of my slavery, the style in which I write is that of Christian Law, the Bible, and I adopted it by free choice, not mere rustic incompetence.'[22]

The *Epistola contra Coroticum* is directed against the actions of a British Christian ruler referred to as a tyrant, possibly Ceretic, king of Dumbarton, whose band of warriors had rounded up some of Patrick's converts, killing some and enslaving others. It complements the *Confessio* since it brings to the fore Patrick's deep sorrow for the victims of violence in Ireland and, naturally enough, his sympathetic feelings for his converts and fellow victims who have suffered and are suffering at the hands of slavers. Like the *Confessio*, it is written with powerful emotion, making use of scriptural allusions. Like the Psalms, it is directed towards different addressees at different times; at one moment he is addressing the soldiers who participated in the slaving raid; at another, good Christians, 'the humble and lowly of heart' whom he enjoins not to eat and drink with these wicked men or receive gifts from them until they have done penance; at another he addresses his suffering converts. He also addresses a prayer to God. He wishes the letter to be read aloud 'before all folk, even Coroticus himself being present' and he ends with a solemn request to any servant of God who can bring his letter to public notice. This was an open letter, designed to denounce the crime of Coroticus and his men and call them to repentance, and was his last attempt to do what he could for their victims, men and women taken by soldiers the day after their baptism. 'On the day after that on which the new converts in white clothing were anointed with chrism,' he wrote, 'it was shining on their brow while they were relentlessly slaughtered and slain with the sword by the above said men.' He had already sent a letter by a priest whom he had taught from infancy, appealing to the raiders to give back the baptised prisoners and some of their loot but that was received with guffaws. He can do nothing for the dead but

---

[22] Charles-Edwards, *Ireland* 232

recall their rewards in paradise; for the women taken off 'as prizes' he can only appeal to consciences and denounce actions.

His abjuration to the Christians to give no support to Coroticus and his men is very like excommunication. He justifies himself, writing, 'I do not go beyond my authority for I have a share with those whom he called and predestined to preach the gospel with no small measure of persecutions unto the very end of the earth'.[23] Coroticus commissioned the raid but, Patrick implies, was not on it. What is certain is that he was British and it was British soldiers who formed the Christian element in the band, although Picts and Irish were also included. It all sounds very like a *fían*, a sworn body of warriors, a feature of the pagan past, marauders without fixed abode, in this instance straddling divisions between religion and kingdom. Members of a *fían* were sometimes distinguished by a mark on their foreheads; if true in this case, it made more poignant the distinction between the mark of a killing and looting band and the chrism on the foreheads of Patrick's converts. Patrick refers to Coroticus as a fellow citizen and calls them 'fellow citizens of demons . . . they live in death', he writes, 'comrades of Scots and Picts and apostates, bloody men who are bloody with the blood of innocent Christians', whom he describes elsewhere as 'the flock of the Lord which was indeed growing most excellently in Ireland with the highest loving care'.[24]

The letter, to encourage or denounce, is addressed solely to Christians, whether free, enslaved by Coroticus or apostate, and one major complaint is that they are enslaving Christians and selling them to pagans. When Patrick addresses his prayer to God, 'What shall I do, Lord?' and sets out the miseries of the situation, he writes, 'Far off from the charity of God is the betrayer of Christians into the hands of Scots and Picts.' A little further on, now addressing the soldiers and contrasting with their wickedness the good deeds of the Gaulish Christians in ransoming, he writes, 'You rather kill and sell them to a remote gentile people ignorant of God.' By Scots he probably means pagan Irish, the immigrants to Argyll who created the kingdom of Dál Riata; the second sentence points to Pictland. A third sentence alludes to the wickedness of deporting men and women to 'far off places' where 'Christians are reduced to slavery, particularly among the most unworthy worst apostates and Picts'. Patrick was not opposed to slavery as such, which is accepted in

---

[23] O'Loughlin, *Discovering* 175–6 (authority); Howlett, *Letters* 27 (converts)
[24] Howlett, *Letters* 27, 33; Charles-Edwards, *Ireland* 226–30; D.N. Dumville, 'Coroticus', id., *Patrick*, 107–27, 'Picti apostataeque' 129–31

Scripture, but felt deeply the sale to pagans and the betrayal of trust in the actions of Christians in Coroticus's band – all thus rightly called apostates.[25]

The letter includes passages of great eloquence, where he speaks of the rewards for the dead in paradise and the likely fate in hell of Coroticus and his men if unrepentant and of his tears over the women converts 'distributed as prizes'. The *Epistola* still more than the *Confessio* reveals one reason why Patrick made converts: he was a preacher of great eloquence. The letter also throws up once more a picture of anarchy in Ireland and of the security problems for a young Church, its converts subject to casual, sometimes lethal violence; Patrick has no secular authority to which he can appeal.

What was his legacy? First, a marked increase in support for Christianity; working with others, Patrick had been building a Church for decades. There is no reason to doubt his statement that he had baptised so many thousand; his writings emphasise the needs of the indigenous Irish, the winning of 'pagans and gentiles', and his care for the most disadvantaged led him to make converts among slaves. The reference to the priest he had taught from infancy suggests the development of an Irish priesthood. Members of Palladius's mission must be assumed to have lived on and cooperated, though their prime field of action lay to the south and east, especially, it may well be, in Leinster with its contacts with western Britain, whereas Patrick's achievement was above all with the Irish who had no contact with Christianity, thus probably in Ulster and North Connaught, in lands 'where the sun set alone in the western sea'. His passion for the conversion of the Irish paved the way for the commitment to Ireland of other missionary priests from Britain and helped to break down the suspicion and hostility of British churchmen generally.[26]

Secondly, he had acquired converts, male and female, who accepted celibacy. He believed celibacy to be the highest form of Christian life and rejoiced that many took it up, though nothing in his writing implies the creation of monasteries, whether for men or for women. He seems to have had a special capacity for drawing aristocratic women to consecrated virginity and was aware that they suffered for it and encountered the hostility of their fathers, living on at

[25] Howlett, *Letters* 33, 35

[26] For Irish Church after Patrick, D. Ó'Cróinín, *Early Medieval Ireland 400–1200* (London, New York 1995); R. Sharpe, 'British missionary activity in Ireland', Dumville, *Patrick* 133–45; Charles-Edwards, 'Britons in Ireland c.550–800'; K. Jackson, *Language and history in early Britain* (2nd edn Dublin 1994) 122–48; B. Yorke, *The conversion of Britain. Religion, politics and society in Britain c.600–800* (Harlow 2006) 112–14.

home and sustaining their way of life despite harassment. The men were likely to have been attached to churches, forming a 'spiritual vanguard' in the process of conversion. This popularising of the celibate state prepared the way for the great flowering of Irish monasticism after Patrick's epoch.

The third legacy was his concept of mission. His appeal is to Scripture and St Paul, to Christ's command to preach the Gospel to all nations and to the visions and revelations which studded his life. The beginnings of a sense of mission can be detected in Celestine and Palladius, but they were only beginnings. Patrick is the first major figure to be impelled by a missionary zeal to reach out to all – even, as he says, to the very ends of the earth.

Patrick's appeal to Scripture as the basis of his own exile from his native land, a secular punishment in Ireland for grave offences, gave a boost to the notion of pilgrimage for the sake of God. He had thrown away the status of the son of a decurion in Britain to become an exile without rights because of a divine call: others followed his example in missions outside their native Ireland. Excommunication imposed by bishops in the surviving canons of the so-called First Synod of St Patrick, a sixth-century collection of decisions, also played a part in the build-up of *peregrinatio*, seen as a penitential exile or a voluntary act of renunciation for God. It reached its full flowering in the seventh century and it helped to bring dedicated missionaries into the mission field of Britain. It was a kind of quid pro quo by the Irish for the major contribution made by British churchmen to their own Christianising. *Peregrinatio* did not necessarily involve mission but in practice it very often did and Patrick's life and fame contributed to that development.[27]

Paganism survived for many years; Christianity in Ireland was not imposed by force, whether by kings, over-kings or a neighbouring Christian power. In Britain in the late sixth century, Aethelberht of Kent speedily incorporated Christian clergy into his law code: not so in Ireland. The brehons long retained their power and native law with its pagan roots remained in being. The long coexistence of paganism and Christianity is shown in its use of pagan terms such as *dia* for God, *cretem* for belief, *ires* for faith.[28] The fact that paganism and Christianity had to exist side by side gave an advantage to those Irish who ventured overseas in pilgrimage and mission, for they had experience in dealing with pagans and paganism on equal terms.

[27] T.M. Charles-Edwards, 'The social background to Irish *Peregrinatio*', *Celtica* II (1976) 43–59
[28] Ó'Cróinín, *Ireland* 38

Though his fame is much the greatest, St Patrick was not the only Briton to play a part in Christian mission to Ireland. Iserninus, reputedly a missionary under Patrick, more probably under Palladius, has a British name and St Mauchteus, founder of a monastery, who foretold Columba's birth, was recorded as a British pilgrim by Adomnán, Columba's biographer.[29] There was evidently a continuing interest by British churchmen and a duty of oversight may well have continued into the sixth century. The existence of a nucleus of Brittonic speakers within Ireland, fruit of earlier spontaneous contacts, facilitated mission from Britain.

The Irish had no common Vulgar Latin as spoken on the continent since it had never been part of the Roman Empire: the Latin necessary for reading the Vulgate, for the liturgy and Christian instruction and learning had to be imparted by missionary churchmen, who, linguistic evidence shows, spoke with a Brittonic accent. There were no secular schools of Latin of the kind which gave Patrick and Gildas their education; as a Christian culture developed, monasteries were the places where education was given. In the course of time, the achievement of these Irish monasteries far exceeded that of the British, but it was British churchmen who gave Ireland its educational grounding.

Archaisms in Irish script – the use of the *et* ligature and methods of preparing the quire – betray British influence. So do place-names. *Domnach* is an Old Irish place-name element denoting a principal church. It derives from *dominicus*, Latin for 'the Lord's dwelling' as pronounced by a Brittonic speaker: it ceased to be used in place-names by the seventh century and is evidence of the existence of a church site in the conversion period. Hypocoristic names, joke-names current among early Irish churchmen, also take their origin from Britain. Some Irish churches were describing themselves as 'churches of the Britons' in the seventh century and the implication of a decision taken to prevent British priests coming to Ireland without permission from their bishop is that there was a spontaneous enthusiasm within the British Church for work in Ireland.

After Patrick's death, British influences stimulated Irish monastic development. The Gildas of the Epistolary Fragments, bearing witness to the growth of monasticism in Britain then seen as a bulwark against corrupt and relaxed

[29] R. Sharpe, 'Saint Mauchteus, discipulus Patricii', A. Bammesberger, A. Wollmann eds, *Britain 400–600. Language and history* (Heidelberg 1990) 85–93

churchmen, influenced Ireland, where he was treated as an authority.[30] Monasticism developed vigorously in Ireland, linking with conspicuous success the ascetic impulse which swept through the western Church with the Irish sense of the importance of kin.

Pilgrimage, mission and the passionate following of the monastic life intertwined in the career of Columba.[31] He was an Irishman of royal rank of the Cenél Conaill centred in Donegal, a branch of the Uí Néill, a dominant dynasty whose power was growing in the sixth century. While Patrick, without local connections or kin, son merely of a British decurion, had to make his way by personal talents, eloquence and contacts with the sons of kings and noblewomen. Columba, trained as a priest in Ireland and his energies in full flower, was deploying the powers and contacts of the members of a leading Irish dynasty.

He might have been born into a pagan family but the convention of hagiography insisted that a child should be holy from the beginning of his life and this may have blurred the facts of his family's religious orientation. As was common in Ireland, he was educated by a foster father, the priest Cruithnechán, studied at Leinster as a deacon and then under St Finnian of Moville, who may well have been the last major figure from Britain to play a role in the development of the Irish Church as it began to look outwards and itself participated in mission.[32]

Columba was in his forties when he chose to travel away from his by then increasingly Christian Ireland. In his case, the impetus for journeying overseas and settling at Iona was ascetic, a form of white martyrdom, a sacrifice of life through monasticism and ascetic practices. This was no pilgrimage to a

---

[30] D.N. Dumville, 'Gildas and Uinniau', M. Lapidge, D.N. Dumville eds, *Gildas. New approaches* (Woodbridge 1984) 207–14; T.J. Brown, 'The Irish element in the Insular system of scripts to *circa* AD 850', H. Löwe ed., *Die Iren und Europa im früheren Mittelalter* (Stuttgart 1982) 101–19

[31] M. Herbert, 'Columba', *ODNB*; D. Broun, T.O. Clancy eds, *Spes Scotorum. Hope of Scots. Saint Columba, Iona and Scotland* (Edinburgh 1999). Clancy, 'Columba, Adomnán and the cult of saints in Scotland', Broun, Clancy eds, *Spes Scotorum* 3–34 esp. helpful; original Life R. Sharpe, *Adomnán of Iona: Life of St Columba* (Harmondsworth 1995); relationship between Adomnán's Life of Columba and his *De locis sanctis*, T. O'Loughlin, 'The tombs of the saints: their significance for Adomnán', J. Carey *et al.* eds, *Studies in Irish hagiography* (Dublin 2001) 1–14; Charles-Edwards, *Ireland*, 282–308; classic is A.O. and M.O. Anderson, *Adomnán's Life of Columba* (Oxford 1991, 1st edn London 1961); broad picture, A.P. Smyth, *Warlords and holy men. Scotland AD 80–1000* (London 1984); J.T. Koch, 'Peregrinatio', *KCC*

[32] Charles-Edwards, *Ireland* 291–3 identifies teacher as Finnian of Moville rather than Clonard

shrine which, however dangerous, takes the pilgrim back home once more. White-martyr pilgrimage meant lifelong exile, plainly with affinities to exile as the most serious of punishments in Irish law. Here it is self-imposed in accord with God's commands, following the precedents of Abraham leaving Ur and the renunciation text of Matthew X 37. It was regarded as a peak of abnegation by Irish monks and Adomnán says simply that Columba 'sailed away from Ireland to Britain, choosing to be a pilgrim for Christ'.[33]

It was not, however, a full white martyrdom, for Columba felt free to return to Ireland and cross to Dál Riata, the Irish kingdom in what is now Argyll, which was already Christian. A late tradition described him receiving the island of Iona from the king of Dál Riata, Conall mac Comgaill; his settlement in the probably uninhabited island has the air of being a carefully planned movement carried out in consultation with his kin and resting on a land grant arranged at the highest level.[34] It was said that Columba made his crossing with twelve companions, the classic apostolic number, but this need not imply any inaccuracy; Columba would have wished to act wherever possible in accord with scriptural precedent. What is significant is that, numbered among the twelve in the list which has come down to us from the early eighth century, were an uncle and two cousins.

Columba was about forty-two when he took up his grant and made the crossing. Adomnán dates his coming to Britain to the second year following the battle of Cúl Dreimne, i.e. 563. Had Cúl Dreimne a dark significance, involving Columba in the crime of instigating the battle? Some of his kinsmen from the northern Uí Néill took part in the fighting against members of the southern branch of the dynasty under the king of Tara and they won. The *Annals of Ulster* say that the battle was won 'through the prayers of Columba'. Nothing suggests a more direct involvement in the battle and there is no evidence of blood-guilt, as some have argued, driving him into a penitential exile. He may well have prayed for his own people's success and, in revenge, the pagan king of Tara could have put pressure on a synod at Tailtiu in his territory to pronounce excommunication on Columba, using some trifling excuse to do so. In the disturbances of Ireland's history, a monk from a leading dynasty would find it hard indeed to occupy an independent stance: the demands made upon him because of his rank would distract him and

---

[33] *Adomnán* 105
[34] I do not believe that Columba received Iona from the Pictish king, as Bede *HE* III 4: arguments of D.A. Bullough, 'The missions to the English and the Picts and their heritage (to *c*.800)', H. Löwe ed., *Die Iren und Europa* (Stuttgart 1982) 82–97 at 82 still hold

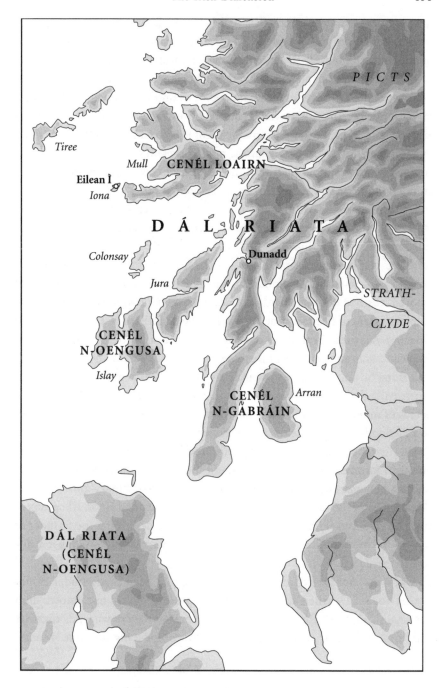

Map 6 The kingdom of Dál Riata. Of the major kindreds (*cenéla*), Cenél nGabráin based in Kintyre was usually dominant. The kings it produced provided a strength and unity lacking among the *tuátha* of Ireland. Iona, near Dál Riata's northern frontier, is well placed for access by water to Pictland and Strathclyde.

interrupt the practice of monastic life. What we know suggests a voluntary withdrawal to achieve a high standard of monastic life free from internal politics but within an Irish settlement on the coast of Britain.[35]

His rank, his strong personality and his obligations as abbot ensured that he dominated the Iona scene, receiving penitents and pilgrims, founding other monasteries, creating a *paruchia*, a confederation of monastic houses under his leadership in Ireland and on the mainland of Britain, subsequently maintained by his successors. At the centre lay the monastery and island of Iona, where, as Adomnán conveys in his picture of the relationship between Columba and the animals, the harmony of creation in the Garden of Eden was restored.[36]

The reminiscences of his own monks form the core of Adomnán's Life, written one hundred years later. In his lifetime Columba was regarded as a saint and incidents in his life came to be given a supernatural aura. Building on these reminiscences and other stories from further afield, Adomnán's purpose was to show Columba as a saint of the same calibre as the saints whose Lives had become standard reading in the Christian world of his day, Sulpicius's Life of St Martin of Tours, the Life of St Benedict in Gregory the Great's *Dialogues*, Evagrius's translation of the Life of St Antony. Like Sulpicius, Adomnán gave his Life two prefaces; like him, he divided his work into three books. The aim was similar – to build up a picture of a saint in touch with the supernatural, already in the society of angels. Biographical details of monastic life and learning, contacts with Dál Riata, kings in Ireland and Pictland are all incidental to the evidence of sanctity.

The first book deals with prophecy: individual examples of Columba's power to foresee events or to understand the future of men flowed from his role as a holy man with access to knowledge denied to ordinary mortals. Book II continues in the same vein, describing his miracles, and Book III speaks of angelic visitations. First and foremost Adomnán is describing the founder of Iona to the monks of his own time when living memory was no longer available to them.

A first attempt at recording Columba's life had been made under Abbot Ségéne (623–52), when a generation was passing which had known him personally; some of these reminiscences were written down and, together with oral evidence, used by Adomnán to compile his account. Monks'

---

[35] M. Herbert, *Iona, Kells and Derry* (Oxford 1988) 28; Charles-Edwards, *Ireland* 294–6 on Irish background

[36] G. Márkus, 'Iona: monks, pastors and missionaries', Broun and Clancy, *Spes* 115–38

memories form the most reliable part of the Life: some betray their origin in written evidence, in stories with genealogical and onomastic detail, very unlikely to have survived over a hundred years in purely oral tradition, about dramatis personae whose only significance lies in their contact with the saint.

The stories about Columba's life with his monks have a sober quality about them and the miracles are not extravagant. Adomnán describes his reception on a visit to Ireland when he came to the monastery of Clonmacnoise; the monks bowed their heads and kissed him; he was protected from the 'pressing crowd of brethren' by four men walking with him holding about him a 'square framed of branches tied together'. A boy touched the hem of his cloak hoping he would not notice; but he did, reached behind him, seized him by the neck, commanded him to put out his tongue, blessed it and prophesied for this insignificant boy a notable future marked by his eloquence, as the boy later testified to Abbot Ségéne.[37]

Adomnán was also writing in an age of controversy between Roman and Celtic parties within the Christian world about the dating of the Easter feast. He was concerned to preserve unblemished the reputation of the saint in an age when leading Churches had decided against the Celtic system, with which Columba was associated. Adomnán himself had decided for the Roman solution but was concerned that the saint's authority should in no way be diminished by the Easter decision. The Life hardly refers to the Easter question, mentioning only the saint's prophecy of division in the future among Irish Churches because of it.

As well as encouraging and informing the monastery of Iona and its *paruchia* about its saint and founder, the Life was designed to buttress Columba's sanctity in the wider world. His portrait, then, dwells on prophecy and the supernatural, rather than asceticism and scholarship. These aspects are brought over much more strongly in the Irish poem composed *c.*600 soon after the saint's death by Dallán Forgaill, 'the little blind man of superior testimony', *Amra Choluimb Chille*, the Wonders of Columba, a eulogy which informs us on his reading, his knowledge of Cassian and Basil's Rule and his skill with the Scriptures. It was said the poem was commissioned by a certain Áed, probably Áed mac Ainmirech of the Uí Néill, Columba's first cousin, part of the tradition of praise-poetry of the Irish world, normally composed in honour of leading members of the aristocracy but here devoted to the praise of one who renounced the world

---

[37] *Adomnán* I 3; J.E. Fraser, 'Adomnán, Cumméne, Faílbe and Picts' *Peritia* 17–18 (2003–4) 183–98 re-examines Adomnán's sources and importance of Pictish monastic audience

and turned his back on secular glory, a man whose battles were inner ones, the battles of the ascetic against his own desires and the demons who beset the Christian rather than against antagonists in war. Miracles are not mentioned.[38]

Adomnán skilfully builds up through three visions a picture of the way in which the saint trained and tested his monks, discerning their differences of character and the stages they had reached in their spiritual journey before they could attain the requisite purity of heart. He writes of Columba's three-day experience on the island of Hinba, where he was illuminated by the Holy Spirit and was enabled to 'see openly revealed many secrets that had been hidden since the world began, while all that was most dark and difficult in the sacred Scriptures lay open, plain and clearer than light',[39] purity of heart being the key.

Virgno the Briton, who later became Iona's fourth abbot, was in the habit of praying while others slept, choosing a side chapel where he would not be seen. When Columba entered the chapel it was so filled with heavenly light that Virgno was dazzled and filled with fear, lowering his eyes. Next day, Columba said, 'Bene filiole', commending his action, for it was 'unimaginable light' that might have blinded him. Another monk, Colcu, chancing to see the light as he approached the chapel, was afraid and fled: as he was but a beginner in the spiritual life he was warned by Columba 'not to see surreptitiously the light from heaven which is not given to you'.[40] He did not stay on Iona. A third case involved a foster son, Berchan, probably a lay youth studying under Columba, who was disobedient. Told by Columba not to come to his lodging as he usually did, he disobeyed, spied through the keyhole, saw the heavenly light round the saint and ran away. Next day Columba revealed that he knew what he had done and told him he was saved from death or blinding only by his prayers; he prophesied that he would live 'lecherously' in Ireland and would only be saved at his death by Columba's prayers.[41] Adomnán's vision narratives were more than casual illustrations of Columba's super-earthly status: they were carefully crafted signposts to the fulfilment of the objectives of the monastic life, based on his own deep reading and the traditions of the Desert Fathers as well as the monks' reminiscences.[42]

[38] T.O. Clancy, G. Márkus, *Iona: the earliest poetry of a Celtic monastery* (Edinburgh 1995); *Amra* 104–28

[39] *Adomnán* III 18

[40] III 19

[41] III 21

[42] J. O'Reilly, 'The wisdom of the scribe and the fear of the Lord in the *Life of Columba*', Broun and Clancy, *Spes* 159–211

The stories illustrate the major role the work of a scribe played within monastic life and its connection with spiritual growth: the work of abbot and scribe ran together. Columba's writing hut occupied a central position. Here he sat writing or reading, perhaps with monks attending on him or learning from him, blessing both tools and those who used them, prophesying, calling on the angels. One story, ostensibly designed to show Columba's prophetic powers, neatly illustrates this. Baíthéne, kinsman and scribe, approached Columba asking him to assign one of his fellows to go through the copy of the psalter he had made, to correct errors. He received the testy reply that he was causing needless trouble, 'For in your copy of the psalter there is no mistake – neither one letter too many nor one too few – except that in one place the letter iota is missing.' 'So it was,' Adomnán comments.[43]

The story has an inner meaning. The Psalms were used to teach literacy, but not that only: they provided more than a physical alphabet – they were a spiritual alphabet as well and Columba was signifying to Baíthéne that he had not yet reached the perfection of a monk's life; perhaps there is a hint of censure on Baíthéne for glorying in his achievement. The missing iota had a strong scriptural echo: there was still something lacking in him. But Baíthéne did advance in the spiritual life and the last scene of Columba's life took place as he was copying Psalm 33 and had reached the verse 'Come, my sons, hear me; I shall teach you the fear of the Lord', and said, 'Here at the end of the page I must stop. Let Baíthéne write what follows.'[44] The verse was a classic allusion to the monastic life: Baíthéne was to be his successor.

Adomnán's Life conveys repeatedly the experiences which lay at the heart of Columba's conduct in Iona as spiritual master – the attaining of understanding through the miscellaneous humble tasks of agriculture, the saying of Psalms, scribal work, the monastic life. He had not come to south-west Scotland primarily for mission but to create a monastic environment for all who wanted to follow his way – provided they were suited. As there were no other inhabitants, the monks sustained their own economic life, having access to boats and the riches of the sea. Penitents who came to seek counsel and expiate sins were transferred to Tiree or Hinba: for pilgrims, postulants and exiles seeking refuge, there was probably a guest house on Iona. The flow of such men coming for spiritual needs provided a source of recruits for the founding of monasteries in other places and a confederation grew under Columba's leadership.

---

[43] *Adomnán* I 24
[44] III 23

Columba's high birth and his knowledge of the dynamics of Ireland made
it natural for him to rule the confederation in the same manner as an over-
king. A connection with Ireland was sustained: emissaries passed to and fro
and Columba was able to found the monastery of Durrow in central Ireland
and was co-founder of another at Derry, near Louth. He kept an ultimate
control by personal visits and often appointed his kin to positions of
authority: of eight abbots who succeeded him in Iona, only Virgno the Briton
was not of the Cenél Conaill. In his lifetime, Columba put his first cousin
Baíthéne in charge of the settlement on Tiree, his uncle Ernan was prior on
Hinba, and Laisrán, another relative from Iona, was put in charge of Durrow.
Such links to kin and the mutual support of Columba's dynasty and confederation fitted a tradition which, as elsewhere in Irish monasticism, was a force
for continuity at Iona, aiding stability and strengthening the constituent
monasteries against hostile forces.

Columba's Life, the stories which circulated by word of mouth before
Adomnán wrote and the *Amra* poem all spread his fame and popularised the
type of Irish monasticism practised so effectively on Iona, and his own lifestyle
popularised pilgrimage and white martyrdom. Mission to non-believers was
no part of it but the journeying from the homeland to alien places inevitably
did have a stimulating effect and led to missionary enterprise. Through his
confident understanding of Scripture and his prophetic gifts, Columba spoke
with power. This tradition of unhesitating decision-making, the discerning of
spirits and the fearless denunciation of error became part of the Irish tradition
and were subsequently carried into the mission field. Iona firmly linked asceticism and scholarship and this was the keynote of Irish monasticism, a magnet
drawing men to Ireland and a potent force in journeys abroad. Iona was not
isolated. In this epoch of frail and slow land transport, water united rather than
divided and there was regular traffic sustained by experienced seamen capable
of dealing with the dangerous currents of Hebridean waters. The Life depicts
Columba on diplomatic journeys; of royal descent, he moved easily among
kings. He was a friend of Rydderch ap Tudwal, Christian ruler of Dumbarton,[45]
and, as Isaac blessed Jacob, he laid hands in blessing on Áedán mac Gabráin,
king of Dál Riata,[46] and played a role in 'the conference of the kings' at Druim
Cett in Ireland between Áedán and Áed mac Ainmirech of his own house, the

[45] *Adomnán* I 15
[46] III 5; D. Woods, 'Four notes on Adomnán's *Vita Columbae*', *Peritia* 16 (2002) 40–67 at
62–7

Uí Néill.[47] Adomnán misunderstood this blessing of Áedán, which he interpreted as an 'ordination' as king whereas Columba never intended to take such
power over the secular world. It is, however, reasonable to suppose that he
negotiated the gift of Iona with the king of Dál Riata from a position of
strength, when his kin were in ascendancy in Ireland and Dál Riata weakened
by a Pictish attack. Annals recorded of Conall that he had given Iona 'as an
offering',[48] i.e. a pious benefaction to a monastic founder, but it would have
been impolitic to refuse Columba's request.

As abbot, Columba travelled widely along the west coast of Scotland as far
as Skye through Pictish territories where he met a monster on Loch Ness which
had already killed a man. He lured it out by setting his companions to swim
across the loch, then with a word of command and the sign of the cross caused
it to flee 'so fast one might have thought it was pulled back with ropes'.[49]
Watching pagans were moved by the evident power of Columba's God.
Adomnán and his monks would have put no limits on the miracles their saint
could perform: the world was divinely ordered and Columba, among the
greatest of saints, could call on divine power as the prophets and apostles had
done. One of Adomnán's most striking passages, marked by vivid and extravagant folklore features, records a journey to the fortress of Bruide near
Inverness. The reader is taken further away from the relatively sober reminiscences of Iona's monks on to pagan territory where Columba faces a situation
comparable to that which Sulpicius records of St Martin: the whole atmosphere
is marked by intense supernatural conflict. Outside the fortress, he said vespers
with his companions but was harassed by 'wizards' who were confounded
through the saint's chanting of Psalm 45, his voice 'miraculously lifted up in the
air like some terrible thunder',[50] and Bruide and his people were filled with fear.
Columba forced his way in, causing the gates to open by making the sign of the
cross.[51] In Bruide's presence, he requested the release of an Irish slave girl but
when the wizard Broíchán refused, Columba prophesied his death. On his
journey home, he learned by his prophetic insight that Broíchán had been
struck by an angel and was struggling for breath, so, when two horsemen
caught him up with the promise that the slave girl would be released, Columba

---

[47] *Adomnán* II 6
[48] Sharpe, *Adomnán* 16
[49] *Adomnán* II 27
[50] I 37. On miracles, Herbert, *Iona* 140–2; D.W. Rollason, 'Columba', *LMA* notes folklore
parallels
[51] *Adomnán* II 35

sent a white healing stone to be immersed in water. Broíchán drank, was cured
and his slave girl released. But Broíchán's fight against Columba was not
finished and he called down mist and storm for Columba's journey home.
Columba defied him and sailed; the natural phenomena dissipated.[52]

In dramatic contests with pagan representatives, Columba never fails and
paganism is humiliated, confounded with miraculous power, yet we are not
told that Bruide was converted and baptised. Had he been, it would surely not
have been hidden from Adomnán and his circle. It seems likely that this was
one of Columba's diplomatic missions designed to obtain safe conduct and
security for Christians within Bruide's lands, though Bede took a contrary
view and believed that he was indeed converted. What Columba did achieve
was to establish a freedom of action for the monks and evangelists who set
about the conversion of the Picts both in his own lifetime and afterwards.[53]

Pictland in the seventh century was part pagan, part Christian. The last of
the British groups or kingdoms in northern Britain to accept Christianity, the
Picts had long lived in comparative isolation. They were originally of the same
stock as other British peoples but the effect of their isolation had been to set
their language in channels of development distinct from the Brittonic of their
neighbours to the west and south and in Wales and Cumbria. A profound
divergence emerged within the period of Roman occupation, so that by
Columba's day a Brittonic speaker would not have been able to understand
Pictish. The problems of the historian investigating Pictish history are
compounded by the near-disappearance of the language and its literature, lost
in a takeover from the ninth century onwards by the Irish (Scotti) of Dál
Riata; there is just a sufficient residue to make plain that the Picts had originally spoken the same language as the rest of the British and were not
intruders who spoke some non-Indo-European tongue.

Isolation had the effect that evangelisation proceeded slowly and piecemeal, in ways not easily recoverable. Adomnán implies as much in the stories
he recounts of Columba's journeys; by Loch Ness, in consequence of a vision
in which he saw angels waiting to receive the soul of an old man, pagan but of

---

[52] *Adomnán* II 33 (Bróichán); II 53 (mist)
[53] I have not accepted arguments of Charles-Edwards, *Ireland* 299–308 in favour of
Columba baptising Bruide: although *Amra* supports this, *Adomnán* omits all mention. See
also K. Hughes, *Early Christianity in Pictland* (Jarrow Lecture 1970), modified in her
'Where are the writings of early Scotland?', D. Dumville ed., *Celtic Britain in the early
Middle Ages* (Woodbridge 1980) 1–21; T. Clancy and B. Crawford, 'The formation of the
Scottish kingdom', R.A. Houston, W.W.J. Knox eds, *The new Penguin history of Scotland*
(New York 2001) 28–95 at 48

a good life, Columba preached and baptised this Emchath, his son and household.[54] In another episode, a whole household 'heard the word of life' and was baptised, a prelude to a miracle in which, like Elisha, Columba brought a son back from the dead. Again, Artbranan, an old warrior of good life, evidently Pictish since Columba had to use an interpreter, was brought to hear the saint on Skye and then was baptised; he died soon afterwards and was buried by the seashore. Irish scholars and writers were particularly aware of the good life of some pagans and admitted them to salvation:[55] the references to good pagans in Adomnán have echoes of this Irish way of thinking. We do not read of Columba addressing and converting mass audiences: he confounds wizards in trials of strength but he brings the word of life to individuals.

Similar episodes involving lesser-known evangelists or casual family contacts leading to a kind of osmotic spread of Christianity will certainly have occurred both before and after Columba. That Christianity had made an impact in the upper echelons of Pictish society is illustrated by the career of Prince Eanfrith. When Aethelfrith died in battle at the hand of Redwald in 617, his sons were exiled; Oswald and Oswiu fled to Dál Riata and were instructed and converted in Iona, while Eanfrith, the eldest, took refuge with the Picts, married a Pictish princess and accepted Christianity. It is fair to say, however, that when he returned to Northumbria as king, he found it politic to shed his Christianity and revert to paganism. He was defeated and killed within a year, a just punishment, in Bede's eyes, for his apostasy.[56]

The earliest beginnings of Christianity in Pictland, however, are hard to elucidate. Long-cist cemeteries without grave goods, with the dead in extended inhumation in coffins made of stones along the sides, top and base of the grave, lying in open countryside and unassimilated to a chapel, may represent an early, pre-Columban Christian presence. Not easily distinguishable from prehistoric burials – which tend to exist in smaller units – they nevertheless may represent the phase before Christian burials came to be associated with church buildings and such cemeteries are to be found north and south of the Forth in both Pictish and non-Pictish areas, with carbon datings suggesting a sixth-century origin.[57]

---

[54] *Adomnán* III 14
[55] II 32 (healing of son); I 53 (Artbranan); M. Richter, *Ireland and her neighbours in the seventh century* (Dublin 1999) 35–7; Romans II 14
[56] *HE* III 1
[57] See I. Smith, 'Origins', J. Blair, C. Pyrah eds, *Church archaeology* (London 1996) 18–42; Yorke, *Conversion* 128–33 perceptive re Picts

As we have seen, revision on Ninian/Uinniau uncovering his evangelising and teaching activities in western Scotland and Ireland leaves him little time for impact in Pictland as well, though some contact by him or his associates cannot be excluded. A fair conclusion will be that there was no one major evangelist for the Picts. Place-names give some clues. *Ecclesia* would have been the term used for church by the Christians of Roman Britain; it occasionally survives in southern Britain in areas dominated by Anglo-Saxon vernacular, as in Eccles near Aylesford in Kent. Transmuted, it was used as a place-name element in languages derived from Brittonic, Welsh, Cornish and Cumbrian. When we meet *egles* place-names in Pictish territory, there is therefore a presumption that they emerged as a result of immigration or evangelisation by Brittonic speakers. With few exceptions, *egles* place-name elements lie in southern and eastern Scotland, northward from East Lothian, Lanarkshire and from Renfrewshire up to Aberdeen, and a significant number of these show 'archaic, fugitive or obsolescent features', precisely what is to be expected from the linguistic history of Pictland, in which the original Pictish was overlaid by the language of its conquerors from Dál Riata. The Brittonic names were, so to speak, preserved as flotsam in a current of Irish-derived names.[58]

Another strand in the place-name evidence is of Gaelic origin, which carries us to Dál Riata and its Irish population or to Ireland itself. The *Annals of Ulster* note that Atholl means New Ireland; its appearance under the entries for 739 suggests peaceful immigration and with it the coming of Christians, settlers or evangelists, in the late seventh and early eighth centuries, well before the forcible takeover of Pictland by Dál Riata's rulers. Atholl is accessible from Dál Riata, lying as it does at the eastern end of a crossing point of the Druim Alban. Adomnán mentions that there were Columban monasteries in Pictland in the 680s and Atholl may well have housed one: Columba's intervention in Inverness could have been intended to ensure they were not subject to harassment. Logierait, a secular and ecclesiastical centre in Atholl, is very likely to have contained in its original form the name of St Coeddi, bishop of Iona, who died in 712; in close proximity are a number of *cill* place-names, *cill* being the Irish-Gaelic term for church, betraying the presence of Gaelic-speaking churchmen. An intriguing aspect of the place-name structure within Atholl is the absence of names which commemorate

---

[58] G.W.S. Barrow, 'The childhood of Scottish Christianity: a note on some place-name evidence', *SHR* 27 (1983) 1–15

Columba.[59] There is only one Columba dedication and that, as one would expect, is at what is now the cathedral church of Dunkeld, which acquired relics of Columba in the ninth century. By contrast, there are seven or eight place-names incorporating Adomnán. He was on close terms with a king of the Picts, Bruide mac Derile, and the dedications can be seen as a tribute to the work of Christianisation both of himself and his associates during his long tenure as abbot of Iona. The continuing contact between Iona and Pictland is shown by the fact that the activities of Pictish rulers were being recorded in Ionan Annals from the 630s. Columba laid foundations: his Ionan family built on them.

A number of *cill* names suggest that another site of a Columban monastery in Pictland lay at Kinrimonth, later St Andrews. The *Annals of Ulster* record the death in 747 of the abbot of Kinrimonth, originally Cinnrigmonaid, who had an Irish name. Other place-names which include the names of abbots of Iona, Baíthéne, Laisrán and Cumméne reflect the presence either of these men and their followers or of churchmen who revered them, and give more evidence of the Ionan influence playing on the Picts. The appearance of place-names including Baíthéne on the Lammermuir Hills route carrying travellers from Iona down towards Lindisfarne offers the possibility of Ionan contacts with pagan Anglo-Saxon Northumbria before King Oswald came to power and called in a mission from Iona.[60]

Both is a little-known place-name element, much less frequent than *cill* and in certain cases having a religious significance. The term derives either from Brittonic or Pictish and a number of place-names which include it witness to Christian influence from churchmen speaking these languages. Evidence of Pictish participation in the work of Christianisation comes from the foundation legend of the Book of Deer, the record of a twelfth-century Cistercian monastery in Buchan; the house came to be associated with Columba but early grants were noted as being made to 'God and St Drostan'. Place-names including Drostan are to be found across much of north-east Scotland; the evidence suggests a Pictish churchman whose cult was supported by Picts and who may have had the centre of his work in northern Aberdour. St Nechtan Ner or Nathalon, who died in 679, is another Pictish saint, dimly glimpsed in the sources, whose name is incorporated in the name of a medieval parish at Fetternear.[61]

---

[59] S. Taylor, 'Place-names and the early Church in eastern Scotland', B.E. Crawford ed., *Scotland in Dark Age Britain* (St John's House Papers 6, St Andrews 1996) 93–110

[60] S. Taylor, 'Seventh century Iona abbots in Scottish place-names', *IR* 48 (1997) 45–72

[61] T.O. Clancy, 'Scottish saints and national identities', A. Thacker, R. Sharpe eds, *Local saints and local churches in the early medieval west* (Oxford 2002) 397–421 at 414–15

St Servan can also be claimed as one of the select band of Pictish saints, but all credible details have been lost, submerged by the fantasies of a medieval Life, which, like Rhigyfarch's Life of St David, stretches the imagination of its readers with such wild tales as Servan's election as pope. We are left with the bare name, Servan, and evidence that he lived in the late seventh century and may have had a significant role in history as a possible leader of the Pictish ecclesiastical reaction against Northumbria in the aftermath of the overwhelming victory of the Pictish army against King Ecgfrith at Nechtanesmere in 685. British, Irish and indigenous elements all played a part in the spread of Christianity in Pictland.[62]

Mission work by others who were independent of the Ionan family has tended to be overshadowed by the great reputation of Columba. But Ireland and its devoted monks continued to have their effect in Britain. To judge by dedications to him in place-names in Kintyre, Arran, Wigtonshire and Ayrshire, St Donnán of Eigg began his career of evangelisation in southwestern Scotland before moving to a sphere of influence northward from that of Iona and Dál Riata. He founded a monastery on the island of Eigg, south of Skye; dedications to him elsewhere in the Hebrides on Skye, South Uist and Lewis and on Wester Ross reflect his and his associates' activities and his influence seems also to have extended deeper into Pictland, into Sutherland and Caithness.[63]

The greatest sacrifice of all evangelists in Britain was made by St Donnán and his community on the island of Eigg, for its location lying beyond the sphere of the authority of the kings of Dál Riata left them without protection. Unfortunately no *Vita* has survived and we are dependent on Irish sources for details of his Passion. The oldest source, the *Annals of Ulster*, says that the community was burned to death: the *Annals of Leinster* and the *Martyrology of Oengus* do not refer to burning but concur in describing them all together singing their psalms of the day when their enemies arrived. Donnán is quoted as saying, 'Let us go into the refectory so that these men may be able to kill us there where we do our living according to the demands of the body; since as long as we remain where we have done our all to please God, we cannot die; but where we have served the body, we may pay the price of the body.' The *Annals of Leinster* records that fifty-four monks died with Donnán, making no

---

[62] A. Macquarrie, 'Vita sancti Servani: the life of St Serf', *IR* 44 (1993) 122–52
[63] T.O. Clancy, 'St Donnán', *KCC*; A.P. Smyth, 'St Donnán abbot of Eigg', A. Williams *et al.* eds, *A biographical dictionary of Dark Age Britain. England, Scotland and Wales c.500–c.1050* (London 1991)

attempt to flee or to fight, having no defenders to call on. True to their vocation, they submitted to the forces of evil and willingly accepted death.

It is the one case of red martyrdom associated with the long process of conversion in the island of Britain. An addendum to the *Martyrology* attributes responsibility for the attack to a rich and avaricious woman, who was accustomed to graze her sheep on Eigg, resented the monks' presence and set marauding bandits from the sea against them. It is not certain whether the inhabitants of the island were Gaelic or Pictish: if the latter, then a pagan Pictish fear that an Irish-led community represented the beginnings of a takeover by Dál Riata expanding at their expense may well have been a motive.[64] Though these murders in 617 would have been a damper on Christianisation, it was only for a time and Eigg reappears in the records in the eighth century. What the episode does is to throw into relief the importance of the lay power in defending vulnerable churchmen from angry pagans, bandits or vicious neighbours. Patrick knew from experience how dangerous attempts to spread Christianity or to practise it in Ireland could be and it puts into perspective the fears which afflicted St Augustine and his fellow monks as they set out on their journey from Rome to pagan England.

Another Irish evangelist, Mael Ruba from the monastery of Bangor seems to have taken up Donnán's work in the north-west, travelling from Ireland in 671 and, two years later, founding the monastery of Applecross, visible from Skye and only a short distance north of Eigg. He did much to restore Donnán's legacy, living on till 722. He had a lasting cult, with church dedications in Skye, Lorn, Knapdale and elsewhere, broadly parallel with those to St Donnán. But he had the advantage of association with one of the dynasties of Dál Riata, the Cenél Loairn.[65]

In the year Columba died, missionaries from Rome arrived fearfully in Thanet. Their petition from Gaul to be released from the task of confronting Kent's pagan Germanic inhabitants had been rejected. In the event they had the protection of a capable and determined ruler and they survived. Nevertheless the Donnán episode shows that their fears were far from baseless.

---

[64] Sharpe, *Adomnán* 368–9 following A. O'Sullivan ed., *The Book of Leinster VI* (Dublin 1983) 1688; see also S. Macairt, G. MacNiocaill, *Annals of Ulster* (Dublin 1983) 109; comment, Smyth, *Warlords* 107–11

[65] D. Maclean, 'Maelrubai, Applecross and the late Pictish contribution west of Druimalban', D. Henry ed., *The worm, the germ and the thorn* (Balgavies 1997) 173–87

CHAPTER 5

The Mission from Rome

Folk tradition had it that Gregory the Great's mission to convert the Anglo-Saxons began in the slave market at Rome when, before his pontificate, he happened to see some boys from the kingdom of Northumbria 'fair-skinned and light-haired'; curious about their appearance, he asked what race they belonged to. The primitive Life of Gregory written over a century later by an inmate of the monastery at Whitby records a crisp, punning dialogue: 'the people we belong to are called Anguli'; 'Angels of God,' replied Gregory. Then he asked who their king was: 'Aelli,' they replied. 'Alleluia' Gregory responded, 'God's praise must be heard there.' His final question asked the name of their own tribe, 'to which they answered 'Deira'. 'They shall flee "de ira dei" from the wrath of God,' said Gregory, 'to the faith.'[1]

There are oddities in the story. Gregory is described as being so moved by the boys' appearance and answers that he obtained permission from his predecessor, Pope Benedict, to set off in person on a conversion mission and was only prevented by the Roman crowd's fierce objections made to the pope. Benedict was not Gregory's predecessor and it is highly unlikely that he determined there and then to set off in person. But Aelle was king of Deira. The incessant wars did lead to the defeated being enslaved; there is nothing impossible in Northumbrian youths being taken to the slave market in Rome.

For all its awkwardness, the anonymous Whitby Life includes facts not generally known, such as the name of Gregory's mother: it tapped authentic traditions and is not simply an assemblage of passages from well-known works. The antitheses Anguli – Angeli, Aelli – Alleluia, Deira – De ira would act as mnemonics to preserve the story over generations. Anglo-Saxons loved

---

[1] B. Colgrave ed., *The earliest Life of Gregory the Great by an anonymous monk of Whitby* (Cambridge 1968) 91; *HE* II 1

puns and word-play and so did Gregory. Angli could turn easily into Anguli. In a triumphant letter of 598 to the bishop of Alexandria alluding to progress made in the Anglo-Saxon mission, he makes play with the name Angli and the Latin *angulum* (corner), writing of the Angles (*gens Anglorum*) lying in a corner of the world (*in mundi angulo posita*) and in his *Moralia in Job* refers to the language of Britain now incorporating the Hebrew Alleluia.

The little story, taken up from the Whitby Life and made famous by Bede, is more likely than not to be authentic and to be one of the spurs to Gregory's action. We know Anglian slaves were in his mind in 595 when in September he issued instructions to Candidus, rector of the papal patrimony in Gaul, to tap papal revenues in order to buy clothes for the poor and to obtain Anglian slaves. He was aware they would be heathen and, with a characteristic pastoral concern, asked Candidus to ensure that priests travelled with them so that should they fall ill they could be baptised before death. It is assumed they would become Christians but there is no sign that he envisaged their returning to their own land; they were to be put in monasteries in Gaul, probably to act as servants to the monks. Nevertheless, it shows that the heathen English were on the pope's mind at this date.

By this time, Palladius's mission had long disappeared into the shadows; the possibility of papal influence across the seas had gone with the Anglo-Saxon invasions. But there was a new opportunity to use papal power in Gregory's day. From early days in the pontificate, he was much concerned with the Frankish Church and its weaknesses; he had become knowledgeable about the Franks and in the formidable Visigoth princess Brunhild, widow of the Merovingian king Sigeberht and at the critical time regent for her grandchildren Theoderic, king of Burgundy and Theodebert II, king of Austrasia, he had a determined supporter driven both by a vein of piety and by political calculation that patronage of a successful mission to the heathen Anglo-Saxons would give prestige to her regency and reinforce her position against her Frankish rivals.[2]

[2] M. Richter, 'Bede's *Angli*: angels or English?', *Peritia* 3 (1984) 99–114 on the slave market preferred to I. Wood, 'The mission of Augustine of Canterbury to the English', *Speculum* 69 (1994) 1–17 at 2; Candidus, N. Higham, *The convert kings* (Manchester 1997) 65–6; mission, R. Gameson ed., *St Augustine and the conversion of England* (Stroud 1999); Gregory, R.A. Markus, *Gregory the Great and his world* (Cambridge 1997); H. Mayr-Harting, *The coming of Christianity to Anglo-Saxon England* (London 1972; 3rd edn 1991) wise perspective, illuminating on Gregory, 51–64; B. Yorke, *The conversion of Britain. Religion, politics and society in Britain c.600–800* (Harlow 2006), 98–136 wide-ranging analytical chapter, excellent bibliography; Higham, *Convert kings* challenges Bede's ecclesiastical interpretation and stresses Aethelberht's secular motivation re Frankish events; R.A. Fletcher, *The conversion of Europe* (London 1977) short account with verve, 110–19

In a letter of July 596, Gregory alludes to 'the desire of the English nation' for conversion and states that it had been neglected by priests from the vicinity (*sacerdotes e vicino*) who had not attempted conversion. The implication is that he had originally wanted a Frankish mission, its priesthood and episcopate lying close at hand and having contacts and interpreters, but it had never got off the ground. So in the end he was led to take the unusual step of sending out a mission himself.[3]

One of the greatest of popes, combining political acumen and acute powers of government with a deep spirituality, Gregory was a man of Rome, where he was born and had served as prefect, later becoming secretary to Pope Pelagius II. He was well aware that the island of Britain had once been part of the Roman Empire. His vision of Empire was that of the emperor Theodosius, for whom Christianity was *tout court* the religion of the Empire to be imposed on all its subjects, and this gave impetus to a mission designed to recover a Christian imperial heritage. Most important of all, Gregory believed passionately in the duty to convert, to spread the Gospel and to bring to the faith the heathen, the backsliders, the idolators and infidels wherever they might be found, a belief given urgency by his sense of the imminent coming of the end of the world and of the Day of Judgment. Gregory's passion for souls was the most important single factor behind the sending of a mission to England.

The exact occasion for its dispatch will always be hidden from us. Kent was the nearest kingdom to Francia and the one most influenced by Frankish culture, and it had a Christian queen, Bertha. She had been an orphan princess of low status in the marriage market, daughter of Charibert I, king of Paris, who died in 567 when she was about five years old. Her uncle Chilperic I is most likely to have been her sponsor in arranging the marriage to the pagan prince Aethelberht, which took place when they were both about eighteen. They lived under the authority of Aethelberht's father, the pagan King Eormenric, a name not indigenous to Kent, but Frankish, suggesting some closer link to the Frankish world in the Kentish royal house than has hitherto appeared. But no whisper of sympathy towards the rival Christianity has reached us from Eormenric's court.

The marriage arrangements made stipulations about Bertha's religious rights. She was to have freedom of worship and she was to include in her entourage a bishop, Liudhard, to serve her and her followers. Was the sending

---

[3] Magisterial analysis, C.E. Stancliffe, 'The British Church and the mission of Augustine', Gameson, *Augustine* 107–51. Her interpretation of 'sacerdotes e vicino' meaning British rather than Franks has not won acceptance; dating of the *Moralia in Job* has implications for T.M. Charles-Edwards's interpretation in D.N. Dumville, *Saint Patrick, A.D. 493–1993* (Woodbridge, Suffolk, 1993) 11–12

of a bishop simply a tribute to the Merovingian connection or was the arrangement designed to provide a foothold for a future advance of Christianity in a pagan land, combined with an intensification of Frankish influence? Liudhard remains mysterious. We have a glimpse of him on a gold coin or medalet found in the nineteenth century in the graveyard of St Martin's church in Canterbury together with sixth-century continental coins, looped for suspension as for a necklace, part, no doubt, of an assemblage of grave goods for a pious woman of the court circle. It was evidently struck by an inexperienced moneyer, thus in Kent rather than Gaul, where moneying skills were high. On the obverse, Liudhard is depicted full face with diadem in the style of an emperor's bust; the reverse has the symbol of the True Cross at Jerusalem, a wreathed double-barred cross on a rounded base in the style of a relief on a reliquary from the Holy Cross convent at Poitiers founded by St Radegund, nun and quondam queen, stepmother to Bertha's father, Charibert. Faulty technique has led to the inscription 'Leudardus Episcopus' being placed retrograde, i.e. running from right to left. Probably struck as Easter money to be distributed at the feast, the coin encourages Liudhard's little flock in Canterbury by associating its leader with the most powerful symbol of Christianity, the cross blossoming into the Tree of Life, incorporating thereby a delicate allusion to a holy kinswoman of Bertha, the bishop's patron. It is an affirmation that here a Christian Church is in being in a predominantly pagan environment, with its cross and the promise of life, its bishop and its link to the Christian world of Gaul.[4] In other words, as long as Eormenric was alive, Bertha presided for years over a small enclave of Christians, mainly her own following and attendants, possibly Frankish visitors and, it may be, stray surviving British Christians, worshipping under Liudhard's direction at a cemetery church, restored from the Roman past and a short distance east of the walls of Eormenric's capital, Canterbury, which, following the traditions of her ancestral house, Bertha dedicated to St Martin of Tours, in which city her sister served long as a nun.[5]

[4] M. Werner, 'The Liudhard medalet', *ASE* 20 (1991) 27–41; Bertha and Gregory, C. Nolte, *Conversio und Christianitas. Frauen in der Christianisierung vom 5. bis 8. Jahrhundert* (Stuttgart 1995) 101–12

[5] Aethelberht's dates, N. Brooks, 'The creation and early structure of the kingdom of Kent', id., *Anglo-Saxon myths: state and Church 400–1066* (London, Rio-Grande 2000) 33–60 at 48; background, B. Yorke, 'Gregory of Tours and sixth century Anglo-Saxon England', K. Mitchell, I. Wood eds, *The world of Gregory of Tours* (Leiden 2002) 113–30; whole context, B. Yorke, 'The adaptation of the royal courts to Christianity', M. Carver ed., *The cross goes north: processes of conversion in northern Europe, AD 300–1300* (York 2003) 243–58; Eormenric still ruling 589? B. Yorke, *Kings and kingdoms of early Anglo-Saxon England* (London 1990) 28

Whatever the intentions of those who originally dispatched Bertha and Liudhard to Kent, there was scant opportunity for any expansion of Christianity in these confined circumstances; Eormenric was a crucial barrier only lifted when Aethelberht became king. Whether he was the eldest son we do not know but even if he was, he would have had no automatic succession and, as was general in this epoch, would expect insecure years before he had fully established his authority. By the 590s he was making his power felt outside Kent and was in a position to risk the dangers of going over to Christianity. Bede confused Aethelberht's dates, giving him a reign of fifty-six years – a figure much more likely to represent his age at death – which has given rise to the erroneous conclusion that Aethelberht had many years in power before he ventured on his Christian project.

Liudhard is never mentioned in Gregory's correspondence; it seems likely that he had died before Gregory's plan took shape. Perhaps Candidus's mediation or Bertha's contacting her relatives was responsible for the news of the desire of the 'English nation' for conversion but she is unlikely to have acted without Aethelberht's consent. He would have seen Christianity as a Frankish religion and on political grounds would have preferred a mission from Italy rather than Francia, as it might have carried implications of overlordship.

The rise of Childebert of Austrasia and Burgundy represented a major shift in the Frankish constellation of power, especially after 593, rendering links with rival Frankish powers originally associated with Bertha no longer advantageous. The fact that Gregory's scheme was backed by Childebert and his mother Brunhild's western Franks might have appealed to Aethelberht on grounds of secular advantage, but, whatever the source of the desire for conversion reported to Gregory, it was not a powerful signal, for the pope himself did not put his full trust in it and dispatched a mission that was in the first instance reconnaissance.[6]

For the missionaries, he used monks from his own foundation, the monastery of St Andrew on the Coelian Hill. Monks were under obedience, accustomed to a life of austerity and abnegation, had freedom from the ties of marriage, children and relatives and from local clerical loyalties. They could also be expected to have scriptural proficiency, which Gregory believed to be an especially important factor in the mission field. He appointed as leader the prior of the monastery, Augustine, known to him personally, who had experience of command in the monastery. Gregory himself knew nothing of the

[6] P.H. Blair, *The world of Bede* (London 1970) 42, 54–6; Higham, *Convert kings* 86–90

Anglo-Saxons or their customs and his correspondence at the outset made no mention of what would now be described as missionary technique and allowed no provision for interpreters. The monks were setting off into unknown territory, with no knowledge of the people they were attempting to convert, whom they thought of as a 'barbarous, fierce, and unbelieving nation'.[7]

On the way, morale broke and they sent back Augustine with the request to be allowed to abandon the project. The pope would have none of it, urged on them the importance of their work and their heavenly reward, but he raised the status of Augustine to abbot, thereby giving him an authority demanding obedience and sent on letters commending the party to the protection of bishops on their journey and to secular rulers such as Brunhild and her grandchildren and asking for interpreters. Obediently, the mission moved on, incidentally fulfilling the pope's wish of reminding the often worldly ecclesiastics they met en route of papal authority and the necessity to respect the papal patrimony.

Some forty strong, they arrived in England in the spring or early summer of 597. The party presumably included Frankish priests as interpreters, though these Bede does not mention, concerned as he was to stress the Italian and papal aspect of the mission. They arrived in Thanet, then a true island cut off from the mainland by the channel of the Wantsum, remaining in a kind of diplomatic limbo till the king came out to meet them. Aethelberht showed himself cautious and diplomatic; significantly, he prudently brought with him the great men of the kingdom whose concurrence would be necessary if the new religion were eventually to be adopted. The tradition which reached Bede was that the king required the meeting with the incoming foreigners to take place in the open air for he feared they might practise magic against him.

There is a simpler explanation. Thunoreshlaew (Thunor's mound) recalls a site of heathen cult on Thanet. The peace of a god extended beyond the place of worship, quite possibly to nearby dwellings and it was a dangerous business to breach that peace. Well aware of pagan sympathies among his aristocracy, Aethelberht, interviewing at a distance in the open air, was playing safe. Caution, too, marked his response at the end of the conference: these were new and uncertain doctrines and he could not suddenly give up the beliefs of his ancestors, but he wished to hear more, he said, and he invited

---

[7] *HE* I 23; R.A. Markus, 'Augustine and Gregory the Great', Gameson, *Augustine* 41–9; L.E. von Padberg, *Mission und Christianisierung. Formen und Folgen bei Angelsachsen und Franken im 7. und 8. Jahrhundert* (Stuttgart 1995) analysis of missionary action and effects in England and on continent

Augustine and his party to his capital, Canterbury, providing them with his protection, residence, provisions and freedom to preach – no small commitment.[8]

Augustine had a capacity for drama.[9] A procession went into Aethelberht's city headed by a priest carrying a silver processional cross, accompanied by another carrying an image of Christ on a board, all singing 'Deprecamur Domini', an antiphon from a Rogation Litany current in Gaul: 'We beseech Thee, O Lord, in Thy great mercy that Thy wrath and anger may be turned away from this city and from Thy holy house, for we have sinned.' The procession echoed the open-air litanies of Rome, the language of the Church and of continental civilisation. The processional cross with its silver and precious stones did honour to Christ but also represented to the Kentings the wealth and power of this continental belief. The cross had become the classic remedy against the demons, which the Christian mission would have believed had their base in the temples of the pagan kingdom whose capital they were entering: it was their protection. The figure of Christ on a board sounds like a Byzantine icon, and perhaps was a Western imitation, but it instantly pointed up the contrast between Christianity and Germanic paganism which did not have representational art.

It was a memorable scene. For monks, whose lives in a monastic house were shaped by the liturgy, memory of the procession, the antiphon, the image of Christ and the ceremonial cross is likely to have lived on in oral tradition in Augustine's monastery, even down to Bede's recording of the occasion well over a century later.[10]

At first, Augustine's group used St Martin's church for their services. They lived simply, holding goods in common, which reminded Bede of the early community of Christians described in the fourth chapter of the Acts of the Apostles. They had the king's support and made converts. Soon it was clear that the reconnaissance had been successful, that there was a basis for a Church which would expand and be something more than a bridgehead in alien territory. Augustine needed to be more than an abbot and travelled to the continent to be consecrated bishop, probably by Syagrius, bishop of Autun, the supporter of Brunhild, together with bishops from Austrasia and Burgundy.

[8] *HE* I 25; Thunor's cult centre, Padberg, *Mission* 109
[9] Higham, *Convert kings* 60 and n. 34
[10] Wood's scepticism on antiphon not accepted, 'The mission', *Speculum* 69 (1994) 3; it was Gaulish, appropriate and readily picked up on journey

In 598 Gregory was rejoicing over a river baptism, allegedly of 10,000 souls, which took place at Christmas 597. Curiously, the date of Aethelberht's own baptism has been lost. It was a step he must have taken, for Gregory later welcomed him to the rank of Catholic kings and held up to him the example of Constantine, who enjoyed both material and spiritual rewards.

Aethelberht showed his support for Augustine and his followers by granting them a better residence, and allowing them to take over a ruined Romano-British church which Augustine dedicated to Christ the Holy Saviour in imitation of the Lateran Basilica in Rome and made his cathedral, a far cry from the confined existence of Liudhard's little group. Aethelberht could easily grant these endowments because land lay idle or had reverted to scrub or water meadows within the walls of Roman Durovernum, now Cantwaraburh, the borough of the men of Kent. Population had shrunk as the infrastructure of Roman Britain was lost, conditions for far-flung trade and specialist industrial production had ebbed away and the villa-dwelling elite had vanished. Parts of the city had been abandoned; the outer walls and a ruined amphitheatre remained and four or five of the Roman gateways were still in use. But the Roman street plan had been obscured as primitive wooden huts with sunken floors (*Grubenhäuser*) cut across the line of Roman streets. There was space left for Aethelberht to be generous, and he was.[11]

Augustine's mission brought back the lost Roman art of building in stone, in the process reinforcing Christian prestige. Outside the walls a monastery arose dedicated to St Peter and Paul, with a church cum burial place. Aethelberht gave special attention to this, for it was designed to take the bodies of himself and his queen. The dedication was significant; it was the same as the Lateran Basilica, the pope's cathedral, and the monastery recalled the great shrine churches of Peter and Paul in Rome. Contemporary popes were buried outside the Aurelian walls; archbishops of Canterbury would be buried outside the walls of Canterbury. Archbishops, kings and queens came to be buried together; it was a vivid realisation of their interdependence in the first age of conversion.

Augustine and his men were recalling the ecclesiastical topography of the Rome they had once lived in and that most of them would never see again: there remained a deep attachment to the papacy and to Rome, its liturgy, its practices and its saints. But not only the Rome of the popes influenced the Anglo-Saxon scene; from the early seventh century, the burial sites of aristocratic Christian women reveal the adoption of Roman-inspired fashion which

[11] N. Brooks, *The early history of the Church of Canterbury* (Leicester 1984) 16–22

abandoned the double brooches securing garments at the shoulders of pre-Christian days and took to necklaces, often with a cross at their centre, and Roman-style dresses, derived possibly from Frankish aristocratic circles. It was a fashion with the highest prestige: the mosaics at San Vitale in Ravenna show the Empress Theodora and her attendants clothed and adorned in this style, and the chasuble of St Balthild, Anglo-Saxon slave girl who became the queen of Clovis II, ruler of Neustria, then abbess of Chelles, has embroidered on it the representation of a necklace with a pendant cross. The change of fashion both followed on the conversion of Kent and gave prestige to the new religion.[12]

Aethelberht promulgated a code of laws in the vernacular 'iuxta exempla Romanorum' (after the fashion of the Romans) in the words of Bede. However, the code owed nothing to Roman law; it is wholly Germanic, putting into writing an ancient oral inheritance, the law of the community; Bede's phrase means that, by setting out this law-code, Aethelberht was putting himself and his Kentings on a level with those civilised peoples, such as the Franks and Romans, who lived by law and issued such codes. What precise role Augustine and, it may be, Frankish priests in his entourage played in the writing of the code cannot now be established: one may say that without the presence of literate churchmen, an orthography for its wording could not have been achieved as hitherto the language could only have been written in runes. The clergy might well have expected to assist in writing in the language of civilisation, Latin, as was the case in other codes such as those of the Franks or Visigoths, and it is natural to see Aethelberht's hand in the decision to promulgate the laws in Germanic vernacular. Though the text we have, the *Textus Roffensis*, dates from the twelfth century, the simplicity of sentence construction, the linguistic differences between Kentish dialect and the West Saxon which became the basis of standard Old English, and the recurrent archaisms reassure us that we have before us the work of Aethelberht, Augustine and his clerical colleagues.[13]

---

[12] A. Thacker, 'In search of saints: the English Church and the cult of Roman apostles and martyrs in the seventh and eighth centuries', J.M.H. Smith ed., *Early medieval Rome and the Christian West* (Leiden 2000) 221–47; A. Thacker, 'The making of a local saint', A. Thacker, R. Sharpe eds, *Local saints and local churches in the early medieval West* (Oxford 2002) 45–73; N. Brooks, 'Canterbury, Rome and the construction of an English identity', Smith, *Rome* 221–47

[13] P. Lendinara, 'The Kentish laws', J. Hines ed., *The Anglo-Saxons from the migration period to the eighth century* (Woodbridge 1997) 211–30, discussion, 231–43; definitive analysis L. Oliver, *The beginnings of English law* (Toronto, Buffalo, London 2002) 3–116; P. Wormald, *The making of English law: King Alfred to the twelfth century* I *Legislation and its limits* (Oxford 1999); J.M. Wallace-Hadrill, *Early Germanic kingship in England and on the continent* (Oxford 1971) learned, pungent and concise

1 Constantine the Great

2 Detail of mosaic at Hinton St Mary: Christ the Saviour is shown with the first letters in Greek of the sacred name, chi rho, and pomegranates, symbolising eternal life.

The Water Newton Treasure

3 The communion vessels and church plate of a congregation, buried close by a major Roman road to the north at the edge of the small town Durobrivae, prominent in pottery manufacture. Votive plaques can be seen at the bottom of the picture.

4 This silver bowl was given by two women, Innocentia and Viventia, who record their donation along the rim. Two Christian symbols, chi rho and alpha and omega, nestling between the chi's strokes, are inscribed in the centre. Innocentia's name lies on one side of the chi rho while Viventia is inscribed at the rear; the remains of a verb – 'runt' – can also be seen on the rim and are conjectured to be the last letters of 'deterunt', 'they gave' or 'dedicaverunt', 'they dedicated'.

5 This silver votive leaf plaque, of a kind usual in paganism, has a gold chi rho and alpha and omega in a roundel with lines in relief radiating from a central rib.

The Baptismal Tank at Walesby

6 Part of a lead tank, standing one foot seven inches high, was found in a field in Lincolnshire, where it was damaged by a plough. It is decorated with three reverse lunettes and a chi rho and shows a Romano-British baptism in the panel, upper left.

7 The redrawn upper-left panel: a woman, naked except for the robe slipping off her right shoulder, comes to baptism with her companions, with the congregation supporting their new convert. The tank, dismembered in antiquity, was of such a size as to presuppose baptism by affusion.

Memorial Stones from the Celtic West

Stones from Wales show standards rising. A ring cross is awkwardly imposed on Voteporix's inscription while the memorial to Ruiallaun and his son integrates a cross with the Latin in book hand with a reference to the Last Judgement. In Cornwall, a conservative society, the simplest references to the descent of the dead remained the norm.

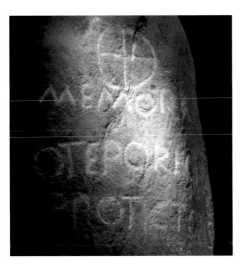

8 Voteporix the Protector is commemorated at Castellwyran near Carmarthen in Latin across the stone and in ogham strokes ascending vertically on the left-hand side of the picture across the arris.

9 *(above)* The King Ruiallaun and his son Ioruerth are remembered in Latin at Llanlywenfel, Brecon: 'In sidone muti Ioruent Ruallainque sepulchres judicii adventum spectant in pace tremendum' – 'In the shroud, silent – Ioruerth and Ruiallaun, in the graves await in peace the dreadful coming of the Judgement'.

10 *(left)* At Fardel, Cornwall, an undressed stone in the most likely interpretation commemorates the Irishman Fanonus son of Maquirinus, both names in the genitive, with a term for 'stone' or 'memorial' implicit. Oghams run vertically up each side of the stone and another Irishman is commemorated in Latin on the back.

The Picts and their Symbols

Finds from Shetland demonstrate that Pictish symbols must have their origin in pre-Christian times. The cross on the Mains of Afforsk boulder marks the coming of Christianity and the emergence of a symbol which on stone slabs comes to dominate Pictish art.

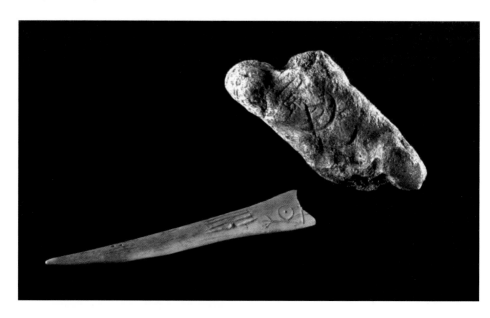

11 (*above*) Bone and bone pin from Pool, Sanday, Shetland incised with Pictish symbols in a context which cannot be later than the sixth century.

12 (*left*) An ogham stone from the Mains of Afforsk, Kemnay, Aberdeenshire bearing the name Necton, which may once have been a boundary marker. A cross has been cut into the upper surface, possibly by the hand of an early Irish missionary.

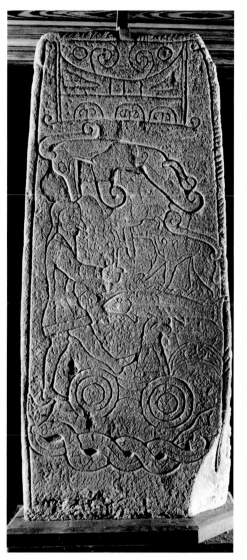 

13 *(left)* At the rear of a cross-stab at Golspie, Sutherland there appears to be an echo of the old paganism. The man, advancing with an implement in his hand, is a mild version of the threatening figure with projecting teeth and an axe hammer visible on stones elsewhere, whose significance, certainly not Christian, is lost to us. On the right of the picture there is an array of Pictish symbols including at the top 'the purse-cover' and below it, the Pictish beast.

14 *(right)* At Raasay, Skye what is probably an early example of a cross-slab has cross-arms like petals.

15 A set of cartoons in the Gospel Books, widely regarded as a book used by St Augustine in Canterbury, illustrates the life and Passion of Christ. At the top left-hand side of the picture is depicted the triumphal entry into Jerusalem and at the bottom right hand Jesus carrying the cross to Golgotha. In the central cartoon at the top, the artist shows the Last Supper.

16 Woden and the Anglo-Saxon warrior: the Finglesham man, a dancing warrior with a Woden head-dress is displayed on a gilt-bronze belt buckle, naked except for head-dress and belt, brandishing spears, buried with a young warrior in a cemetery near Sandwich, Kent.

17 The Sutton Hoo Helmet: dancing warriors in pairs are shown in Woden head-dresses brandishing their spears on panels, together with another scene on different panels, where a cavalryman rides down a victim who stabs his horse from below, on the magnificent parade-ground helmet from the great ship-burial at Sutton Hoo, Suffolk. This replica helmet is made of steel with electrotype panels.

18 The battle of Nechtanesmere: at Aberlemno, Angus in the kirkyard the reverse of a cross-slab shows beneath Pictish symbols, a sequence of battle scenes in which Ecgfrith, the Northumbrian king, on the right hand side of the picture in a distinctive helmet, is worsted by the Pictish king Bridei and his men and ends as a corpse on the battlefield, pecked by a raven, bottom right.

19 The hermits and the bread of life: on the pediment of the cross-slab at Nigg, Ross and Cromarty the Desert Fathers Antony and Paul kneel as a raven carries down the consecrated host to them. A chalice stands on the top of the cross as though on an altar; below, the cross is ornamented with a remarkable array of patterns, knots, interlace and thin, twined animals while the sides of the stone are covered with massive bosses, delicately intertwined with slivers of stone and lesser decoration. The combination of subtle thought in the design and the virtuosity of the craftsmen who carried it through make it one of the masterpieces of Pictish art.

Kingship, Pictish and Anglo-Saxon

Pictish churchmen backed monarchy, bringing order and security in a troubled world. So did Anglo-Saxon churchmen. But a remarkable feature of the Anglo-Saxon world is the emergence of saints within their royal houses. In this the cult of Oswald was a portent.

20 The St Andrews Sarcophagus: part of a magnificent post-shrine for a Pictish king is dominated by the figure of David, larger than life-size, while on the left of the picture a high-ranking cavalryman hunts a lion, a man pursues a deer and a mule has been brought down by a griffin: scenes of violence in an anarchic world, which needs to be mastered by a royal authority.

21 King David: the King of Israel at the height of his powers breaks a lion's jaws with massive bulging hands in high relief. Once a shepherd boy, his past is recalled by a sheepdog above his left shoulder and a ram above his right.

22 St Lachtin's Arm: a twelfth century bronze reliquary with silver and gold inlay gives an impression of the appearance of St Oswald's arm, exhibited for veneration at Bamburgh. The hand is more likely to have been extended in prayer or in blessing than clenched.

St Matthew in Two Versions

The Lindisfarne Gospels, now convincingly dated, have been more touched by Mediterranean art than the Book of Durrow has. Both are profoundly influenced by the emergence of an insular style in Britain.

23 St Matthew, Book of Durrow: the cloak on this stiff schematic figure with its millefiori decoration reveals its debt to the traditions of Irish jewellery. There is a Celtic tonsure.

24 St Matthew, Lindisfarne Gospels: St Matthew, bearded in a Byzantine style, writes his gospel while a mysterious figure peeps out from a tabernacle curtain and a man-angel blows a trumpet, echoing Revelation I, 10–11. He is named 'o agios Mattheus' in Greek, using Roman capitals. The figure looking out from the curtain may be Moses with a tablet of the Law.

25 A cross-carpet page from the St Chad's Gospels: a stylised cross is filled – as are the surrounds on the page – with intricate ornament, loops, spirals and intertwined animals, such pages being known as carpet-pages because of their resemblance to oriental carpets. A practical function is that of a text-divider and a spiritual one that of stimulating the 'ruminatio', contemplating the sacred page and feeding the spiritual life. These Gospels found a home as a result of a benefaction in the church of Llandeilo Fawr.

26 An eighth-century whalebone casket from Northumbria named after the antiquary who discovered it in the nineteenth century in France.

27 The back panel, including two sets of scenes. Titus in a crested helmet assaults Jerusalem. Jews occupy the roof of the Temple, shown as an Ark, then flee the city. Within the sequence of scenes below, the story of Weland the smith, begun on the front panel, is concluded (*see left*), as the wicked King Nithad, enthroned, who lamed and maltreated Weland, holds a cup. Below him the tiny figure of Weland holds another cup, ready to give Nithhad. It is a cup of poison – his revenge. Titus fulfils the prophecy of Jesus; Weland does justice on an evil master.

The Ruthwell Cross

A masterpiece of Northumbrian art in the eighth century, this great cross of red sandstone north of the Solway Firth in the former British territory of Reghed, though marred by weathering and iconoclasm, has a unique combination of Latin, runic verse and scriptural imagery.

28 *(left)* The north side from a drawing of 1833 includes in a sequence passing up the shaft the following major scenes: Christ returning as a baby on Mary's lap from Egypt, Christ in the bread of the Eucharist received by hermits in the desert, Christ adored by beasts, Christ singled out by John the Baptist as the Lamb of God.

29 *(centre)* In one scene from the north side Christ is adored by beasts in the desert, who cross their paws to form the Greek letter chi.

30 *(right)* On the western side there is vinescroll, inhabited by birds and animals and symbolising the Eucharist.

The code is concerned with regulation for warding off the blood feud, a cement in society in which kindred took responsibility for their members' crimes and the community laid down tariffs to compensate a wronged kindred for crimes against its members, removing the ancient requirement to exact vengeance. Elements of alliteration, the methodical enumeration of ranks in society from the top to the bottom, and the *wergilds* which they commanded, the equally methodical setting out of tariffs for personal injury, from the head to the feet, betray the code's origin in an oral tradition held together by the use of mnemonics. Christianity per se plays no part: the fact that there are no injunctions on Sabbath observance, tithe-paying or the keeping of Lent shows that the code was drawn up at an early stage in conversion. The grades of clerical hierarchy are fitted into the pattern of compensations with great generosity. The first clause of all, for example, runs, 'God's property and the Church's with twelve-fold compensation' and the second is hardly less generous, 'A bishop's property with eleven-fold compensation'. These are levels exceeding anything else in the code and are in collision with Gregory's advice to Augustine on theft from churches, which expressed horror at the Church making a profit from theft and expanded on the necessity to distinguish between wilful bandits and the genuinely needy. 'God forbid', he writes, 'that the Church should make a profit out of the earthly things it seems to lose and so seek to gain from such vanities.'[14] Augustine was not responsible for these clauses; with the zeal of a convert, Aethelberht was honouring the Church and churchmen in the one way he knew. The Church had an auxiliary role in these decisions: it was pursuing an aim which recurred over centuries – the attempt to curb revenge and minimise bloodshed.

A more direct action by churchmen is to be inferred from the institution of the Anglo-Saxon charter. Roman land law lay behind this development. The charters were Latin texts, generally on single sheets of parchment recording a grant of land or privileges from a king to a religious house or to an individual, very precisely and formally laid out according to strict conventions. This was of vital importance for the future. The earliest extant examples of charters come from the late seventh century but it is quite likely that they were inaugurated in Aethelberht's time and that the pattern emanated from Augustine and his circle advising the king and, as with the law code, the charters gave documentary backing to his authority. The earliest examples are written in stately uncials of a kind usual in religious texts.

[14] Oliver, *Beginnings* 61; *HE* I 27

The special dependence on Rome and the papacy, which sprang from Gregory's initiative and the personal wishes of Augustine and his team, was a factor in the creation of a new Church based on the support of Aethelberht, his leading men and the kings they assumed he could bend to his view. It was a Church of the English coming into being – and one which incidentally, and perhaps all unconsciously, paid no attention to the surviving British Christians. Gregory's view of the situation in England was simplistic; even before his mission was launched, he referred to 'the English nation' and called Aethelberht the 'king of the English'.[15] All this was wholly to neglect the divisions between ethnic groups from the continent, the volatility of kingdoms and the fighting between kings and contenders for their thrones. Aethelberht, indeed, did hold an overlordship and for a time might exercise persuasion on other kings but he had only a personal authority which in any case did not extend beyond southern England.

In 600–1 the mission moved forward. Augustine felt confident enough to send to Rome two of his leading men, Laurentius, who succeeded him as archbishop of Canterbury, and Peter, later first abbot of the new monastery, to ask for more men and materials, including books, liturgical equipment, vestments and relics. He also asked for advice. The request found Gregory in the summer of 601 in a positive state of mind: he sent men headed by the abbot Mellitus, who proved to be important in the furtherance of mission, and responded to the desire for equipment. Relics might mean cloths laid against the remains of saints, thereby held to receive virtue from them. Books were vital for the conduct of services – he sent 'very many manuscripts', Bede tells us[16] – psalters, commentaries, biblical texts, mass books and devotional reading essential for missionary endeavour and books for the instruction in Latin of Anglo-Saxon boys with whom the future of the priesthood lay.

In his *Cura pastoralis* Gregory stressed the need for the preacher to be supported by the sacred word: he should never cease to set aside time for sacred reading. He should drink first, then give to others to drink from his preaching. One illustrated Gospel book from approximately mid-sixth century, north Italian in provenance and given in 1575 by Archbishop Parker to his Cambridge college, has long been associated with Augustine and probably either travelled with him in 597 or was dispatched with Abbot Mellitus.

---

[15] *HE* I 32; P. Chaplais, 'Who introduced charters into England? The case for Augustine', F. Ranger ed., *Prisca munimenta* (London 1973) 88–107
[16] *HE* I 29

Originally there were miniatures of the four evangelists under arches with scenes from the life of Christ and at least two separate pages of scenes from the Gospels. The portrait of Luke has survived and one of the illuminated pages, arranged as a tailpiece to St Mark's Gospel in the manner of a strip cartoon, has miniature scenes from Christ's Passion, giving us a glimpse of the way in which Augustine and his colleagues would probably have instructed Aethelberht and aristocratic converts, commanding respect for the Christian message with the spectacle of a manuscript book, an object of prestige in an illiterate society and a reminder of the association of literacy with the civilisation of the continent.[17]

A flurry of letters was written in June 601 to accompany Mellitus's party. Gregory also answered in detail questions of Augustine who had sought answers to problems on such matters as a bishop's relationship with his clergy, on offerings, theft from churches and the puzzle of differing liturgies, on the proper procedure for consecrating bishops, given that Augustine was alone and could not readily call on Gaulish bishops to assist him, and on his relationship generally with Gaulish and British bishops; questions on marriage, menstruation and the pagan practice of marrying a stepmother were problems of morality in Germanic life which Augustine, a Roman monk, would be meeting for the first time; others concerned the applicability of Old Testament laws to seventh-century practice.

Gregory's answers were humane, based on a broad understanding of the Bible and episcopal authority. The status of Old Testamental rules on ritual purity was a problem discussed in the Church of Gaul and did not simply represent a fine scruple on Augustine's part; though minor, the other problems were queries natural to a monk suddenly thrust into a leading role in an alien society with an uncertain relationship with the senior, contiguous Church of Gaul. The nature of communication between Canterbury and Rome was such that Augustine cannot have expected answers within a short time: a monk bound to obedience and an archbishop who owed fealty to the pope was seeking information on points on which he would already have had to reach decisions.[18]

---

[17] Gameson, *Augustine* 23, 29; R. Marsden, 'The gospels of St Augustine', Gameson, *Augustine*, 285–312

[18] I have not accepted R. Meens, 'Questioning ritual purity', Gameson, *Augustine* 174–86, adducing British rather than Gaulish background to queries. S. Hollis, *Anglo-Saxon women and the Church. Sharing a common fate* (Woodbridge 1992) interesting analysis disputing that Christianity raised women's status; hostile to Augustine on queries 16–25 – but is not Old Testament authority key issue? Just description of Gregory's attitudes on religious freedom; authenticity of source, R. Flechner, 'The making of the canons of Theodore', *Peritia* 17–18 (2003–4) 121–43 at 135–8

One question, about the status of the British saint Sixtus, on whom Augustine had been consulted by a surviving British congregation who had managed to keep their faith but no longer knew the history of their own saint, throws into relief the lack of Gregory's understanding of the old British Church. Timid about recognising relics of a saint otherwise unknown, Augustine thought it wise to consult Gregory in the hope of obtaining relics of certain provenance, that is, of the Roman martyr pope St Sixtus, which it seems he intended to put with the British ones, thereby creating an authenticity without offending or condemning the British and their unknown saint. Gregory was less accommodating. He required Augustine to take the Roman relics, shut off access to the British Sixtus and entomb the authentic Roman relics at another site where they could be venerated. It was a snub to the British deputation and shows unawareness of the British Christians' long history, their martyrdoms under the Empire and their sufferings at the hands of the Germanic invaders.[19] In a letter instructing him on the future episcopate for the Anglo-Saxons, Gregory referred only perfunctorily to the British. 'You are to have under your subjection all the bishops of Britain', he wrote, assuming here, as elsewhere, that the British could be bundled up with a Roman episcopate yet to be appointed. Gregory's casual phrases, looking forward to the bishops seeing from Augustine's words and actions 'what true faith and good living are like',[20] concluded a deeply flawed set of instructions. It is hard to imagine any words of guidance less likely to ensure harmonious relations.

The replies to Augustine's queries are measured enough but other letters have a sense of haste. Gregory wrote to Aethelberht a letter which would have needed interpretation by Augustine as it spoke of the signs of the imminent end of the world. 'Many things threaten which have never happened before . . . changes in the sky, unseasonable tempests, wars, famine, pestilence and earthquakes'. Aethelberht was told that if he recognised them as happening, he was not to be 'troubled in mind; for these signs of the end of the world are sent in advance to make us heedful of our souls'. The end of the world should come when the Christian message had reached all parts of the world and Anglo-Saxon England lay near the rim. The example of Constantine was held up to Aethelberht and he was urged to use force to make belief prevail. 'Hasten to extend the Christian faith . . . suppress the worship of idols; overthrow their buildings and shrines; strengthen the morals of your subjects by outstanding

[19] Stancliffe, 'The British Church' convincing
[20] HE I 29; T.M. Charles-Edwards, 'Conversion to Christianity', id., After Rome (Oxford 2003) 103–39 at 128

purity of life, by exhorting them, terrifying, enticing and correcting them, and by showing them an example of good works ...'[21] It is not clear what Aethelberht would have made of Constantine.

On the same day, 22 June, he wrote to Bertha urging her to influence her husband. The letter to Aethelberht was on all fours with Gregory's attitudes on the continent; he made scant distinction between lapsed or half-hearted Christians and outright pagans. He had no experience of a totally heathen land and it was natural to him to apply to Anglo-Saxon England the model he was accustomed to elsewhere. Aethelberht was to coerce the sluggish and unwilling just as secular authorities were expected to do in parts of Italy, Sardinia and Corsica where the pope exerted pressure, and as Brunhild was expected to do in her lands.

Less than a month later, Gregory had changed his mind. On 18 July he sent post-haste a letter to Mellitus, already on his journey to England: his messenger was expected to catch up with him somewhere in Gaul and deliver a message which reversed the strategy so earnestly recommended to Aethelberht. Mellitus was to tell Augustine that Gregory 'after long delibera-tion' had decided 'that the idol temples of that race should by no means be destroyed, but only the idols within them. Take holy water and sprinkle it on these shrines, build altars and place relics in them. For if the shrines are well built, it is essential that they should be changed from the worship of devils to the service of the true God. When this people see that their shrines are not destroyed they will be able to banish error from their hearts and be more ready to come to the places they are familiar with ...' Relics would aid Christian reuse of a pagan site for their power would ward off demons. From coercion to adaptation and persuasion: we have no idea how Gregory came to make his volte-face, 'diu mecum cogitans' (after long consideration).[22]

He had manifestly first felt that Aethelberht could do more; had he come to see that the king lacked the power to compel obedience and that the situation in England differed from that in Gaul and Italy? Aethelberht held in greater affection those who accepted Christianity, Bede tells us, but he did nothing to inhibit pagan practice. He and a group of high-born supporters faced an entrenched paganism. Place-names tell us there were no fewer than five heathen sanctuaries within twelve miles of Augustine's monastery base in

---

[21] HE I 32
[22] HE I 30; R.A. Markus, 'Gregory the Great's pagans', R. Gameson, H. Leyser eds, Belief and culture in the Middle Ages (Oxford 2001) 23–34; R.A. Markus, 'Gregory the Great: a missionary strategy', SCH 6, 29–30

Canterbury.[23] Archaeology confirms this. Probably dating from the second half of the sixth century, the grave goods of a young warrior of about eighteen in grave 95 of the cemetery at Finglesham near Sandwich, not far from a royal estate at Eastry, includes a gilt-bronze belt buckle. It has little signs of wear: it was most likely made for the young man as a protective charm as he settled into his warrior career. On it is portrayed a warrior brandishing a spear in each hand and wearing a headdress or helmet with curved horns culminating in eagles' beaks. They are the symbols of Woden, god of war, under whose protection he will go into battle; how powerful that protection would be is shown by the nakedness of the man deliberately portrayed. He wears only his helmet/headdress and a waist belt. Devotees of Woden went to fight with only their weapons, scorning body armour, trusting in the god and demonstrating their faith in him for all to see, battling in an ecstasy, oblivious of wounds, in a state well known to those who study the psychology of war. The paganism of the battlefield supported a leading class in an age of warfare and was a dangerous and long-lasting enemy to Christianity. With a ferocious vitality, it was certainly no passive fertility cult which could quietly be absorbed in a Christian agricultural calendar marked by saints' days and religious festivals. The pagan grave goods, of which the Finglesham belt buckle is such a notable example, help to explain Aethelberht's cautious actions and the pagan reaction which followed under his son Eadbald.

Kings themselves were children of the Germanic propitiation religion. How profound a hold that had on the leading class in barbarian kingdoms both in Anglo-Saxon England and on the continent is demonstrated by Guy Halsall's examination of attitudes to war-making, choice of battle timing and procedures before battle, all profoundly influenced by the supernatural. For pagan rituals, Christian rituals were substituted in due time: our knowledge of these enables us to draw inferences about what happened before the conversion to Christianity. Aethelberht, his contemporaries and successors were generally shrewd, capable men, tested by their struggles for power. But their thought-world was far from a modern one. They were influenced by their belief in invisible powers and made decisions, whether in war or diplomacy, which cannot be wholly accounted for by Realpolitik.[24]

---

[23] F.M. Stenton, 'The historical bearing of place-name studies: Anglo-Saxon heathenism', *TRHS* 4th ser. 23 (1941) 1–12
[24] S. Chadwick Hawkes, G. Grainger eds, *The Anglo-Saxon cemetery at Finglesham, Kent* (Oxford 2006) 21, 78–81, 263–6; G. Halsall, *Warfare and society in the barbarian west* (London, New York 2003) illuminating and wide-ranging

The letter on the episcopate unfolded Gregory's long-term plan for the English Church, which was to have two provinces headed by archbishops at London and York, with twelve bishops under each metropolitan. Augustine's pallium, a woollen band with six black crosses, a symbol of papal authority, entitled him to act as metropolitan and to set about consecrating more bishops. There were shrewd arrangements for the future precedence of York or London, Augustine remaining the senior ecclesiastic for his lifetime and, presumably, transferring his see from Canterbury to London.[25] It was Gregory at his most confident and most imperial, looking back to a vanished past, the pattern of rule of third-century Roman Britain with its two governing centres of London and York. It bore no relation to the realities of the clashing kingdoms of 601.

Some time after the arrival of the party of reinforcements from Rome, and stimulated no doubt by his will to move on with the mission and gain more helpers, Augustine set about contacting the British Church to gain their aid, meeting with representatives from the neighbouring British *provincia* at a site on the borders of the lands of the Hwicce and the West Saxons. As Bede describes it, Augustine 'proceeded to urge them with brotherly admonitions, that they should preserve catholic peace with him and undertake the joint labour of evangelising the heathen for the Lord's sake'.[26] The question of mission to the Germanic settlers was probably not a major point of controversy: we have seen the evidence of some imparting of Christianity by the British to the Hwicce and Magonsaetan. But there was a clash of traditions. The British wished to remain faithful to their system of calculating Easter because it was hallowed by the usage of their holy men, while Augustine believed there were flaws in their administration of the rite of baptism. The British, with their holy men and their learning – acknowledged by Bede – were being asked to surrender their customs which they 'stubbornly' defended. Discussion was inconclusive and the conference ended with a trial by miracle. The British, challenged to heal a blind Anglo-Saxon, failed; Augustine succeeded. This story, something of a standard ingredient in hagiographical tales, is a metaphor for the superiority of the Roman side: Augustine had right on his side and therefore could heal, while the British had no such right and could not heal. The story stems in all likelihood from an oral tradition tapped by Bede through his contacts with Abbot Albinus of the Canterbury monastery and must therefore have been over a hundred years old when it reached him.

[25] Above, n. 20
[26] *HE* II 2

As Bede describes it, this miracle convinced the British that Augustine was right but they asked for the opportunity to consult with their own people and for a second and fuller conference to be held. For this second meeting, the British sent a more substantial and representative delegation including seven bishops and 'many learned men', notably monks from the monastery at Bangor-is-Coed then 'ruled over by Abbot Dinoot'. With their characteristic veneration for the ascetic life, the British consulted an anchorite on what to do when they met Augustine again; he ruled that they should be ready to abandon their own traditions if Augustine was a man of God. The anchorite advised that they should arrange for Augustine and his followers to arrive first, the test being that if at their approach Augustine rose courteously he would be showing the necessary humility of a man of God, who should be followed; if not, he would show himself 'harsh and proud'[27] and was not of God. Augustine stayed seated. There was anger. The British accused Augustine of pride and rejected him and his proposals; the meeting broke up and relations were not resumed. The rhetor in the classical world taught sitting in his chair. To sit was a sign of authority and in this Augustine was doing no more than Gregory required of him – asserting his overriding jurisdiction over the British. Authority was the key point.

The description of the second meeting is significant because it can be shown to emanate not from oral tradition but from a document written in the British interest. Bede includes phrases he habitually uses for uncertain sources of information: the seven bishops and learned men are 'said' to have attended ('ut perhibent'); Dinoot is 'said' ('narratur') to have been abbot; Augustine is 'said' ('fertur') to have made his prophecy. This is not surprising: Bede would not have felt a source emanating from the schismatic British worthy of the same credence as a source from the Roman side. Still, he incorporated it and we can tell that he was dealing with an independent British source because of its style and language and because of the names which could hardly have come to him through an Anglo-Saxon tradition. The exception is Dinoot; as it stands it is neither Brittonic nor Latin in origin but it could have been an Anglo-Saxon attempt at the Brittonic Dunawd derived from oral reminiscence in Canterbury.

In one of the darkest passages in the *Ecclesiastical History*, Bede describes Augustine, having had his proposals and authority as archbishop rejected, turning to condemn the British because of their failure to cooperate and

---

[27] Ibid.; J.T. Koch, 'Bangor-is-Coed (Bangor on Dee)', *KCC*; N.J. Higham, *NH* 38 (2001) 12

warning them that 'if they would not preach the way of life to the English nation they would one day suffer the vengeance of death at their hands'; which prophecy, he continued, was fulfilled at the battle of Chester against the British in 615 or 616 when King Aethelfrith of Northumbria, observing a host of monks from Bangor praying for a British victory, ordered them all to be slaughtered. The guards appointed to defend them under Brocmail, their leader, all 'took to their heels at the first assault'.

For the battle of Chester, Bede also had access to special information from the British side, for he knew the name of the cowardly guard, refers to the battle under the British name for Chester, knew the number of monks slain, 1,200, and gave his readers detail about the organisation of the Bangor monastery and its commitment to manual labour. Using a little arbitrarily the materials he had to hand, Bede created an ecclesiastical saga, moving from the Canterbury tradition in which Augustine is shown to be God's rightful representative, to a British narrative in which his remaining seated at the meeting led to breakdown and thence to Augustine's prophecy of judgment on the British fulfilled at last in the death of the Bangor monks at Chester. Bede praised the Bangor monks' way of living but demonstrated that their prayers and three-day fast could not bring victory because their cause was wrong. This is a construction by a masterly storyteller, which, for all its flaws, still conveys the underlying reasons for the breakdown of trust between the Roman archbishop and the British episcopate.

Whether a man of wider vision and independence than Augustine could have prevented a wholesale rupture cannot now be established. Tenacious obedience, the regard of a monk for his superior's wishes and a will to make Church life in all respects conform to canon law and the Gospel shines through the records of Augustine's life, and meant that even if he had wished, he could in no way modify Gregory's demand that he as archbishop should exercise rights over the British. One other factor to which Bede would not have been sensitive was the British political and military fear that adherence to Augustine would perforce aid the power of his sponsor, the wily and powerful Anglo-Saxon ruler from the alien Germanic world which had brought so much destruction to the British cause and its Church. That was always liable to put paid to any prospect of high-level cooperation between Aethelberht's archbishop and the British bishops.[28]

[28] I follow principally Stancliffe, 'The British Church' 107–51 at 128–34; ecclesiastical saga, P. Sims-Williams, *Religion and literature in western England 600–800* (Cambridge 1990) 9–10, 78; rhetor's chair, M. Deanesly, *The pre-conquest Church in England* (London 1961) 59

Gregory's postscript letter of 601 to Mellitus is his last recorded intervention in the affairs of the English mission; Augustine had to digest his directions and his detailed advice in response to queries. Thereafter Augustine, his band of Italians, trainee Anglo-Saxon monks and clergy, Aethelberht and the converts were on their own. Nothing more is heard of the proposal to transfer the archbishopric to London, which lay in the kingdom of the East Saxons, now a shadow of its power and status in the Roman epoch. Could the plan have owed something to Aethelberht's political ambitions? The East Saxons were in some relation of dependence: a connection went back to Eormenric's day when he married his daughter, Aethelberht's sister Ricula, to its king and Aethelberht may have wished to turn a loose overlordship into a relation of much greater dependence and make London his capital. Shrunken though it was, it was still a nodal point in the surviving Roman road network and a worthwhile prize.

The East Saxon king, Aethelberht's nephew Saeberht, accepted Christianity and Aethelberht built a cathedral church in London dedicated to St Paul. After a period of acculturation and, no doubt, language learning, Mellitus was consecrated its bishop in 604. Rochester was made the seat of a second bishopric, designed, it may well be, to meet the aspirations of the West Kentings. There is some evidence that West Kent, with its distinct archaeology, had once had some independence from the East, the seat of Aethelberht's power. Its cathedral was dedicated to St Andrew, patron of Gregory's church on the Coelian Hill, and Justus, another member of the 601 mission, was consecrated bishop.[29] Christianity advanced no further in Aethelberht's reign.

Aethelberht outlasted his Christian wife and remarried; he outlasted Gregory, who died in 604, and Augustine, who died some time between 604 and 609: the fruitful relationship between them seems to have continued without friction under Augustine's successors. Aethelberht was buried with his erstwhile queen in 616 in a position of honour in the porticus of St Martin contiguous with the monastery of St Peter and St Paul, subsequently dedicated to St Augustine, outside the walls of Canterbury. Placing his burial site as close as possible to the prayers of the monks argues for a core of genuine commitment to Christianity. The record suggests a man of skill and resolution who, with tactful determination, managed an acceptance of the new religion, understood the limitations of his power, but faithfully backed Augustine with endowments and buildings and was capable of innovation, as in the case of

---

[29] For London, Higham, *Convert kings* 94–6; Rochester, Brooks, *Myths* 52–3; Aethelberht's death, S.E. Kelly, 'Aethelberht', M. Lapidge ed., *The Blackwell encyclopaedia of Anglo-Saxon England* (Oxford 1999)

the law code. Where he could, he recommended Christianity and achieved a real success in the conversion of his nephew Saeberht.

New evidence casts light on this otherwise little-known ruler. He is the most likely of all candidates to be identified with the man in a magnificent chamber at Prittlewell, Southend, uncovered in 2003, who was buried in a coffin containing two gold foil crosses, which their position shows were most likely laid over his eyes. There is thus a small but definite Christian presence among the immense wealth of the rest of the tomb – drinking vessels, a standard, a lyre, a gaming board with antler-bone pieces and a gold belt buckle; in a word, the apparatus of Anglo-Saxon kingship. The crosses, a flagon and a bowl attest to the Christian belief of the man commemorated but the rest, displaying with extraordinary exuberance the wealth and far-flung contacts of a warrior-king, was a tribute to the paganism of what was likely to be still the majority of the population in 616 when Saeberht died. Tradition had its way and those who staged the burial left open the chamber, then boarded it and raised a mound above it, but only after they had given time for mourners and subjects to view both the commemoration of a Christian and the pagan display, demonstrating to all the remarkable wealth that this society was prepared to commit to the ground in memory of its ruler. Christianity had no specific condemnation of grave goods; nonetheless, the display forcibly proclaims the continuance of pagan customs and gives a glimpse of the old religion's passive power with which missionaries and converts long had to grapple.[30]

Saeberht's conversion was a major success; the attempt on Redwald, king of East Anglia, was a failure. Bede places Aethelberht third on a list of Anglo-Saxon kings who held authority over other kings south of the Humber, using the Roman term *imperium* for their authority. The first two, Aelle of the South Saxons and Ceawlin of the West Saxons, are shadowy figures from the time of the invasions, an oral epoch when events were interpreted by harpists in the mead-halls, praising their patrons and calling up semi-mythical heroes from the Germanic past as ancestors for them.[31]

By contrast, the achievements of Aethelberht are documented. He may, in fact, have been the first to exercise a real authority amongst the southern rulers, aided by the wealth of Kent and its continental contacts. But even he was unable to make his commands effective at a distance and over a long

---

[30] *The Prittlewell prince. The discovery of a rich Anglo-Saxon burial in Essex*, Museum of London Archaeological Service (London 2004). I owe advice to Dr J. Blair; gold-foil crosses, V. Bierbrauer, Carver, *Cross* 429–42

[31] *HE* II 5

Fig. 4 The Prittlewell burial.

period of time. His authority was sufficient to bring Redwald to Canterbury and induce him to accept baptism: no doubt the mission hoped it would be the prelude to an invitation to spread the faith into new territory. This did not happen. The baptism does not seem to have been prepared for on any scale, Redwald was not accompanied by sons and there is no evidence that clergy went back with him; alternatively, aware of the failure of this attempt at conversion, Bede did not mention them.[32]

Returned home, Redwald fell under the influence of his queen and 'certain evil counsellors'[33] and contented himself with putting one new altar to the Christian God into his heathen temple. He could afford to let his baptism remain ineffective as Aethelberht's power faded in his later years. Choosing his words carefully, Bede said that Redwald was winning *ducatus*, i.e., military power, over his own people in Aethelberht's lifetime. He could not be coerced.

After Aethelberht's death, Redwald obtained the southern overlordship and so a pagan held the position of greatest prestige and authority, doubtless with a supporting war band of calibre. Treasure bought warriors and their equipment; booty and tribute reinforced the treasure-chest and so long as a king kept his strength and his war band, he could dominate his fellow kings and, at least for a time, beat off rivals. Redwald was able to do this and dominated at least from the time of Aethelberht's death till his own death in 624–5. It was not a fortunate epoch for the Christian mission.

Just what treasure and equipment Redwald had is revealed by analysis of the ship-burial in which his body was interred, a ninety-foot boat drawn up from the river Deben in Suffolk to a commanding site at Sutton Hoo on the threshold of the kingdom and buried under a mound.[34] It was once thought that there was never a body and that the whole ensemble was a cenotaph, perhaps for a king whose body had been lost or buried at sea; it is now clear from chemical traces that there was one. No evidence suggests that Redwald had anything other than a natural end and soil analysis has thus made the

---

[32] Padberg, *Mission* 252–3

[33] *HE* II 5

[34] Major research reports: R.L.S. Bruce-Mitford, *The Sutton Hoo ship burial* I–III (1975–83); M.O.H. Carver, M.R. Hummler, *Sutton Hoo. The early medieval cemetery and its context* (forthcoming); A. Care Evans, *The Sutton Hoo ship burial* (London 1986) helpful summary; M.O.H. Carver, *Sutton Hoo. Burial ground of kings* (London 1998) distinctive analysis, views whole site; id., 'Sutton Hoo in context', *Sutton Hoo. A seventh century burial ground and its context* (London 2005) 489–503; I. Wood, 'The Franks and Sutton Hoo', I. Wood, N. Lund eds, *Peoples and places in Northern Europe* (Woodbridge 1991) 1–15 inc. Scandinavia

traditional identification with Redwald more probable. The magnificence of the grave goods and the paucity of Christian artefacts suggest the burial to be that of an Anglo-Saxon ruler with exceptionally wide authority, as Redwald had, and the strongly pagan cast of the ensemble makes him a more likely candidate than later East Anglian kings. The body was laid out within a wooden hut amidships: in the coffin beside the corpse were intimate personal items including a washing bowl, spare socks, knives for trimming nails and beard and some keepsakes.[35]

Outside the coffin lay the equipment for feasting: a great cauldron with chains to hang from beams in a mead-hall, buckets, meat and a lyre in a beaver-skin bag, which a scop could use to entertain the company. Parade-ground equipment of a great warrior included helmet, shield and sword in magnificent display, with a great golden buckle inlaid with niello and garnets, the helmet being adorned with bronze sheets depicting warriors whose helmets with eagle heads, together with the conventional representations of Woden, recall the warrior of the Finglesham belt buckle. There are echoes of Rome as well, for Late Antiquity provides the ultimate model for the helmet, and the clasps of the Emperor Augustus's armour for the splendid Sutton Hoo shoulder clasps.

A whetstone of Celtic provenance with eight carved heads near its apex was surmounted by a delicate bronze stag on an iron ring, so made that it could swivel independently on a pedestal base. Symbolising virility and energy, it was never intended to be used: it was a symbolic object comparable to the ceremonial staffs of West Africa, derived from European silver-topped walking canes of the seventeenth century, which had no function but were simply symbols of authority.[36] The technique of niello, the gold and garnets, the writhing, snake-like objects redolent of the curvilinear abstract art of the Celts impose on the modern observer a vision of a leader capable of drawing on great reserves of wealth and summoning into his service a smith, a weapon-maker and adorner of great talent and sophistication, likely to have been British.

One aim of those who assembled the grave goods seems to have been to show how great the range of contacts of the dead king and warrior had been. There were Frankish coins from thirty-seven different mints in a purse on the

---

[35] Carver, *Burial ground* pagan characteristics 165, personal items and queen's influence 169
[36] M.J. Enright, 'The Sutton Hoo whetstone sceptre: a study in iconography and cultural milieu', *ASE* 11 (1983) 119–35; M.O.H. Carver, 'Burial as treasure: the context of treasure in Anglo-Saxon graves', E.M. Tyler, ed., *Treasure in the medieval west* (York 2000) 25–48 at 35

top of the coffin together with three blanks and two gold billets; a Syrian cloak; a Coptic bowl; a bowl from Alexandria; bowls from Byzantium with crosses on them; a great dish with the stamp of the emperor Anastasius; hanging bowls, shallow bronze bowls with ornamented hooks and escutcheons, the most notable of which is likely to be of Irish workmanship; the whetstone of silty greywacke stone most commonly found in the uplands of southern Scotland is derived from the world of Celtic royal symbols, while the workmanship of helmet and shield betray Swedish origins. In a brilliant reconstruction, Philip Grierson has explained the coins and blanks in the purse as payment for the forty oarsmen and the two gold billets as the reward for the skill of the helmsman needed to carry the ship into the realms of the dead.[37]

An overwhelmingly costly burial, involving the dragging of a great vessel over the dunes, the construction of trench and mound and the commitment of vast treasure to the ground in commemoration of one man is an emphatic assertion of pagan, kingly power just at the time in which Christianity had secured a place in Kent, with the blessing of Christian Frankish kingdoms. Sutton Hoo was a counterblast to the Franks, the Christians and the Roman world. The evidence of the helmet, old when it was put in the ground, and the construction of the shield suggest that the young monarchy of East Anglia had had Swedish connections; the Scandinavian past helped to draw those who made up the treasure, moved the ship and constructed the mound to look to Sweden, where the Vendel graves were ship burials. In face of Rome, the Franks and Christianity, they looked to a totally pagan land which had never known Christianity. Ship-burials continued for centuries in Scandinavia; in Anglo-Saxon England, in the present state of knowledge, they are both few and short-lived. Only three are known, one other from Sutton Hoo, one from Snape, all in East Anglia.

There is a slight Christian presence. Two spoons of late classical silver, both with a cross and a Greek inscription apparently reading, respectively, Paulos and Saulos, were once hailed as baptismal spoons, high-level presents to a convert, designed to mark a baptism of great importance and provide a reminder of the civilisation with which Christianity was associated, conceivably presents from Aethelberht. Paulos/Saulos were natural inscriptions on a pair of baptismal spoons, recalling St Paul's Christian and Jewish names. Close analysis cannot support this. One spoon is of Byzantine workmanship and it

---

[37] P. Grierson, 'The purpose of the Sutton Hoo coins', *Antiquity* 44 (1970) 14–18; Carver, *Burial ground* 169; mints, Wood, 'The Franks' 10

is not impossible that it was a baptismal present: the other is most likely to be an incompetent copy and is certainly not of Byzantine workmanship. The workman knew no Greek and may well have muddled a Greek P and S in trying – perhaps from memory – to reproduce the original. In what circumstances this poor copy was made, it is impossible to conjecture.[38]

The finest hanging bowl in the treasure has a fish and has sometimes been interpreted as a Christian artefact, but this is unlikely. Hanging bowls, once surmised to have had a liturgical purpose, perhaps holding holy water and being an artefact of the British Church, are now believed to have had a secular use, possibly as tableware. If the former, then one would have expected to see chi-rho monograms on them but this is not the case. What is significant is that the craftsman who made the bowls used late Roman or Celtic motifs which originated outside Anglo-Saxon England. The technique and design of the rims of the hanging-bowl mount certainly carry us over to Ireland, where there is a parallel at the monastery of Ballinderry.[39] A mould for an escutcheon has been found at Craig Phadrig, a Pictish fort near Inverness, and there have been significant finds at Dunadd in Argyll and near an Irish monastery. Plainly the East Anglian court had links with the world of Celtic craftsmanship but nothing of Celtic Christianity passed over to those who commissioned their work. Christianity was the religion of the defeated.

The meagre Christian presence at Sutton Hoo contrasts with the situation at Prittlewell where Saeberht's relatives compromised, leaving signs of the new religion within a treasure which looked back to the pagan kingly past. There was no such compromise at Sutton Hoo and one is tempted here to look back at the queen with Bede's 'evil counsellors', who dissuaded Redwald from following up his Kentish baptism. Women were responsible for burial arrangements and the queen's hand is surely shown in the care for kitting out her husband for feasting and fighting in the other world at the high level he was accustomed to enjoy in this life.

---

[38] M.O.H. Carver, 'Reflections on the meaning of monumental barrows in Anglo-Saxon England', S. Lucy, A. Reynolds eds, *Burial in early England and Wales* (London 2002) 132–43; R.E. Kaske, 'The silver spoons of Sutton Hoo', *Speculum* 42 (1967) 670–2

[39] M. Ryan, 'The Sutton Hoo ship-burial and Ireland: some Celtic perspectives', R. Farrell, C. Neuman de Vegvar, *Sutton Hoo fifty years after* (Ohio 1992) 83–105 esp. 90–5. I am indebted for ref. and comments to Professor G. Henderson; J. Brenan, *Hanging bowls and their contexts*, BAR Brit. ser. 220 (Oxford 1991); H. Geake, 'When were hanging bowls deposited in Anglo-Saxon graves?', *MA* 43 (1999) 1–18

Touched by the mission from Kent, Redwald had nonetheless rejected Christianity's unique claim and contented himself with the mild polytheistic gesture of adding a Christian altar to the pantheon in his temple. He and his people remained in the past and consequently the years of his supremacy were years in which the paganism which had lain passive and undefeated could again show itself and cast off Christianity.

The mission held, albeit by a thread. Among the East Saxons there was complete disaster. Saeberht's three sons who formed the collective leadership demanded the right to receive communion, though unbaptised. 'Why do you not offer us the white bread which you used to give our father ... and yet you still give it to the people in church?'[40] they said. Mellitus could not compromise and refused them; whereupon they expelled him. It was evident that if the protection of the mission at royal level faltered, the forces of paganism were ready and waiting to fill the gap. Bede comments that the sons of Saeberht 'allowed their subjects to worship idols'[41] and when there was a subsequent revival of mission under Eadbald, the people of London were still 'preferring to serve idolatrous high priests'.[42] The infrastructure of paganism had not been put out of business by one individual conversion, even of a king. Mellitus went back to Canterbury and conferred with other leaders. Aethelberht's successor, Eadbald, seems at the outset not to have accepted Christianity. The bishops despaired. Mellitus and Justus of Rochester went over to Gaul. In Bede's account, Laurentius, Augustine's successor, prepared to spend his last night in the monastery church before following them, when, in a legendary story which probably came down from the traditions of the monastery, St Peter appeared, scourged him and reproached him with desertion. Shown the weals next morning, Eadbald, according to Bede, repented of his paganism, abandoned his wife and accepted baptism. So, in his account, the mission was saved.

Bede's chronology is confused and he has foreshortened events. There is evidence that Laurentius was censured 'by apostolic authority', an odd phrase in a much later account which may well reflect a hostile papal reaction to Laurentius's will to flee – as it were, an oral scourging. Eadbald's pagan phase, in fact, lasted a long time but somehow, partly through Frankish or papal influence, the mission continued. Laurentius died in office and was succeeded

---

[40] *HE* II 5
[41] Ibid.
[42] *HE* II 6

by Mellitus and then by Justus. Eadbald shifted his policy. There was a flurry of action. He abandoned his first wife and accepted a Merovingian noble-woman, Ymme, daughter of the mayor of the palace of Neustria and thus from the Christian world, and founded a church, consecrated by Mellitus. Pope Boniface V wrote to Justus conferring on him the pallium and praising him for Eadbald's conversion.[43]

Though he had never been able to recover the *imperium* his father had, Eadbald still ruled a prosperous kingdom in contact with the continent and minted gold coins in his own name: it was evidently advantageous for Edwin, pagan king of Northumbria, a rising power in the north, to seek a marriage alliance with Kent. Though at this time Eadbald was still pagan, his sister Aethelburh was Christian and the Canterbury mission was strong enough to stipulate the same conditions for her as Bertha had enjoyed: that she should have freedom of worship and take her own chaplain with her, Paulinus, one of the reinforcements sent by Gregory in 601. Families were commonly divided over the acceptance of Christianity.

In the wake of Eadbald's conversion, Boniface wrote both to Edwin and his queen commending Christianity and sending gifts including a 'garment from Ancyra', a Byzantine gift that was a discreet reminder of the civilisation of Christian states, urging him 'with all affection ... to hate idols and idol worship, to spurn their foolish shrines and the deceitful flatteries of their soothsaying':[44] to Aethelburh he sent a silver mirror and a gold and ivory comb, urging her to use her powers of persuasion on her husband.

In Edwin, Boniface was dealing with one of the major figures of seventh-century Anglo-Saxon history, a shrewd, tenacious candidate for kingship with a keen eye for both the trappings and the realities of power. As a Northumbrian monk, Bede had access to an oral tradition which relates the insecurities of Edwin's early years as an exiled prince trying to maintain himself in the face of Aethelfrith of Bernicia, one of the greatest figures of the Germanic aristocracy which was by now in control of scattered British settlements north of the Tees. More thickly settled by Angles in the plains of York, Deira was the seat of Edwin's rival royal house which had been absorbed by Aethelfrith, a success sealed by his marriage to Acha, Edwin's sister.

After long wandering to escape Aethelfrith's power, Edwin took refuge in Redwald's territory. Warned by a friend that under pressure from Aethelfrith

---

[43] J.M. Wallace-Hadrill, *Bede's Ecdesiastical history of the english people: A historical commentary* (Oxford 1988) 61–3; *HE* II 8
[44] *HE* II 10; R. Cramp, 'Eadwine', *ODNB*; J.T. Koch, 'Eadwine / Edwin', *KCC*

Redwald was about to betray him, he followed the heroic tradition of fidelity to a lord and was unwilling to abandon Redwald and the promises exchanged between them. Sitting anxiously outside the palace, Bede recounts, he was approached by an unknown man, whom he later understood to have been a celestial visitor, who drew him into conversation about his fears and hinted at a future deliverance from his earthly troubles, gave guidance for his life and salvation and, after receiving Edwin's promise to obey him if his promises for the future were fulfilled, vanished. Just then, Edwin's friend reported that, influenced by his queen, Redwald had decided against betraying him.[45]

It was the turning point in Edwin's career. Redwald advanced against Aethelfrith and defeated him in the battle of the river Idle in Mercian territory. Edwin then took his kingdom and established his power over both Deira and Bernicia, expelling Aethelfrith's sons. He married Aethelburh and went on to continue Aethelfrith's policy of expansion against the British, driving into their heartland of Powys and conquering Anglesey and Man, exercising both naval and military power and establishing a supremacy around the Irish Sea. In Bede's list, he succeeded Redwald as overlord south of the Humber.

Bede believed the mysterious visitor at Redwald's court to have been Paulinus, who at this juncture went to Edwin, laid his right hand upon him and reminded him of his promise. The *Historia Brittonum* reports that as an exile at a British court, Edwin had already received baptism from Rhun, king of Rheged.[46] It reads like a confused version of the mass baptisms which in fact took place under Paulinus, but it is by no means unlikely that Edwin had been baptised for diplomatic reasons. In Viking times multiple baptisms played a part in diplomatic negotiations over land and security.

Bede depicts him as a man who came slowly to decisions – sitting outside the palace 'with his mind in a tumult, not knowing what to do or which way to turn' and then, after the approach of Paulinus, hesitating – 'he used to sit alone for hours at a time, earnestly debating within himself what he ought to do and what religion he should follow'.[47] A move from paganism to Christianity was second in danger only to commitment to battle for a king of

---

[45] *HE* II 12

[46] N.K. Chadwick, 'The conversion of Northumbria. A comparison of sources', id. ed., *Celt and Saxon: studies in the early British border* (Cambridge 1963) 138–66; J.T. Koch, 'Rhun fab Urien', *KCC*. If Eanflaed included, story unlikely. C. Corning in *NH* 36 5–15 argues for Rhun as godfather/sponsor

[47] *HE* II 1

this age. While Redwald held power, it was certainly too dangerous. Redwald was his protector and had failed to accept Christianity. After his death it was possible: but Edwin was still isolated. Kent alone had Christian representatives among Anglo-Saxon kingdoms.

Redwald's son, Eorpwald of East Anglia, remained pagan, as did the Mercians. Christianity was the religion of the British against whom Edwin fought. A man of caution, as Edwin clearly was, needed to proceed slowly and be sure to carry his aristocracy with him. In one of the masterly narratives of the *Ecclesiastical History*, Bede depicts Edwin putting the matter to debate among 'his loyal chief men and his counsellors'. He set his debate in the Yorkshire lowlands, in Deira, the heartland of Edwin's power, and gives one speech to each of the protagonists; Coifi, the pagan chief priest, takes the role of the Vicar of Bray, condemning his pagan gods for their failure to bring about his own advancement. 'None of your followers,' he is described as saying, 'has devoted himself more earnestly than I have to the worship of our gods, but nevertheless there are many who receive greater benefits and greater honour from you than I do and are more successful . . . If the gods had any power, they would have helped me more readily'.[48] At the end of the debate, he volunteered to be the first to set about the destruction of the old temples and, in a gesture which throws a ray of light on paganism, asked the king for a stallion and arms, thereby ostentatiously breaking with the tradition which allowed a chief priest to ride only on a mare and never carry arms, and set off for Godmundingham – Goodmanham, east of York – cast a spear into the sacred enclosure and ordered his companions to fire the temple. It was a 'rehearsed drama'[49] designed to move Edwin's leading men, the kind of vivid episode likely to have been handed down in folk memory.

At Goodmanham, the present twelfth-century church stands on what looks uncannily like an artificial mound, very possibly a prehistoric barrow on which the pagans, ever fond of using existing sacred places, had erected their shrine. The assumption is that the Christians had put a church on top of the site of Coifi's temple. Probably from about 580, more developed shrines had begun to appear among the Anglo-Saxons and, from Bede's description of

---

[48] *HE* II 13. Pagan priesthood remains controversial. D. Page, 'Anglo-Saxon paganism: the evidence of Bede', T. Hosfra *et al.* eds, *Pagans and Christians: the interplay between Christian Latin and traditional Germanic cultures* (Groningen 1995) 99–130 argues that Bede played down role of kings in paganism. If pagan priests had significant role, would they not have had a *wergild*?

[49] M. Truran, 'The mission from Rome', D. Rees ed., *Monks in England* (London 1997) 19–36

enclosure, idols and temple, Goodmanham was one of these. It is a sign of paganism's continuing vitality that in the latter half of the sixth century at a time of growth of ideas of kingship, of increasing prosperity and what has been referred to as a growing monumentality, shrines emerge of a character which is not detectable in the Germanic homelands of the invaders.[50] Bede uses the same term, *fanum*, that Gregory uses in his letter to Mellitus urging him to destroy the idols in temples when he describes Redwald's gesture of putting in an altar to Christ in his temple, which was still standing in the 660s or 670s, some thirty years or more after its abandonment. This indicates full-scale building of substantial structures. He again uses *fanum* when he describes the pagan reaction under one of the kings of the East Saxons, Sighere, who, after a visitation of plague, began 'to restore the derelict temples'. As we have seen, Aldhelm remembered animal pillars standing in *profana fana* ('profane shrines'), and rejoiced that the *fana* had been replaced by Christian structures – churches, or perhaps monasteries where Anglo-Saxon youth were trained.[51]

There is archaeological evidence of the appearance of square-ditched enclosures associated with burials, or, probably, worship, of a kind not detectable on the continent. John Blair argues that the emergence of the 'temples' described in the literary sources was the fruit of the Anglo-Saxon elite's imitation of the remains of Celtic and classical Roman temples as seen in Britain. It was once suggested that migration away from the sites of ancient worship hallowed by generations of usage in the Germanic homelands had weakened the force of heathenism; Coifi's Goodmanham and other sites such as Slonk Hill in Sussex or Blacklow Hill in Warwickshire are evidence that, so far from weakening, the old religion was capable of innovation and development and had the confidence to borrow from and imitate the structures of worship it found in conquered lands.

To an unnamed noble, Bede gave one of the finest of all passages in his *History*:

This is how the present life of man on earth, King, appears to me in comparison with that time which is unknown to us. You are sitting feasting with

---

[50] J. Blair, 'Anglo-Saxon pagan shrines and their prototypes', *ASAH* 8 (1995) 1–28; I. Wood, 'Some historical reidentifications and the Christianisation of Kent', G. Armstrong, I. Wood eds, *Christianising peoples and converting individuals* (Turnhout 2000) 27–35; comment, Higham, *Convert kings* 25

[51] *HE* II 15; III 30; Aldhelm, above 63

your ealdormen and thegns in winter time; the fire is burning on the hearth
in the middle of the hall and all inside is warm, while outside the wintry
storms of rain and snow are raging; and a sparrow flies swiftly through the
hall. It enters in at one door and quickly flies out through the other. For the
few moments it is inside, the storm and winter tempest cannot touch it, but
after the briefest moment of calm, it flits from your sight, out of the wintry
storm and into it again. So this life of man appears but for a moment; what
follows or indeed what went before, we know not at all.[52]

He went on to argue that if this new teaching brought any more certain
knowledge, the assembled counsellors should follow it. This was an argument
which missionaries would certainly have been putting to converts, contrasting
the ordered Christian explanations of creation and the purpose of man's life,
the choice between heaven and hell, with the limited hereafter of paganism.
Edwin's own reactions in what were probably years of negotiation and discussion with Paulinus, smacked initially more of Coifi's approach than the
noble's.

Bede reports that on the occasion of his marriage, Edwin made a
conditional promise that 'he might accept the same religion himself if, on
examination, it was judged by his wise men to be a holier worship and more
worthy of God'.[53] The growth of his power was clearly resented by Cwichelm,
king of the Gewisse of the Upper Thames Valley: he sent an assassin to his
court with a double-edged poisoned dagger, who gained entry to the royal
residence by pretending to deliver a message and would probably have ended
Edwin's career but for Lilla, the king's counsellor, interposing his body and a
courtier, Fordhere, who also perished in the struggle. It was a heroic scene, the
stuff of a scop's narration, demonstrating a retainer's loyalty to the death in the
Germanic tradition. It was Easter Day; on the same night, the queen gave
birth to a daughter, Eanflaed. Edwin, still pagan, gave thanks to his gods:
Paulinus gave thanks to Christ.

Taking another cautious step, Edwin 'gave his infant daughter to Bishop
Paulinus to be consecrated to Christ'. It was a species of thank-offering. At
Pentecost, Eanflaed was baptised together with twelve of her entourage.
Edwin, wounded by the force of the assassin's dagger through Lilla's body,
recovered and made a final promise that he would renounce heathenism

[52] *HE* II 13
[53] *HE* II 9

if God gave him victory over Cwichelm. An expedition was successful and the king then moved on to 'learn the faith systematically from the venerable Bishop Paulinus' and to submit the case for Christianity to his leading counsellors. One day, the anonymous Life of Gregory relates, as the king and his companions walked towards church for this instruction, they were disturbed by the calls of a crow. Conscious of paganism's reliance on foretelling the future by the flight of birds, Paulinus reacted by calling on one of his youths to shoot the bird on the wing. The Christian candidates could proceed undisturbed to hear Paulinus's exposition, who at the end of the session displayed the arrow, drawing the moral that the bird who could not avoid death could not foretell the future.[54] Finally, on Easter Day 627 or 628, Edwin accepted baptism at York in a timber church. Afterwards he set about building a stone basilica around it, so creating a church in the Roman style.

Edwin was aware of the wider implications of his policy. He had chosen to ally himself with the kingdom most closely in touch with the continent and take to wife a princess of part-Merovingian descent. He received from Boniface's successor, Honorius I, a letter with the blessing of St Peter, describing him as the 'King of the English' and recommending with lack of realism study of the writings of Gregory.[55] A standard in Roman style was carried before him when on progress through the land. Bede described with admiration the peace he created and the generosity of a great ruler setting up posts with water in brass bowls for travellers to slake their thirst.

Edwin was not content for Paulinus to remain simply bishop of York and combined with Eadbald in requesting the pallium for him, thus bringing into being the archbishopric at York envisaged by Gregory the Great in his master plan for the English Church. This was late in Edwin's reign and his death prevented any further action, but the request suggests that he had an unusual capacity for seeing the implications of his carefully crafted movements towards Christianity: the second archbishopric would redound to the glory of the northern kingdom.

Meanwhile Edwin used his position to spread the faith. Paulinus preached in Deira and performed mass baptisms in the river Swale near Catterick. Bede

---

[54] Colgrave, *Earliest Life* ch. 15; M. Richter, 'Practical aspects of the conversion of the Anglo-Saxons', P.N. Chattáin, M. Richter eds, *Ireland and Christendom* (Stuttgart 1987) 362–76 at 371–2
[55] *HE* II 17

picked up oral evidence from the abbot of Bardney, using reminiscences of an old man who remembered just such a mass baptism carried out by Paulinus in the river Trent and gave a rare description of him as a tall man having a slight stoop, an ascetic face, a thin, hooked nose and 'a venerable and awe-inspiring presence'.[56] Paulinus also preached in Lindsey, a dependent territory of Edwin's below the Humber, and built the stone church at Lincoln, where he consecrated Honorius as archbishop of Canterbury in succession to Justus. Edwin used his status as overlord to persuade Eorpwald of the East Anglians to accept baptism though it brought Eorpwald no advantage. Bede reports that he was soon after killed by a pagan named Ricbert and the kingdom relapsed into paganism for three years, thus knocking away a prop to Northumbrian power.

Paulinus accompanied the king and queen to provide a mission at the royal residence at Yeavering.[57] Bede describes Edwin's palace as lying at 'Ad Gefrin', meaning hill of the goats. It is significant that he gave a British name, for the site had a long history of ritual significance before the Anglian occupation. The British name obviously applied originally to the hill of Yeavering Bell, a defensive position and a place for ceremonial gatherings in prehistoric times. Anglian kings chose to build substantial timber structures along the whale-back running away from Yeavering Bell; they deliberately built along a line linking two prehistoric sites, the western and eastern ring ditches at each end of the ridge, in early times used for burials. The conquerors of the territory wished to arrogate to themselves something of the sacral quality of this landscape. The site was used as a centre for tribute-taking, feasting and decision-making, and by Edwin for Christianisation. Bernicia is a Celtic name, there is a significant survival of major strongholds with Celtic names throughout the kingdom and an allusion in the Gododdin seems to imply that it had once been a British kingdom. Literary sources on this should not be cast aside: fighting for conquest there will certainly have been but there are nevertheless indications of a more peaceful British–Anglian coexistence long term within Bernicia than has sometimes been supposed.

Two halls of the kind described in the sparrow story put up on open ground where there was no defence and on a site where no midwinter sun fell witness to a remarkable sense of security in a conquered land and a respect for the

---

[56] HE II 16; L. Sherley-Price trans., History of the English Church
[57] J.T. Koch, 'Brynaich (Bernicia)', KCC; A. Woolf, 'Bernicia', Lynch, Companion; Dumville, 'Origins of Northumbria', Bassett ed., Origins of Anglo-Saxon Kingdoms, Kirby, Earliest English Kings; on settlement, D. Rollason, Northumbria 500–1100. Creation and destruction of a kingdom (Cambridge 2003) 98

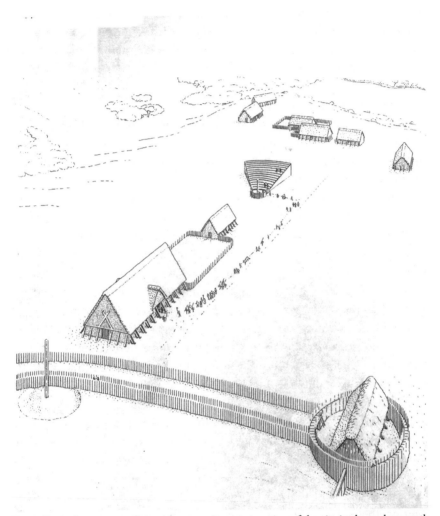

Fig. 5 Yeavering: a centre for royal power. A reconstruction of the site in the early seventh century from above the palisades of the great enclosure, a corral for cattle or horses to be trained for cavalry duties. Beyond lies the great hall and then the tiered theatre for assemblies. Yeavering Bell lies off the drawing on the left-hand side and the river Glen on the right.

ancient associations of this territory. They were lofty structures with white plastered walls and wide gables, approaching as near as possible classic Roman buildings. The first, which may date from *c*.600 was succeeded by one of more assured workmanship and design measuring eighty by thirty-seven feet with a roof apex which may have been as high as thirty-six feet. The two halls are the grandest so far to be discovered in the Germanic world before the Viking age. At the eastern entrance of the larger of the halls there is a burial, so aligned as to make it seem that the corpse was guarding the building; with it was buried a goat skull and what seems to be a ceremonial staff. This might be a priest's burial, the goat skull recalling the ancient British title of the place, and the long staff being an imitation of the *groma* of Roman surveyors, used by the priest honoured here to align the great halls; or possibly we have here the surveyor himself and the symbol of his office.

Elsewhere on the site there was a segment of a wooden imitation of a Roman theatre, possibly derived from the surviving stone amphitheatre at Canterbury, with tiered seats facing a tall post comparable to the *stafolus* of Frankish law codes and a platform from which a ruler could address his notables or deliver legal decisions. The theatre was another demonstration of royal power, for acres of woodland were required for such structures. Another timber building lacking the scattering of detritus or animal bones which denote human occupation, and housing a mass of ox bones, predominantly skulls, indicates pagan temple worship of the kind described by Gregory the Great in his letter to Mellitus.[58] Graves run up into intimate contact with the building, one containing a single ox tooth and the skeleton of a child in a crouched position.

From early days, it had been adapted to the movements of a ruler with his entourage and in this last, Christian phase of his career, Edwin with his queen was doubtless following in the footsteps of his pagan predecessor, Aethelfrith, but combining with a barbarian royal progress the opportunity for Paulinus to instruct and baptise. Bede tells us Paulinus spent thirty-six days there. 'During these days ... he did nothing else but instruct the crowds who flocked to him from every village and district in the teaching of Christ. When

[58] B. Hope-Taylor, *Yeavering: an Anglo-British centre of early Northumbria* (London 1972); modifications P. Frodsham, C. O'Brien eds, *Yeavering, people, power and place* (Stroud 2005); L. Alcock, *Kings and warriors, craftsmen and priests in northern Britain AD 550–850* (Edinburgh 2003) 234–56 cogent on dating; I have followed A. Meaney, 'Pagan English sanctuaries, place-names and hundred meeting-places', *ASAH* 8 (1995) 29–42 at 29 arguing against Hope-Taylor, that Yeavering temple is of Anglo-Saxon pagan origin; see J. Hines, 'Religion: the limits of knowledge', id., *Anglo-Saxons 375–401* at 388

they had received instruction he washed them in the waters of regeneration in the river Glen, which was close at hand.'[59]

It was a great occasion, set in the context of an ancient point of assembly. Two powerful personalities, Edwin and Paulinus, were in action. Given the number of British in the population, there must have been converts in this early mission phase who were British, some perhaps already Christian. Inhumation in close proximity to the temple continued after Paulinus's visit, the style of burial with grave goods from the past being in no way in conflict with the new Christianity. Hope-Taylor, the excavator of Yeavering, notes that the Paulinus mission involved effectively 'reconsecration ... people were allowed to go on doing much the same things and were merely asked to feel differently about them.'[60]

The careful, quasi-geometric layout on the ancient site, the mysterious tall post with its ritual significance, the long history of assembly and worship at the same place had a potency which a crowded, no doubt exciting mission with the powerful symbol of adult baptism could not be expected wholly to displace. Paulinus would have expected to return to lead a long process of acculturation, of prayer and instruction well beyond this revivalist movement. It was not to be.

Edwin was a king of the heroic age who lived by the sword and died by the sword. Earlier so effective, his moves against the Britons of the north and west ended in catastrophe. Cadwallon, king of Gwynedd,[61] combined with Penda, a Mercian aristocrat, perhaps with assistance from Aethelfrith's heirs and even from Picts and Scots. At Hatfield Chase near Doncaster, Edwin was defeated and killed. His kingdom of Northumbria fell apart. Cadwallon and Penda ravaged the land. Penda was a consistent pagan, though not hostile to those who accepted conversion; Cadwallon was Christian. This was politics and war in a secular context. Using Roman political vocabulary, Bede contrasts the British ruler's 'insane tyranny' with the honourable *imperium* of the Christian Edwin, refers angrily to Cadwallon's 'beast-like ferocity', and accuses him of intending genocide. Cadwallon, nevertheless, once driven by Edwin from Anglesey, possibly even forced into temporary exile in Ireland, had everything to fight for.

---

[59] *HE* II 14
[60] Hope-Taylor, *Yeavering* 250; continuity with Celtic past 280–1
[61] J.T. Koch, 'Cadwallon ap Cynan', *KCC* using Welsh literature, reinforces the traditional case, and T. Charles-Edwards, 'Cadwallon' *ODNB* with comment on Bede, preferred to A. Woolf, 'Caedualla *Rex Brettonum* and the passing of the Old North', *NH* 41 (2004) 5–24 arguing Edwin's killer came from the Old North

Aethelburh did not feel safe in Kent against the menace of Aethelfrith's heirs and with her children sought protection in Gaul. Paulinus became bishop of Rochester, taking with him mementos of Edwin's Christian rule, including a great gold cross and a golden chalice. James the Deacon remained in a village near Catterick maintaining a Christian presence, baptising and teaching music, singing from memory 'after the manner of Rome and the Kentish people'.[62] It was a slight, fragmentary result of Edwin's short-lived Christian epoch. Belief fell away. Paulinus's mass baptisms had not been consolidated; Edwin and Aethelburh's court, where one might expect a greater depth of commitment, was shattered by his defeat.

[62] *HE* II 20

CHAPTER 6

Oswald and Oswiu

In the kaleidoscopic manner of the politics of the heroic age, war, which destroyed Edwin's curtain-raiser to Christianisation, was also responsible for a lasting commitment to Christianity by Northumbrian rulers. But at first the situation looked black. Bernicia and Deira fell apart, Edwin's cousin Osric claiming Deira, and Eanfrith, son of Aethelfrith of the rival royal house, who had lived in exile among the Picts, Bernicia. Both had been baptised; both refused the risk of carrying their commitment to Christianity into the rule of lands still largely pagan; one after the other, both fell victim to Cadwallon, the last notably successful British leader against Anglo-Saxon power. Osric had taken action against Cadwallon and besieged his forces, only to be surprised and killed by a British sally. Eanfrith sued for peace but was killed by Cadwallon, who thus made a clean sweep of leading candidates for kingship, from both the Bernician and the Deiran sides. Bede saw these killings as a judgement on candidates who had abandoned their Christianity.[1]

Oswald of the Bernician dynasty, which had been forced into exile by Edwin, now came to power. A son of Aethelfrith by his diplomatic marriage with Acha, Edwin's sister, Oswald was approximately eleven when forced to flee. The Irish kingdom to which he and his brother fled was Dál Riata in Argyll; there, during some seventeen formative years, Oswald accepted the faith, was baptised, learned his craft as a warrior, and learned to speak the Irish language fluently. Oswald moved to confront Cadwallon, who with Penda had killed Edwin, ravaged the land and may well have been advancing north

[1] *HE* III 1

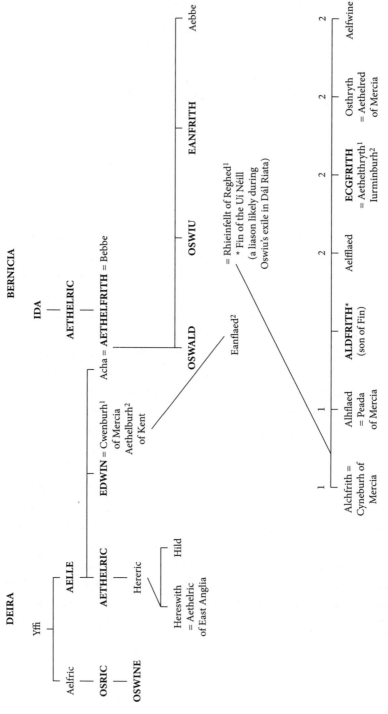

Fig. 6 The ruling houses of Northumbria.

Note: sons of Edwin and Aethelburh of Kent died in childhood; Oswald had a son Oethelwald who died at the Winwaed

to crush Bernician resistance when he was checked by Oswald and, in a decisive battle at Heavenfield, near Hexham in 634 or 635, defeated and killed.[2]

Columba's biographer Adomnán reported what he had heard from Faílbe, his predecessor as abbot of Iona, who in turn had been present when another abbot heard Oswald recall how Columba had appeared to him in a vision before the battle, had promised his support, foretold victory and encouraged Oswald with words from the Book of Joshua. Oswald put his faith in the Christian God: those of his war band who had been in exile with him in Dál Riata could be expected to be Christians but the bulk of his Bernician force would have been heathen.[3]

Like their counterparts in the Christian West, Irish churchmen had in general come to terms with the warrior societies in which they lived. Warfare was inescapable in contemporary Ireland as in Anglo-Saxon England; Adomnán describes Columba leading his monks in prayer for victory in battle for King Áedán of Dál Riata but there are some signs that Irish traditions brought out moral aspects of kingship which were not characteristic of the heathen Anglo-Saxons and it was their tradition which Oswald would have assimilated in his long Dál Riata apprenticeship. Bede is at pains to observe that in fighting and defeating Cadwallon at Heavenfield, Oswald was fighting for the salvation of his people – a not unreasonable proposition given the danger presented by Cadwallon to the Germanic North and his elimination of would-be rulers from both the Bernician and Deiran royal houses.[4]

As Bede describes the battle, Oswald set up a cross, himself holding it upright while his troops drove it into the earth: he and all his army knelt in prayer before it. In Bede's time, the place was an objective of pilgrimage and splinters of the cross were used for healing men and animals. Whether Bede was right to think that the cross which survived into his own time was the original or simply a marker to commemorate the battle and whether Oswald did indeed use a Christian symbol – some may see echoes of Constantine – is not of the greatest importance. Bede and Adomnán agree that Oswald committed his army to the Christian God and the reality of that commitment is shown by the immediate sequel. He sent to Iona for a mission to his people. At first this was not a success as Iona was a centre of asceticism and the first

[2] *HE* III 2; C.E. Stancliffe, 'Oswald, "most holy and most victorious king of the Northumbrians"', C.E. Stancliffe, E. Cambridge eds, *Oswald: Northumbrian king and European saint* (Stamford 1995) 33–83; *HB* 64; J.T. Koch, 'Oswald, St', *KCC*
[3] *Adomnán* I 1
[4] *HE* III 2

missionary underestimated the problems of what he called 'a people who were intractable, obstinate and uncivilised' and returned defeated. Among the monks to whom the failed candidate reported was one, Aidan, who spoke for the need to meet would-be converts halfway and temper the message of Christian living to them and was, in consequence, sent himself.[5]

Following the pattern of Iona, he took up residence on the island of Lindisfarne near the Bernician fortress of Bamburgh. Accessible only via a causeway at low tide, it was a missionary base characteristic of Ionan monasticism, with emphasis on withdrawal and austerity. Monks of the Ionan *familia* came to support Aidan, and Bede reports widespread preaching, though Aidan was not fluent in Anglo-Saxon and Oswald interpreted for him. Aidan fulfilled Bede's ideal of the devoted shepherd to his flock, normally travelling on foot, despising wealth: 'all who accompanied him,' Bede says, 'whether tonsured or laymen, had to engage in some form of study, that is to say to occupy themselves either with reading the scriptures or learning the psalms'. He is pointing the contrast to 'our modern slothfulness'.[6]

Not the least of Aidan's achievements was his success in securing for English monasticism the talents, devotion and connections of the young Hild; probably no one else at the time would have had the personality and aristocratic links to bring it off. Hild was descended from a brother of Edwin: her mother had connections with the East Anglian royal house and her exiled father Hereric had sought refuge with a British king as shelter from Aethelfrith's ferocity. His stay ended in disaster – Bede says he was poisoned. He does not tell us which kingdom was harbouring Hereric, though he gives the king's name as Ceretic, but it has been conjectured that it was Elmet, a small British kingdom in the area of modern Leeds, which had contrived to keep itself alive in face of Anglian pressure into the seventh century, and that Edwin's elimination of its independence was a consequence of his wrath at the death by poison of his kinsman.

Hild and her mother had benefited by Edwin's rise to power; no doubt Hild, at about fourteen, was one of the distinguished company which accepted baptism with Edwin at the hands of Paulinus in 627. She spent years thereafter in obscurity as a laywoman before becoming inspired by a wish to enter the monastic life. It was early days and nunneries were not developed in England but her widowed sister, who had married into the East Anglian royal house,

[5] *HE* III 2 (battle), 5 (Aidan)
[6] *HE* III 5

had gone into the religious house at Chelles in Gaul, which had been refounded by the quondam English slave Balthild after the death of her husband, the king of Neustria. After a stay in East Anglia, Hild was preparing to cross the Channel to join her sister when, it seems, Aidan intervened. 'Bishop Aidan called her home', Bede says. She was given one hide of land by the river Wear and there she began to live as a nun with a few companions: a considerable sacrifice on her part, exchanging for the settled existence of an established religious house in Merovingian Gaul the raw spiritual landscape of a Northumbria still close to paganism.

She persevered by the Wear, then became abbess at Hartlepool and, after Aidan's death, received a site at Whitby, which she developed into one of the leading religious houses of Anglo-Saxon England, a double monastery in which she, as abbess, presided over both monks and nuns – a form of monastic life adopted from Gaul. It was distinguished by its regular observance and emphasis on study, was a training ground for no less than six bishops and the home of the anonymous monk or nun who wrote the first Life of Gregory the Great. Hild's wisdom and her high birth made her a confidante of aristocrats and rulers.[7]

Bede describes how the gift of verse-making in Old English came by a miracle while she was abbess. A shy and illiterate cowherd employed on the Whitby estates, Caedmon, was accustomed to slip away on the occasion of lay feasts where participants were expected to entertain their fellows, 'when he saw the harp approaching him'. In his stable after one such occasion, he was visited in a dream by a man who commanded him to sing and when he objected that he could not do so replied, 'Nevertheless you must sing to me.' He was commanded to sing of the creation and found that he had the skill to do so. On awaking, he found he could compose, went to the reeve, his superior, who took him to the abbess, who heard his story and the verses he was now able to sing 'in the presence of the more learned men'. They concluded that he really had miraculously gained the power to compose and sing religious verse in the vernacular, so they instructed him and gave him the materials for composing. He became a monk at Whitby and continued to exercise his gift there until his death. Poetry, so beloved of Anglo-Saxon society from the heathen age and used to convey the stories of kings, heroes and monsters from the past, was an ideal medium to convey the stories of Scripture to a largely illiterate world.

[7] *HE* III 23, 24; D. Breeze, 'The kingdom and name of Elmet', *NH* 39 (2002) 158–71; J. Campbell, 'The first century of Christianity in England', id., *Essays in Anglo-Saxon history* (London, Ronceverte 1986) 49–67 (Gaulish influences and comparisons)

Hild was one of a number of high-born women who founded or presided over both nunneries and double houses, using their wealth and their influence with relatives to provide strongpoints for the faith. They were aided by the high status of women in Germanic aristocratic society and encouraged by Gaulish monasticism. Hild herself left no *Vita* and when Bede described her life, he was writing fifty years after her death. The main lines of his composition are convincing enough and they show a balanced and devoted personality who presided over an open-minded community anchored in the aristocratic world, which eschewed a withdrawn asceticism and was ready to foster the learning so necessary for a fast-developing Church. Whatever the underpinning provided by the role of women in her society, it was the authority of the holy man in the person of Aidan which prevented her talent and devotion draining away across the Channel.[8]

A common background brought a natural intimacy to the relationship between the Gaelic-speaking Oswald and Aidan, who probably sprang from the Dál Riatan aristocracy with which Oswald had so long been at home, and they worked easily together. There was generosity in endowment of monasteries and Aidan was supported in his preaching on royal estates. When the servant in charge of almsgiving told Oswald, dining with Aidan at an Easter feast, that 'a very great multitude of poor people' was sitting outside in the road asking for alms, Oswald responded by at once ordering his own food to be taken out to the poor and the silver dish from which he was about to eat to be broken up and distributed among them; Aidan took hold of the king's right hand saying, 'May this hand never decay';[9] in fact, hand and arm, severed from the body when Oswald was killed in battle, remained uncorrupted as a relic in a silver casket kept at Bamburgh. It was evidently not a solitary gesture because Bede's story incidentally reveals that Oswald had an officer whose duty it was regularly to relieve the poor. He describes Oswald as a man of prayer: 'very often he would continue in prayer from matins till daybreak; and because of his frequent habit of prayer and thanksgiving, he was always accustomed, wherever he sat, to place his hands on his knees with the palms turned upwards'.[10] He was uninhibited in his description of Oswald as 'sanctissimus';

[8] *HE* IV 24 (quotations) 23 (Hild); P.H. Blair, 'Whitby as a centre of learning in the seventh century', M. Lapidge, H. Gneuss eds, *Learning and literature in Anglo-Saxon England* (Cambridge 1985) 3–32; H. Mayr-Harting, 'Aedan', *ODNB*
[9] *HE* III 6
[10] *HE* III 12

to attribute sanctity to a warrior-king at this time was an unusual thing to do. Oswald's violent death at the hands of his enemies along with the tradition that he died with a prayer for his army on his lips, spontaneous veneration by the laity, miracles after death and the backing of the royal house created a saint, but Bede gives enough evidence in his account based on the traditions of Northumbria to justify this description.

Though he tells us nothing of Oswald's other battles, Bede with justice puts him into his list of great kings who held overlordship south of the Humber. This would not have been possible had he not been able to hold disparate elements in Northumbria together. Caedualla's activities had made it easier to hold Bernicia and Deira in unity than it might otherwise have been and the fact that Oswald was Edwin's nephew was an added cement, though tensions between these two very distinct areas of Anglo-Saxon settlement could not be entirely eliminated. Bede's phraseology on Oswald as heir is misleading, designed with a certain blandness to blur the central fact that Oswald had succeeded by force of arms to the difficult inheritance of both Bernicia and Deira. He calls him Edwin's heir; he was not. Anglo-Saxon understanding of kingship gave a right of inheritance to all who were descended from the line of a kingdom's founder. Oswald belonged to a rival line at enmity with Aethelfrith and his descendants.[11]

The removal of rivals for kingship coupled with the tradition of kin-vengeance was a powerful strand in Anglo-Saxon politics. It is significant that Aethelburh did not feel that her sons would be safe from Oswald or even from her brother Eadbald of Kent, as she feared the kind of pressure a more powerful king could impose on another, such as Aethelfrith had once brought to bear on Redwald for the surrender of Edwin. Penda's killing of Edwin's son Eadfrith, who would have had the duty of vengeance against Penda, eliminated another potential rival to Oswald. Division between Bernicia and Deira continued to be a major factor in northern history but for the time being Oswald's power ensured peace.

Against the British, Oswald continued the aggressive policies of both Aethelfrith and Edwin and with success. His main thrust was to the north towards the Firth of Forth against the Gododdin, where his connection with Iona meant that its success was likely to be less destructive of British

[11] *HE* III 1, II 5 (over-kings); T. Charles-Edwards, 'Bede, the Irish and the Britons', *Celtica* 15 (1983) 42–52 at 49–51

Christianity than was the case later in the days of the Anglo-Saxon bishop Wilfrid, for Irish and British Christians had much in common. South of the Humber, Oswald survived an earlier confederacy of those reluctant to accept the re-establishment of Edwin's overlordship but Penda was a hostile force which Oswald was never able to eliminate. He was endeavouring to build a bulwark against the expansion of Penda's power when he made a marriage alliance with the daughter of King Cynegils of Wessex and was godfather to Cynegils at his baptism. The two kings joined in giving Birinus Dorchester-on-Thames as a base for mission. Political need and sponsorship of Christianity came together in Oswald's initiative.[12]

The aid given in Wessex to the Christian cause was not the most important aspect of his work for his faith: the crucial decision to call in Iona was the major step forward. After the first failure, Iona sent some devoted missionaries and the Northumbrian Churches became part of the family of Iona under the leadership of its abbot; the founding of monasteries provided the basis for a deeper Christianity. Aidan is described by Bede as using his resources to redeem slaves and recruit them. Individual Irish missionaries played a part elsewhere south of the Humber, but in an idiosyncratic, volatile manner: in Northumbria the Ionan organisation sustained its contribution, which over time made it a cradle for Christianity in a way which had not hitherto occurred either in Kent or Edwinian Northumbria.

In death, Oswald came to have a great potency for the Christian cause. Penda had allied with British Christian forces and in 642 overwhelmed Oswald at the battle of Maserfelth, to be identified as Oswestry, where Oswald's body was hacked in pieces and his head and forearms mounted on stakes. This smacks of pagan ritual, perhaps a sacrifice to Woden. Bede is precise: it was Penda the pagan who killed him and displayed these remains, perhaps originally on the battlefield, perhaps subsequently in a pagan sanctuary, not a British warrior.[13] A year later, Oswald's brother Oswiu came with an army and rescued the head and arms, placing the head in Lindisfarne and encasing the hands and arms in a silver casket at Bamburgh. The rest of the body was presumably left on the battlefield and then buried. Years later

---

[12] *HE* III 7

[13] *HE* III 13; siting, C.E. Stancliffe, 'Where was Oswald killed?', Stancliffe and Cambridge, *Oswald* 84–96; D. Rollason, *Saints and relics in Anglo-Saxon England* (Oxford 1989) 23–129; W.A. Chaney, *The cult of kingship in Anglo-Saxon England: the transition from paganism to Christianity* (Manchester 1970)

Oswiu's daughter Osthryth with her husband the king of Mercia decided to secure the bones for the monastery at Bardney in the minor kingdom of Lindsey, approximately modern Lincolnshire. There had been contention between Deira and Mercia over Lindsey and Oswald was disliked by the Bardney monks as an alien ruler who had attempted to impose his power at the expense of Mercia. So when the bones were disinterred, put on a wagon and taken to Bardney for burial and veneration, the wagon was denied entrance and left for a night under an awning outside the gates. It took the miraculous appearance of a pillar of light the whole night long to persuade the monks to abandon their hostility and accept the bones. Once convinced, they gave Oswald his due. They washed the bones, made a casket for them and placed it in the monastery church; the water from the washing was poured into the earth and created a remedy against demonic possession. Oswald's banner of purple and gold was hung over the tomb. The remains thus found three different homes – in the royal centre of Bamburgh, the monastery of the Ionan mission at Lindisfarne and the monastery at Bardney, all under the influence and with the active support of Oswald's royal relatives. It was an early example of a durable tradition: the encouragement of the cults of members of royal houses. Though diminished by the destruction of paganism, the sacral quality of kingship and the aura which it gave to kings was in some way recovered by the emergence of saints within the royal houses of Anglo-Saxon England.[14]

Bede tells us of popular lay devotion to Oswald's remains: both the crucial battle sites of Oswald's life, Heavenfield and Maserfelth, were a focus for healing miracles. At Heavenfield, splinters from the cross which Oswald set up before the battle were put into water and used to heal men and animals. At Maserfelth, so many took away earth for its curative properties from the site where Oswald was killed that a hole was eventually created, so deep that a man could stand in it. In one early episode, a horse collapsing with the pain of colic rolled on the death site whereupon the pain ceased, the horse lay recovering on its side, then got up and began to graze: the owner marked the site, went on to the inn where he proposed to stay, found that the niece of the innkeeper suffered from paralysis and recommended the healing power of the death site. The niece was put into a cart, taken to the site and laid on

[14] *HE* III 11

the earth, where she slept for a time, then recovered. Animal cures were characteristic of the farming world, where so many lived close to subsistence and
the loss of stock was a heavy blow to a farm's viability. In another story, a
Briton, chancing to pass over the battlefield, noticed a spot greener than the
rest, inferred that someone of greater sanctity than anyone else in the army
had been killed there, took some earth, wrapped it in a linen cloth, then called
that night on neighbours holding a village celebration. He hung his bundle on
a beam; when the thatch caught fire, the whole house burned down apart
from the beam made safe by Oswald. Peasants at a village feast; a Briton; an
innkeeper's niece; a solitary horseman – these are lay people of low rank, who
recognised the sanctity of the dead king before ecclesiastics developed the
cult, cutting more slivers of wood and creating shrines where devotions were
formalised. There are intriguing echoes of paganism in the Oswald cult. It was
the horse, not the rider, who revealed the miracle-working properties of the
place of death; horses had a special role in pre-Christian beliefs, had sacral
qualities, were protectors and companions, escorts to paradise.[15]

Heroic deaths in battle were a prime feature of Anglo-Saxon poetry, and the
death of a warrior-king, who was also a Christian was a natural starting point
for a saint cult. Wooden posts had a role in paganism too; on them farm
animal heads were displayed as votives. The early devotees of Oswald cutting
slivers off the wood of his cross were acting, perhaps subconsciously, within a
long-established tradition. In subsequent developments of Oswald's cult associations with sacred wells play a part and this may not be pure coincidence,
given the Celtic pagan penchant for sacred wells and springs and the importance of the severed head in Celtic mythology. It may be significant that
Lindisfarne with its understanding of the Celtic world, though it received
Oswald's head with honour, simply buried it and did not enshrine it for veneration, aware, it may be, of the Celtic use of severed heads displayed in temples
or on fortresses to bring good fortune.[16]

Oswald's place as a saint, then, was given its first impulse by a spontaneous
lay reaction to his death on a battlefield, a bare site which had no ecclesiastical
presence – there was no control by churchmen and the faithful spontaneously
collected earth from the spot where he fell. It was soon taken further by

---

[15] *HE* III 9, 10; C. Cubitt, 'Sites and sanctity: revisiting the cult of murdered and martyred
Anglo-Saxon royal saints', *EME* 9 (2000) 53–83; A. Thacker, 'Membra disjecta: the division
of the body and the diffusion of the cult', Stancliffe and Cambridge, *Oswald* 97–127
[16] Ibid.

Oswald's kin. The needs of a dynasty led to a division of Oswald's remains, rare in Christendom at this time and forbidden by the papacy, as the head was deposited at the ecclesiastical site of greatest importance to Northumbria, Lindisfarne, and the arms at the key dynastic site for Bernicia, Bamburgh, where Oswiu built a chapel for the relics. In boldly presenting Oswald as a saint-king, Bede was breaking new ground. He was presenting a case not simply for martyrdom, which in contemporary understanding wiped away all previous sins, but for a saint whose life was worthy of veneration and whose prayers would be efficacious in heaven.

Edwin fared less well. Visions instructed an Anglian priest to seek out a witness who would tell him where Edwin's remains lay and, possibly after some lay veneration, at some time between 680 and 704 they were recovered from the Hatfield Chase battlefield and transferred to a shrine at the abbey at Whitby, presided over by his daughter Eanflaed and granddaughter Aelflaed; here again royal relatives played a major role. His head was buried at York, his body at Whitby. Yet, despite the similarities between the kings, both Christian, both killed fighting for their people, Edwin's cult faded while Oswald's flourished, finding support widely in Anglo-Saxon England, in Ireland and on the continent. Willibrord, the apostle to the Frisians, possessed a piece of the stake on which Oswald's head was affixed and, while studying in Ireland, used it to heal a fellow monk. Long after his kingdom had accepted Christianity, Offa, the eighth-century king of the Mercians, adorned Oswald's shrine despite the fact that it was the Mercian Penda who had killed him.[17]

The vision of a young Saxon convert at Selsey led its community to honour Oswald and ward off an attack of the plague. An essential boost to Oswald's fame was given by the monks of Hexham, a community presided over by St Wilfrid, who inaugurated an annual pilgrimage to the battlefield of Heavenfield and made available splinters from Oswald's battle cross; and his successor, Acca, was a source for Bede's healing stories. Hexham's concern for Oswald's fame may well have owed much to the inner politics of Northumbria and Wilfrid's decision in his long and controversial relationship with descendants of Oswald to back the young Osred, boy heir to Aldfrith, for the throne of Northumbria; a new emphasis on the saintly power of Oswald was, it has been suggested, the natural outcome of Wilfrid's decision to come to terms

[17] *HE* II 20 (Edwin) III 13 (Oswald cult)

with Oswald's descendants at the Synod of the Nidd. What this resilient and resourceful personality decided generally had a major impact. Edwin's cause had no such backing.[18]

It has been rightly pointed out that Bede's narrative of the reigns of Edwin and Oswald is, in effect, a narrative of the conversion process in one kingdom from the first beginnings under Edwin to the full unfolding of the Christian mission under Oswald and Aidan. The portrait of Edwin with his cautious step-by-step acceptance of Christian belief throws into clearer relief Oswald's unrestricted commitment to the Christian cause, his exercise of the virtues of humility and charity, his devotion to prayer and his early decisive backing of the Church's mission. How far Bede's narrative idealises Oswald as 'a most holy king' can never entirely be settled: his modern biographer notes that he may have been a 'rougher diamond' than one could ever guess from Bede's polished account. Yet it is unlikely that Bede's description of his virtues, with the oral traditions still alive in his own Northumbria, is a falsification. Curiously, the British descriptions of the three Northumbrian kings go some way towards bearing out Bede's characterisation. Aethelfrith, Oswald's father, the Saul of Bede's *Ecclesiastical History*, was in the *Historia Brittonum* known as 'Flesaur' the twister, Edwin as 'deceitful' and Oswald as 'Lamnguin', 'bright blade'.[19]

The reign and legacy of Oswald, his cult, his Life and his fame were of major importance. Christianity was established firmly in the dominant kingdom in the nine years of his reign and mission was encouraged outside it; most important of all, the growth of devotion to his life and ideals marked a stage in the assimilation of Christianity and Anglo-Saxon society. The fighting hero of Germanic legend had found a place within the Christian scheme of things. This would have been broadly in accord with Gregory's ideal of service in the world by kings and bishops. Bede himself, however, still praises kings who took the opposite course and resigned in order to enter monastic life. This most probably had its roots in Irish spirituality, a potent influence in the Northumbrian Church.[20]

A highly personal structure, Oswald's overlordship broke as soon as its creator perished. His brother Oswiu, who had shared exile on Iona and had

---

[18] A. Thacker, 'Wilfrid', *ODNB*

[19] Stancliffe, 'Oswald', Stancliffe and Cambridge, *Oswald* 61; *HB* 57; J.T. Koch, '*Historia Brittonum*', *KCC*

[20] C.E. Stancliffe, 'Kings who opted out', P. Wormald *et al.* eds, *Ideal and reality in Frankish and Anglo-Saxon society* (Oxford 1983) 154–76; *HE* I 32

similar experience, succeeding him at the age of about thirty, was hard pressed to restore it. The perennial tensions between Bernicia and Deira resurfaced, and Oswiu was unable to control Deira, which passed to Oswine, Osric's son and last hope of Edwin's dynasty, who bade fair to be, in his way, a worthy successor. A tall, handsome man, he had one crucial attribute of a fighting king, the ability to draw to himself warriors. Bede tells us that noblemen from almost every kingdom flocked to serve him. He grew close to Aidan, a tribute in itself to Aidan's capacity to work for the Christian cause irrespective of political affiliations: he had come as a missionary at the invitation of a son of Aethelfrith, yet succeeded in working harmoniously with Oswine, a hereditary enemy of that dynasty.

Oswine once clashed with Aidan over the gift of a horse. It was a classic collision between the assumptions of the Germanic gift-giving society, in which the gift advertised the power and generosity of the giver, and the other-worldly asceticism combined with uncalculating generosity of an Ionan missionary – the spirit of the Irish churchmen and their missionary offshoots. Oswine gave Aidan a horse of high calibre, fit for a king, to use in emergencies or on difficult journeys, a complement to his normal humble mode of travel on foot. Meeting a beggar who asked for alms, Aidan, the protector of the poor, got off his horse and gave it to him. The king was angry, Aidan obdurate. 'Surely this son of a mare is not dearer to you than that son of God?' he replied. Going into dinner, the bishop sat in his place while the king, who had come in from hunting, warmed himself at the fire, then, impulsively unbuckling his sword, knelt at the bishop's feet and asked for forgiveness. Forgiven, the king was merry at the meal while Aidan grew sad and wept. Aidan's chaplain asked in Gaelic, to ensure the king and his circle would not understand, why he wept. Aidan replied, 'I know that the king will not live long: for I never before saw a humble king. Therefore I think that he will very soon be snatched from this life; for this nation does not deserve to have such a ruler.' Incidentally illustrating Bede's artistry as a Latinist, this anecdote encapsulates both his understanding of the prophetic power of the holy man and his awareness of the perennial division between the call of the Gospel and the demands of the position of king in a ruthless warrior society.[21]

After Osric's death, the young Oswine had been taken to Wessex for safety. The friendly relationship established by Oswald with Cynegils of Wessex, his

[21] *HE* III 14

baptism and Oswald's marriage with his daughter, all made Wessex an outpost of Northumbrian power and a check against the expanding force of Penda. As guest of Cynegils, Oswine was neutralised as claimant to Deira – it could perhaps be called a benevolent detention. But all such arrangements broke down at Oswald's death.

Oswiu had been married to Rhieinfellt, princess of Rheged in the line of Urien, probably early in his brother's reign, furthering Oswald's expansionist policy in the north by putting a seal on the long-standing infiltration and takeover of this once-powerful British kingdom. She died and soon after he became king, in an astute diplomatic move Oswiu sought from Eorcenberht, king of Kent, the hand of Eanflaed, Edwin's daughter, whose birth on Easter Day had marked a stage in his conversion. The alliance which established a useful link with Kent was designed to mollify Deiran sentiments and end the dangerous attachment to Edwin's dynasty. It failed to do so. Instead, Oswine came out of exile and emerged as ruler of Deira, conceivably at the invitation of the Deirans; Bede says that Oswiu was 'a partner in the royal dignity' with Oswine who in his province was 'beloved by all'; but there was a lasting tension.

In 651 armies were raised; seeing Oswiu's Bernician army was the more powerful, Oswine determined to live to fight another day and went into hiding with a trusted thegn in company with one faithful follower. The thegn betrayed him and both Oswine and his companion were put to death on Oswiu's orders. It was a savage act designed to put an end to the Deiran threat, remembered by Bede as a great crime. Mourning her relative, Eanflaed insisted that Oswiu found a monastery at the site of the murder and Oswine's relative Trumhere became its first abbot. The killing still did not eliminate Deiran separatism and a son of Oswald, Oethelwald, came to rule there. Oswiu may have had a hand in this, but soon found his nephew exercising his independence.[22]

Maserfelth had been the making of Penda. He was exceptionally gifted as a warrior, a 'vir strenuissimus', who held together by military power the conglomeration of peoples which made up seventh-century Mercia, and attacked at various times Northumbria, Wessex and East Anglia. He ravaged repeatedly in Bernician territory; Bamburgh itself suffered attack and a

[22] Ibid.; C.M. Scargill, 'A token of repentance and reconciliation: Oswiu and the murder of king Oswine', SCH 40 (2004) 39–46

burning of the town was only averted by the intercession of Aidan. From Maserfelth till his death in 655, Penda was the effective overlord of the kingdoms south of the Humber and remained an obdurate pagan.

Oswiu seems to have attempted to deal with this menace by alliance, arranging a marriage between his son Alchfrith and Penda's daughter Cyneburh, while Penda's son Peada asked for the hand of Oswiu's daughter and accepted Christianity as the price of the alliance. It was a major step forward. The baptism took place at one of Oswiu's estates near Hadrian's Wall at the hands of Fínán, bishop of Lindisfarne, successor to Aidan, and was followed by the entry into Peada's lands of a mission comprising one Irish and three English priests, Diuma, Cedd, Adda and Betti. Oswiu also used his influence with Sigeberht the Good, king of the East Saxons, persuading him to baptism at the same site.

In Bede's judgement, Penda, though personally obdurate, was not an aggressive pagan: he did not, he said, 'forbid the preaching of the Word even in his own Mercian kingdom if any wished to hear it'.[23] But he is likely to have viewed with misgiving his son's approaches to Oswiu, and his baptism in Northumbria. Mercia was a fissile kingdom, which could easily spring apart and independent moves by Peada could be dangerous. It is likely that the sequel to these events was Penda's most serious attack of all on Oswiu, who, driven back to the northern end of his territories, probably Stirling, by a substantial army which included Cadafael, king of Gwynedd, was forced to buy off Penda with a heavy tribute and hand over his son Ecgfrith as a hostage. Oswiu then risked his son and his future, promising twelve estates for the building of monasteries and the offering of his one-year-old daughter to God as a nun if he was victorious, and with his son Alchfrith gave battle against heavy odds. Oswiu may have had help from Dál Riata, even from the Picts, ruled from 653 by Talorcan, his nephew, but Penda had had more than a decade to create a dominating position south of the Humber and had support from Oethelwald of Deira as well.

Against all expectation, Penda's army was devastated in 655. Oswiu's courageous strike against a numerically superior force was greatly aided by his choice of time and place, taking the host by surprise when Oethelwald and the king of Gwynedd had departed. He attacked at a point close to the Mercian frontier where the Roman road north-west of Doncaster crossed the river

[23] *HE* III 21; D.J. Craig, 'Oswiu', *ODNB*

Winwaed, probably the Went, a tributary of the Don. The army was home-
ward bound; Penda was returning late in the season from a triumphant expedition to the north and his host, turning to defend itself, was caught with the
river at its back. Swollen by heavy November rains, the water table had turned
into marsh the low-lying land around the causeway leading to the bridge.
Many drowned in the flooded river. Penda was killed and decapitated by
Oswiu, avenging his brother at the battle of Maserfelth. Courage, ruthless
determination and generalship had won the day.[24]

It marked a stage in the conversion. Oethelwald is never heard of again; in
his place Oswiu's son Alchfrith, who stood by his father's side in the battle,
ruled as sub-king in Deira. Oswiu gave 120 hides for monks, sixty in Bernicia
and sixty in Deira, as a symbol of reconciliation as well as an expression of
gratitude for victory, using for part of the gift the lands of the treacherous
thegn who had betrayed Oswine. In a similar position, Peada ruled southern
Mercia for three years on behalf of Oswiu till he was assassinated in a plot in
which his wife had complicity, while Oswiu kept northern Mercia directly
under his own power. Such immediate control seems to have come up against
Mercian feeling, so, after a revolt, Wulfhere inherited his father's kingdom.
Oswiu thus held his great power both north and south of the Humber only for
some three years, between the Winwaed and Wulfhere's accession. Thereafter
Oswiu's expansionist ambitions turned north, leading to a subjection of the
Picts and the exaction of tribute from them.[25]

But the military and political landscape had changed. Passive as a pagan
Penda might have been, but his aggressive moves disrupted mission:
Wulfhere, by contrast, had accepted baptism. Circumstances were much more
favourable to the cause of Christianity when the major power in Anglo-Saxon
England, still Oswiu's Northumbria, was an active supporter of mission:
Northumbria's authority gave a springboard to the monks who spread the
faith from court to court. Christianity had survived the death of Oswald and
the dominance of Penda, supported by the force of its own message and the
calibre of its missionaries; but Penda's death removed an obstacle. Wulfhere
married a daughter of Eorcenberht of Kent, became a patron of monasticism
and was served by a succession of bishops who set up their see at Lichfield.

[24] D.P. Kirby, *The earliest English kings* (2nd edn London, New York 2000) 78–81; D. Breeze,
'Notes and documents. The battle of the *Uinued* and the river Went, Yorkshire', *NH* 41
(2004) 377–83; *HE* III 24
[25] Ibid.; Kirby, *Kings* 82

Sigeberht the Good's baptism near Hadrian's Wall had borne fruit and Cedd came down from the Middle Angles to evangelise the East Saxons. In 654 he was consecrated bishop by Fínán of Lindisfarne. His church at Bradwell on Sea in a former Saxon Shore fort is to this day a reminder of his enterprise.[26]

Kings remained of critical importance. Those who made the decision for the faith still ran great risks. The fate of Sigeberht in the days when Penda dominated the scene is a case in point. He fled from East Anglia after conflict with Eorpwald and became a Christian in exile in Gaul, returning at the end of the phase of pagan relapse following on Eorpwald's assassination, to divide the kingdom with a certain Ecgric. Felix the Burgundian came to the East Angles at the instance of Archbishop Honorius of Canterbury and under Sigeberht conducted mission, setting up his bishopric at Dunwich; later, an Irish pilgrim, Fursey, stayed for a time and set up a monastery. Sigeberht's reign was thus significant for the embedding of Christianity in his kingdom. He himself may well have learned his Christianity in circles influenced by the Irish reformer Columbanus and inherited from him the uncompromising idealism which made no concessions to the special circumstances of kingship. He took the decision to abandon his kingship for a monastery and leave Ecgric as sole ruler. But an attack by Penda created a crisis. In his time, Sigeberht had been an excellent warrior; aware of their own inferiority in military skills, his people dragged him from his monastery to reinforce Ecgric in battle. True to his monastic obligations, he declined arms, went into battle carrying only a wand and, together with Ecgric, was killed.[27]

The missionary situation grew more complex. As we have seen, Felix the Burgundian came as a volunteer, went to the archbishop and then by his own request to the East Angles. Fursey was also a volunteer, an ascetic who had turned to the highest stage of self-renunciation in lifelong exile from Ireland, and East Anglia appealed because of Sigeberht's active Christianity. There he founded a monastery, passing it on his abdication to his brother and two priests with Irish names, turned first to the hermit life and then left for Gaul where he built another monastery. Birinus was another volunteer with high connections, perhaps even with Merovingian kings, a missionary bishop consecrated in Italy who arrived in England in the 630s on the advice of Honorius I, 'having promised in the pope's presence that he would scatter the

---

[26] *HE* III 22
[27] *HE* III 18

seeds of the holy faith in the remotest regions of England, where no teacher had been before', and ended up with King Cynegils in Wessex. His successor bishop Agilbert was Frankish; his, too, was an individual intervention, partly due to Gaulish interest in the Anglo-Saxon missionary field and partly to a general awareness of England's need acquired while he was studying in Ireland. He followed Birinus in the see at Dorchester-on-Thames. Bede believed that Cynegils's son Cenwalh grew tired of Agilbert because he disliked his 'barbarous speech' and invited in 'a bishop who spoke the king's own tongue' called Wine, a Saxon who had been consecrated in Gaul. Without consulting Agilbert, he proceeded to divide his kingdom into two dioceses and gave Wine the new see at Winchester. Agilbert was gravely offended and left. Some historians believe that the principal motive lay in Cenwalh's desire to create a secure ecclesiastical base in the southern part of the kingdom, as his people were pressed hard by expanding Mercia. Whatever the reason for Agilbert's departure, the overriding authority of the king is apparent.[28]

These pioneer figures in conversion history have little or no connection with either Canterbury or Lindisfarne. Progress was often made in casual, individual ways. Sigeberht was baptised as an exile; Cenwalh of Wessex, although the son of Cynegils, to whom Oswald stood godfather, had apparently never been baptised until, forced out of his lands c.645, he became an exile in the court of Anna of East Anglia; Felix and Fursey followed their own missionary impulses; Birinus did the same but was influenced by the pope, possibly aware of the damage done to the Christian cause by Edwin's death and anxious to bring in a reinforcement; Agilbert, though Frankish, came from Ireland to a kingdom which may have established an informal link with the Gaulish Church, possibly with the archbishop of Rouen. Canterbury may well have been isolated from Wessex: certainly its archbishops played but a small part at this stage in the forward movement of Christianity, kingdom by kingdom.

A multitude of factors were at work. Bede's story in the *Ecclesiastical History* revolves round personalities, missionaries and kings, some holy, some not. His story needs to be completed by the story of monasteries. Whether of the Irish and Ionan or the Roman tradition, monks formed the overwhelming majority of the missionaries: monasticism was seen as, and was for them, the

---

[28] *HE* III 7; B. Yorke, *Wessex in the early Middle Ages* (London 1995) 58; id., *Kings and kingdoms of early Anglo-Saxon England* (London 1990) 136

Map 7 Anglo-Saxon kingdoms, *c*.550–650.

highest form of Christian life and it was natural for their patrons to found monasteries and for the most zealous of the converts to enter monastic life. Monasteries underpinned the conversion and performed a miscellany of functions, of prayer, of study, of patronage. They could be founded as an act of expiation, as in the case of Oswiu; they could enshrine relics and be a focus for lay as well as monastic devotion; they could be a refuge for dowager queens; they were centres for scriptural study and for all the ancillary learning of the day; and they were springboards for continuing evangelisation.

In 680, the seven-year-old Bede was brought as an oblate to the monastery of Monkwearmouth and a year later was transferred to its sister house at Jarrow, where apart from a few trips away, he spent his whole life. His *History of the Abbots* is a history of his own monastery, but it throws a flood of light on monastic life generally. Lindisfarne was dear to his heart and he describes how Fínán built a church of oak there 'after the Irish method', thatched with reeds, and how Eadbert, a later bishop, sheathed roof and walls in lead. A monastery was a fortress against demons and Bede's description of Cedd's exacting preparation of a monastery site at Lastingham in North Yorkshire shows how such a fortress of the spirit was built up.

Though his sphere of work lay among the East Saxons, Cedd still returned to Northumbria and preached, and accepted a grant of land from Oethelwald, then sub-king of Deira, for a monastery where prayers could be said for him and where he might be buried. The site, while not remote – a Roman road ran not far away – was desolate. Prayer and fasting were needed to make the site holy and Cedd followed a most demanding Lenten regime in imitation of the forty days of fasting by Christ in the desert, taking no food till evening except on Sunday and then only 'a small quantity of bread, one hen's egg, and a little milk mixed with water'. He was called away by the king of the East Saxons and handed over the duty of fasting to his brother for the last few days of Lent; whether the fast was completed by Cedd in person was not the crucial issue.[29] Contemporaries would see the founding of monasteries as the creation of a network of prayer for the benefit of kings, bishops, priests and laity, for the

[29] D.H. Farmer, J.F. Webb eds, *The age of Bede* (Harmondsworth 1965 rev. edn 1983) inc. Bede's Life of Cuthbert (*VSC*) and History of Abbots (*HA*) and Stephen of Ripon's Life of Wilfrid (*VW*); intro. Farmer 9–38; *HE* III 25 (Lindisfarne) 23 (Lastingham) Texts: B. Colgrave, *Two Lives of St Cuthbert* (Cambridge 1940); *HA*; C. Plummer, *Baedae Venerabilis opera historica* 2 vols (Oxford 1896); B. Colgrave, *The Life of bishop Wilfrid by Eddius Stephanus* (Cambridge 1927)

kingdom's spiritual and temporal welfare and for the confounding of devils. Bede only mentions a few monasteries: it is likely that there were many more. Some would have been active in evangelisation, others, such as the little house of Irishmen in Bosham in pagan Sussex, incidentally mentioned in Stephen of Ripon's Life of Wilfrid, quietly existed without ever, it seems, influencing or seeking to influence the inhabitants.[30] *Peregrinatio* – exile for Christ – did not necessarily lead to missionary activity. But monasticism generally did lead to mission and was a vital part of the conversion process.

Another factor touched on but not fully illuminated by Bede is the evangelisation of the countryside through Christian courts. Duties of royal service and the custom of military apprenticeship aided the spread of Christianity, as young men from leading families served their king and attended court; if it was a Christian kingdom, they would come into contact with missionaries and the Christian practices of the royal circle. When in the normal course of events, they received or inherited land, they would in turn become patrons of monks and clergy, found monasteries and carry forward the Christian cause. The courts of Oswald and Oswiu provided such a training ground and point of recruitment for an elite in their kingdom. Benedict Biscop and Wilfrid are examples of men of aristocratic background who were not content to remain patrons, but went on to devote their lives to the Church. Biscop, originally Biscop Baducing, who took the name of Benedict in religion, was a layman in Oswiu's court, who in 653 determined to travel to Rome.[31]

The harshness of his stepmother caused Wilfrid to leave his ancestral house at the age of fourteen, albeit with a substantial following. Throughout his life, he showed a remarkable ability to attract powerful patrons and this was apparent very early on, when, recommended by noble contacts from his father's house, he was presented to Eanflaed, Oswiu's queen, who became his first patron and his protector as he pursued his wish to serve God. First he went to Lindisfarne and looked after a nobleman, a former companion of the king, afflicted with paralysis, and in the monastery followed the life and learned the psalter. Then he determined to make a journey to Rome to the see of Peter, encouraged by some of the monks, and recommended by Eanflaed to

[30] Below, 258
[31] Role of aristocracy, J.N. Hillgarth, 'Modes of evangelisation of western Europe in the seventh century', P.N. Chattáin, M. Richter eds, *Ireland and Christendom* (Stuttgart 1987) 311–31

her relative, King Eorcenberht of Kent: he waited a year, furthering his education till he could find a fellow traveller to accompany him. Such a one arrived, Benedict Biscop, the Northumbrian aristocrat. At Lyons they parted, perhaps after a quarrel, as Wilfrid's biographer compares their parting with that of Paul and Barnabas. Wilfrid stayed on for a year and earned the favour of the archbishop Annemundus; here he began his acquaintance with episcopacy as understood by the great Merovingian bishops, with their broad lands, their high aristocratic connections and sense of office.[32]

Passing on from Lyons to Rome, he entered on one of the memorable emotional experiences of his life as he visited its great shrines and developed a special devotion to St Andrew, patron of missions. 'In the oratory dedicated to St Andrew the Apostle' he 'besought the Apostle . . . that the Lord, by his intercession, would grant him a ready mind both to read and to teach the words of the Gospels among the nations'.[33] His gift for friendship emerged once again as he fell in with Boniface, the archdeacon of Rome, who took him up and instructed him in canon law and in the prevailing Roman mode of calculating Easter via the Dionysiana which was then dominant and superseding regional collections in Gaul and Ireland. This collection stressed the papal primacy. He had an audience with Pope Martin I who was deeply involved in a conflict over Monotheletism with the Byzantine emperor, who ended the pope's career by kidnapping him and sending him to the Crimea, where he died. It was an example probably not lost on the young Wilfrid of steadfastness in the face of bullying by a secular power.

He returned only slowly to England, spending another three years continuing his education at Lyons where he received the tonsure. This further, prolonged stay in one of the major centres of Gaul ranked second only to Rome in the impact it had on his thinking. Annemundus was characteristic of the Merovingian bishops of the day. Part of the ruling elite, his brother being the count, he was reared in a tradition of public service which blurred the lines between sacred and secular and was accustomed to the use of power and wealth. Bishops were founders of monasteries and accustomed to using their riches to educate the young and relieve the poor. High office could be and sometimes was combined with personal austerity and devotion: Gregory the

[32] VW 3
[33] VW 5; M. Laynesmith, 'Stephen of Ripon and the Bible: allegorical and typological interpretations of the Life of St Wilfrid', EME 9 (2000) 163–82

Great, who had been much concerned with the reform of the Frankish episcopate, recommended combining power and authority in the office of bishop
with a private austerity and self-denial.

But sometimes political needs catapulted unsuitable candidates into the
office of bishop, men hardly distinguishable from the lay aristocrats from
which they sprang. A Frankish bishop expected to be deeply involved in politics and to have the ability to confront rulers and defend the interests of his
see. All in all, it was a far cry from the austerity and passionate avoidance of
the secular wealth and power of bishops in the tradition of the Irish and of
Iona, which Wilfrid would have known in his adolescence. He lacked personal
self-indulgence – his biographer described him as given to fasting, vigils and
prayer throughout his career[34] – but it was the Merovingian style of episcopacy which gripped his imagination and which he sought to follow for the rest
of his life. The continental journey, combining the experience of Lyons with
Rome, its law and its shrines, shaped Wilfrid's outlook permanently.

On his return to England, another friendship drew him into Northumbrian
monasticism and politics when Cenwalh, king of Wessex, introduced him to
Oswiu's son Alchfrith. Soon taken with Wilfrid's charisma and his knowledge
of continental ways, and influenced by Cenwalh's bishop, the Frankish Agilbert,
an adherent of the Roman Easter, Alchfrith began to favour the Roman Easter
also. He gave Wilfrid endowments and pressure began to build up against
monks who followed the Columban Easter, including Eata, abbot of Melrose
and Cuthbert at the monastery of Ripon which Alchfrith had founded; they
were eventually expelled as they were unwilling to accept the Roman Easter.[35]

The Easter controversy was a peculiarly difficult one for all concerned. Its
roots lay far back in time, part of a complicated series of events involving
ambiguities over a decision of Constantine and the first Council of Nicaea in
325. Biblical exegesis, difficulties in managing systems required to combine
solar and lunar time, and ecclesiastical authorities changing decisions about
methods of finding Easter created a confused situation. Sharpened by the
great importance of the cult of saints and the attachment of Easter to great
names and Churches with long and honoured traditions, the controversy
came to have a momentum of its own.[36]

[34] *VW* 21
[35] J.T. Koch, 'Alchfrith', *KCC*; R. Cramp, 'Alchfrith', *ODNB*
[36] Synod and problem, T.M. Charles-Edwards, *Early Christian Ireland* (Cambridge 2000),
391–415; classic accounts, *HE* III 25; *VW* 10

In the early days of the Church, the Christian holy day became Sunday, the day of resurrection, yet the commemoration of Christ's Passion still had to be linked to the Jewish Passover, which in turn was linked to the vernal equinox and full moon and was celebrated on any day of the week. The mapping out of sacred time concerned both rulers and clerical leaders as, given the frailties of barbarian kingdoms, uncertainties over the correct timing of Easter, leading to clashes over the timing of Lent and Pentecost, could act as a cloak for challenges to kings and local separatism. Nowhere was sacred time more significant and nowhere did it touch daily life more acutely than in the monastery, with its liturgy anchored to the festivals of the Christian year. Awareness of the symbolism of light and darkness, of the contrast between the Old and New Testaments, between Judaism and Christianity and the desire to ensure that the festival of the Resurrection was celebrated at a time within the lunar month when the proportion of light from the moon exceeded the darkness, were factors working in men's minds behind the technicalities of astronomy and biblical exegesis, which combined to make an academic, reassessed solution among churchmen particularly hard to attain.

A solution by authority turned out to be the answer, tilting the balance against the Irish Easter but relieving the anxieties of those who, under the pressure of controversy, were troubled and, in Bede's terms, 'feared that they might have received the name of Christian in vain'. In Northumbria, the crisis brought into prominence one eloquent and forceful advocate of the Roman cause, Wilfrid, who now began his meteoric career at the highest levels of the Anglo-Saxon Church. He had powerful patrons: Agilbert was a constant source of support and ordained Wilfrid priest and Alchfrith made him abbot of Ripon.

Both Wilfrid and Alchfrith were uncompromising. Alchfrith's enthusiasm for the Roman calculation of Easter had dangers for Oswiu whose upbringing had been at Iona and who had inherited from his brother a predominantly Iona-trained clergy. Alchfrith was sub-king of Deira, and Oswiu cannot have been unaware of the dangers of Deiran separatism, basing itself on what was by this time a significant division within the Church. Eanflaed, clearly a woman of independent personality, as her reaction to the murder of Oswine shows, had never wished to adapt to the Columban Easter and had kept in her entourage her chaplain, Romanus, as well as the survivor of Paulinus's day, James the Deacon. Bede put forward an anecdote that because of the clash of custom, it sometimes happened 'that the king had finished the fast and was keeping Easter Sunday, while the queen and her people were still in Lent and observing Palm Sunday'. It made a good story and fairly reflected the emotions surrounding the issue but modern research has not found any relevant year in which this could have happened.[37] For Oswiu the main source of anxiety was political. In England, the question of Easter and the other sources of division came to matter as the numbers of continental clergy increased and links with Gaul and Rome grew stronger; loyalty to the Ionan tradition threatened Oswiu's contacts with other kingdoms and his interest in ensuring that Deira did not once again break away from his own power base in Bernicia. Rome remained a source of ecclesiastical power and prestige; if the Columban tradition was turning out to be politically damaging, then Oswiu was ready to abandon it. His decision would be made in the interests of his kingdom and his kingship.

In 664 he presided over a royal council for the kingdom of Northumbria, an assembly of churchmen and leading laity at Whitby; Alchfrith was present but Oswiu was in charge and made the decision though the debate fell solely to the churchmen. Colmán, bishop of Lindisfarne, spoke for the Irish party; Agilbert, bishop of Dorchester, of the same rank to balance the debate, was to speak for the Roman, but felt that his grasp of the language was too frail. Rather than speak through an interpreter, he asked permission for Wilfrid to present the case on his behalf. Colmán spoke first and appealed to the precedent of Columba and those who had sent him to Lindisfarne as bishop and, behind them, to the apostle John. It was an appeal to precedent and to holiness of life validating precedent.

In his answer, Wilfrid ranged widely, recalling his travels in Gaul and Italy, the observance of Easter in Rome, and denouncing those who did not accept the Roman Easter. 'The only exceptions are these men and their accomplices in obstinacy, I mean the Picts and the Britons, who in these, the two remotest islands of the Ocean and only in some parts of them, foolishly attempt to fight against the whole world'. In this Wilfrid was right. By the time of Whitby, the southern Irish Church had gone over to the Roman Easter and so had Columba's monasteries; the Picts, the British, Iona and its confederate monasteries in northern Ireland, together with those in Anglo-Saxon England who followed Columba's Easter, had become a small section of the Church, albeit

---

[37] *HE* III 25; D.A. Bullough, 'The missions to the English and the Picts and their heritage (to *c*.800)', H. Löwe ed., *Die Iren und Europa* (Stuttgart 1982) 82–97 at 91

still including men of high calibre and holy life. They were, in geographic terms, to use the harsh phrase of Cummian writing to Ségéne, abbot of Iona in 632/3, 'but pimples on the face of the earth'.

But their method of calculating Easter using an eighty-four-year cycle was not in itself an inferior one. It was a venerable inheritance, going back in the first instance to the old British Church, which with its high respect for St Martin of Tours probably derived the method from the saint's biographer, Sulpicius Severus. From the British Church, it passed to their converts in Ireland, who held a common means of reckoning Easter till about 500 when the Irish and British Churches became separate. Victorius of Aquitaine, using a nineteen-year cycle, was the sixth-century scholar whose tables and methods were taken up by the papacy and by the Frankish Church, which made the decision in 541, a decision that neither the Irish nor the British Church followed. Disunity on Easter had emerged as a factor in the tensions between the Roman mission dispatched by Gregory and the British and Irish clergy and sparked off a letter from Laurentius, Augustine's successor, in association with Mellitus and Justus, appealing for unity. Dagan, an Irish bishop passing through England, followed St Paul's advice on the proper treatment of heretics and refused even to eat with Laurentius and his colleagues. Nonetheless, at this stage the tensions were not overwhelming: an early Irish missal included Laurentius, Mellitus and Justus amongst the dead to be commemorated.[38]

What did intensify feeling was the work of St Columbanus, in personality not unlike Wilfrid, who had an impact on the Frankish Church and created a confederation of monasteries in France and Italy. The Easter question soured his relations with the Frankish episcopate; he was no compromiser and was unwilling to modify the observance he had inherited, though after his death his monasteries quietly abandoned the eighty-four-year cycle and accepted the Victorius tables. But the conflict on the continent had raised the temperature and it had become acute by the time of Whitby. The evidence is that the Irish were not ignorant of Victorius, but did not believe that his table and method were superior to their own. There were ambiguities in it and by 640 the papacy itself had turned over from Victorius to Dionysius Exiguus.

Both the eighty-four- and the nineteen-year cycles had their problems. Each had to find some means of reconciling the solar year, 365.24 days, and the lunar

---

[38] *HE* II 4; H. Mayr-Harting, *The coming of Christianity to Anglo-Saxon England* (London 1972; 3rd edn 1991) 105

year, 354.37 days, which the conflicting cycles did by intercalating extra lunar months. How and where these months were to be intercalated effectively forced decision-making by some authority – as indeed Constantine had seen, back in 325. First Nicaea left a loophole. Quartodecimans, as they were called, were condemned as not making the rightful and necessary distinction between the Jewish Passover and the Christian Easter and for celebrating Easter on 'quarta decima luna', the fourteenth day of the lunar month, whether it fell on a Sunday or not. Quartodecimans became a term of abuse, a label like that of Arian, and much play was made in the controversy with this term from the past. The search for a rightful solution in biblical exegesis was bound to be inconclusive because of the contradictions within Scripture, between the definitions of 'day' and 'feast day' in the Old Testament and in Jewish practice and between the timing of the events of the Passion in the Synoptic Gospels and John.

In Bede's reconstruction of the debate at Whitby, Wilfrid is depicted as pinning his opponent back to a reliance on Anatolius and the apostle John and displaying a polemical mastery of the technicalities of the rival cycles and the days of the moon unmatched by Colmán. John, he agreed, lived at a time when the Christian Church had not yet emancipated itself from observing Jewish practices: he and the other Christian leaders conformed so as not to give offence at the time to Jews. Columba and his successors, though not keeping Easter at the rightful time, acted with sincerity. 'Nor do I think', Bede quotes him as saying, 'that this observance of Easter did much harm to them while no one had come to show them a more perfect rule to follow'.[39] Nonetheless, Columba and his colleagues, he argued, were 'without doubt committing sin' if they rejected 'the decrees of the apostolic see, or rather of the universal Church'. Columba could not take precedence over Peter. It was a contribution in which Wilfrid showed his high debating ability, but he had raised the issue from one of discipline to one of faith and heresy and this was the dangerous path which the controversy subsequently followed.

Oswiu concluded the assembly by first asking Colmán whether the power of the keys had been given to Columba, then asking both if they accepted the Petrine texts. In Stephen's account, when they both assented, 'smiling', he concluded that he would obey the commands of Peter, lest when he came to the gates of heaven, Peter turned him away.[40] This half-humorous decision

[39] *HE* III 25
[40] *VW* 11 ('subridens')

bypassed arguments from astronomy and Scripture. Oswiu had made up his mind before the meeting was called: a decision from him was absolutely neces- sary, otherwise it would not have been prudent to hold the meeting at all as it would merely have exacerbated feeling. He gained on two fronts. He obviated the danger of a split in his kingdom and he secured the ultimate authority for appointing his bishops, which passed from Iona to the king of Northumbria. Colmán, faithful to Iona which had approved him, could not assent to the deci- sion and withdrew with some of his followers to Ireland, taking with him some of Aidan's bones and clearly having a marked effect on the number of monks at Lindisfarne. Relations with Oswiu were not broken off. Colmán asked that Eata, formerly abbot of Melrose, should become abbot of Lindisfarne; he had been one of the twelve Anglo-Saxon boys trained by Aidan and thus the emotional link to the father of Northumbrian Christianity in the reign of Oswald was retained.

Tuda, who had studied in southern Ireland where the Roman Easter was accepted, became bishop of Northumbria. There was evidently a policy of retaining those of the Irish strand amongst Northumbrian clergy, provided they could accept the decision of 664. But Tuda did not survive the plague which raged the same year as the Whitby assembly. Alchfrith and Wilfrid then acted. Wilfrid was to be bishop; he had received ordination from the Gaulish bishop Agilbert and now set off for Gaul to be consecrated bishop with the unimpeachable authority of Agilbert and the Gaulish episcopate. The impli- cation was that he could not obtain a secure and valid consecration in Anglo- Saxon England.

Both Bede and Wilfrid's biographer stressed the Easter problem but they were aware that there were other sources of tension as well. About the tonsure Bede reminds us 'there was no small argument'.[41] Like the date of the celebra- tion of Easter, discussion of tonsure carried with it emotional implications. Removal of hair was a solemn act, associated with mourning, with the status of slaves, with entry to the monastic or clerical life. There were echoes in Scripture; Job cut off his hair in his tribulations, Isaiah wrote of baldness as a sign of mourning: the Irish tradition of tonsuring, where the hair was shaved ear to ear across the front of the head contrasted with the Roman practice of shaving the crown, leaving a circle of hair round the head, its likeliest source lying in the conventional iconography of St Peter, which represented him with

[41] *HE* III 26; E. James, 'Bede and the tonsure question', *Peritia* 3 (1984) 83–93

a bald patch. The effect was to provide at a glance in any clerical gathering an immediate sign of the party affiliation of the participants. Opponents of the Irish tonsure sometimes insulted it by calling it the tonsure of Simon Magus and exalted the Petrine tonsure by treating it as a symbol of the crown of thorns. Such symbols were of great importance in the early medieval world and held an emotional significance that is now wholly unfamiliar. Like the Easter question, it could only be dealt with by an act of authority.

Wilfrid's determination to secure a Gaulish consecration and the leisurely pace of the proceedings removed him from the Northumbrian scene for years. Alchfrith disappears from history. Oswiu acted. He chose as bishop, with his see to be at York, the Irish-trained Chad, who had earlier been chosen by Cedd to succeed him as abbot of Lastingham. He was continuing a line of policy apparent in the earlier choice of Tuda – selecting a candidate in the Ionan tradition who had nonetheless accepted the Roman Easter and tonsure.[42]

York was a significant choice. There is little doubt that York had also been the choice of Wilfrid and Alchfrith, the quondam choice of Gregory the Great for his northern archbishopric, the see of Paulinus in the brief flowering of Christianity under Edwin and a one-time legionary fortress. The choice of York reinforced acceptance of the Roman tradition. Bede attributed this second appointment to Wilfrid's long delay on the continent, but a more immediate factor is likely to have been a quarrel between the king and Alchfrith. Oswiu was seizing full control of his kingdom ecclesiastically and seeking to build further on the platform created by Whitby as he dispatched Chad to Canterbury, the archbishopric of the Roman mission, for consecration. On reaching the south, they found that the old archbishop, Deusdedit, had died of the plague. Chad was inexperienced; neither he nor, probably, Oswiu realised the vital importance of having a consecration which would indubitably be valid in the aftermath of Whitby. Chad's party went on to Wine of Winchester who, at this time, Bede tells us, was the only bishop in all Britain who had been canonically consecrated. Wine drew in for the rite two British bishops, probably from Devon and Cornwall, who were adherents of the Columban Easter and consequently unacceptable to all who followed the Whitby decision.[43]

---

[42] D.P. Kirby, *The earliest English kings* (2nd edn London, New York 2000) 211; J.M. Wallace-Hadrill, *Bede's Ecclesiastical history of the English people: a historical commentary* (Oxford 1988) 129, 133; R.A. Fletcher, *Who's who in Roman Britain and Anglo-Saxon England 55 BC–AD 1066* (London 1989, repr. Mechanicsburg 2002) 52
[43] *HE* III 28

Plague exposed the frail foundations of early Anglo-Saxon Christianity: churchmen had spoken confidently of the temporal as well as spiritual benefits faith brought to converts – victory in war, prosperity, safe childbirth and the like. But what if acceptance of Christian belief brought misfortune? Did not the plague demonstrate that the promises were false and the old gods could bring down punishment on their apostates? Such was the inference drawn by some East Saxons as plague visited them and killed their bishop while on a visit to Lindisfarne. Sighere, joint ruler with Saebbi, sought to propitiate the gods by rebuilding temples and restoring idols. Fortunately for the Christians, Saebbi held to the new faith and Wulfhere, king of Mercia, asserted his overlordship and sent in his bishop Jaruman to restore the situation, which he did, travelling and preaching and ensuring temples were destroyed.[44] But the event made apparent the need for energetic bishops and priests to give sustained instruction. Unfortunately, the number of bishops had declined. In Mercia, Jaruman died and was not replaced; in Wessex, King Cenwalh's stormy relations with his bishops led to Agilbert's departure and later to the loss of Wine from the see created at Winchester, which remained vacant; Damian at Rochester was not replaced and Berhtgils (Boniface) for East Anglia, who had been consecrated by Honorius in 652/3, died in 669/70. Thus by the end of the decade Kent, Wessex, Mercia and the East Saxons had no bishop. London's vacancy was filled by Wine who purchased the see from Wulfhere.

Meanwhile Wilfrid was made bishop at the royal palace at Compiègne in a glorious setting, enthroned, carried shoulder high in a golden chair in a ceremony presided over by Agilbert with eleven other bishops.[45] He lingered on in Gaul; if Alchfrith had fallen from power, he would no longer have a protector in Northumbria. Then, being stranded on the coast of pagan Sussex on his return c.666, he narrowly escaped death at the hands of a gang of looters bent on stealing booty and enslaving the ship's company. Persuasion and offers of money did not dissuade them. In the account of Wilfrid's biographer, the scene is full of Old Testament echoes. A chief priest of the pagans, who stood on a mound both to curse his victims and use magical arts against them, was killed by a stone from a sling wielded by one of the bishop's men, as Goliath was slain by David. The bishop's force numbered 120 men, just the years of Moses's life, Wilfrid and his clergy on their knees lifted their hands to

---

[44] *HE* III 30
[45] *VW* 12; Wilfrid's delay, N.J. Higham, *The convert kings* (Manchester 1997) 260

heaven to secure victory in the manner of Moses at the battle against the Amalekites. In a phrase characteristic of both Wilfrid and the heroic Anglo-Saxon tradition in which he was so much at home, they resolved 'that they would either win death with honour or life with victory'.[46] They beat off the pagans and God caused the tide to turn 'before its usual hour', enabling the ship to be floated off. It was one of the sequence of trials to which Wilfrid was subjected in Stephen's narrative. It was also a reminder that while Whitby discussed the liturgical calendar and the shape of the tonsure, in the south, Sussex and the Isle of Wight had barely been touched by Christianity.

Wilfrid returned quietly, took up his post as abbot of Ripon and undertook periodically casual episcopal duties for King Wulfhere of Mercia and Egbert of Kent. Wulfhere became a benefactor and his endowment enabled Wilfrid to found a monastery at Oundle. Wilfrid believed that with the appointment of Chad to York 'a wrong deed had been done'.[47]

Oswiu built further on his decision at the synod and wrote to Pope Vitalian asking for his intervention to secure an archbishop of Canterbury. We only know of his letter because Bede reproduced a part of the pope's reply. It was written in the style the papacy used for dealing with Anglo-Saxon kings, persuading, flattering, encouraging, urging Oswiu to observe 'the holy rule of the chief of the apostles in all things, both in the celebration of Easter and in everything delivered by the holy apostles, Peter and Paul';[48] in other words, to ensure that the decisions made at Whitby were fully implemented. Presents of relics reinforced the message both for Oswiu and his queen, who was sent a cross made from the fetters of Peter and Paul, with a golden key.

The letter alludes to Oswiu's request for an appointment and observes that the pope has not yet been able 'to discover a man wholly suitable'. A quotation from Isaiah, 'Listen, O isles, unto me; and hearken, ye people, from far' and a reference towards the end of the pope's letter to the whole island of Britain – 'We trust that your Highness will speedily fulfil our desire and dedicate the whole of your island to Christ our God' – and the pope's allusion to Oswiu's seeking that 'all his islands' should be subject to God suggests another signif-icant aspect of Oswiu's exchange with the pope.[49] The texts, the assurance of divine aid, the reference to 'the whole island' give the air of a papal blessing of

[46] *VW* 13
[47] *VW* 14
[48] *HE* III 29
[49] Isaiah XLIX 1

a hegemony yet to be achieved by Oswiu. He and the pope would be aware that the British, the congregation of Iona in northern Ireland, Iona itself and the Picts had not accepted the Roman Easter. If acceptance was a matter of faith, as Wilfrid argued at Whitby and the papacy itself did in 640 in reply to a letter about the calculation of Easter sent by northern Irish Churches, the whole controversy became much more serious, with possibly sinister political and military overtones.

The northern Irish were concerned about the proper dating of the coming Easter of 641 according to the tables of Victorius of Aquitaine but it was a problematic year which showed up their contradictions. The pope-elect, John, and his colleagues wrote back expressing concern at the date proposed, which they believed involved celebrating the feast on the fourteenth day of the moon – as the Jews did. This answer was a forceful negative and may indeed have led some northern Irish churchmen to abandon Victorius's tables for the Dionysian being used at Rome. The significant point is that the pope-elect's letter denounced what he and his colleagues saw as a faulty calculation as equivalent to Pelagianism. It was heresy because celebration on the fourteenth 'pre-empted' Easter; it implied a lack of basic belief in the sole efficacy of the Passion and Resurrection just as Pelagius did. This was a forced interpretation but it raised the spectre of heresy. A resolute ruler in Anglo-Saxon England with a record of victory and strong resources had in his hand, it seems, the weapon of a heresy accusation. Charles-Edwards sees in this curious episode a possible foretaste of the attitudes implicit in the Bull *Laudabiliter* addressed to Henry II supporting his invasion of Ireland in order to subject its people to law and root out from them the weeds of vice.[50]

Oswiu remained a fighting king, who campaigned against the Picts, winning the kingdom of Fortriu and possibly Fib and Fortriv. His general overlordship south of the Humber established after the battle of the Winwaed was of short duration, ended by the revival of Mercia under Wulfhere, but papal backing and his emergence as the natural leader of the Roman cause could still be useful both south and north of the Humber. Bede believed that the Scots of Dál Riata paid tribute to Oswiu. This may not have been true. It is nonetheless the case that the relative strengths and weaknesses of Northumbria and Dál Riata left the latter in a state of dependent alliance: it

---

[50] Charles-Edwards, *Ireland* 434

may even have sent troops to aid Oswiu in battle against the Picts.[51] Iona remained the ecclesiastical centre for Dál Riata, yet committed to the Columban Easter; might it fall in the future under York and might Dál Riata be subject to a closer control by Oswiu as the protagonist of the rightful Roman Easter? Isaiah spoke of 'isles'; might the isles in question in the pope's letter include the island of Iona? In various ways Vitalian's letter opened attractive vistas for a Northumbrian king.

The relationship of the exchanges between Oswiu and Pope Vitalian, and Bede's information that Egbert, king of Kent, dispatched an Anglo-Saxon candidate to Rome to be consecrated as archbishop of Canterbury and to receive the pallium is not clear. To send to Rome was a natural proceeding in the situation in which there were few bishops to officiate in England, and Whitby had cast doubt on the validity of the orders of bishops of the Ionan tradition. To choose an Anglo-Saxon candidate was equally natural since the suitability of indigenous candidates had been fully established since Deusdedit's appointment to Canterbury and Bede informs us that Egbert was anxious to have a bishop of his 'own race and language' and did not want to have to use an interpreter.[52] Wighard, one of Deusdedit's household, was thus chosen and set out with his entourage to Rome, only to succumb there with his men to plague. It was the pope's right to appoint in cases where a candidate died in Rome, and thus Wighard's death had the same effect as Oswiu's lost letter in causing the pope to make his own choice.

Bede characterised Oswiu and his brother Oswald very differently: he did not forget the assassination of Oswine. Whereas the brother was 'most holy', Oswiu was only 'most noble'. Nevertheless Oswiu's achievement for the cause of Christianity was considerable. Ruthless, courageous, cunning, he kept Northumbria together and despite setbacks maintained the strength of his kingdom. Unlike only too many Northumbrian rulers, he died in his bed in 670 at the age of fifty-eight, seeking to end his days with a pilgrimage to Rome – in effect, a form of resignation. He used Northumbrian power to bring missionaries to kingdoms south of the Humber by requiring Peada of the Middle Angles to accept baptism as the price of marrying his daughter and used his friendship with Sigeberht king of the East Saxons to bring about the king's baptism by his bishop Fínán of Lindisfarne and to introduce

---

[51] Ibid. 434–5
[52] *HA* 3

missionaries to his court. Oswiu's defeat of Penda removed a major force disruptive of Christianisation and raised the prestige of Northumbria in the eyes of possible converts. A kingdom with a Christian court had, in the end, been victorious against one of the greatest and most powerful warriors of the age. He acted skilfully at Whitby in 664 despite his own Ionan and Irish training and his personal links to Colmán, his bishop, and warded off the perennial threat of Deiran separatism. He rescued his brother's remains and gave royal backing to the new cult. He was a founder of monasteries and helped to make Whitby a centre for training and monastic life as well as a royal mausoleum. His actions after Whitby and the death of Deusdedit opened the way to a revivification of the authority of Canterbury.

What Oswiu could not do was prevent a heavy blow being dealt to the traditions of Columba and Lindisfarne. Bede recalled that 664 was the thirtieth anniversary of the coming of the Irish bishops to Northumbria. At a stroke, three decades of membership of the congregation and tradition of Iona had been brought to an end: Iona would no longer appoint the bishops and in liturgical and clerical practice was divided from the Northumbrian Church. Colmán's departure with monks from Lindisfarne to found a monastery at Mayo in Connaught, English but part of the congregation of Iona, was more than a symbolic blow to the Northumbrian Church. It drew off from the Lindisfarne community dedicated men whom it would take time to replace.

Wilfrid's assault on the Ionan tradition left a legacy of uncertainty and mistrust. Though no doubt Bede recreated the Whitby debate as one of the great set-pieces of his *History*, we have the witness of all of Stephen's Life to assure us that Bede had got the caustic tone right. What was now the status of Aidan, the founder of Lindisfarne, or of Columba, the protector and patron of his congregation of monasteries? Deep divisions remained. Colmán and his followers solved their problem by departure. Nonetheless the spectacle of the sacrifice of their monastic home by these men for the sake of their loyalty to Columba could only disturb those who chose to remain.[53]

One party in Northumbria, given voice and leadership by Wilfrid, were the uninhibited Romanisers, fascinated by continental Christianity, who meant to press on and eliminate the Irish past. A majority stood between, accepting the

[53] J. Gameson, 'Why did Eadfrith write the Lindisfarne Gospels?' Id., H. Leyser ed., *Belief and culture in the Middle Ages* (Oxford 2001) 45–58

Whitby decision but still valuing the ascetic, spiritual tradition of Aidan and Lindisfarne, anxious that it should not be cast aside. Given emotional force by such party groupings, these sentiments and local rivalries brought suffering in the short term to Church members, but in the long run bore fruit in unexpected ways in art and architecture, and issued in a multifaceted Northumbrian Renaissance, one of the glories of the conversion epoch.

CHAPTER 7

Conflict and Reconciliation

WILFRID AND THEODORE

A combination of events and a forceful, gifted pope brought about a sharp upward turn in the fortunes of Anglo-Saxon Christianity. Around 666, Wighard, the Anglo-Saxon candidate for Canterbury, left with his entourage for Rome to secure the pallium and to be consecrated by the pope himself. He left behind him great gaps in the episcopate, caused especially by the plague of 664 and an uncertainty about the validity of the orders of missionaries from the Ionan tradition. Consecration as archbishop in Rome itself was designed to issue in an appointment to Canterbury of unimpeachable Roman orthodoxy. Wighard was to be a fount of orders and of orthodoxy in the confused situation following on Oswiu's decision at the Synod of Whitby. The choice of an Anglo-Saxon was in itself a sign of the greater maturity of the indigenous Church, as was its ability to train its men at home to the standard requisite for a bishop or archbishop. The first Anglo-Saxon bishop had been Paulinus's successor, Ithamar of Rochester, and he had consecrated Deusdedit, the first Anglo-Saxon archbishop of Canterbury. The dominance of the Italian mission was over and a native episcopate was coming into being.

How Wighard might have measured up to his task can never be known, since, as we have seen, he perished with most of his following in an epidemic of plague in Rome. The tragedy nonetheless put the appointment of a successor into the hands of a distinguished pope, Vitalian (657–72), one of the most Eastern-orientated popes, a skilful diplomat who had initiated a reconciliation with the Byzantine emperor in the long dispute over Monotheletism and borrowed from Byzantine ritual for papal masses. Vitalian had shown his hand in his letter to Oswiu exhorting him to observe the holy precepts of the Prince of the Apostles and was certain to look for a candidate who would enforce orthodoxy and build on the decision of Whitby, and the evidence is that he looked for scholars who would be fully informed on such matters. He may also have felt, as Gregory the Great did when he sent Augustine, that the mission field demanded a churchman with a full understanding of Scripture.

England was an unattractive posting, out on the rim of civilisation, at the end of a long and potentially dangerous journey, and Vitalian admitted to Oswiu in his letter that 'in view of the lengthy journey involved' he had at that time been unable to find a suitable candidate. He chose first Hadrian, a Greek-speaking refugee from the Muslim conquest of North Africa, who had long been settled in the bilingual Latin–Greek environment of Naples and had become abbot of the monastery of Nisida in the bay. He had contacts with the Franks, having served on two missions to Gaul, and had been an intermediary between the pope and the Byzantine emperor. He had scholarly powers and was an international figure. But he said that he was unfitted and recommended a chaplain to a nunnery, who pleaded ill health and refused. Vitalian approached Hadrian again, who asked for time to find a suitable candidate.[1]

This time he succeeded. With a similar bilingual background, Theodore of Tarsus was a Greek monk born in the birthplace of St Paul, who on the evidence of his biblical commentaries had studied in the ancient Christian centre of Antioch before fleeing in face of Persian invasion, then studying in Constantinople and finally settling in Rome, where at the time of Vitalian's call he was a monk in a Greek-speaking monastery, probably the Cilician house at Tre Fontane outside Rome dedicated to St Anastasius, a martyr victim of the Persians. He straddled worlds, was a linguist and, above all, a scholar. There is good evidence that he was one of the monks of St Anastasius who assisted in drawing up the proceedings of the Lateran Council of 649 rejecting Monotheletism.[2]

Although he had not been Vitalian's first choice, as he was nervous that a Greek archbishop might introduce Greek custom and confuse an already unstable situation, the pope was reconciled to his appointment when Hadrian agreed to accompany him to England and Theodore decided to let his hair grow, abandoning Greek-style head-shaving and giving himself time to acquire the Petrine tonsure on the crown of the head. This caused delay but, given the intensity of feeling in some quarters over the issues discussed at Whitby, it was a wise move. The pope required Hadrian to accompany

[1] *HE* IV 1; M. Lapidge, 'Hadrian', *ODNB*
[2] M. Lapidge, 'The career of Archbishop Theodore', id., *Anglo-Latin literature 600–899* (London, Rio Grande 1996) 93–121; id., 'Theodore of Tarsus', *ODNB*

Theodore and commanded Benedict Biscop to go as well and act as interpreter. Biscop was in Rome for the third time from his adopted monastery of
Lérins in southern Gaul where he had been tonsured and had expected to
spend the rest of his days; he abandoned his plans and was in consequence
won to further and vital service to Anglo-Saxon monasticism.

Together the trio travelled, but slowly. For six months they stayed with
Agilbert, formerly bishop in Wessex and now bishop of Paris: it was the opportunity for Theodore to learn more about his future flock. At last, in May 669,
he arrived at Canterbury, at sixty-seven an old man by medieval standards.

It was an improbable appointment, especially as Egbert, king of Kent, had
wished for an archbishop of his own race and language who would not need an
interpreter;[3] but on the other hand he and the other kings acquired a
commanding leader with wide horizons and the energy of a man decades
younger, who built the authority of Canterbury to a level never seen before.
In its early years, Canterbury necessarily had but limited authority as
Christianisation spread slowly. The death of Edwin destroyed the Roman
bridgehead in the north and the rise of the Ionan connection through Oswald's
seizure of power in Northumbria left Canterbury with limited influence north
of the Humber. Moreover Kent's power sank in the seventh-century competition between kingdoms and Canterbury's role was thereby diminished.

This now began to change. Theodore had lived in a monastery at the gates
of Rome in an age in which, alongside the great doctrinal controversy with
Byzantium, much practical business was conducted at the papal court: he may
have seen more of the world of power and politics than one might at first sight
have expected of a scholarly oriental monk. He was not unworldly in office. A
fair assumption is that his commission from Vitalian was to restore or bring
into fresh vitality a metropolitan authority in England, to re-create a territorial episcopate and bring about a unity of custom and of orders under the
authority of Rome.[4]

When Hadrian – who was delayed in Gaul by the unjust suspicion of Ebroin,
the tyrannical Merovingian mayor of the palace, that he was engaged on some
mission for the Byzantine emperor to the detriment of his kingdom – finally
reached England, he joined Theodore in a visitation of his whole province,

---

[3] *HE* IV 1; *HA* 3
[4] T.F.X. Noble, 'Rome in the seventh century', M. Lapidge ed., *Archbishop Theodore.
Commemorative studies on his life and influence* (Cambridge 1995) 68–87

north and south of the Humber. This had no precedent but Theodore received, Bede says, 'a ready welcome'.[5] Arrived in Northumbria, he deposed Oswiu's appointment, Chad, and reinstated Wilfrid. This established two points: that the authority of an archbishop overrode that of a king and that consecration involving two British bishops not recognised by Rome could not be accepted. Chad, a man of humility, accepted as such by both Bede and Wilfrid's passionate partisan, his biographer Stephen of Ripon, quietly accepted his removal and went back to being abbot of Lastingham. Theodore nonetheless wished to have him as a bishop and saw to it that he was 'consecrated fully . . . through all the ecclesiastical degrees'.[6] With Oswiu's and Wilfrid's consent he appointed him as bishop to the Mercians in a kingdom which now included Lindsey, where Wulfhere gave him land for a monastery. Lichfield became his seat, where he took estates by a friendly arrangement with Wilfrid, who had been granted them originally by Wulfhere.

Chad followed Aidan's custom of travelling on foot as a sign of humility and also, it may be, as a means of reaching Christians and potential Christians more easily and personally. Theodore commanded him to ride over great distances in the interests of more effective leadership and in a symbolic gesture helped him personally on to his horse. Chad was a man of magnetic sanctity, known for his practice of intensive prayer during storms, which he saw as God's warnings to mankind of wrath and judgment. He foretold his death, probably in 672, to his fellow monks. His body was housed in a shrine 'in the shape of a little house',[7] with an aperture from which pilgrims could take out some dust for its curative properties, both for mankind and farm animals, who would drink the dust mixed with water. Anglo-Saxon England was building up relics and shrines of its own. Theodore was making use of the personal qualities of men of the Ionan tradition provided only that they accepted Roman order. A first task was to appoint to the vacant bishoprics, the more important at an early phase of missionary activity because of the close relationship of bishops with kings, the vital role of their immediate households as training places for young priests, their activity as preachers and their duty of baptising and ordaining. They were a fulcrum of Church life. Theodore rapidly filled the vacant places at Rochester, Dunwich and

[5] *HE* IV 2
[6] *VW* 15
[7] *HE* IV 3

Winchester and when Chad died, appointed to Lichfield Wynfrith, formerly of Chad's household.

While Theodore brought new order and vitality to the Church, Wilfrid used his influence and his wealth to build and adorn. He restored Paulinus's stone cathedral at York, neglected in the years of Lindisfarne's pre-eminence so that the roof ridge let in water and birds flew in and out of the windows, nested and fouled the walls. Wilfrid leaded the ridge, glazed the windows, whitewashed the walls and gave an endowment.[8] The monastery at Ripon, Alchfrith's gift to Wilfrid, was provided with a stone church dedicated to St Peter, lying in a prominent position on a ridge with a crypt which survives, where as abbot he introduced a Kentish singing master with knowledge of Roman chant. Defending his achievements as bishop before the hostile Synod of Austerfield in 702–3, he recalled his liturgical contribution: 'Did I not instruct them in accordance with the rite of the primitive Church to make use of a double choir singing in harmony, with reciprocal responsions and antiphons?'[9]

Hexham, on a promontory overlooking the river Tyne with a stone church dedicated to St Andrew, was a community founded by Wilfrid in 671–3 on estates granted to him by Aethelthryth, wife of King Ecgfrith of Northumbria, who with Wilfrid's encouragement had insisted on preserving her virginity despite the marriage bond, till at length Ecgfrith yielded to her wishes and allowed her to take the veil and become a nun, first at Coldingham and then at Ely, where she was abbess. It was another example of Wilfrid's great ability to draw to himself pupils, patrons and followers. The churches at Hexham and Ripon were declarations of Wilfrid's religious affinities with Gaul and Rome and seem to have been aisled basilicas on the pattern of great Roman churches. Stone-building was a rare skill in Anglo-Saxon England and there may also have been an intention to hark back to great buildings of ancient as well as Christian Rome. Certainly at Ripon Wilfrid's men reused ancient Roman dressed stone from nearby Corbridge and the floor was of opus sign-inum, another reversion to the Roman past. Hexham's crypt closely resembles Ripon's: both were designed to create a worthy resting place for the relics which Wilfrid had collected, to facilitate the entry of pilgrims venerating relics and shrines and to provide an evocative scenario for both monks and

[8] *VW* 16
[9] *VW* 17, 47

visitors. Hexham had three entrances rather than two, and two passages tunnelled under the church walls, which probably enabled visitors to enter by a *porticus* outside the chancel and so pass in to venerate the relics without being obliged to enter the church.[10]

Both crypts would evoke a wholly unknown world of stone, so little seen in the Anglo-Saxon England of timber structures, with dark, twisting passages and candle-lit embrasures, a setting full of awe for the veneration of the relics of the saints, an echo of the catacombs with memories of the early martyrs.[11] Given Wilfrid's passionate Rome-ward gaze, these are the likeliest models for the fundamental layout, together with practical experience of the working of a shrine. The dedication of the stone church at Ripon was a magnificent occasion, held in the presence of Ecgfrith and his young brother Aelfwine, under-king of Deira, 'together with the abbots, the reeves and the sub-kings' and 'dignitaries of every kind'.[12] The dedication of the altar seems to have followed a Gaulish rather than a Roman ritual, in which holy water was poured on to the altar bases. Everywhere there was a display of riches and strong colours: the altar was vested 'in purple woven with gold' and Wilfrid commissioned illuminated Gospels 'written out in letters of purest gold on purpled parchment' housed in 'a case all made of purest gold and set with most precious gems'. Such conspicuous display, well known to the Anglo-Saxon world through the display apparatus of war and kingship, was here deployed for God and the saints on the precedent of the Old Testament, as Moses had built an earthly tabernacle 'of divers varied colours', in the words of Stephen of Ripon, 'according to the pattern shown by God in the mount'. At the ceremony Wilfrid stood in front of the altar and read out a list of the lands presented to him for Ripon by the kings and a list of 'consecrated places' deserted by British clergy fleeing from Northumbrian warriors, a reference to Ecgfrith's successful military action against the British kingdom of Rheged as revealed by Stephen of Ripon's listing of lands round Ribble and Yeadon and the region of Dent and Catlow as part of the generous landed endowment made available by Ecgfrith and Aelfwine. There followed three days and three nights of heroic feasting, the kings, Stephen reports, 'rejoicing amid all their people, showing magnanimity towards their enemies and humility toward the servants of God'. The list of

---

[10] *VW* 22
[11] R.N. Bailey, *Saint Wilfrid's crypts at Ripon and Hexham* (Gateshead 1993)
[12] *VW* 17

endowments which Wilfrid read out at the dedication of Ripon were not only a means of glorifying the abbey and, above all, its patron Peter, but also of ensuring acceptance of the abbey's title to these lands. It was a list presented to the kings 'with the agreement and over the signatures of the bishops and all the chief men'; in other words, a form of documentation for the future.

As Wilfrid's biographer, Stephen was intensely conscious of his hero's likeness to the great figures of Scripture, so he describes the fall of Bothelm from the top of Hexham church during construction, how the victim lying on the stone pavement with broken limbs, apparently breathing his last, was healed by Wilfrid leading the prayers of the community 'after the manner of Elijah and Elisha'[13] with an invocation remembering Paul's healing of the young man Eutychus of Troas who, having fallen asleep during his sermon, fell to the ground from a high window.

The years from 669, when Theodore restored Wilfrid to his see of York, until 678, when Ecgfrith turned against him and drove him out of the Northumbrian kingdom, were Wilfrid's golden years during which he held great authority, was enabled to unfold his style of Gaulish episcopacy, to build, adorn, commission great works and lead a monastic confederation which included not only Ripon and Hexham but monastic houses outside the Northumbrian kingdom as well. He claimed to have introduced the Rule of St Benedict to Northumbria; a magnificent manuscript of it, attributed to his patronage, survives.[14]

The secular power which Wilfrid exercised is best illustrated by the case in 676 of the Merovingian king Dagobert II. Begged by the Franks of Austrasia to secure his return from twenty years of exile in Ireland, Wilfrid, no doubt with the aid of his contacts with the Irish Churches that celebrated the Roman Easter, used his good offices to bring Dagobert back. Reproached four years later, after Dagobert's assassination, by a Frankish bishop for having brought them so unsatisfactory a ruler, Wilfrid defended his action on scriptural precedent. 'In accordance with the command of God to the people of Israel which dwelt a stranger in a strange land, I helped and nourished such a man living as an exile and sojourner and I raised him up for your good and not for your harm'.[15] Wilfrid travelled in state with armed followers; with his riches and his

---

[13] *VW* 23
[14] *VW* 47; defence of Wilfrid, E. John, *Reassessing Anglo-Saxon England* (Manchester 1996) 32–7, 42
[15] *VW* 33

entourage, he resembled a great aristocrat whose powers and contacts through his monastic confederation, and his gift for acquiring patrons and friends, extended widely in England and even into Gaul and Ireland. It was this power extending across kingdoms and an abrasive, commanding personality which roused enemies and led to the conflicts and controversies of his later career.

But he was by no means a merely secular figure, a Wolsey of the seventh century. There is no reason to doubt Stephen of Ripon's tribute to his asceticism amidst the outward grandeur of his living, for Stephen had been in close contact with him. 'He was habitually temperate at feasts,' Stephen says, 'and even when alone, never drank a full glass no matter how small the vessel might be. In praying and keeping vigil, in spiritual reading and in fasting, where will we find his equal? Every night, summer and winter, he washed himself in holy water until Pope John of happy memory advised him to forgo such rigours on account of his age.'[16] A miracle story in Stephen gives a glimpse of him in action as bishop out riding, 'going round on his various duties as bishop, baptising and confirming', when among the baptismal candidates in a village, he found a woman whose first-born son had died and whose body she was carrying. Uncovering the face, she asked Wilfrid to baptise him. For a moment he was disconcerted, for it was plain he believed that the child was dead but he yielded to the importunate pleas of the mother, prayed and laid his hands on the child, who recovered. The sequel to the story illustrates Wilfrid's firm hold on his people. The healing was accompanied by a condition – that the mother should present the child as an oblate when he was seven years old. When she broke her promise and fled, the boy was searched out by the bishop's reeve, found living with 'a gang of Britons' and brought to Wilfrid, who ensured that the promise was fulfilled.[17]

It was a vast diocese, not easy to cover even when the bishop had the energy and determination of a Wilfrid. Alan Thacker notes that Wilfrid ordained priests and deacons but consecrated no bishop to assist him. He showed no inclination to divide the territory, evidently inclining to believe, as Gaulish bishops did, that he required the endowments of so substantial a bishopric to sustain him and his followers in the style he believed appropriate.[18] That assumption led to conflict in his later career.

[16] *VW* 21
[17] *VW* 18; see above ch. 6 n. 29
[18] A. Thacker, 'Wilfrid', *ODNB*

Wilfrid made no challenge to Theodore during these years but seems to have maintained a respectful distance, being content to exercise a semi-independent role in the north. When Theodore summoned a council of the bishops of Anglo-Saxon England to Hertford in 672, Wilfrid sent his legates to represent him. There had not been a synod in the real sense of the word in the English Church before Theodore entered office; missionary bishops had conferred together in a corner of Anglo-Saxon England, Augustine had conferred with British bishops; and a council of one kingdom, Northumbria, with ecclesiastics and magnates presided over by the king had made a momentous decision over Easter and obedience to Rome; but Hertford was the first true synod of the whole Anglo-Saxon Church north and south of the Humber. Unlike Whitby, Hertford was presided over by its archbishop and it legislated not for a kingdom but for the whole Church, carrying forward Theodore's policy of integrating the mission field of England in the structures and law code of the Roman Church. We learn from another passage in Bede that Ecgfrith was also present but he did not preside and he is not mentioned in the record of the synod.[19]

The record of the Council came from Theodore himself and no doubt knowledge of it reached Bede via his informants in Canterbury. It followed Italian norms and in the contemporary Italian style the completion clause names the notary responsible: having been brought up in the written culture of the Mediterranean world, Theodore, like other Graeco-Roman bishops, expected to have his own notary. The ten canons of the Council blend shrewd practicalities relevant to the condition of the English Church with statements of principle. The proceedings opened with an exhortation by Theodore 'that we all should deliberate in common for the benefit of the faith; so that whatever has been decreed and defined by holy fathers of proved worth may be preserved incorrupt by us all.'[20] The canons agreed at the synod were indeed based on these earlier decisions.

The first canon harked back to Whitby and also to Pope Vitalian's wish to appoint as archbishop a candidate who would enforce obedience to the Roman Easter: it ran 'that we all keep Easter Day at the same time, namely on the Sunday after the fourteenth day of the moon of the first month', i.e. the equinox.[21] Theodore was unyielding on this point. Other canons were

---

[19] C. Cubitt, *Anglo-Saxon Church councils c. 650–850* (Leicester 1995)
[20] *HE* IV 5
[21] Ibid.

concerned with establishing the norms of episcopal activity and the clergy under their obedience – no bishop was to intrude into the diocese of another; no clergy were to wander about at will and they were not to be received anywhere without letters of commendation from their own bishop; monks were not to wander except with letters dimissory from their own abbot and they were to keep their promise of obedience made when they were professed; travelling bishops and clergy were to be 'content with the hospitality afforded them' and to exercise no priestly function without permission from the bishop of the diocese. Synods of the bishops were to become a permanent feature of Church life. The first inclination had been to meet twice a year but various obstacles led them to decide to meet once a year on 1 August at a place called Clofeshoh, now unidentifiable but, some believe, located near London. Even that proved far too ambitious.

The synod was largely amenable to Theodore's wishes – this was hardly surprising since he was a commanding personality and he had appointed most of them, Bisi for the East Angles, Putta for Rochester, Wynfrith, successor to Chad, for the Mercians. The exception was Leutherius for the West Saxons, who was not of indigenous origin but was Agilbert's Frankish nephew, dispatched in his stead when, as an act of repentance, the king invited Agilbert to return. Cenwahl's kingdom had remained for a time without a bishop as Wine, whom he had appointed bishop of Winchester, had also fallen foul of the king and left to purchase the bishopric of London. Bede reflected that during this interval Cenwalh who 'was continually suffering heavy losses in his kingdom at the hands of his enemies' had come to realise that his action had left his kingdom without God's protection. Leutherius was accepted and consecrated by Theodore. This was an old-style appointment of a nephew of a former bishop with the decision being made by the king, but it worked. Bede says he ruled 'wisely'.[22]

There is no mention of the simoniac Wine in the synod's proceedings. With Wilfrid's legates, there were only five bishops present or represented; with the exception of Putta of Rochester, there was one bishop per kingdom, indicating that large tracts of mission territory fell under one man. This was not the tradition of episcopacy in which Theodore had been reared, for his earlier experience was of the multitude of sees in the Greek world, with their intimate connection between the bishops and their cities. A predilection for small

[22] *HE* III 7

dioceses would be reinforced by Theodore's experience of the Roman, as opposed to Gaulish, liturgy where bishops participated directly in the baptismal rite itself, making regular episcopal visitations necessary and in turn requiring manageable sees where closer pastoral care was possible.[23]

Hertford began to grapple with the problem. It was recorded 'that more bishops shall be created as the number of the faithful increases'. But the statement continues, 'This chapter received general discussion, but at the time we came to no decision on the matter'.[24] Here, it is probable, Theodore met some resistance, based in part on the problems of adequate endowment and the necessary role of kings in supporting the physical needs of a bishop and his *familia*. Without royal help, direct support and patronage, the bishop's position was shaky indeed and the assembled episcopate would certainly have been aware of this.

At the back of the deliberations at Hertford, moreover, lay a clash of assumptions between the Germanic rulers' understanding of a bishop as a follower from whom a king would expect the fidelity due from his great aristocrats, and the established, canonical concept of the bishop as an independent leader of the Church with his own objectively understood rights and duties. The latter was not likely to prevail easily. Episcopacy had to accommodate to the realities of Germanic kingship. Theodore was concerned to achieve a unity amongst his bishops, requiring from them their signatures to the decisions taken and laying down sanctions for those who disobeyed. 'If anyone therefore shall attempt in any way to oppose or disobey the decisions confirmed by our consent and ratified by our signatures . . . let him know that he is excluded from exercising any priestly office and from our fellowship'.[25] Towards this aim of unity, he had a note in canon eight that precedence among bishops should be determined solely by seniority of consecration. The bulk of the deliberations was evidently concerned with building a coherent, territorially based, disciplined episcopate and banishing the Irish tradition of the wandering preacher, valuable as it had been in the pioneer days of mission – or indeed in Theodore's own time. In the fourth canon we glimpse the realities of the pagan society into which Christianity had been inserted and with which the bishops and their priests had to contend. Theodore

[23] H. Vollrath, 'Taufliturgie und Diozesanteilung in der frühen angelsächischen Kirche', P. Ni Chatháin, M. Richter eds, *Ireland and Europe* 377–86
[24] *HE* IV 5
[25] Ibid.

reaffirmed the sanctity of Christian marriage: 'that nothing be allowed but lawful wedlock', says the tenth canon. 'Let none be guilty of incest and let none leave his own wife except for fornication, as the holy gospel teaches.'[26] In sexual matters lay a major source of friction between the old world and Christian teaching.

The synod was a publicising event. At the centre of attention lay, certainly, the bishops, since a prime aim was the establishment of a territorial episcopate and, of the ten canons, no less than seven were concerned with the rights and duties of bishops. But others were present to hear and disseminate the new understanding of the role of canon law. Bede describes those summoned as consisting not only of the bishops but also of 'many teachers of the Church who knew and loved the canonical statutes of the Fathers':[27] their function plainly was to make known the role of canon law in the mission Church. Theodore brought out his book of canons, a version of the collection of Dionysius Exiguus, and showed them the places he had marked and which he believed to be most relevant to Anglo-Saxon England, giving the impression that he was not intending to make new law but to make effective the decisions of the Church in the past.[28]

Hertford shows the thrust of Theodore's thinking: canon nine might put it diplomatically and refer to an increase in the episcopate 'as the number of the faithful increases' – a proposition which could hardly be rejected in itself – but Theodore's consistent aim was to have smaller dioceses wherein the bishop's influence and authority could be more effective, and he set about subdividing the great dioceses wherever opportunity occurred. Bisi's illness gave him the chance in the mid-670s to split the diocese of the East Angles into two, putting beside the old see at Dunwich a new one at North Elmham with accompanying new bishops. The division corresponded to a division between North Folk and South Folk, the latter keeping Dunwich while the former had the new bishopric.[29]

When Wine died, Theodore appointed Earconwald, founder and abbot of Chertsey, to be bishop to the East Saxons with his see at London. Bede praises his holiness and that of his sister Ethelburga, for Earconwald had founded a monastic establishment at Barking, a double monastery for men

---

[26] Ibid.
[27] Ibid.
[28] M. Brett, 'Theodore and the Latin canon law', Lapidge, *Theodore* 120–40
[29] *HE* IV 6

and women distinguished by visions, miracles and courage in the face of death. Earconwald's horse litter, used to carry him about when he was ill, became a healing relic to which the sick were taken to be placed under or beside it. In Ethelburga's convent a boy of three being brought up by the nuns, too young even to be an oblate, sickened of plague and, dying, called out three times to one of the nuns. The convent gave the nun's death a supernatural interpretation and believed that the little boy was summoning her to the kingdom of heaven; children, in fact, were often the most vulnerable to infection and the boy may well have infected the nun who had most contact with him. Bede expands his narrative stories of healing, edifying deaths and the appearance of brilliant, heavenly lights in and around the convent, resembling the supernatural lights of Adomnán's Life of Columba. These were not irrelevant to Bede's account of Earconwald. Holiness was for him above all the mark of the episcopate, and the mention of the brother led him naturally to an account of the holiness of his sister. Both were bulwarks of the Church and the miracles and the signs showed God's favour to it.[30]

This makes the more poignant Bede's entry on Wynfrith, the former member of Chad's household consecrated by Theodore to succeed him at Lichfield. 'Not long afterwards Archbishop Theodore, displeased by some act of disobedience of Wynfrith, bishop of the Mercians, deposed him from the bishopric which he had held only a few years.' He goes on to describe how Wynfrith went back to his monastery at Barrow in Lindsey, 'and there lived a very holy life until his death'. In his place, Theodore appointed another abbot, Seaxwulf, founder and abbot of Peterborough, probably also subdividing the bishopric at this point. Theodore was a masterful old man in a hurry: the entry on Wynfrith implies a rebuke.[31]

In 678 Theodore made a mistake. In the pursuit of the objective of securing smaller dioceses, he seized the opportunity of King Ecgfrith of Northumbria's quarrel with Wilfrid to break up his massive diocese in the north, enlarged still further since the time when Wilfrid took office by Ecgfrith's conquests in his campaigns against the British, the Picts and the Scots. Wilfrid's power over and above kingdoms was in any event likely to cause disquiet, the more so in view of his friendly relations with Mercia. He had been on good terms with Wulfhere, one of his benefactors, and friendly relations continued after 675

---

[30] Ibid. 6 (Earconwald) 8 (Ethelburga); comment, S. Crawford, *Childhood in Anglo-Saxon England* (Stroud 1999) 84

[31] *HE* IV 6

when Wulfhere died and was succeeded by his brother Aethelred, just at a time when tensions between Mercia and Northumbria were on the increase. Under abbess Hild, Whitby, a royal foundation and burial place of the Northumbrian kings, was a focus of hostility to Wilfrid; Hild's sympathies at the time of the great synod had been with Lindisfarne against Wilfrid's party, and her continental links were with the western Franks, in contradistinction to Wilfrid's connections with the eastern Franks. A hidden factor could have been some attachment to other potential royal claimants, whether from Bernician or Deiran houses.[32]

No doubt the most acute source of tension was personal. Ecgfrith could not be expected to bear with equanimity Wilfrid's successful encouragement of his queen's sustaining her virginity; after the issue had been finally resolved by Aethelthryth taking the veil and entering Coldingham, his second queen Iurminburh took against Wilfrid and, in Stephen of Ripon's account, poisoned the king's mind, troubling him with her descriptions of Wilfrid's wealth and power and, most significant, 'his countless army of followers arrayed in royal vestments and arms' like a king's retinue. In his crude fashion, Stephen alleged that the king and queen proceeded to bribe Archbishop Theodore to fall in with their plans. It was not so. The archbishop was eager to take the opportunity to use Wilfrid's fall to create smaller dioceses in the north and he failed to anticipate the hornet's nest that his actions would stir up. Bede puts the responsibility firmly on Ecgfrith: 'there arose a dissension between King Ecgfrith and the most reverend bishop Wilfrid with the result that the bishop was driven from his see'.[33]

However, Bede disliked recounting unedifying quarrels within the Church and is remarkably reticent about Wilfrid's dispute with Theodore. After alluding to the conflict, Wilfrid's expulsion and his subsequent travelling, including a journey to Rome, he notes that on his return, the hostility of Ecgfrith made it impossible for him to go back to his own diocese. Bede then gives an extended description of Wilfrid's missionary work among the South Saxons and later his dealing with the people and rulers of the Isle of Wight; it is a strangely cavalier way of noticing a major conflict between a leading Anglo-Saxon churchman and his archbishop and two successive kings of

[32] Wulfhere, D.P. Kirby, *The earliest English kings* (2nd edn 2000) 94–8; gen. comment, Kirby, 'Northumbria in the time of Wilfrid', id., *St Wilfrid at Hexham* (Newcastle 1974) 1–34
[33] *HE* IV 12

Northumbria. Bede's *History* was intended to edify and this was not an edifying story, so he omitted much of it and concentrated on Wilfrid's remarkable gifts as a converter of pagans.

Wilfrid was angry at his expulsion and the loss of his bishopric and probably the more angry because of the nature of the appointments made by Theodore, as he used the quarrel to break up the great diocese. Bosa was appointed to York with responsibility, in effect, for the ancient kingdom of Deira; Eata was appointed to Hexham for Bernicia, Eadhaed was given Lindsey and then, after Mercia took Lindsey from Northumbria, Ripon. Hexham was officially designated as the see (though in practice Eata often preferred Lindisfarne) and Hexham was Wilfrid's monastery – as was Ripon. Bosa was a monk from Hild's abbey of Whitby and thus emanated from a milieu unsympathetic to Wilfrid; Eata came from Melrose and Lindisfarne, i.e. monasteries from the former Ionan congregation; Eadhaed had served Oswiu, who had appointed Chad in place of Wilfrid at York. This made it all the more disagreeable. What Wilfrid would have wanted were monks from his own establishments or men who had served in his episcopal household, knew his mind and were part of his following. This would have sweetened the pill and could have reconciled him to the division of his over-extended diocese. Stephen commented querulously, 'In the absence of our bishop he consecrated, by himself, over parts of Wilfrid's own diocese, irregularly and contrary to all precedent, three bishops who had been picked up elsewhere and were not subjects of this diocese.'[34]

Theodore was a passionate reformer and he was seventy-six when the crisis blew up. He would not have been able to stop Ecgfrith's reaction against Wilfrid, but feeling it too good an opportunity to miss, was precipitate in cooperating with Ecgfrith against Wilfrid in Wilfrid's absence and failed to act in consultation with the English bishops. Wilfrid went off to appeal to the pope against uncanonical proceedings. It was the start of a long conflict.

In the following year, 679, Ecgfrith and the Northumbrian cause received a sharp check when he met Aethelred of Mercia in battle at the river Trent, was defeated and lost his younger brother Aelfwine in the fight. It ended Northumbrian ambitions against Mercia and undid Ecgfrith's earlier success against Aethelred's brother, Wulfhere, who had done so much to revive

---

[34] *VW* 24; C. Cubitt, 'Wilfrid's usurping bishops: episcopal elections in Anglo-Saxon England *c*.600–*c*.800', *NH* 24–5 (1988–9) 18–38

Mercian power, Lindsey, always something of a shuttlecock between these powers, passing back to Mercia. Stephen of Ripon interpreted the loss of Aelfwine as punishment for the rejection of Wilfrid's appeal to the king and archbishop to rescind the decision to take away his bishopric and describes his hero turning away from the royal tribunal and, 'amid the mirthful laughter of the king's flatterers' prophesying that 'on this day twelvemonth you who now laugh at my condemnation through malice, shall then weep bitterly over your own confusion'. 'And his prophecy was true,' wrote Stephen, 'for on that day twelve month the body of the slain king Aelfwine was carried into York, and all the people with bitter tears tore their garments and their hair.'[35] Aelfwine had been loved in both kingdoms, Northumbria and Mercia.

Strong emotions were in play and the feud to avenge a dead brother was a matter of honour for Ecgfrith. Blood feud was a major sanction in Anglo-Saxon England, as it was among the Franks, indispensable in a society without police. Theodore now showed what a powerful personality accustomed to working with kings could do in the bloodstained politics of the seventh century as he brought together Ecgfrith and Aethelred to avert the feud. Despite his victory, Aethelred showed himself willing to pay the blood price and so ward off war. Bede gives Theodore the credit for making peace after 'prolonged hostilities between the kings and between these war-like peoples': he had the advantage of being a complete outsider, with no family links to any of the protagonists. Whether he was invited as arbitrator or whether he simply intervened is not clear; the great point is that he succeeded and thereby introduced a period of peace between the kingdoms. But Mercia kept the fruits of its victory and Theodore transferred Eadhaed from Lindsey to Ripon, discreetly allowing high-level politics and war to have their influence, the Northumbrian being unacceptable to the conquering Aethelred.[36]

A second synod was held in September 679 at Hatfield, the site probably close to Doncaster, in Wilfrid's quondam sphere of influence: it was to give the formal support of the English Church to Pope Agatho in his attempt to settle the long-lasting Mediterranean controversies over the Council of Chalcedon's definition of the two natures in Christ and the attempt by Byzantine emperors to settle matters by imposing their own solution of Monotheletism, which had

[35] VW 24
[36] HE IV 21; T. Charles-Edwards, 'Anglo-Saxon kinship revisited', J. Hines ed., The Anglo-Saxons from the migration period to the eighth century (Woodbridge, Suffolk, 1997) 170–204; Kirby, Kings 93

led to the arrest and torture of Pope Martin I in 653. The issue was the more poignant because of Theodore's expert knowledge and his likely involvement in the official rejection of Monotheletism in 649.[37]

Agatho was eager to cooperate with the emperor Constantine IV, who had begun to have doubts about his predecessor's embracing of Monotheletism and to show how the Churches in the barbarian kingdoms were sound in opposition to Monotheletism in contrast to the more uncertain attitudes of Churches in the East. Visited by a legate, Anglo-Saxon England readily fitted in with the pope's plan. Theodore used the opportunity to secure the members' commitment to orthodoxy through assent to the five ecumenical councils and rejection of Monotheletism. John the arch-chanter, a liturgical expert who had come to instruct English monks, carrying the report of the synod home to the pope, died on the journey and, being a devotee of St Martin, was buried as he had wished, at Tours.

But the report went on to Agatho, who informed the emperor that he had wished Theodore 'our fellow-bishop and philosopher from the large island of Britannia' to join the leaders of the Italian Church in conferring on Monotheletism. Theodore was too old to accept the invitation but it was a compliment to him and to the Anglo-Saxon Church. Nonetheless a scintilla of doubt remains about the initial attitude of the pope to Theodore, and consequently his bishops. Why was it needful for Agatho to send John the arch-chanter to England; would it not have been simpler to send a message asking for the support of the Church of the Anglo-Saxons? Had Wilfrid, in pursuit of his claim against Theodore, suggested a doubt about the Syriac Theodore's full orthodoxy on a predominantly Eastern issue, and was John dispatched to ascertain in person Theodore's views?

As reported in Bede, the synod ended in declaring their faith in the Trinity, including therefore the Holy Spirit 'ineffably proceeding from the Father and the Son'; that phrase 'and the Son', 'filioque', an addition of Augustinian origin to the Nicene Creed, albeit initially acceptable to the Greek Churches as well, had become controversial in the course of the Monothelete controversy. Amongst its decisions, the synod in England formally declared itself for the Western, Augustinian side, which may have been an implicit reply to Wilfrid, refuting any allegations about Theodore's Western orthodoxy. There was no further problem: in his decisions and his will to make peace with

[37] *HE* IV 17

Constantinople, Agatho made no mention of the 'filioque' clause, which could have created further tensions. The Hatfield Synod is customarily seen as an event entirely separate from the long conflict with Wilfrid: that may not have been the case.[38]

Theodore's claims for his office reached a high point in the opening of his synodical letter recording the decision of 679 when he described himself as 'Archbishop of the island of Britain and of the City of Canterbury'.[39] No mention here of an archbishop of York, as in Gregory the Great's master-plan of two archbishoprics with twelve bishops in each province. Theodore meant to rule north and south of the Humber. Although he did not mention the second archbishopric, it is no accident that he fostered the cult of Gregory the Great in Britain, which had followed on the gift of relics of Gregory dispatched by the pope Vitalian to King Oswiu and designed to record the English Church's indebtedness to the pope and its continued commitment to the papacy.

Partly through Theodore's influence, Gregory emerged as the apostle of the English, with his cult not limited to Canterbury. Canterbury certainly had an altar dedicated to Gregory in its monastery; but it seems that in Theodore's time a cult also developed at Whitby and at York and issued in the odd, anonymous Life of Gregory written by an inmate of the double monastery at Whitby in about 700, to whom we owe the anecdote of Gregory's punning response to the sight of Anglian slaves in the market at Rome. The high title now claimed by Theodore corresponded to the realities of his actions and was reminiscent of the role of the archbishop of Alexandria (known in the West but not the East as Patriarch), who expected both to approve and consecrate all bishops in the provinces under his authority. Theodore expected to make the choices.[40]

Wilfrid went on a leisurely journey to Rome to make his appeal and, remembering the hostility stirred up by his support for Dagobert in Austrasia, made sure that he avoided the most direct route through Gaul via the port of Quentovic, which would have carried him into territory dominated by Ebroin, mayor of the palace in Neustria, Western Francia, and his enemy.

[38] H. Chadwick, 'Theodore, the English Church and the Monothelete controversy', Lapidge, *Theodore* 88–95
[39] *HE* IV 17
[40] A. Thacker, 'Memorialising Gregory the Great: origin and transmission of a papal cult in the seventh and early eighth centuries', *EME* 7 (1998) 59–84 at 76

Behind him he left monks of his confederation who mourned the departure of their patron and protector; before him, as he took his circuitous route, lay the pagan Frisians, who had once formed an element in the multifarious forces that over years invaded sub-Roman Britain, bone of the bone of their Christian Anglo-Saxon relatives in England and speaking a language with affinities to the speech of Wilfrid and his men.

The Frisians stimulated all Wilfrid's missionary instincts. In the west of Friesland, Stephen of Ripon tells us, Wilfrid and his companions arrived 'to be received with all ceremony by Aldgisl and vast crowds of the heathen'.[41] He preached and baptised, aided in his mission by an unusually large catch of fish and a fruitful year. Conversion clearly brought prosperity. It was nonetheless a flash in the pan for Christian mission; there was no planned initiative and no backing from England. Despite strong trading links with Anglo-Saxon England, Frisians associated Christianity with the neighbouring Franks, feared their politics and were reluctant to accept Christ; Aldgisl was succeeded as king by Radbod, who was less sympathetic; serious inroads into Frisian paganism were only made years later under St Willibrord. But Willibrord had been a monk under Wilfrid at Ripon: when his master left for Rome, he went to study in Ireland and fell under the influence of Egbert, the Englishman who had accepted lifelong exile for Christ, who reinforced the missionary zeal he gained from Wilfrid and led him and a party of eleven monks to Frisia in 690.[42] It was the first step in an effective long-lasting missionary enterprise.

Arrived at Rome, Wilfrid presented his petition only to find that Theodore's messenger had preceded him. He defended his position with his customary skill before Agatho and a council of bishops in 679 and the decision went in his favour. Wilfrid was to return to York. With the help of a Church council, he was to choose bishops for the other sees, and they should be consecrated by Theodore, whose appointees were to leave their posts. However, the total number of sees in Anglo-Saxon England was not to exceed twelve; Theodore's target may well have been higher and the pope and his synod were thus not following his subdividing policy without restriction. They were, however, granting a great deal to Wilfrid, perhaps more than they realised, since it was

---

[41] VW 26; Frisia, H. Mayr-Harting, 'Wilfrid in Sussex', H.M. Kitch ed., Studies in Sussex Church history (London 1981) 1–17 at 9

[42] M. Costambeys, 'Willibrord', ODNB; W. Levison, England and the continent (Oxford 1946) 45–69

evident that a bishop of Wilfrid's temperament would only appoint his own partisans. Wilfrid's request for papal protection of his monasteries and their exemption from the authority of the bishop was also granted.[43]

Wilfrid stayed on in his beloved city, visited again the great shrines and collected relics and ornaments for his churches. In 680 he made for home with the decision in his hand, a document 'with its bulls and stamped seals,'[44] Stephen says, to present to King Ecgfrith. The king flew into a rage. Iurminburh confiscated Wilfrid's reliquary, which she proceeded to wear as a necklace when out in her carriage or even in bed; Stephen uses the term 'chrismarium' for it, which strictly means a container for the holy oil used in baptism, but also for relics. There is a poignancy here, as the queen sought a baby and hoped the reliquary would provide the needful fertility, but it did not work and she brought Ecgfrith no heir.[45] The king put Wilfrid in solitary confinement. The conflict moved into a new phase.

Biscop's career, which had briefly intertwined with Wilfrid's, has a contrasting tone. Both were Northumbrian aristocrats, both passionate enthusiasts for Rome and monasticism, both frequent travellers into and through Francia to Rome and both were dedicated collectors. Each in his way helped to draw their native land into Mediterranean civilisation and a wider Christian and aesthetic world. Biscop lacked the larger-than-life quality of Wilfrid, his capacity to captivate followers and to build an empire and his taste and talent for converting pagans, but also his acerbity and intense political interest. While Wilfrid's battles developed, Biscop moved quietly from his post at the Canterbury monastery where he had stayed as abbot for two years and, as Hadrian succeeded him, went in 671 again to Rome and then to Vienne in pursuit of books.

On his return in 672 he planned to draw on his friendly relationship with Cenwalh, king of Wessex, and cooperate with his bishop Leutherius in founding a monastery. Cenwalh's death in 674 led him to turn instead to his native Northumbria, where King Ecgfrith gave him an endowment of seventy hides and he founded a monastery dedicated to St Peter at the mouth of the river Wear. He was determined to have a stone church in Roman and continental style and sent to Gaul for craftsmen. With the collapse of Roman

---

[43] *VW* 32
[44] *VW* 34; Thacker, 'Wilfrid', *ODNB* doubts imprisonment
[45] *VW* 39

civilisation, even the ability to lay mortar had been lost and as the building neared completion he had to use his contacts with Gaul to bring in glaziers, who not only glazed the windows but taught their craft to the English. His collecting abilities paid off: he interested Ecgfrith in the first instance by telling him about his continental acquisitions of books and relics and, as need arose in his new plan, obtained more of the equipment necessary for a major Church centre. He moved with speed. Bede relates with admiration in his *History of the Abbots* how he had the gable-ends of the church in place after only a year 'and you could already visualise mass being said in it'.[46]

A major visit to Rome in 679 obtained more materials over a broad front; books of every sort, relics to be used not only for his own monastery but also 'for many churches in the land', knowledge of Roman liturgy and chanting aided by John the arch-chanter, a grant of exemption for his monastery protecting it against external interference and many pictures of saints including Mary, the twelve apostles, scenes from the Gospels and the Apocalypse. The building, the monastery and its rich adornment impressed Ecgfrith and in 681 or 682 he gave another endowment of forty hides which was used under Biscop's erstwhile prior Ceolfrith to build a sister monastery at Jarrow dedicated to St Paul. Biscop made another journey to Rome in 685, his sixth and last, in pursuit of yet more books and equipment. Endowment, the king's favour, Biscop's extraordinary ability to assemble books and materials and the popularity of the two sister monasteries created a community of high calibre large enough to throw up a certain number of men of unusual, specialist talent, and its powerful library made it a centre of learning.

Biscop was determined that there would be no friction between the two communities and made good appointments of leaders: Ceolfrith to Jarrow and, in his absence, Eosterwine to Monkwearmouth. Though a cousin of Biscop and once a thegn of Ecgfrith, Eosterwine was praised by Bede for his determination to take no advantage either of his rank or his relationship to the founder and for his readiness to take his full share of winnowing and threshing, milking, work in bakehouse, kitchen and garden and to eat with the rest of the monks and sleep with them in the common dormitory. Eosterwine died while Biscop was abroad and Sigfrid was elected in his place.

As Biscop's health sank in the years after his return from his last journey, he was consoled at the end by having Job read out to him and a number of monks

---

[46] HA 5; P.H. Blair, *Northumbria in the days of Bede* (London 1976) 28

singing the Psalms antiphonally at his bedside. At his death in 689, he solemnly enjoined his monks not to depart from their Rule compiled by him, with a strong admixture of St Benedict's, or from the customs of the seventeen monasteries which he had visited during his travels; they were also to keep the library intact and to avoid ever electing an abbot because of his rank and connections. Specifically he warned them against the temptation of electing as his successor his brother, 'who has not entered on the way of the truth'.[47] Biscop evidently had the enthusiasm of many of his class and background for beautiful and striking objects but, with that, an unusual awareness of the dangers of attachment to kindred, so powerful a force in the society of his time. He was on easy terms with kings, no less with Ecgfrith than with his successor Aldfrith, and never appeared to them as a threat.

Wilfrid evidently did seem to be a threat to Ecgfrith and on his return from Rome inspired in him an exhibition of power and anger. In prison, Wilfrid's dungeon had no light at night so he consoled himself by singing psalms, resisted Ecgfrith's offer of rewards and gifts if he would accept the king's commands and reject the authenticity of the papal document containing Agatho's decisions, healed the wife of the sheriff in charge of the prison and, when transferred to harsher conditions in Dunbar, continued to defy his captors. Fetters designed to bind him somehow failed to do so: God worked against his captors and the smiths they employed, says Stephen of Ripon, having in mind St Peter's escape from his fetters in Acts. Eventually, an intervention by Ecgfrith's aunt, abbess Aebbe of Coldingham, when the queen fell ill as the court on progress visited the nunnery, led to Wilfrid's release and the return of his reliquary. The illness was a punishment, Aebbe said, for the king's treatment of Wilfrid. Ecgfrith relented to a limited degree but still would not accept the papal decision in favour of Wilfrid, who had to go into exile. He was helped by Berhtwald, a nephew of Aethelred of Mercia, but his long friendly connection with Mercia could not stand against the hostility of Aethelred's queen, who happened to be Ecgfrith's sister. The one concession was from a sub-king of Mercia, Oshere, king of the Hwicce, who granted land in Worcestershire to one of Wilfrid's monks. Wessex seemed a possible refuge but King Centwine was Iurminburh's brother. Wilfrid was checkmated by queens and passed on down to Sussex, the last unconverted kingdom of the Anglo-Saxons.[48]

[47] *HA* 11; S. Coates, 'Ceolfrith', *ODNB*
[48] *VW* 36, 37 (Wilfrid's defiance) 38 (fetters) 39 (Aebbe)

It had been but lightly touched by Christianity. Aethelwalh the king had married Eaba, a Christian princess from the Hwicce, and had himself been baptised, Wulfhere of the Mercians standing as godfather. But Wulfhere, though apparently sincere enough for he had dispatched his bishop Jaruman to check a defection of East Saxons, was a strong king exerting overlordship and was inclined to play off the minor power of Sussex against Wessex. Baptism and overlordship might be acceptable, even unavoidable for Aethelwalh but the overlordship was resented by his South Saxon nobles, who were consequently unwilling to accept the Christianity associated with it. Wulfhere died in 674 or 675 and it would seem the issue lapsed. The role of a small monastery at Bosham remains uncertain: what Bede says is that the indigenous people were not willing to listen to these monks.[49]

A stray bishop with his entourage, Wilfrid carried no political baggage. He brought with him only his experience of pagans and his undoubted eloquence. For many months he preached to them, Stephen says, describing 'with great fulness of words the works of Almighty God to confound idolatry, from the beginning of the world down to the day of judgement'.[50] The pagan Anglo-Saxon world was being set into a full historical context based on biblical narrative: to the right audience, this would have considerable appeal. It was an all-embracing interpretation and in its simplicity and emphasis on the one Creator God cut through the complexities of polytheism. Moreover, the message was being preached just after a three-year drought and consequent famine had come to an end: the old gods had not saved their adherents from want and suffering; relief could be seen as coming from the new God and His preacher. Cut off from the rest of the Anglo-Saxon world by the forest of the Andredesweald, Sussex was backward. Its people had not learned adequately to supplement food from the earth by tapping the plentiful supplies of fish in the region. Apparently they could only catch eels. Wilfrid's men collected the eel nets and used them for fishing in the sea, dividing the catch three ways, among the net-owners, the poor and Wilfrid's entourage, so winning hearts and, by implication, teaching the lesson that Christianity brought higher skills and prosperity.

Aethelwalh responded to Wilfrid's work by granting him eighty-seven hides of land at Selsey with tenants and slaves. Wilfrid baptised the slaves,

---

[49] *HE* IV 13; Mayr-Harting, 'Wilfrid', illuminates missionary opportunities and techniques
[50] *VW* 41

gave them freedom and founded a monastery where followers of his joined the community. No doubt the freed slaves would become estate workers and Wilfrid may also have hoped to train some of them for the priesthood. Aethelwalh, however, did not last. An exiled prince, Caedualla, son of King Cenberht of Wessex, emerged from the forests of the Chilterns and the Andredesweald, drew to himself a formidable war band and began a rise to power. His was the most ferocious talent to surface in a period of power politics, fighting and instability among the kingdoms of the south in Theodore's later years. This instability may have owed something to Theodore's ill health and failing strength, which inhibited his ability to mitigate barbarian warfare, especially in his home kingdom of Kent. There in 685 Eadric, son of Egbert, who had played a part in the coming of Theodore, made war on his uncle Hlothere, who died of his wounds. Eadric gained his power with the aid of resurgent South Saxons and may have ruled, in effect, as their client.[51]

Caedualla, however, destroyed South Saxon hopes. Exiles have affinities with other exiles and when, in Stephen of Ripon's account, Caedualla sought Wilfrid's friendship, promising to be an obedient son if Wilfrid would be 'his true father, to teach and help him', the precarious status of both prince and churchman no doubt brought them together in a solemn compact, 'which they called God to witness',[52] though Caedualla remained pagan. Having established his authority over much of West Saxon territory, Caedualla attacked the South Saxons; initially beaten off, in his second attack he killed Aethelwalh, thereby checking the possibilities of further expansion by Sussex, which in Aethelwalh's earlier years had been a power in the south-east; he ravaged Kent and attacked the Isle of Wight, formerly acquired by Aethelwalh, and still pagan. In a fierce plan Caedualla aimed to exterminate the inhabitants and after the ethnic cleansing replace the population with families from his own kingdom. He had promised a quarter of the land and spoils to God if he won the island and fulfilled his vow by offering it to Wilfrid. By Bede's calculation, this amounted to three hundred hides, which Wilfrid handed over to his nephew, leaving one of his priests named Hiddila to preach and baptise. The Isle of Wight was thus the very last part of Anglo-Saxon England to fall to Christianity and that as the by-product of ruthless campaigning by a Wessex prince who had remained a pagan.[53]

[51] Kirby, *Kings* 98–104; B. Yorke, 'Caedualla', *ODNB*
[52] *VW* 41
[53] *VW* 42; *HE* IV 15, 16

Closely intertwined with Wilfrid's, Caedualla's career illustrates the degree to which churchmen found themselves subject to the will of barbarian kings, carried along in the wake of their internecine disputes or personal whims. J.P. Kirby does not suppose that Wilfrid behaved treacherously to Aethelwalh and doubts whether warfare between the two could have been controlled by him; by contrast, Alan Thacker calls it a 'murky episode' and believes that it was treated with 'considerable circumspection' by both Bede and Stephen.[54]

Arwald, king in the Isle of Wight, perished at the hands of Caedualla and so did his two young brothers, who, having escaped by crossing to the mainland and hiding in Hampshire, were betrayed and scheduled to be executed, when the abbot of Redbridge, an otherwise unknown monastery, intervened and asked Caedualla, nursing his war wounds in seclusion nearby, for a stay of execution while he instructed and baptised them. They accepted baptism and then were killed: mercy was not often shown to dynastic rivals.[55]

Caedualla's land grants and his subjection of Sussex and Kent show that his years of campaigning had given him a dominant power in the south. By his own choice he removed the opportunity to sustain and consolidate this newly won authority; instead, perhaps in part driven by illness or the effect of wounds, he resigned his kingdom, went to Rome, was baptised with the pope standing godfather, and died in the spring of 689 ten days after the rite. He was only about thirty. It was the most dramatic of a sequence of resignations by Anglo-Saxon rulers, which was unique to England, characteristic of a certain stage in the conversion process.[56]

A journey to Rome, contact with the pope, the assumption of the name Peter, all smack of Wilfrid's influence – but also that of bishop Earconwald of London. Caedualla had given land in Battersea to the monastic house at Barking founded by the bishop's sister; he granted land in Kent to a monastery and land to Aldhelm at Malmesbury: Earconwald may have made the charter in which he granted land at Farnham in Surrey. He was thus both accessible and generous to churchmen and aware of the civilising functions of a ruler for he issued charters in Latin and may have struck coins. He had achievements beyond that of the terror created by his war bands. Bede cites his epitaph in Rome ordered by the pope 'so that the memory of his devotion might be

[54] Kirby, *Kings* 101; Thacker, 'Wilfrid', *ODNB*
[55] *HE* IV 16
[56] C.E. Stancliffe, 'Kings who opted out', P. Wormald *et al.* eds, *Ideal and reality in Frankish and Anglo-Saxon society* (Oxford 1983) 154–76

preserved for ever and those who read it or heard it read might be kindled to religious zeal by his example', and says that he ruled 'most ably'. Viewing his life, R.A. Fletcher writes of the 'paradoxes and surprises' which the historian meets in the history of the conversion.[57]

Ecgfrith of Northumbria was killed in battle in 685. Pursuing the policy of active expansion to the north initiated by Oswiu, he attacked the British and the Picts. In 684, in a move heavily criticised by contemporaries, he had sent an expedition against Ireland to Brega in Co. Meath, perhaps because the Irish had given refuge to British warriors fleeing from his army. Bede calls him 'temerarious'[58] and recorded Cuthbert's vain attempt to restrain him from war against the Picts. No doubt he had an ambition to wipe out the humiliation of his defeat by the king of Mercia at the battle of Trent and may have been disturbed by the moves of Bruide, ruler of Fortriu. He was, moreover, an experienced warrior, victor in battle against Pictish forces at the Two Rivers in 671. So, trusting in his skill and his army, he pressed on deep into Pictish territory along the Loch of Forfar on to dangerous ground, where he was defeated at Nechtanesmere, a disaster which ended the greatest days of Northumbria in political and military terms and, there being no longer pressure to pay tribute, opened the way to a wealthier and more effective Pictish kingship.

In the kirk yard at Aberlemno one of the finest of all Pictish inscribed stones, a little over seven feet tall, schematically records the battle, in effect the clash between the two greatest war machines of the seventh century. But the patron who put his mason to work chose to represent it as a personal battle between Bruide and Ecgfrith, distinguished by his distinctive helmet. They are shown mounted at the top, where Ecgfrith drops his sword and shield; on the line below he is confronted by Pictish infantry; at the bottom he clashes directly with Bruide with the result shown in the far right corner, a corpse being eaten by a raven. Art-historical indications place this sculpture of a Pictish triumph in the early eighth century, long after the event.[59]

---

[57] HE V 7; R.A. Fletcher, Who's who in Roman Britain and Anglo-Saxon England 55 BC–AD 1066 (London 1989, repr. Mechanicsburg 2002) 61

[58] VSC 27; Cuthbert as Gregory the Great's ideal pastor, A. Thacker, 'Bede's ideal of reform', Wormald et al. eds, Ideal and reality 130–53 esp. 137–49

[59] Aberlemno interpretation, S.M. Foster, Picts, Gaels and Scots: early historic Scotland (London 1996) 104; Lloyd Laing, 'The date of the Aberlemno churchyard stone', M. Redknap et al. eds, Pattern and purpose in Insular art (Oxford 2001) 241–51; J.E. Fraser, The Pictish conquest. The battle of Dunnichen 685 (2nd edn Stroud 2006); Bridei and Ecgfrith, A. Woolf, 'Pictish matriliny reconsidered', IR 49 (1998) 147–67; G. Cruickshank, The battle of Dunnichen (Balgavies 1991)

This defeat removed Wilfrid's irreconcilable enemy; the stolen reliquary had done nothing for Iurminburh's fertility, and in the absence of a male heir kingship passed to Aldfrith, illegitimate son of Oswiu by an Irish princess, Fin of the Uí Néill. Illegitimacy was disregarded in a remarkable coup for the house of Ida and Oswald, aided, it may be, by influence from the Uí Néill, from Dál Riata and even the Picts, all anxious to end the Northumbrian militarism which had flourished at their expense. Within the kingdom, Aldfrith had the support not only of Aelflaed, Oswiu's daughter and abbess of Whitby, but also that of St Cuthbert. Originally destined for the Church, Aldfrith was the most learned of Anglo-Saxon kings. He had long studied in Ireland and was living in Iona when Ecgfrith was about to launch his fatal campaign against the Picts.

As king, he did not seek to continue the policy of northern expansion. Dál Riata threw off Northumbria's supremacy, as probably did the Britons of Dumbarton, while the Picts regained lost territory, and the bishopric of Abercorn, founded to support Northumbrian rule, was lost. In the words of Bede, Aldfrith 'ably restored the shattered state of the kingdom although within narrower bounds' and maintained it as a kingdom of wealth and cultural vitality despite its defeat, capable in his hands of providing the sinews for a phase of remarkable and precocious Christian achievement in art and literature.[60]

In 685–6, he was visited by his quondam teacher Adomnán and agreed to release sixty prisoners from Ireland, taken by Ecgfrith in his raid of 684; in return, this scholar-king received Adomnán's work on the Holy Land pilgrimage, De locis sanctis. Northumbria finally had a king sympathetic to reconciliation.[61] In the south Theodore, now in chronic ill health, took an initiative for peace with Wilfrid at a conference in London, offering to nominate Wilfrid as his successor. This act, described by Stephen of Ripon, is corroborated nowhere else, yet is not wholly improbable. At the time of the conference, Caedualla was still the dominant figure in the politics of southern England and Wilfrid could have been the ideal personality to work with him and sustain his interest in the Church. Wilfrid diplomatically referred the matter to a future Council.

Theodore wrote on Wilfrid's behalf to abbess Aelflaed, who had evidently inherited the Whitby tradition of hostility to Wilfrid. To Aethelred of Mercia

---

[60] HE IV 26
[61] T.M. Charles-Edwards, Early Christian Ireland (Cambridge 2000) 341

he wrote a moving letter which has survived, telling the king that he has 'made peace in Christ' with Wilfrid and urging Aethelred to support him 'because for a long time he has been working among the pagans on the Lord's behalf, having been deprived of his own possessions'. Theodore referred bluntly to 'wrongs inflicted upon him', describing Wilfrid as a man who 'possesses his soul in patience', and quoted from the text of Genesis which he knew so intimately from his commentary to the pupils at Canterbury, from the passage where, aware of his approaching death, Jacob calls on Joseph to see that he is buried in the land of his ancestors. Theodore is Jacob and, in another allusion, Isaac, near blind, seeking to bless Esau. Conscious of his age and frail health, he went on to ask Aethelred to journey down to see him. 'Come, despite the discouraging length of the journey and let me see your joyful face and let me bless you before I die.' He ended with a paternal plea to help Wilfrid: 'Now, my son, do as I ask concerning this most saintly man and your charity will stand you in good stead in the world to come.'[62]

The appeals were successful. Wilfrid's exile ended, he regained his great monasteries of Hexham and Ripon and Aethelred returned his Mercian possessions. Bosa was even expelled from Wilfrid's old see, and from late 686 or early 687 the former bishop reigned at York once more. But his great diocese no longer existed. Lindsey had been lost to Mercia, and Hexham and Lindisfarne, carved out of York, were still bishoprics, which by a curious arrangement he administered for about a year after their bishops, Eata and Cuthbert died. It was a partial, imperfect settlement lasting only a short time beyond the archiepiscopate of Theodore, an intermission in Wilfrid's long fight for his rights.

Wilfrid's tenure at Lindisfarne, 687–8, brought trouble. St Cuthbert was seen as a saint in his own lifetime, representing a fusion between Celtic ascetic and pastoral ideals and the Roman requirements of Whitby. Coming immediately after him, Wilfrid, the trenchant and uncompromising Romanist, was a great shock. Though he chose to gloss over the episode in his *Ecclesiastical History*, Bede unmistakably alludes to it in his prose Life of Cuthbert, describing how he went to his hermit refuge on the Farne Islands for the last months of his life. Some Lindisfarne monks accompanied him and as they were singing lauds came to the appointed psalm just as Cuthbert died. It begins, 'O God, thou hast cast us off and hast broken us down; Thou hast been

---

[62] *VW* 43. I have not accepted Colgrave's doubts on authenticity

angry and hast had compassion on us.' As arranged, a monk came out on Farne and stood with a lighted candle in each hand to signal the death to the Lindisfarne monk in the watchtower awaiting the news; when he ran to the church, he found the monks there also singing the same psalm. It was, Bede writes, providential. The psalm gave prophetic warning of what was to come and comfort that the troubles would not last. He goes on: 'For after Cuthbert was buried such a storm of trouble broke out that several monks chose to depart rather than bear the brunt of such danger.'[63]

Wilfrid's monks had suffered under the bishops imposed in 678; now he was exercising power over monks of the other party. To Lindisfarne, struggling to maintain its spiritual power and authority after the Synod of Whitby, he represented the alien power of York. Although Wilfrid had himself first made contact with monasticism as a youth at Lindisfarne and there conceived the plan to make a pilgrimage to Rome, much water had flowed under the bridge since then and the appointment was a disaster. Any abbot of Lindisfarne had admittedly no easy task: Bede describes how Cuthbert needed all his self-control to master the recalcitrance of some monks when he was prior. Old tensions and associations and, no doubt, Wilfrid's temperament made his period of rule barren and alien. Theodore resolved the problem by appointing in Wilfrid's place Eadberht, as Bede says, 'a man of outstanding virtues . . . It was with his accession that the trouble and disturbances were quelled. The Lord, as the Scriptures tell us, did build up Jerusalem.'[64] The cause of the storm can only have been Wilfrid.

Cuthbert's fame grew: it was a crucial element in sustaining the fame of Lindisfarne as a holy place, making up for the loss of prestige in the rejection of the Columban and Ionan method of Easter calculation. Although the young Cuthbert was guarding sheep when he had a vision of the soul of Aidan being taken up to heaven by choirs of the heavenly host, his function may have been that of a young warrior protecting the flock against rustlers. He was probably a member of the minor aristocracy for he rode with a spear and a servant to the monastery of Melrose as a postulant.

Cuthbert began his life as a monk in 651 under the direction of the prior, an Irishman called Boisil, at the Ionan foundation of Melrose in the borders,

---

[63] VSC 40; C.E. Stancliffe, 'Cuthbert and the polarity between pastor and solitary', G. Bonner et al. eds, St Cuthbert, his cult and his community to AD 1200 (Woodbridge 1989) 21–42 analyses differences between Lives of Cuthbert
[64] VSC 40

then transferred with his abbot Eata to a new foundation at Ripon where he became guest-master, only to suffer from Alchfrith's decision as founder to throw in his lot with Wilfrid and accept the Roman calculation of Easter. Eata, Cuthbert and others would not accept the decision and went back to Melrose. Boisil died of the plague; Cuthbert survived, became prior and followed Boisil's example of engaging in preaching tours, some lasting as long as a month, and taking his message, sometimes on horseback, more often on foot, into the remote villages and hills, hearing confessions and drawing back-sliders back to the faith. His was a powerful, ascetic style of monasticism combined with a zeal for preaching and converting, especially country people.

Melrose accepted Oswiu's decision on Easter. When Colmán and his followers left Lindisfarne for Ireland rather than accept the decision, Eata came as abbot to Lindisfarne and took Cuthbert with him as prior. Cuthbert thus had impeccable qualifications as a passionate adherent of the Ionan monastic tradition. He was trained in the life by an Irishman, was pastorally active, but was nonetheless ready to accept the Roman Easter and tonsure, and his life was marked by intense prayer and miracles. Though himself of Biscop's foundation at Jarrow, Bede was sympathetic to the Lindisfarne tradition and venerated Aidan. In Cuthbert, he saw another Aidan who was orthodox on the Easter tradition and a sustainer of all that was best in the Columban tradition. It was the view of the Lindisfarne monks reflected in the first Life of Cuthbert commissioned by bishop Eadfrith of Lindisfarne and written by a member of the community, then it was refined by Bede in first a verse and then a prose version.[65]

Cuthbert's appearance in seventh-century Northumbria was a demonstration that Anglo-Saxon England could produce saints with all the virtue and miraculous power of the greatest figures of Christian history, whose prayers would continue to accompany and sustain members of the Church on earth. Cuthbert's Life is shaped and expounded in the light of biblical texts. As Benedicta Ward has taught us in an illuminating passage, Cuthbert is introduced by Bede in his first chapter with a quotation from Lamentations. It forms the very first sentence and makes little sense in this place until one realises the echoes that that sentence would set up in the mind of a monk

---

[65] D.P. Kirby, 'The genesis of a cult: Cuthbert of Farne and ecclesiastical politics in Northumbria in the late seventh and early eighth centuries', *JEH* 46 (1995) 383–97; J. Campbell, 'Elements in the background to the Life of St Cuthbert and his early cult', Bonner *et al.*, *Cuthbert* 3–19

reading or listening; it is a verse quoted in the night office of Good Friday, words attributed to Christ in His passion. Bede is conveying at the outset that, in its suffering and renunciation, Cuthbert's life resembles that of Christ.[66]

Similarly when he recounts the mysterious cure of Cuthbert's knee as a child: a passing horseman asked Cuthbert for hospitality and, being told his knee prevented him from doing anything, dismounted, inspected the knee and told the boy to boil some wheaten flour in milk and bathe the tumour, which then disappeared in a few days. Bede confidently identifies the horseman as an angel sent by the same power who had dispatched the Archangel Raphael to cure Tobit's blindness. Bede's commentary on Tobit gives a clue to the meaning he wishes to convey: when Raphael heals a devout Jew, he is a type of Christ granting salvation 'to those who were already devout but not yet wholly given to Christ', exactly the position of the young Cuthbert, already leading a good life but about to progress to a new level of commitment. 'Henceforth', Bede says at the opening of the next chapter, 'the boy devoted himself to God.'[67]

The healing has both a physical and a spiritual dimension; while using monks' reminiscences and checking facts and sources, Bede was concerned to show how, from his earliest years, Cuthbert's life corresponded to the patterns of Christian living shown in Scripture and so far from being casual ornaments, the texts and allusions are designed to summarise and characterise the events of the Life so as to demonstrate this conformity with Scripture. He was aware of a likeness to St Martin and knew Sulpicius Severus's Life. There are echoes of Gregory's *Dialogues*. Yet, despite its literary clothing and hagiography in general, the authentic traits of an ascetic holy man in the Irish tradition, with powers of second sight and a remarkable affinity with the natural world, comes over. The Irish predilection for islands and the zeal for the hermit life are unmistakable.

In about 675 or 676, Cuthbert withdrew from Lindisfarne to live as a hermit on Inner Farne, an island several miles to the south-east. 'No one', Bede wrote, 'before the Lord's servant, Cuthbert, had been able to live alone on this island without trouble as it was haunted by evil spirits', but it was purified by Cuthbert, just as Lastingham had been by Chad, and 'the wicked foe himself,

<hr>

[66] B. Ward, *The Venerable Bede* (London 1990, 2nd edn 1998) 98–9 deceptively simple, understands Bede's mind
[67] VSC 2, 3

together with the whole crowd of his allies, was driven away'.[68] The building erected by Cuthbert had the characteristics of Irish practice, 'almost round in plan, measuring about four or five poles from wall to wall: the wall itself on the outside is higher than a man standing upright; but inside he made it much higher by cutting away the living rock so that the pious inhabitant could see nothing except the sky from his dwelling'. He built a dwelling place and an oratory using turf, rough-hewn timber and straw. Farther away at the landing place, there was a house and a well for the use of guest brothers, whom Cuthbert would visit and whose feet he would wash, but as time passed he withdrew more and more into a complete solitude, with a minimal diet, to free himself for prayer and contemplation.

Despairing of obtaining assent by conventional means, Ecgfrith and his party sailed to the Farne in 684 to beg Cuthbert to accept a bishopric; the arrival would have been a shock, but it followed a synod presided over by Theodore and the object was to fill a vacancy at Hexham. Cuthbert's resistance went far beyond the conventional gesture of an episcopal candidate – 'at last he came forth', says Bede 'very tearful, from his beloved hiding place'. But he gave way, succeeding in persuading authority to make him bishop of Lindisfarne, not Hexham, which was taken by Eata.[69]

Ecgfrith's views were clearly somewhat different from those of his father and more sympathetic to the Irish tradition than Oswiu felt he could be in his last years. The appointment to Lindisfarne of Cuthbert, an indisputably holy man, made it incidentally more difficult than ever to give heed to the papal judgment on Wilfrid's case: it would have been embarrassing indeed for a saint to be dismissed to open the way for Wilfrid's return. Cuthbert was consecrated in March 685 in a ceremony attended by seven bishops; he died two years later on the Farne, having retired to the hermitage for the last month of his life. Despite the continuing difference with them over the dating of Easter, he maintained a connection with the Picts. This gave added weight to his plea to Ecgfrith not to ravage Pictland in 685 in the disastrous campaign which ended at Nechtanesmere but, despite veneration for the Northumbrian holy man, Ecgfrith would not listen to him on matters of war and peace. With equal lack of success, Cuthbert had attempted to dissuade Ecgfrith from his attack on Ireland in the previous year.

[68] *HE* IV 28; *VSC* 17
[69] *HE* IV 28 Sherley-Price trans.

Cuthbert moved easily among the great; in this, despite some striking differences, he resembled Wilfrid. The great also consulted him. Ecgfrith's sister Aelflaed, then with her mother joint abbess of Whitby, sought out Cuthbert who had come with some of his brethren to a meeting place at Coquet Island where she appealed to his powers of prophecy to tell her about the succession to the throne of Northumbria. As Bede describes it, she 'flung herself before him, abjuring by the awful name of the King of Heaven and His angels to tell her how long her brother Ecgfrith would last and who was to rule after him'.[70] Cuthbert forecast his death and in reply to her question about succession (for Ecgfrith had neither brother nor son) gave a riddling answer understood by her to indicate Aldfrith. Was Aelflaed seeking to use Cuthbert's power of prophecy or hoping to enlist his aid in keeping the succession in Oswald and Oswiu's line? She was a friend who influenced him to accept the episcopate and she clearly deferred to him in great matters of state.

In Carlisle, whither he had come to give comfort and companionship to Iurminburh awaiting the outcome of Ecgfrith's Pictish campaign in 685, its citizens were showing Cuthbert a Roman fountain built into the city walls, when he had a premonition of disaster, looked up to the sky and said 'almost in a whisper', 'Perhaps at this moment the battle is being decided.'[71] It turned out to be the hour in which the Picts slaughtered the king and his bodyguards at Nechtanesmere, Bede says. He advised Iurminburh to travel on the following morning to York to await news: he was a royal adviser at the highest level.

Prophecy and second sight and the working of miracles were the marks of a holy man: the likeness between Cuthbert and Columba is unmistakable. So too is the likeness between the saints in their affinity with the natural world and their power of commanding the elements and receiving obedience from creatures. At Coldingham near Berwick, invited by the abbess Aebbe, Oswiu's sister, to stay and exhort the community, Cuthbert was in the habit of stealing out of the building at night to pray waist-deep in the sea. He was observed by one of the monks as he came out of the water and knelt down on the sand, attended by two otters who 'warmed his feet with their breath and tried to dry him on their fur' and when they had finished, received his blessing. The immersion in the sea, a traditional remedy for the desires of the flesh, has a special significance in view of the erotic atmosphere among some young nuns at Coldingham. On a

[70] VSC 24
[71] VSC 27

journey, he prophesied that an eagle would bring food and sent his companion to fetch a big fish caught by the bird. He then told the boy to go back with half of it to ensure that the eagle received his reward. On the Farne, birds set on eating his barley were ordered to desist. Like Columba, he could command the elements. A saint, it was believed, had power over the natural world because he or she could transcend the limitations of ordinary mortals and return to the state of harmony between man and beast which prevailed before the Fall.[72]

Some aspects of Cuthbert's life may have been blurred or underplayed. He was evidently obedient to Theodore's insistence on adherence to canons and on the Roman calculation of Easter, but his continuing contact with the Picts suggests he was not fanatical on the issue. A journey to Pictland with a company of monks, described by Bede as though it had been prolonged by a great storm, may have been intended from the first to be a major expedition designed to enable Cuthbert and his party to spend Epiphany with the Picts in friendship. His alleged deathbed declaration enjoining his followers to have nothing to do with those who had wandered from the unity of the Catholic faith through not celebrating Easter at the proper time, is likely to be a falsification.[73]

But, whatever the caveats of historians about the Lives and some details of the record, it is plain that Cuthbert was an extraordinary man with a deserved reputation as a saint and that his long contact with Lindisfarne and his time as bishop, coupled with the miracles both contemporaneous and posthumous, ensured that Lindisfarne never lost its position as an especially holy place in Northumbria. He was but a short time bishop, yet it was the culmination of his life in religion and disseminated his influence more widely than ever – and it was a synod presided over by Theodore which decided on his appointment. Fame grew after his death and miracles at his shrine proliferated: a major impetus to the cult was given in 698 by the translation of the body to a tomb chest above the original burial place and the discovery that it had remained incorrupt. Thereafter his position was firmly established as a Northumbrian saint and an adherent of the middle party, as it might be called, which sustained itself after Whitby, preserving the Columban tradition of spirituality together with the Roman tonsure and Easter calculation against criticisms of the extreme Romanist party.[74]

---

[72] VSC 10, 12, 19
[73] Kirby, 'Genesis', JEH 46 (1995) 389
[74] Ibid., 391–2; D. Rollason, Saints and relics in Anglo-Saxon England (Oxford 1989) 35–41

Theodore's energies by this time were at last running down. He left behind him not only a much more effective network of dioceses but also a distinguished library and a prestigious school at Canterbury. Two men, Theodore and Hadrian, educated in Christian centres of learning with centuries of tradition and great libraries, came in maturity to the mission field in a country dominated by a warrior aristocracy and combative kings, only partially Christianised and with a very limited apparatus of learning. The elite of the infant Church, whom they trained in the Canterbury classroom, were thus exposed to teachers of calibre who commented on the Bible in the light of a knowledge of places and libraries wholly outside their range. As Michael Lapidge notes, they were men who had never seen a melon or, in most cases if not all, had never travelled outside England. For these pupils it must have been an extraordinary and often exhilarating experience. Theodore and Hadrian evidently brought with them or subsequently acquired a substantial library of Greek and Latin Fathers, the Septuagint and the Greek New Testament and works of classical learning ancillary to biblical learning. With these and with their memories of their own studies, they created an unusual milieu dominated by the Antiochene school of biblical exegesis, hardly known in the West, in contrast to the reigning school of Alexandria.[75]

The Antioch tradition sought to establish the meaning of the scriptural text as intended by the authors, using philology, delving into the origins of the words, comparing the Vulgate with other texts and referring to topography, history, medicine, rhetoric and philosophy to establish the context of sacred writing and its full implications. Typology, the seeking of foreshadowings of the Christian dispensation in the Old Testament, was also important. This style of biblical exegesis required an immense range of information and provided for the students privileged to hear Theodore and Hadrian an encyclopaedic education.[76]

It attracted an elite. Lapidge is a little wary of Bede's famous description of Theodore and Hadrian's effect in the field of education: 'They attracted a large number of students into whose minds they poured the waters of wholesome knowledge day by day. In addition to instructing them in the holy Scriptures, they also taught their pupils poetry, astronomy, and the calculation of the

---

[75] B. Bischoff, M. Lapidge eds, *Biblical commentaries from the Canterbury School of Theodore and Hadrian* (Cambridge 1994) 133 (wooden churches) 274 (lack of travel)
[76] Ibid. 243–9; J. Stevenson, *The Laterculus Malalianus and the School of Archbishop Theodore* (Cambridge 1995) 43–7

Church calendar. In proof of this some of their students still alive today are as proficient in Latin and Greek as their native tongue.' Bede, the devoted scholar, viewed with passionate enthusiasm the scholarly success of Theodore and Hadrian and may have exaggerated numbers. 'We would be wiser to think in contemporary terms of an Institute of Advanced Studies drawing in pupils who already have considerable attainments', Lapidge writes.[77]

Prestige and the calibre of the teaching reversed the flow of scholars: earlier in the seventh century the English crossed to Ireland to study but now the Irish came to Canterbury. A former pupil, Aldhelm, later abbot of Malmesbury, in a letter to a scholar he probably hoped to attract as a pupil, praised Britain for having Theodore and Hadrian and described Theodore triumphing over critical Irish students,

> ... although Theodore who pilots the helm of the high priesthood be hemmed in by a mass of Irish students, like a savage wild boar checked by a snarling pack of hounds, with the filed tooth of the grammarian – nimbly and with no loss of time – he disbands the rebel phalanxes, and just as the warlike bowman in the midst of battle is hemmed in by a dense formation of enemy legions, then, when his bow is tensed by his powerful hands and arms and arrows are drawn from the quiver, that is, from the obscure and acute syllogisms of chronography, the throng, ... their shield wall having been shattered, turn their backs and flee headlong.[78]

The tone is not sympathetic to Irish learning. Clearly the reference to chronography means that Theodore was worsting Irish pupils on the means of reckoning the Paschal cycle. A coolness to the Irish, at least those who had not accepted the Roman Easter, was characteristic of Theodore. Charles-Edwards calls his policy 'harshly anti-Quartodeciman'.[79] His mission had been to establish Roman administration and the Roman liturgical year as against the Columban reckoning and the Irish tradition: at Canterbury he could feel that he and Hadrian had instituted a tradition of learning as good as or better than the Irish.

The manuscripts which inform us on the teaching of Theodore and Hadrian make plain that both participated and that Theodore did not simply leave scholarly work to Hadrian in consequence of his heavy administrative

---

[77] *HE* IV 2; Bischoff and Lapidge, *Biblical commentaries* 268
[78] Aldhelm, *The prose works*, trans. M. Lapidge, M. Herren (Ipswich, Cambridge 1979) 163
[79] Charles-Edwards, *Ireland* 437

duties. A pupil, recording a commentary on II Chronicles where the text mentions the doors of the temple and gold plates fastened to them, noted that Theodore thought the Latin term *valuas* in the Vulgate referred to aqueducts, while Hadrian believed they were walls around the Temple. For him and Hadrian our principal sources are commentaries on the Pentateuch and the Gospels as recorded in pupils' lecture notes and glossaries on a wide range of biblical books and Patristic and grammatical texts.[80] In a major feat of scholarship, these have been recognised, correctly attributed to the Canterbury School and analysed so as to provide an insight into the minds of Theodore and Hadrian and a picture of the works studied by their pupils. Here and there we have a glimpse of the protagonists; so we find Theodore telling his pupils of the twelve baskets of fragments gathered after the feeding of the five thousand, preserved by St Helena and kept at the base of the Porphyry Column in the Forum of Constantine in Constantinople, which he had seen; and Hadrian shuddering at the memory of the wild gourds 'as bitter as bile', which he knew while he lived in Africa, or alluding to the porphyrio, 'the most beautiful of birds' found in Libya, the land of his upbringing. Both Theodore and Hadrian had a common experience, for both had been compelled to flee in the face of Arab attack and it is therefore not surprising that the Saracens are referred to as 'a race which is never at peace with anyone but is always at war with someone'.[81]

The method of instruction can be reconstructed from these pupils' notes. The Vulgate was the basic text but it was illuminated with reference to the Septuagint and the Greek New Testament and overwhelmingly by the Greek, rather than the Latin, Fathers. To judge by their students' notes, Greek was being conveyed to them in speech rather than reading: their mistakes make plain that they had no independent grasp of Greek. The orthography of Greek words transliterated by these Anglo-Saxon students reveals their teachers' Byzantine Greek style of pronunciation, and gives the reader an eerie sense of listening to the two great masters across more than fourteen centuries.

Bede wrote enthusiastically about two pupils of the Canterbury School: Tobias, who became bishop of Rochester, and who, he says, 'is also said to have

[80] M. Lapidge, 'Theodore and Hadrian in England', Bischoff and Lapidge, *Biblical commentaries* 133–89; M. Lapidge, 'Abbot Hadrian', Bischoff and Lapidge, *Biblical commentaries* 82–132

[81] Bischoff and Lapidge, *Biblical commentaries* 42 (Porphyry Column) 178 (gourds) 84 (porphyrio) 92 (Saracens)

learned Latin and Greek so thoroughly that they were as well known and as familiar to him as his native tongue'; and Albinus, the successor to Hadrian as abbot of the Canterbury monastery, who 'was so well trained in scriptural studies that he had no small knowledge of the Greek language and that he knew Latin as well as English, his native tongue'.[82] But men such as these were in a small minority.

The *Laterculus Malalianus* based on the *Chronographia* of the Antiochene scholar John Malalas, part translation, part original reflections on redemption and the life of Christ, though possibly put together by Theodore's class under his control and supervision, is more likely to have been translated and written by Theodore for purposes of class teaching. Malalas was not a distinguished writer but his emphasis on Christology and his 'patient repetition of information' were eminently suited for the instruction of an unsophisticated class who needed a firm underpinning in narrative and historical context as a backing for Christian learning. Chronographic data are important in the *Laterculus* and would have been valuable for a teacher needing to initiate pupils from a wholly alien tradition into both Christian and classical learning and to provide them with historical background. It shows Theodore's diplomatic skill and tact in maintaining a traditional and Athanasian Western Christology while using Antiochene exegesis and Greek writers who often had very different assumptions.[83]

It also reveals, incidentally, Theodore's knowledge of medicine: Bede records how St John of Beverley, seeing that the swollen arm of a nun of Watton, near Beverley, had been bled, said to the abbess, 'You have acted foolishly and ignorantly to bleed her on the fourth day of the moon; I remember how Archbishop Theodore of blessed memory used to say that it was very dangerous to bleed a patient when the moon is waxing and the Ocean tide flowing.'[84] His biblical commentaries are permeated with medical knowledge which is likely to have been the fruit of his stay in Constantinople and attendance at the lectures of Stephen of Alexandria.

Theodore was sought after by pupils for judgements on ethical matters and for decisions on penances. He became an authority transcending national boundaries, influencing penitential practice in Ireland, Brittany and Francia, an honoured figure in an important, fluid and informal development of a

[82] *HE* V 23
[83] Stevenson, *Laterculus* 272–4
[84] *HE* V 3

form of canonical authority in such matters. At first sight, a contribution by Theodore to the development of penance and private confession originating in a Hiberno-British tradition and popularised by Irish monks is a surprising development, given his lack of sympathy for the Irish tradition in general and his occasional hostile remarks on the Irish. One clue may lie in the Syriac practice of private confession, which as it lay within a tradition familiar to him in his formative years may well have made him more sympathetic to Celtic practice.[85]

The manuscript tradition is complicated: no text of his judgements has come to us in an unimpeachably original form but there is sufficient material to observe his use, characteristically, of St Basil and his willingness to adapt to barbarian usages. He is notably moderate in the penances he believes appropriate for killing in war under orders, harsher in his attitude to revenge killings but willing to make substantial concessions when *wergild* is paid. Irish penitentials required a sinner who planned homicide to relinquish arms for the rest of his life; Theodore, who knew his Anglo-Saxon warriors, was not ready to insist on this although it was in accord with the practice of early centuries. Sometimes Irish rulings and Theodore's judgements came close to each other. Theodore knew about the role of the feud in Anglo-Saxon society and Irish churchmen knew about the feud in Ireland: here the similarities were due to a pragmatic understanding of the realities of the societies in which they had to live.

Theodore is also moderate on dietary pollution and concerned that unintentionally eating something that is polluted by blood or anything unclean is not adjudged a sin. He may well be reacting against more austere Irish ruling. Anglo-Saxon practice allowed marriage partners to divorce when one decided to enter the monastic life: Ecgfrith of Northumbria and his obstinately virgin queen make a case in point. It was not a practice acceptable to the Latin Fathers. Theodore discreetly deployed a ruling of St Basil to provide a permission for Anglo-Saxon custom, while carefully avoiding any suggestion that Basil as a Greek was superior to a Latin authority. He preferred wherever possible not to interfere with local custom – an attitude illustrated by his acceptance of double monasteries in England despite his personal dislike of monks ruling over nuns, or vice versa.[86]

---

[85] T. Charles-Edwards, 'The Penitential of Theodore and the *Iudicia Theodori*', Lapidge, *Theodore* 141–74; Stevenson, *Laterculus* 12 n. 15
[86] Charles-Edwards, 'Penitential'

Both Theodore and Hadrian influenced the liturgy and martyrology of the Anglo-Saxon Church. Hadrian evidently brought with him a Gospel book with Neapolitan pericope lists and a Campanian sacramentary; Neapolitan pericopes found their way into the Lindisfarne Gospels and Campanian saints into the Calendar of Willibrord and the Old English Martyrology. Theodore popularised the cult of St Anastasius Magundat martyred at Kirkuk by Persians in 628, introduced Antiochene saints into the Anglo-Saxon tradition and caused the litany of saints to become a part of the Western liturgical tradition.

Four Greek prayers which originated in the patriarchate of Antioch were translated in Anglo-Saxon England, in all probability by Theodore. One of the four, the litany of saints, which consists pre-eminently in a series of petitions to individual saints, was a form of Greek and Eastern prayer not known in the West which through Theodore and the Anglo-Saxon Church passed into general Western usage. Theodore, familiar with the churches of Syria, which used the vernacular in worship and for biblical translation, may have been sympathetic to the use of written English; there is a possible indication of this in Bede's description of Tobias as 'a scholar of Latin, Greek and Saxon'.[87]

We know less of Hadrian than of Theodore, but he was manifestly an able scholar and successful abbot. Theodore was a polymath whose devotion to Antiochene exegesis and his record as a scholar in Tarsus, perhaps Edessa, certainly Antioch, Constantinople and Rome gave him an extraordinary range of knowledge and raised the prestige of Canterbury. Greek learning passed on in force probably to Tobias and Albinus and perhaps Oftfor, later bishop of Worcester; others would at least have had their horizons widened by attendance at memorable lectures. Biscop spent two years as abbot before Hadrian succeeded him and would have gained by his contacts. Hadrian lived on till 709.

Albinus was a stalwart support and inspiration to Bede. But the school inevitably lost distinction. It had been reborn by an unusual event, the arrival of two major figures from the world of Greek learning, and there was thereafter no comparable reinforcement from the Greek world. Knowledge of Greek was an unusual attainment in the contemporary Western world of learning – Bede himself, though he knew Greek, had not advanced much

---

[87] Bischoff and Lapidge, *Biblical commentaries* 155–60 (Neapolitan pericopes) 160–72 (Campanian saints) 168–72 (litany); St Anastasius, C.V. Franklin, 'Theodore and the *Passio S. Anastasii*', Lapidge, *Theodore* 175–203

beyond the New Testament – and it did not last in Canterbury after the generation trained by Theodore and Hadrian passed away.

Bede, who was aware of the darker side of Theodore's archiepiscopate, nonetheless saw his long tenure as a golden age. Theodore was, as he said, 'the first archbishop whom the entire Church of the English obeyed'. With Hadrian he created a school whose activities were a high-water mark in Anglo-Saxon literary culture and he made Canterbury a centre of learning and administration. As an Anglo-Saxon patriot, Bede rejoiced in the success of Anglo-Saxon kings, for although Northumbria had lost much ground in the north, the time had long passed in which the English settlement could be shaken by their old enemies, the British. Christianity had advanced. 'Never', he commented, 'had there been such happy times as these since the English first came to Britain.'[88]

[88] *HE* IV 2

CHAPTER 8

Christian Britain

The Picts were the last to enter the family of Christian peoples within Britain, the finest of their work and their conversion coming together in the late seventh century. To the secular scenes of the hunt, the animals and hybrids are now added the cross-slab, demonstrating emphatically an adherence to the faith, and scriptural scenes and symbols reveal the presence of thoughtful, trained indigenous clergy directing the high-calibre work of the sculptors. A skirted figure flanked by two pairs of lions in the centre of a cross-slab at Meigle in Perthshire suggests Daniel in the lions' den, commonly used as a prototype of Christ's suffering and resurrection. Jonah and the whale depicted in a panel at Dunfallandy, also in Perthshire, is another well-known Old Testament story interpreted as foreshadowing the death and resurrection of Christ.[1] In other words, the Pictish clergy were fully equipped with the learning of the time, the systems of analysis of the standard commentaries interpreting the Old Testament as prefiguring the New.

The greatest age of Christian sculpture in Pictland is the eighth and early ninth centuries: its quality may be illustrated by an example from Nigg in Ross and Cromarty. A creative mind has transformed a conventional scene derived from Jerome's Life of Paul the Hermit where Paul and Antony are being fed by a raven in the desert, into a representation of the mass. The hermits are bent low over their books while above them a raven carries down, not the conventional loaf, but the consecrated Host above the chalice, already broken to be delivered to them in communion. Learning, represented by their books, devotion as they lead their consecrated lives in the desert and the sacred gifts of the

---

[1] I. and G. Henderson, *The art of the Picts* (London 2008) no. 194, pp. 133–4, 143, 156, 201–2 (Meigle no. 2); no.149, pp. 142–3 (Dunfallandy)

Holy Mysteries brought down from heaven are all conveyed to the observer. Below the figures are two lions, recalling the wild beasts of the desert, here shown not as threatening but as standing patient and passive, the chalice and Host commanding their quiescence. A cross beneath the pediment dominates the stone, intricate displays of 'interlace spirals, fret and zoomorphic ornament' resembling nothing so much as a carpet page from one of the great Gospel books produced further south; while the bosses which originally existed above and below the cross-arms, ten at the left and twelve at the right, may well stand for the Old and New Testaments, the Decalogue at the left and the Christian message on the right, preached by the twelve apostles. Here is a fine combination of hagiography, liturgy and symbolism.[2]

S.T. Driscoll has a wise comment on the forces at work when he remarks on the significance of the stage in Pictish history when 'the importance of the Church [superseded] that of the ancestors'[3] A key point was the conversion of the aristocracy, who acted as patrons and put their resources into Christian stones. While never surrendering its individuality, the opening of Pictland to the outside world provided new stimuli, bringing more book learning and Mediterranean contacts.

It is common to associate this move out of isolation with Nechtan, over-king of the Picts, who, in his first period of rule between 706 and 724, took his subjects over to the Roman Easter, a move spurred on by a desire to break from a politically dangerous isolation and enter into closer relations with the Northumbrian Church. The victory of Nechtanesmere had stopped the payment of tribute to Northumbria,[4] altered the balance of power and helped the build-up of Fortriu as a centre of government. Although in 711 Nechtan suffered defeat at the hand of a Northumbrian ealdorman, he did not counter-attack but rather continued to seek rapprochement on the ecclesiastical front and sought to obtain fuller information from Ceolfrith, the abbot of Bede's own monastery, Jarrow. He then received a long exposition on the Easter question, stating the Roman position, which could have been written by Bede: it forms the longest chapter in his *History*.[5]

---

[2] Ibid., nos 202–3, pp. 41, 50, 131, 139–40, 211, 217, 227
[3] S.T. Driscoll, 'The relationship between history and archaeology: artefacts, documents and power', Driscoll, M.R. Nieke eds, *Power and politics in early medieval Britain and Ireland* (Edinburgh 1998) 162–87 at 184
[4] HB 57
[5] *HE* V 21; S. Coates, 'Ceolfrid: history, hagiography and memory in seventh and eighth century Wearmouth-Jarrow', *JMH* 25 (1999) 69–86

The letter was translated and read aloud in the presence of Nechtan and 'many learned men', the nobility also being present. Nechtan was committing his case for the approval of as wide a body as possible. Nechtan then ordered the tables of the old Columban and Ionan eighty-four-year cycles to be replaced by the new. He also made a request for architects to enable him to build a stone church in honour of St Peter as a symbol of Pictland's transference of obedience from St Columba.

Bede gives no date for Nechtan's initiative but 710 is traditional. It was a thoroughgoing business. Having sought advice on the correct form of the clerical tonsure, Nechtan decreed that the tonsure of St Peter was henceforth to be the norm. In 717 he took another drastic action and expelled Columban monks. It is not clear whether the Easter question was directly involved in this episode since Iona itself had accepted the Roman Easter in 716 but it may have been that a faction within the Ionan *paruchia* declined to accept the decision either of their mother house or of Nechtan and so were put out of Pictland. More likely is the hypothesis that the Columban monasteries were at odds with the power over Church matters which Nechtan was assuming, manifestly in conflict with the Ionan tradition of rule by abbot. Nechtan also had a personal interest: Bede implies that he had studied the problem of Easter before he got in touch with Ceolfrith. In a subsequent vicissitude in 724 he went into a monastery, not necessarily voluntarily, for tonsuring was a way of getting rid of rivals and it seems not to have been a coincidence that in 726 he was imprisoned by his successor, Drust. Thereafter he had one period of renewed rule before being again displaced.[6]

This tangle of events illustrates the common insecurity of Pictish over-kings. They had established their position vis-à-vis Northumbria but had to reckon with succession disputes within Pictland and periodic hostilities with Dál Riata; progress had been made under Bruide, building up both monarchy and Church, but still there were tensions and the reinforcing of monarchical authority by churchmen was an antidote. The figure of David, ancestor of Christ, great warrior and king blessed by God, appears on Pictish stones, which used the scriptural and artistic expertise of churchmen as a reinforcement of royal powers. David had a dual role. On the one hand he reminds the

[6] M.O. Anderson, 'Nechtan mac Derile', *ODNB*; id., 'Picts, Kings of the', *ODNB*; id., 'Picts – the name and the people', A. Small ed., *The Picts: a new look at old problems* (Dundee 1987 repr. 1996) 7–14

viewer of the powers of a just king in defending his people against their enemies and oppressors and on the other he is a symbol of Christ leading believers to salvation. A sarcophagus at St Andrews, probably commemorating Nechtan's successor Oengus who ruled from 732 to 761, or conceivably Nechtan himself, is dominated by a representation of David on the surviving long panel of a post-shrine, which was a magnificent royal memorial. If it is that of Oengus, reputedly the founder of the monastery at St Andrews, the sarcophagus, which may have lain in the monastery church, was clearly intended as a celestial makeweight for an otherwise bloodthirsty career.[7]

Behind this representation lies the story of David the shepherd boy from I Samuel who defied the giant Goliath, killed him with one slingshot and rose to be king of Israel, but the man shown here is an experienced warrior, king and statesman, over life size, who demonstrates his power under God's protection by breaking open a lion's jaw and killing it. The massive figure of the sarcophagus is still the shepherd – a sheepdog above the left shoulder reminds us of his youthful status – but the historical David of the Goliath episode has been subsumed in the powerful king of David's maturity. The David figure stands for security and protection in this life and salvation in the next. The other scenes, apparently so disparate, are in fact integrated into the whole, conveying the clash of life and death and the struggle for order in a threatening and uncivilised world.

After Nechtan's initiative and signs of effective common endeavour of ruler and churchmen, the ninth century saw the beginning of the end of Pictish independence, their resistance beaten down by Viking attack, and the opportunity given by their weakness seized by the rulers of Dál Riata. Gaelic so overwhelmingly supplanted Pictish that all we have are a few stray words and a number of place-names. Books, records and liturgical vessels of the Pictish Church disappeared.

One stone, the Dupplin Cross, in the heartland of southern Pictland overlooking the Water of May and the royal site of Forteviot, has been dated by Katherine Forsyth after skilled work with chalk and charcoal on a replica. Part of the worn inscription reads CUSTANTIN FILIUS FIRCUS, Constantine son of Fergus, and identifies the man commemorated as Constantine, originally of

---

[7] S.M. Foster ed., *The St Andrews sarcophagus* (Dublin 1998) coll. essays of distinction reviewed by R.N. Bailey, *Antiquity* 74 (2000) 246–7; see esp. I. Henderson, '*Primus inter pares*: the St Andrews sarcophagus and Pictish sculpture', Foster ed., *St Andrews sarcophagus* 97–167

the royal house of Dál Riata, who died in 820 and in his lifetime negotiated for the transfer of Columba's relics to Dunkeld, ruled both kingdoms and began the process of Gaelic takeover. It is the only extant complete cross of the Ionan type in Pictland: the Constantinian family chose it deliberately in a wish to boost the fame of Columba, patron of Dál Riata, in Pictland.[8]

One purely ecclesiastical factor hinted at in the sources which may have operated in the early tenth century to destroy the old Pictish Church was a conviction among members of the Céli Dé movement that it needed reform. Of the justice of this one cannot judge. Patrick Wormald believed that so complete a destruction of Pictish language and artefacts could only have occurred as a result of a heavy application of force, suppressing the Pictish elite.[9] At the very end little but the stones, damaged by the rain and winds of centuries and religiously inspired vandalism, have remained to bear witness to the Pictish clergy and their patrons.

The career of Adomnán shows that for all the loss of Iona's power through the decision at Whitby, its spiritual influence across Britain had not been forfeited. He has been overshadowed by the towering figure of Columba but he was a major personality in his own right, a worthy successor in his spirituality and his gift for making contact with rulers, and in his twenty-five years as abbot did much to restore Iona's reputation. He was concerned to show the world that it was possible to venerate Columba's memory while holding views other than his on the Easter question. His other master achievement was the enactment of the Law of the Innocents in 697 which sprang directly from his desire as a devout churchman to mitigate the effects of warfare. Like Theodore, Adomnán was aware that fighting was an integral part of the society in which he lived but was concerned to limit its effects to those who fought; in practice, to adult males. Women, children and clergy should be exempt. What was striking was the great geographical scope which the law was designed to have – the whole of Ireland and lands deeply influenced by Iona. A great assembly at the monastery of Birr brought together forty churchmen or abbots and fifty kings or their representatives from Ireland, Dál Riata and Pictland and these leading men gave their

---

[8] K. Forsyth, 'The inscriptions on the Dupplin cross', C. Bourke ed., *From the isles of the north. Early Mediterranean art in Ireland and Britain* (Belfast 1995) 237–44; L. Alcock, *Kings and warriors, craftsmen and priests in northern Britain AD 550–850* (Edinburgh 2003) 391–3

[9] P. Wormald, 'The emergence of the *Regnum Scottorum*: a Carolingian hegemony', B.E. Crawford ed., *Scotland in Dark Age Britain* (St Andrews 1996) 131–53

guarantees. Not only that. Guarantors were to be provided from each kindred: in effect, the nobility was being mobilised against the harming of these helpless groups. Stewards of the law collected debts due for a killing against the terms of the *Lex innocentium* on behalf of the lord or kindred in question. The saints in heaven were also brought to bear to provide their sanctions: the *Annals of Ulster* has the entry for 727, 'The relics of Adomnán are taken across to Ireland and the Law is renewed.'[10]

Although in the turbulent conditions of the ninth century, the Scots, i.e. the Irish from Dál Riata, took over the Pictish Church, remodelled it and drove its language into extinction, the strength of its Christianity was not diminished. It had come to stay. The British Churches of what is now Wales, children of the old Romano-British Church adapted to the very different circumstances of a rural society, continued their Christian life and sustained it with a resolute conservatism. They long continued to think of themselves as part of a British nation driven out of their lands by the pagan invaders of the fifth and sixth centuries, but not, for all that, finally defeated, never losing the awareness of the island of Britain as territory they once held and might yet regain. It is significant that it was amongst these British that the traditions of the Men of the North were preserved, most probably in Gwynedd, where in the court of its ruler, Merfyn Frych, the *Historia Brittonum* was written, compiled in the form we have it in 829/30.

Its central theme in a disorderly collection of information and legend is a reconstruction of the origins and early history of the British, given unimpeachable legitimacy by being linked to the Bible through Brutus, a Trojan immigrant whose genealogy is traced back to Japheth, son of Noah. The fight against the Anglo-Saxons is embellished with an account of Vortigern's great feast to which British leaders were invited and there treacherously murdered. The assertion is that it was not the British people as a whole who failed to resist the enemy but their betrayal by one leader who stabbed them in the back.[11]

'Then Arthur fought against them in those days, together with the kings of the British; but he was their leader in battle.' The Latin translated here as 'leader in battle' is 'dux bellorum'. In this way, the author gives support and comfort to

[10] T.M. Charles-Edwards, *Early Christian Ireland* (Cambridge 2000) 280–1, 564 (quotation); R. Sharpe, 'Adomnán', M. Lapidge ed., *The Blackwell encyclopedia of Anglo-Saxon England* (Oxford 1999)
[11] *HB* 18, 46; D.N. Dumville, 'The historical value of the *Historia Brittonum*', *Arthurian Literature* 6 (1986) 1–26; D.E. Thornton, 'Nennius', *ODNB*

the theme of British resurgence, giving a list of twelve battles, a biblical number, culminating in Mount Badon, in which 'nine hundred and sixty men fell in one day, from a single charge of Arthur's, and no one laid them low save he alone; and he was victorious in all his campaigns'.[12] Ostensibly describing events of the fifth century, the author has taken up the established hero of poetic sources, so well known that Áedán mac Gabráin of Dál Riata named his son Arthur, and has fleshed out the story to produce a super-hero who cannot be beaten. The most plausible hypothesis is that the original was a Welsh battle-catalogue poem, arbitrarily assigned to the great name of Arthur: the *Historia* spreads itself on one battle, Castellum Guinnion, in which 'Arthur carried the image of the Holy Mary the everlasting Virgin, on his [shield] and the heathen were put to flight on that day and there was a great slaughter upon them through the power of Our Lord Jesus Christ and through the power of the Holy Virgin Mary, his mother'. The original text speaks of carrying the image of the Virgin on his shoulder. That is almost certainly a misreading of the Welsh for shield. What is striking here is the Christianisation of the Arthur story. If Arthur did exist and fought the Anglo-Saxon enemy, then it is not very likely that there was so strong a Christian element in his wars. What we know of these fifth/sixth-century encounters is that individual chieftains fought one another, sometimes in alliance with pagan Anglo-Saxons, sometimes not, religious tensions between them not being a prominent factor.[13]

All unsuspectingly, the *Historia*'s author was launching the concept of the Christian hero-warrior, subsequently transmitted to a wider world through various channels. The tenth-century *Annales Cambriae* included a passage on Arthur, legends passed from Brittany into France till, in the hands of a twelfth-century fiction writer of genius, Geoffrey of Monmouth, they became a classic story of a chivalric knight that has held the European imagination down to this day. N.J. Higham has shown how knowledge of the Bible played a role in the compiler's work. 'Dux bellorum' is not a quasi-Roman title for a supreme cavalry commander moving between different theatres of war. It is a biblical title of honour adopted from the 'dux belli' of the first verse of the Vulgate version of the Book of Judges, where, after the death of Joshua, the heroic leader of the Israelites, they ask the Lord 'Who shall go up for us

[12] *HB* 56; K. Jackson, 'The Arthur of history', R.S. Loomis ed., *Arthurian literature in the Middle Ages* (Oxford 1959) 1–30
[13] *HB* 56; J.T. Koch, 'Arthur', *KCC* (adds little-known lit.); id., '*Historia Brittonum*', *KCC*; O. Padel, 'The nature of Arthur', *CMCS* 27 (1994) 1–31

against the Canaanites and be the "dux belli"?'[14] Arthur was another Joshua
with the hand of God upon him. The implication was that Merfyn Frych
could assume the mantle of Arthur, the victories of Arthur's day could be
repeated and British successes come again – if only the treachery that had
brought down Arthur could be avoided. Merfyn was an ambitious ruler of the
most powerful of the kingdoms in Wales, successful in battle and with a will
to unite others under his leadership against the Anglo-Saxon enemy. But he
did not succeed. The rise of dominant kingdoms, a perennial feature of
Anglo-Saxon history, is not replicated within Wales, the kingdoms remaining
small and disunited. Welsh churchmen long remained aware of the links
between them and the British of all parts of Britain and left a precious legacy
of information on the vanished heroes of the Old North in Cumbria and
southern Scotland, and in Arthur a literary hero of compelling power.

As it lived on in Wales, the British Church was distinguished by resolute
independence and conservatism. There is evidence from a ninth-century text
that a version of the *Vetus Latina*, the Latin text of Scripture before Jerome's
Vulgate, was still being used. Another sign of fidelity to the past lies in the
unchanged liturgy for the Vigil of Easter, which takes no account of its major
revision by Gregory the Great.

Fidelity to the past is also reflected in British churchmen's attitude to the
Easter question. Only in 768 was the decision made to accept the Roman
Easter: the *Annales Cambriae* has a laconic entry recording the decision and
noting that it was due to the influence of Elbodus, bishop of Bangor. How it
came about, what pleas were made by the bishop or by scholars and what influence secular politics had, all remains unknown. The decision bound Gwynedd,
possibly also kingdoms further south. It removed a barrier between the British
and the rest of the Churches but it did not seem to have made much difference
at the highest levels, for acceptance of the Roman Easter did not lead to acceptance of the jurisdiction of the archbishop of Canterbury: instinctively the
British Church looked west rather than east and remained in contact with the
Irish Church which it had done so much to found.

The British maintained their sacred sites, their shrines and their saints and
there are signs of an indigenous hagiography emerging *c.*800, which has not
come down to us. They valued illuminated Gospels. One of the finest, written

---

[14] Judges I 1; N.J. Higham, *King Arthur. Myth-making and history* (London, New York
2002) 142

perhaps about 730, and known both as the Gospels of Chad and the Lichfield Gospels, arrived after unknown vicissitudes in Llandeilo Fawr. In the style of the Lindisfarne family it has a carpet page for three of the evangelists, finely illuminated initials with their symbols, John being no longer extant and Luke incomplete. It uses runes and is therefore much more likely to have been made in an Anglo-Saxon monastery rather than in Wales or Scotland but a note in Welsh explains, 'Here it is shown that Gelhi, son of Arihtiud, bought this gospel from Cingal and gave him for it his best horse and gave for the sake of his soul this Gospel to God and St Teilo upon the altar.'[15] Gelhi made his gift in the early ninth century, and it is likely that it came on the market as Viking loot, so enabling him to make this generous gift to his church: on the other hand, the fragmentary Hereford Gospels may well have been the work of a monastic foundation in Wales. Lost some time after 1594, the Book of St Berino allegedly copied by St Twrog in the reign of the seventh-century king Cadfan, and in its secure casing the survivor of a fire at Clynnog church, is an intriguing might-have-been, perhaps a Gospel book of calibre. Manuscripts from Wales have tended to survive when they proved to be of interest to the English and much has been lost; nevertheless, sufficient literary and ecclesias-tical material survives to show the existence of varied scriptoria and scribal traditions within Wales which continued through the early Middle Ages.[16] Rulers supported Welsh churches and monasteries generously but the limited nature of the Welsh economy, the lack of towns and substantial urban markets inhibited the growth of the monasteries and the building of churches.

The Book of Llandaff, a compilation including much early material made in the interest of a twelfth-century bishop in his battle for the rights of his see, suggests the early existence of a substantial number of religious foundations in the south-west of Wales, probably over fifty small communities with limited resources but lying on fertile land. The area is fortunate in the survival of char-ters providing information about earlier centuries but the suspicion remains that documentation on religious communities further north and west is slight simply because there were fewer of them on poorer land with a lower population.[17]

[15] P. Lord, *The visual culture of Wales: medieval vision* (Cardiff 2003) 25–7; Easter decision, H.R. Loyn, *Society and peoples. Studies in the history of England and Wales, c.600–1200* (London 1992) 43–4

[16] P. Sims-Williams, 'The uses of writing', H. Pryce ed., *Literacy in medieval Celtic societies* (Cambridge 1998) 22

[17] W. Davies, *Wales in the early Middle Ages* (Leicester 1982) 141–8; J.T. Koch, 'Llandaf, Book of', *KCC* dissipates doubts on evidence

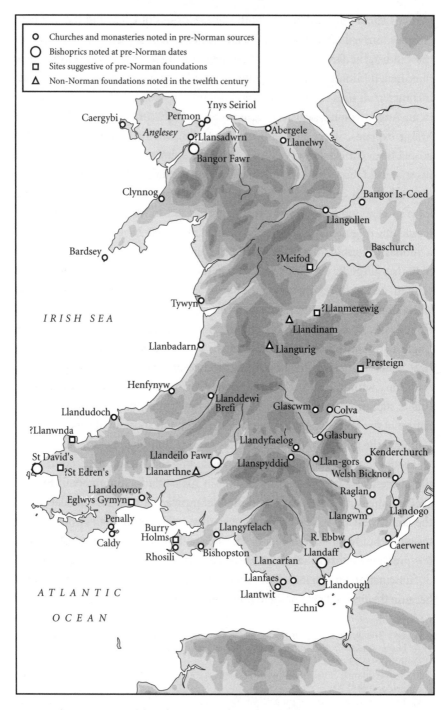

○ Churches and monasteries noted in pre-Norman sources
◯ Bishoprics noted at pre-Norman dates
□ Sites suggestive of pre-Norman foundations
△ Non-Norman foundations noted in the twelfth century

Caergybi
Anglesey
Permon
Ynys Seiriol
?Llansadwrn
Bangor Fawr
Abergele
Llanelwy
Clynnog
Bangor Is-Coed
Llangollen
Bardsey
Baschurch
?Meifod
IRISH SEA
Tywyn
?Llanmerewig
Llandinam
Llanbadarn
Llangurig
Henfynyw
Presteign
Llanddewi
Brefi
Glascwm
Colva
Llandudoch
?Llanwnda
Glasbury
St David's
Llandyfaelog
Kenderchurch
?St Edren's
Llandeilo Fawr
Llanspyddid
Llan-gors
Llanarthne
Welsh Bicknor
Llanddowror
Eglwys Gymyn
Raglan
Penally
Llangwm
Llandogo
Caldy
Burry
Holms
Llangyfelach
R. Ebbw
Caerwent
Bishopston
Llandaff
Rhosili
Llancarfan
Llanfaes
Llandough
Llantwit
Echni
ATLANTIC
OCEAN

Map 8 Christian sites and foundations in Wales before the Normans.

On the great monastery of Bangor described by Bede in his account of the massacre at the battle of Chester, we have no information: there is more than a suspicion that Bede was using a British source where the vivid description of the multitude of monks was influenced by the rhetoric of praise-poetry. Standards and expectations were variable. A bishop would have his household and it is clear that a distinction was originally made between such a household and a true monastic community but a fragment of evidence from the Welshman Asser, bishop of Sherborne and biographer of Alfred, shows that by his time the situation had deteriorated and this distinction had been lost. Communities remained and were vital support points for Church life but were not necessarily communities of monks in the sense understood by St Samson or St David. Celibacy weakened and there was much influence of family and intrusion of hereditary rights over office and property. These developments would help to explain the emphasis on the fierce asceticism of the hermits and founders of monasteries in the Age of Saints as described by the *Vitae*, such as that by Rhigyfarch in a later age. The authors were looking for reform and a return to a more traditional monastic life.[18]

The impact of Christianity on the Anglo-Saxon kingdom of Northumbria was the crucible for an explosive burst of creativity through its opening of links with the cultural world of Gaul and the Mediterranean, which mixed with Celtic, Pictish and Anglo-Saxon traditions and art forms.[19] Four remarkable works and one scholarly career may be allowed to illustrate the whole wide-ranging achievement of the Northumbrian Church. They are the Lindisfarne Gospels, the *Codex Amiatinus*, the Franks casket, the Ruthwell cross and the achievements of Bede. A key precondition lies in the sequence of seventh-century kings Oswald, Oswiu and Ecgfrith, their great wealth and generosity to the monasteries they founded and patronised, and the work of converted aristocrats who contributed their own resources and powers of leadership, staffing, leading and endowing churches and monasteries. Northumbrian kings ruled wide lands, had at various times under their power many British Christians and some Picts, had contacts with Dál Riata and Pictland and from the time of Aidan's mission, intimate links to Iona and its federation of monasteries in Ireland.

---

[18] Davies, *Wales* 149

[19] Whole picture C. Neuman de Vegvar, *The Northumbrian renaissance. A study in the transmission of style* (London, Toronto 1987)

Artistic traditions within the island had earlier begun to fuse: the Sutton Hoo ship burial included both jewellery and arms from the Germanic tradition and techniques derived from British smiths while display goods, coins and miscellaneous artefacts came also from Gaul and the Mediterranean. At Dunadd in Dál Riata, where traditions of Celtic jewellery were paramount, a mould and jewellery fragments of Anglo-Saxon provenance have been found, and there is similar evidence at the fortress of Mote of Mark near Dumfries in the former kingdom of Rheged. The Insular style, formed from Christian and pre-Christian traditions, was brought to a masterly synthesis in the seventh- and eighth-century Latin Gospel books, created in monastic communities to the glory of God and in honour of their saints, using the skills of the calligraphers and illuminators amongst them, the devotion of monks making the long and solitary labour part of their sacrificial lives.[20] Scholarly and pacific, Aldfrith was one of the few Anglo-Saxon kings who could read. He gave eight hides of land to the monastery of Jarrow in exchange for 'the magnificently worked copy of the Cosmographers which Benedict [i.e. Biscop] had bought in Rome', striking evidence of wealth and generosity when one recalls that the whole island of Iona measured five hides.[21]

Great libraries, built up through the book-buying tours of Biscop and Ceolfrith, were both a condition and a stimulus for scriptural study, work on the Fathers, hagiography and the maintenance of liturgy. At Hexham, Wilfrid helped to create a notable library, while at Ripon he commissioned illuminated Gospels, in Stephen of Ripon's words 'a marvel of art hitherto undreamt of', probably produced in Italy.[22] It has now vanished but it may well have been one factor working in favour of the production of Gospel books elsewhere, part of the competition for excellence among leading monasteries.

Wilfrid played a pivotal role in stimulating creative reactions to his abrasive personality and chequered career. Troubles did not end with the reconciliation at the end of Theodore's life but broke out again during the tenure of his successor, Berhtwald. After his conflict with and banishment by Aldfrith in 672, Wilfrid took refuge in a long exile in Mercia; then in 703 Berhtwald took

[20] G. Henderson, *From Durrow to Kells. The Insular Gospel books 650–800* (London 1987); id., *Vision and image in early Christian England* (Cambridge 1999); I. Wood, 'The transmission of ideas', L. Webster, M. Brown eds, *The transformation of the Roman world* AD *400–800* (London 1997) 111–26
[21] *HA* 15; R. Cramp, 'Aldfrith', *ODNB*
[22] *VW* 17

the decision in Council to confine him to his abbey at Ripon. This Wilfrid declined to accept, went again to appeal in Rome and received a cautious decision in his favour, but on his way home had a seizure at Meaux. In 705 he was reconciled to Berhtwald and five years later died at Oundle. In his will he left the largest amount to two basilicas in Rome, one of the passions of his life; then his faithful followers who had laboured with him in his long exile were remembered and, most significantly, a portion was given to the abbots of Hexham and Ripon 'so that they might have something in hand wherewith to secure the favour of the kings and bishops'.[23] He left more wealth and a wider body of estates than some kings.

Wilfrid continued to have passionate supporters who believed he had been mistreated by authority in England and took him to be a saint, views faithfully represented in the partisan hagiography of his companion Stephen of Ripon, which came out between 710 and 720. Ranged against him were those who feared his party and their influence in the Church, remembering the abrasive effects of his time as abbot of Lindisfarne. Their hero was St Cuthbert, whom Bede saw as the kind of bishop he wished to see leading reform in his own Church: his Life of 720 had a defensive function against the Wilfridians, intended to aid the development of Cuthbert's cult and preserve the status of Lindisfarne as a holy place.

The Lindisfarne Gospels had a similar aim: though its colophon dates from the tenth century, it surely reproduces the contemporary entry and reads, 'Eadfrith, Bishop of Lindisfarne Church, originally wrote this book, for God and for Saint Cuthbert and jointly for all the saints whose relics are in the Island.' It was a cult book designed as a source of power and protection: the immense effort which went into making it was a call to God and His saints, specially St Cuthbert, to defend the monks and the holy islands where his relics lay. Its balance of Insular art, derived above all from the Irish tradition via Iona and its powerful presence in Northumbria, combining with elements of Mediterranean art, especially in the evangelists' portraits, implicitly made a statement about the position of Lindisfarne. It had accepted the Whitby decision and the Roman Easter, it had surmounted the damage caused by Wilfrid's rule and dissensions among the monks, it had held fast to the Ionan tradition, its vigour manifest in the superb ornament of the Gospel pages, blending the high-calibre jewellery skills, which came originally from pre-Christian Irish

[23] *VW* 63

smiths, with Germanic ornament of the kind shown in Sutton Hoo and incorporating something of the Pictish tradition of animal representation.[24]

Plausibly attributed to the Ionan scriptorium, the Book of Durrow represents an earlier stage in the evolution of the Gospel book with its fine marriage between jewellers' skills and calligraphy, utilising by paint on vellum the styles evolved over the years in jewellery-making. Jewels had multiple functions in early societies as bribes, ransoms, security, decoration, declaration of status, gifts and pawns in diplomatic exchanges and were a forcing-ground for the skills of smiths, men who thereby acquired major status in their societies. It was one of the achievements of Christianity in the island of Britain that within the context of violent clashes between kingdoms and individuals struggling for power, it called together skills derived from these colliding political entities, whether from Ireland, Dál Riata, Pictland, Anglo-Saxon kingdoms or, via hanging bowls, late Roman Britain, to produce the Insular style, not strictly part of a renaissance, as is sometimes said, but a new creation.[25]

The Gospel book evolved as a spin-off from the necessity to manage the transition from scroll to codex, where signs were needed to enable the reader to navigate his way through a text, particularly important in the case of psalters because of their role in monastic life. The process can be seen developing in the Cathach, a psalter attributed by some to St Columba, with aids to find the way through long, unpunctuated word sequences. A whole series of such earlier scriptural texts, now vanished, in which scribal techniques and illuminator skills were refined, lay behind the Lindisfarne Gospels: when, after the dramatic moment of the translation of Cuthbert's body in 698 and the discovery that it was incorrupt, the monastery decided to embark on the making of a supremely valuable Gospel text, it was drawing on an expertise spanning back over decades. It was also drawing on a remarkably wealthy institution, with wide estates supporting many calves to provide the necessary vellum and with a manpower some six hundred strong which enhanced the possibility of a calligrapher and illuminator of genius emerging within the community and flourishing in an atmosphere that placed such emphasis on copying and calligraphy as a high duty of a monk.

---

[24] M.P. Brown, *The Lindisfarne Gospels. Society, spirituality and the scribe* (London 2003) definitive analysis; colophon 103–4; J. Backhouse, *The Lindisfarne Gospels* (Oxford 1981) factual intro.
[25] M.P. Brown, 'Durrow, Book of', Lapidge, *Blackwell encyclopedia*

Eadfrith, bishop of Lindisfarne from 698 to 721, was just such a man; that he alone was responsible for the great bulk of the Gospel, Michelle Brown's research has proved. She shows that only a very small proportion was the work of another scribe, competent but wholly undistinguished, probably detailed to finish it after Eadfrith's death.[26] It is a mark of Eadfrith's genius that he so ably assimilated Mediterranean models for the evangelists and combined them harmoniously with the German and Celtic tradition of ornament which forms the bedrock of his Gospel. With their intricacy and profusion of images and ornament, the carpet pages convey the element of complexity in contemporary scriptural study, discerning beneath the letter of Scripture layer upon layer of allegory, prophecy and allusion. Jane Hawkes recalls the importance of *ruminatio*, the meditation of a mature monk contemplating the sacred text with the aid of the Fathers and, above all, of prayer, the pre-eminent pathway to understanding. The calligraphy and illumination would have been an extraordinarily demanding, solitary task, taking anything between five to ten years. It casts an interesting light on what Lindisfarne expected from a bishop, for Michelle Brown opines that Eadfrith made the Gospels when he was bishop and not before. It also casts light on the high valuation laid there on the eremitical strand in monastic life and the intimate link between spirituality and the making of a sacred book.[27]

Although Monkwearmouth-Jarrow's ethos was very different from Lindisfarne's, there was nevertheless collaboration between them, indicated by their loan to Lindisfarne of a Gospel text with Neapolitan pericopes, undoubtedly a text brought originally from Italy by Abbot Hadrian. Pandects, that is whole bibles, were the mark of the scriptorium of Monkwearmouth-Jarrow, inspired by one of Ceolfrith's greatest prizes from the continent, the *Codex Grandior* from Cassiodorus's sixth-century south Italian monastery Vivarium, a whole Bible in a mixture of versions. It was Ceolfrith and his senior monks' ambition to create in their scriptorium another pandect in the best, most correct version, i.e. the Vulgate translation of St Jerome, superseding the Cassiodorus text but using tables and miniatures from the *Codex Grandior*. It imposed immense demands on scribes and a cost of materials only bearable in monasteries of great wealth, 1,550 calf skins being

[26] Brown, *Lindisfarne Gospels* 244, 299
[27] M.P. Brown, 'Carpet pages', Lapidge, *Blackwell encyclopedia*; Celtic background S. Youngs ed., *The work of angels. Masterpieces of Celtic metalwork 6th–9th centuries* AD (London 1989)

required for each volume. Moreover the monks made two in order to bring the fruits of the latest scholarship to each of the twin monasteries. Nothing has survived of one; the other is extant in a few leaves recovered in the nineteenth century, enough to make plain that it was not so fine as the third and last pandect, designed as a ceremonial gift to the see of Peter in a majestic uncial, reminiscent – and surely this is no accident – of the high script of Gregory the Great.

At some stage, Ceolfrith decided in secrecy that he would himself, in the evening of his days, take the great book to the pope. When he announced his departure on 2 June 716, there was consternation in his monasteries but no one could stop the abbot and two days later he set off taking ship with the pandect, other gifts and eighty of his monks. Bede was so shocked at the departure of an abbot he loved that he had to stop work on his scriptural commentary for a time. On the journey Ceolfrith recited the psalter and the canonical hours twice daily, but he was seventy-four, the travel was too much and in September he died at Langres in southern Gaul. Some monks stayed there, some returned and some travelled on with the pandect, which survives in full as the *Codex Amiatinus*, so perfectly made that it was long thought to be a product of an Italian monastery.[28]

Ceolfrith appended a verse to the *Codex* describing himself as an abbot from the furthest parts of the earth. The work was designed to show what a monastery at the very rim of the world could do and how a full orthodoxy and mastery of scriptural scholarship was in existence there – a message of hope, of the approaching fulfilment of the prophecy of the Second Coming when the Gospel would have been preached in all corners of the earth; perhaps also designed to show what peace, orthodoxy and scholarship prevailed in Northumbria, the papal court having been for so long subject to appeals from Wilfrid alleging injustice and malpractice in the English Church.

Assigned to eighth-century Northumbria, the Franks casket has no exact precedent. It stands alone, a small finely worked whalebone casket, nine inches long, seven and a half wide and five deep, a treasure box or reliquary with panels depicting an extraordinarily miscellaneous set of scenes, biblical, historical, legendary. The patron who commissioned it exhibits an exuberant delight in Northumbria's new learning, blending in his mind with the German

[28] Coates, 'Ceolfrid', *JMH* 25 (1999) 69–86; *HA* 16–18, 21–3

legends of his own people. The use of runes alongside inscriptions in Latin demonstrates his linguistic virtuosity and his will to straddle both worlds.[29]

It offers a set of puzzles, which hold the scenes together: the Magi bringing gifts to the Christ child; Titus assaulting Jerusalem in AD 70; Romulus and Remus suckled by a she-wolf; Weyland the Smith taking revenge on the evil king Nithad who had lamed him, holding the skull of Nithad's son and offering his daughter a drugged drink before raping her; Egil the archer, Weyland's brother defending his house against warriors and a scene from an unknown Germanic legend played out in a forest and marsh with a monster, a warrior, a great horse and a skeleton in a mound, with two persons laying hold on a third to lead into captivity.

Two words 'dom' (judgment) and 'gisl' (hostage), curt signposts on the far left and right of the back panel, give the key to the work. Judgment is given both against the Jews, fulfilling Jesus's lament for the city of Jerusalem, and against the evil Nithad, Weyland the avenger depicted sitting beneath the throne holding the poison for the king in his hand. 'Gisl' has echoes of imprisonment and exile, with the Jews fleeing from Titus's destruction and the twins in exile in a wood. Marsh and woodland are dreary and dangerous places, and the Germanic scene, where a certain Hos is described in the accompanying inscription as sitting on a 'sorrow mound', in 'a wretched den of sorrows and torments of mind', can be explained as a depiction of paganism, an exile for the recalcitrant from which there is no escape. The twins can be rescued from the woodland but the pagans can never escape from their den of sorrows. Treasure and kingship also link the scenes contrasting the Magi bringing good gifts to the Christ with the pagan Weyland who presents a deadly gift to an evil king.

Anglo-Saxons loved riddles and this patron explains his casket in a riddling phrase round the front: 'The fish beat up the seas on to the mountainous cliff, the king of terror became sad when he swam around on the shingle.'[30] Then comes the solution: 'whale's bone', the casket having been made from a whale stranded on the Northumbrian coast. There is determined erudition here: the whale features in the *Physiologus*, the destruction of Jerusalem in Josephus,

---

[29] Earlier work superseded by L. Webster, 'The iconographic programme of the Franks Casket', J. Hawkes, S. Mills eds, *Northumbria's golden age* (Stroud 1999) 227–46; J. Lang, 'The imagery of the Franks Casket: another approach', Hawkes, Mills eds, *Northumbria's golden age* 147–55; J. Hawkes, 'Symbolic lives: the visual evidence', J. Hines ed., *The Anglo-Saxons from the migration period to the eighth century* (Woodbridge 1997) 311–38, discussion 338–44, subtle analysis of pagan and Christian symbolism inc. Franks casket
[30] Webster, 'The iconographic programme' 232

the Ark of the Covenant is depicted empty since the Mosaic covenant has been superseded. The patron not only shows his learning but demonstrates how pagan Germanic legend can be made to yield moral lessons and stand beside Scripture and Roman and Jewish history. It is another remarkable product of the Northumbrian Renaissance.

The tall cross-pillars of Bewcastle in Cumbria and Ruthwell in Dumfries in the former British kingdom of Rheged are outstanding examples of figural sculpture which demonstrate the ability of Anglo-Saxon churchmen and patrons to assimilate Late Antique models, using them for their own Christian purposes, as much for the consolidation of the faith as for the instruction of the laity. These dominate the landscape, the former being about sixteen feet in height and Ruthwell's over seventeen: their impact would have been all the more powerful in their original splendour in bright colours, inset with glass and metal, suggesting the replacement of the vanished Roman Empire by the Christian Church producing stone monuments for a society whose buildings were overwhelmingly made of wood. This would have been particularly true of the Bewcastle cross which stands close to the ruins of an auxiliary Roman fort in which, it is conjectured, was a monastic community which played a part in its erection. It is the more conventional of the two, depicting an aristocrat with a bird, perhaps a falcon, and a runic inscription, just decipherable as an acknowledgement of donors and request to pray for their souls.[31]

These great crosses have much in common: each has John the Baptist enfolding the Lamb of God, pointing as if in recognition of the Christ, each has vine scrolls with birds and animals symbolising the Eucharist. There are signs that the same craftsmen worked on both, though the Ruthwell cross exceeds all others in the sophistication of its iconography, its intimate relationship to the liturgical developments of the eighth century and the originality of its extracts from vernacular poetry. This is eighth-century work, its runes anticipating the tenth-century poem, *The Dream of the Rood*, in which the cross speaks, and shows again the confident integration of Christianity and the Germanic tradition. It is in stone what the Gospel books are in vellum: a focus for meditation, a demonstration of the truths of the faith and an expression of the Christian liturgy.

[31] R.N. Bailey, 'Bewcastle', Lapidge, *Blackwell encyclopedia*; Alcock, *Kings* 379; J. Hawkes, 'Sacraments in stone: the mysteries of Christ in Anglo-Saxon sculpture', M.O.H. Carver ed., *The cross goes north* (Woodbridge, Suffolk 2003) 351–70; B. Cassidy, ed., *The Ruthwell Cross* (Princeton, N.J. 1992)

The broad side panels bear Latin inscriptions, the narrow lower sides runes, which tell the story enshrined in the sculptures, linking the Virgin's acceptance of the will of God as expressed by Gabriel at the Annunciation to the cross's acceptance of the will of Christ, albeit with deep reluctance, as it bears His body through the tortures of the Crucifixion. In the words of the poem *The Dream of the Rood*, the cross bows in order to present Christ's body to the veneration of his followers. The sculptor has put in parallel the growth of Christ in Mary's womb with the growth of the soul through conversion, symbolised by the healing of the blind man and the repentant sinner washing Christ's feet with her tears. The natural world is also represented: vine-scroll patterns recall the Eucharist and the worshipping animals have their paws crossed in echo of the chi half of the Greek symbol of Christ's name. The classic representation of the Eucharist is there, with the hermits receiving bread from heaven. They are in the desert, a reminder of what the Northumbrian and British Churches had in common, a veneration for the monastic, eremitical life, 'the desert'.

This is not a Bible for the poor: explanation at a high level would be needed to convey its meaning. It is rather a demonstration of the truths of the faith, a focus of meditation, an expression in stone of the Christian liturgy. It is natural to attribute the work to a monastery nearby, otherwise unknown to us. It is up to date, plausibly to be linked to the development of Marian feasts in the eighth century, and remarkably original. It is not clear that the theme of the cross speaking of its own suffering, its obedience and the courage of its Lord has any precedent. It would seem to be an original product of the Anglo-Saxon world. Christ is the master who voluntarily accepts His fate, powerfully expressed in a runic line typical of Anglo-Saxon heroic literature, describing how 'The young Hero, who was God Almighty', ascended the gallows.[32]

It is all the more noteworthy that so sophisticated a work of art should have been erected in a Northumbrian borderland without deep roots in Northumbrian Church life. Neuman de Vegvar has detected at Ruthwell signs of a rapprochement with the British Church and a tendency to ecumenical

[32] É.Ó. Carragáin, 'The Annunciation of the Lord and his Passion', J. Nelson ed., *Essays in Anglo-Saxon and related themes in memory of Lynne Grundy* (Exeter 200) 339–81; É.Ó. Carragáin, 'The necessary distance: Imitatio Romae and the Ruthwell cross', Hawkes and Mills, *Northumbria's golden age* 191–203, offer definitive interpretation; E. Okasha, 'Literacy in Anglo-Saxon England', *ASAH* 8 (1995) 69–74 at 73

reconciliation. It may be that the siting in just such a borderland, far from the
polemics and tensions of the heartland, made possible so mature and calmly
contemplative a monument. Here, as with the Franks casket, the two worlds,
Latin-Mediterranean and Anglo-Saxon, both have their place and contribute
to a confident and sophisticated synthesis.

In Bede we recognise the most learned man of his age, a polymath, humble in
mind, an exegete, poet, translator, historian and scientific observer, whose tables
on the tides remained long in use, and he may have had more to do with the
making of the *Codex Amiatinus* than hitherto realised. It seems he took up
compass and ruler and dry-pointed the portrait of Cassodorus, equipping him
with high priestly garments believing him to be Ezra, a hero of Bede's because of
his renewal of the Israelites after their return from Babylon, his work with their
Scriptures and reform of the priesthood, causes dear to his own heart.[33] Little
doubt, he was a major influence in the decisions about the pandect and the
notion of transporting one as a present to the pope: Scripture and fidelity to
Rome were the two pillars of Bede's scholarly career. He would himself have
valued most highly his commentaries on the books of the Bible, largely verse by
verse analysis based on the works of the Fathers, which he wrote throughout his
life to convey to the young Church the riches of past learning from the Latin
Fathers, above all his own revered master Gregory the Great. The daily round of
Jarrow's liturgical prayer would have familiarised him with a great array of
scriptural passages from both Testaments, which his commentaries link together
in a variety of ways. His purpose was pastoral and he sent many to his friend
Acca, bishop of Hexham, for the monks and clergy to spread learned knowledge
in order to form a proper basis for their preaching. Linguistic knowledge was
essential. Bede had a mastery of Latin, a lucid, elegant style superior even to
Gregory's, and he composed Latin verse. He knew Greek; a Greek manuscript of
Acts which he used to correct his first commentary on the Acts of the Apostles
is still extant. No doubt Acts would have especially interested him as the story of
the spread of the Gospel among the Gentiles; in just the same way as Paul and
his companions, a small body of missionaries worked among his pagan predecessors generations before his day. It is their story which he narrates in the
Ecclesiastical History, his greatest achievement.

---

[33] S. DeGregorio, '"Nostrorum socordiam temporum": the reforming impulse of Bede's
later exegesis', *EME* 11 (2000) 107–22; P. Meyvaert, 'The date of Bede's *In Ezram* and his
image of Ezra in the Codex Amiatinus', *Speculum* 80 (2005) 1087–133

His popularising of the use of *Anno Domini*, his textbooks of Latin grammar, suitably expunged of unsuitable material, were notable achievements but his *History* was a stimulus to the German mission field, whence some of the earliest manuscripts come, and an immediate success. He was concerned to tell the story of the English people as a new Israel chosen by God, thereby instilling the notion of one nation, not a very obvious concept given their varied origins, dialects and kingly rivalries.[34] At times leading to distortion, it nevertheless had a real and lasting effect, though the story does not end victoriously.[35]

Bede falters when he comes to write about his own time. Book V lacks narrative drive, being dominated by disparate stories and visions, such as Drycthelm's description of purgatory and the fate of a monk who repented too late to be saved from the pains of hell. There is a reason for this. Bede had long been troubled by the state of his own Church, an anxiety clearly seen in his work on Ezra, and at the end of his life he wrote to his former pupil, Egbert of York, pleading for reform, denouncing the setting up of monasteries for family interests to take advantage of tax exemption, and the feasting and laxity of bishops who took tribute to maintain their status and failed to visit their flocks. He was never a withdrawn Latin elitist; his learning was always designed to serve the Church. When he died he was engaged on a translation, now lost, of St John's Gospel, a favourite of Anglo-Saxon churchmen since of all the Gospels it conveys most clearly Christ's power and majesty. By tradition, Cuthbert actually placed the book of this Gospel on the sick for healing.

The attitude of kings and aristocrats in this hierarchical society was inevitably crucial for the initial acceptance of Christianity and their assent, sometimes a deep and personal commitment, produced patrons responsible for the churches, monasteries and major works of art, as we have seen.[36] How far Anglo-Saxon courts could go in passionate acceptance of the faith is apparent from the number of kings who abdicated for conscience's sake, most probably, as Clare Stancliffe suggests, under influence from the Irish rather

---

[34] On Bede, above ch. 1 n. 10; J. Campbell, 'Bede', *ODNB*; R.A. Fletcher, 'Bede', *Who's who*; J.T. Koch, 'Beda/Bede', *KCC*; W.M. Stevens, 'Bede's scientific achievements', *Jarrow Lectures 1985, Bede and his world* (Aldershot 1994)

[35] As noted by N.J. Higham, *The English empire. Bede and the Anglo-Saxon kings* (Manchester 1995) but see rev. H. Vollrath, *Deutsches Archiv* 52, 718

[36] Analysis, J. Blair, *The Church in Anglo-Saxon society* (Oxford 2008) 108–12; penetrating on problem of aristocratic values, P. Wormald, 'Bede, Beowulf and the conversion of the English aristocracy', R.T. Farrell ed., *Bede and Anglo-Saxon England BAR* 46 (1978) 32–95

than the Roman tradition and from the royal houses who produced saints, the sacral kingship of paganism giving way to prestige for those royal houses which produced holy men and women. After the first potentially dangerous transition phase was passed, Christianity aided rather than hindered kingship, contact with missionaries bringing access to skills not hitherto available in Britain after the collapse of Rome: literacy and books, law codes, the recording of land transactions, building in stone and glazing, all stimulating links to classical art and Mediterranean culture, which no doubt formed part of the attraction of the faith for rulers.

It was not only men who had high responsibility at this time. Queens mattered whether pagan or Christian.[37] Redwald's queen, together with 'evil counsellors', dissuaded her husband from following up his Kentish baptism, influenced him against betraying Edwin and for taking on Aethelfrith, the greatest warrior of the day. The evidence of Sutton Hoo suggests she also had a hand in setting up the most magnificent of burials and an overwhelmingly pagan one. Ecgfrith's queen retained her virginity with steely resolve and proceeded to become St Aethelthryth, abbess of Ely; her successor, Queen Iurminburh, inflamed Ecgfrith against Wilfrid and through her network of female connections checkmated Wilfrid's plans while it was the abbess Aebbe who persuaded the royal pair to cool the quarrel. Hild at Whitby appears as a model ruler of a double monastery, successfully sustaining a Gaulish type of monasticism on English soil, counselling at the highest level and providing a training ground for bishops. Princess Bertha, though an unknown personality, faithfully maintained her bishop and a Christian circle under the rule of a pagan father-in-law and may have influenced her husband more than the sources tell us. Women in these years exerted power both through their husbands and in direct rule over nunneries and double monasteries. How far their powerful role stemmed from the pagan age, how far Bede tended to underplay their importance and how far the position of women deteriorated through the Christian centuries continues to be a subject of debate. What is clear is that they mattered in the conversion age.

Aristocratic leadership was also of great importance and wise rulers made no decisions without the support of their nobles. Young warriors who learned of the faith during their service at court took their beliefs back with them and used the resources of their estates to sponsor endowments and influence those

---

[37] S. Hollis, *Anglo-Saxon women and the Church. Sharing a common fate* (Woodbridge 1992)

dependent on them. Monasteries involved lay servants and tenants, the majority learning by word of mouth and through the services of the Church. There will have been many like Caedmon the cowherd, simple, devout, illiterate, and unrecorded.

Clearly there were areas where the new religion had barely penetrated, which needed such men as Aidan and Cuthbert, devoted preachers who journeyed to reach them, Aidan using royal support points. Memorial stones, crosses and sculptures across Britain were used as preaching stations. Commanding personalities were there to call forth response in the early years. A common line can be seen between St Martin of Tours, St Patrick, St Wilfrid and St Boniface, fearless, larger than life, able to command their audiences with dramatic acts or eloquence, uncowed by opposition or danger, challenging the pagan gods to do their worst. The work initiated by these natural leaders and motivators needed to be followed by consolidators to instruct and sustain. When centuries later in Sweden a period of successful revivalist preaching was not followed up by the founding of monasteries, the recruits fell away and the attempt at conversion had to begin all over again. Structures, endowments and institutions had a vital role.

In the conversion of England, efforts of churchmen from the Irish and Roman traditions intertwined but, as John Blair reminds us, the Irish had a certain advantage in coming from a rural rather than an urban society with an affinity to that of Anglo-Saxon England.[38] The importance of the Irish tradition in Northumbria may well have been underestimated; there was a real, potential danger after Whitby but somehow it was got over and the Church recovered. This gives weight to Bede's joy over the acceptance of the Roman Easter and his exposition on the Englishman Egbert, who decided to undergo white martyrdom in Ireland and there instructed the monk Willibrord from Wilfrid's Ripon monastery, influencing him to go as a missionary to Frisia. Wilfrid was influenced throughout his life by his devotion to St Andrew, patron of mission. It can well be argued that the sending of Anglo-Saxon missionaries back to pagan Germans was a major event, fit to be put beside the process of conversion within the island of Britain. There seems to have been a general feeling among their Christian compatriots in England that the pagans on the continent were 'bone of our bone' and should be aided. It was a dangerous business. Willibrord himself came close to death and the Hewald brothers were killed in Frisia for their faith.

[38] J. Blair, *The Anglo-Saxon age. A very short introduction* (Oxford 2000) 7

Boniface had a long career in Germanic lands and became archbishop of Mainz: he was as much reformer as missionary to raw paganism but he can fairly be called a martyr for he knew very well that he was working in areas of danger and took his shroud with him. He and his following fell victim to looters at Dokkum in the modern Netherlands in 754, succumbing to men grabbing treasure, who scattered their prize over the ground when they discovered they had captured books. According to tradition, Boniface attempted to shield himself from the axes of his killers with a Gospel book. There is a book to this day in the treasury at Fulda with cut marks on the text but it appears that these are not likely to have been caused by the looters' blows though the book itself is Boniface's, the *Codex Ragyndrudis* containing passages explaining the doctrine of the Trinity and also the *Synonyma* of Isidore of Seville, a manuscript serving as a missionary handbook.[39]

In sum, all the Churches of the island had major achievements behind them by the time of Bede's death in 735. All classes were affected by them. The monuments created gave to all an impression of the power of God. Overall a new spiritual and intellectual climate had arisen, in which the old sacrifices, temples and idols were replaced by churches, saints and relics, which became protection for the fearful and gave hope of healing. Prayers for the dead created a nexus between the generations and linked patrons to monasteries. While recognising the inevitability of warfare, churchmen worked with some success to mitigate its worst effects. Help to the poor was considered, in a way not apparent in paganism, a proper duty of a believer – seen in the tradition of hospitality by monasteries, the symbolic episode of Oswald's breaking up of the silver dish and the endeavours of Wilfrid to use his wealth and his skills for the poor. The preaching of churchmen offered, indeed insisted on, moral choice by the individual, vividly illustrating the fate of those who persisted in sin or disbelief.

Via the monasteries, religious poetry flourished and, with the Psalms, music, sometimes to the highest level of the continent. With Christianity came book learning and contact with the riches of Mediterranean Christian and Jewish minds. Here were many gains, however much tyranny reigned, the

---

[39] R.A. Fletcher, 'St Boniface', *Who's who*; I. Wood, 'Boniface', *ODNB*; I. Wood, *The missionary life. Saints and the evangelisation of Europe 400–1050* (Harlow 2001); M. Imhof and G.K. Stasch eds, *Bonifatius. Vom angelsächsischen Missionar zum Apostel der Deutschen* (Petersberg 2004), esp. M.A. Aris, 'Der Trost der Bücher Bonifatius und seine Bibliothek' 95–110

more potent because it was local, and however often kings took full advantage of their powers for reckless and licentious behaviour, as Bede well knew.

There was a dark side, the consequence of the marriage – a very successful marriage – between Christianity and the ancient pagan values of the Anglo-Saxon aristocracy. The heroic feasting, the heavy drinking, the crude display, the joy in warfare were all there, and often unchanged. By and large, paganism had been defeated, but belief remained in demons, evil spirits which could bring on illnesses and warp lives. Ancient practices such as burning grain on the roof are treated to heavy penalties in Theodore's Penitential, and some superficially Christian prayers and rites have a strong flavour of the old paganism.

These were centuries of real change and improvements in many lives, but were only part of a long, slow change of belief and practice.

Index

Aaron, martyr, 9, 10, 83
abaton, 32
Abercorn, Anglo-Saxon bishopric, 262
Aberdaron, 90
Aberdeen, 160; Aberdeenshire, 115
Aberdour, 161
Aberlemno, 261
Aber Lleu, 129
Abraham, 28, 180
Acca, bishop of Hexham, 211, 296
Acha, queen of Northumbria, 131, 190,
    201, 228
Acts of the Apostles, 257; pattern for
    Augustine, 170, and for *Ecclesiastical
    History*, 296; and text for Patrick on
    preaching, 140
Add, river, 113
Adda, 215
Ad Gefrin, 196
Adomnán, abbot of Iona, 114, 148; restores
    Iona's reputation, 153, 281; influence in
    Pictland, 161; persuades Aldfrith to
    release prisoners, 262; inspires Law of
    Innocents, 281–2; relics, 282; Life of
    Columba, 111, 119, 150, 152–5, 156,
    158–9, 160, 202–3, 248; interpretation of
    miracles, 157; misunderstanding r.e.
    blessing of Áedan mac Gábráin, 156–7;
    Easter question, 153; *De locis sanctis*, 262
Adversus Judaeos, 4
Aebbe, abbess of Coldingham, 257,
    268, 298
Áed mac Ainmirech, 153, 156
Áedan mac Gábráin, ruler of Dál Riata,
    defeated by Aethelfrith, 132; blessed by
    Columba, 156–7, and prayed for, 203;
    names son Arthur, 283

Aelflaed, abbess of Whitby, 211; supports
    Aldfrith, 262, approached by Theodore
    for Wilfrid, 262; consults Cuthbert on
    Ecgfrith's successor, 268
Aelfwine, underking of Deira, attends
    dedication at Ripon, 241; killed at Trent,
    250; mourned at York, 251; feud over,
    averted by Theodore, 251
Aelle, king of Deira, 164
Aelle, king of South Saxons, 183
Aeneid, 46
Aethelberht, king of Kent, 147, 181, 187,
    189; becomes king, 168; marriage,
    166–7; receives Augustine, 169–72, 178;
    correspondence with Gregory, 174–8;
    his *imperium* and baptism of Redwald,
    183, 185; converts Saeberht, 183; Parker
    Gospels, 175; laws and charters, 172–3;
    cathedral for London, 182; remarriage,
    death and burial, 182
Aethelburh, Edwin's queen, origins, 190;
    marriage alliance, 190; gives birth to
    daughter, 194; and Paulinus, 190, 196,
    198; departs after Edwin's death,
    199–200, 207
Aethelfrith, king of Bernicia, 123, 199,
    200, 207; conquers Deira, 131; marries
    Edwin's sister, 131, sires Oswald,
    Oswiu, 132, 159; defeats Áedan mac
    Gábráin, 132; threatens Redwald,
    191, 298; victory at Chester, 131–2,
    181, massacres Bangor monks, 131,
    181; Hereric's flight from, 204;
    damages Rheged, 131; barbarian
    progress of, imitated by Edwin,
    198; death, 133, 159, 191; nicknames,
    131, 212

Aethelred, king of Mercia, 249; defeats
    Ecgfrith 250–1; and Theodore 250–1,
    262–3; and Wilfrid, 257, 262–3
Aethelthryth, queen of Northumbria, 240,
    249, 298
Aethelwalh, king of South Saxons, marries
    Eaba of the Hwicce, 258; acquires Isle of
    Wight, 259; grants land to Wilfrid,
    258–9; killed by Caedualla, 259; see
    Kirby, J. P.; Thacker, Alan
Aetius, consul, refuses to help British, 52
Africa, 272; West Africa, 186
Agatho, pope, 251, 252, 253, 254, 257
Agilbert, bishop of Dorchester-on-
    Thames, 228; expelled, 218, invited to
    return, 245; dispatches Leutherius, 245;
    background, 218; influences Alchfrith,
    223; ordains Wlfrid, 224; hands over to
    Wilfrid at Whitby, 225; presides at
    consecration of Wilfrid, 230; as bishop
    of Paris, receives Theodore, 238
Agricola, 45
Aidan, St, origins, 203–4, 206, 287; and
    Lindisfarne, 204; Hild, 204–5, 206;
    relationship to Oswald, 204, 206, to
    Oswine, 213; style of mission, 204, 299;
    saves Bamburgh, 215; redeems slaves,
    208; personality, 204, 265, and Bede's
    ideal, 265; status and effects of Whitby,
    234, 235; vision of Cuthbert, 264;
    bones, 228
Ailred of Rievaulx, St, 108, 109
Alban St, 80; martyrdom, 5–9, 10; shrine,
    39, visited by Germanus, 49; Passio, 5–8,
    origins and anti-Pelagian function, 47
Albina, 45
Albinus, abbot of Canterbury, linguistic
    powers, 273; informant and inspiration
    of Bede, 179, 275
Alchfrith, son of Oswiu, 215, 225; at
    Winwaed, 216; underking in Deira, 216;
    and Wilfrid, 222, 224, 230; founds
    Ripon, 223, 240; supports Roman
    Easter, 223, 265; attends Whitby, 225;
    disappears from history, 229
Alcock, Leslie, 77
Aldfrith, king of Northumbria, 211;
    parentage, 262; student in Ireland, Iona,
    262; chosen as king, 262, 268; releases
    prisoners, 262; Jarrow and
    Cosmographers, 288; relations with
    Biscop, 257; relations with Aelflaed, 268;
    banishes Wilfrid, 288

Aldgisl, Frisian ruler, 254
Aldhelm, St, abbot of Malmesbury, bishop
    of Sherborne: denounces worship of
    animal pillars, 63, 193; letter to king of
    Dumnonia, 103; granted land by
    Caedualla, 260; Theodore's triumph
    over Irish students, 271
Alexandria, bishop of, 165; patriarchate,
    253; bowl from, 187; school of exegesis,
    270, and Origen, 4
Alfred, king of Wessex, 64, 287
Alfriston, 68
Allectus, emperor, 8, 9
Allen, R., 99
alpha and omega: at Lullingstone, 20; at
    Water Newton, 22, 23; at Poundbury,
    30; at Mildenhall, 42; miswritten
    versions, 21; at Long Wittenham, with
    the cross, 28; on Welsh epitaphs, 87;
    at Kirkmadrine, 105
Alps, 3
Altarnun, 99
Alt Clut, 123, see Dumbarton
Altyre, 121
Amalekites, 231
Ambrosius Aurelianus, 73
Ammianus Marcellinus, 48
Amra Choluimb Chille, 153, 156
Anastasius, Byzantine emperor, 187
Anastasius Magundat, St, 237, 275
Anatolius, 227
Ancyra, 190
Andredesweald, 258, 259
Andrew, St, patron of Wilfrid, 222, 299;
    oratory of, Rome, 222; see also Hexham;
    Rochester
Angles, 211; invaders, 55; monastery of, at
    Whithorn, 107; targets of Gododdin
    raid, 127; in word-play of Gregory the
    Great, 164–5, 253; in Deira, 190; occupy
    Yeavering site, 196; pressure of, on
    Elmet, 204; see Middle Angles
Anglesey, 90, 191, 199
Anglo-Saxon Chronicle, 54
Anglo-Saxons: invaders, of London, 15, as
    analysed by Bede, 53–4, 55; revolt against
    Vortigern, 56; legend of three 'cyuls', 74–7;
    and Romano-British elite, 79–80; as
    instruments of God's wrath, 74; language
    eclipses Brittonic, 57; enclaves of security
    from, 7, 10; and Gildas, 81–2; burial
    practices, 64–72, 76, 89, 102; ceremonial
    graves, 183, 185–8; belief in efficacy of

animal symbols, 63, 67, 69–70, 116; heathen beliefs *see* paganism; and British memorial stones, 81–2; advance of, against Dumnonia, 100, 103; Aethelfrith's success against British leaders, 131–3, economic factors in, 133; slaves and Gregory the Great, 164–5; Christianisation of, and British clergy in West Midlands, 75–6; pagan Northumbria and Iona, 161; women and Roman fashion, 171–2; and Arthur, 285; and Merfyn Frych, 283; fidelity to lord, 191, 194; heroic ideal, 231, like that of Men of the North, 126; blood feud restrained by Aethelberht's code, 173, in clash of Northumbria and Mercia, 250–1; attitude to dynastic rivals, 260; attachment to kin and Biscop's warning, 257; kings' assumption that bishops were their followers, 246; tradition of display for war and kingship, adapted to Christian use, 241; world view challenged by Wilfrid, 258; emergence of warrior saint, 212; Christian relics and shrines, 239, *see esp.* Cuthbert; first Anglo-Saxon bishop *see* Ithamar; first Anglo-Saxon archbishop *see* Deusdedit; lack of tradition of glazing, 256, and of building in stone, 240; love of poetry and Caedmon, 205; heroic literature as source for *Dream of the Rood*, 295; love of beautiful things, 257; love of puns and riddles, 164–5, 292–4; ornament at Sutton Hoo, 186, in Insular style, 290, Lindisfarne Gospels, 291; development of national pride *see* Bede; Ceolfrith; traditions of, in synthesis with Christianity, 301

Angus, 118

Anna, king of East Anglia, 177

Annales Cambriae, 283, 284

Annals (Book) of Leinster, 162

Annals of Ulster, 74, 110, 150, 160, 161, 162, 282

Annemundus, bishop of Lyons, 222

Annianus, 37

Antioch, 237, 273; school of biblical exegesis, 270; Antiochene saints and Theodore, 275; patriarchate, 275; *see* Malalas, John

Antonine Wall, 47, 104, 123

Antony, St, 277; Life of, 152

Antrim, 110, 111

Apollo, 17

Applecross, 163

Aquae Sulis, 34, 41

Aquaticus, 92, *see* David, St

Arberdour, 161

Archenfield, 91

Ardwall Island, 38

Argyll, 145, 150, 188, 202, and Bute, 110, 111

Arimathea, Joseph of, 2, 10

Ark, 294

Arles, 44, council of, 11

Arminium (Rimini), Council of, 12

Arminius, 11

Arran, 162

Artbranan, 159

Arthur, 125, 282–4

Artognou, 98

Arwald, king of the Isle of Wight, 260

Ashton, baptismal tanks at, 27; cemetery, 31

Asser, 287

Atholl, 160; *see* New Ireland

Attacotti, Irish raiders, 48, 50

Attila, 52

Atys, 15

Audiva, 74

Augurius, bishop of London, martyr, 10

Augustine, St, 75, 163, 189, 226; monk in Rome, 168–9; Scriptural proficiency, 169, 237; mission to Kent, 169–70; settlement in Canterbury, 170–2, 174–8, 182; building, 171, 182; queries to Gregory, 175–6, 177; and law code, 172–3; and charters, 173; and Parker Gospels, 174–5; cathedral, 39; contacts with British, 11, 179–81, 244, *see also* Sixtus, St; made abbot, 169; consecrated bishop, 170; pallium, 179; death, 182

Augustine of Hippo, St, condemns *refrigerium*, 29, doctrine of grace, 44–5, effects, 139; and filioque, 252; *Confessions*, 143

Augustus, emperor, 186

Austerfield, Synod of, 240

Austrasia, 165, 168, 170, 242, 253

Autun, 36; bishop of, 170

Auxerre, 8, 46; and Alban's *Passio*, 47; bishop of *see* Germanus

Aylesford, 160

Ayrshire, 108, 162

Babylon, and Ezra, 296; Harlot of, 143

Bacchus, 14–15, 17; spoons, 35

Baíthéne, abbot of Iona, 155, 156, 161

Ballinderry, monastery, 188

Balthild, St, 172, 205

Bamburgh, 116, 130, 204; attacked by
    Penda, 214; saved by Aidan, 215; shrine
    for Oswald's relics, 206, 208, 209, 211

Bampton, 63

Bangor, bishop of see Elbodus

Bangor, Irish monastery, 163

Bangor-is-Coed, British monastery, monks
    massacred at Chester, 131, 181, 287; and
    Abbot Dinoot, 180

Bannavem Taburniae, 51

baptism, in Roman Britain, 24–8; role of
    bishop, 24; affusion, 24; fonts, 24–6; lead
    tanks, 26–8; and St Martin, 37; rejected
    by Radbod, 62; repudiated by Redwald,
    184–5; administered by Columba, 159;
    administered by Paulinus, 198–9;
    administered by Wilfrid, 258–9; in
    dispute between Augustine and British,
    179; and Sutton Hoo spoons, 187–8

Bardby, 162

Bardney, abbey, 196, 209

Barflat, near Rhynie, 118

Barking, double monastery: founded by
    Earconwald, 274; sister for abbess, 248;
    supernatural light and healing, 248

Barnabas, St, 222

Barrovadus, 104–5

Barrow, monastery, 248

Basil, St, 274; Rule of, 153, 274

Bassaleg, 83

Bath, temple of Sul Minerva, 3; Aquae
    Sulis, 34; curse tablet, 37; possible site
    for Gildas, 81, 82; monastery at,
    founded by St David, 92

Battersea, 260

Bede, 114, 129, 172, 177, 189, 191, 208,
    229, 244, 258; oblate at
    Monkwearmouth, 220; transfer to
    Jarrow, 220; languages, 275–6, 297; Acca
    and biblical commentaries, 296; Ezra
    and Codex Amiatinus, 296; Anno
    Domini, 297; affection for Ionan
    tradition and Lindisfarne, 220, 265;
    beliefs on Easter, 108, 299; papacy, 107,
    296; attitude to British, 75, 131, 179–81,
    276; use of Gildas, 54, 75; evidence on
    paganism, 59–62, 64, 193–4, 210; St
    Alban, 7–9; origins of Anglo-Saxons, 55;
    imperium and Anglo-Saxon kings, 183,
    185, 199; Ninian, 107–8; Dál Riata, 110;

Columba, 158; Eanfrith's apostasy, 159,
    201; Augustine's mission, 39, 165–77,
    178–82; battle of Chester and British
    contacts, 131, 179–81; Roman and Irish
    missions, 185, 189–96, 199–200, 201–15,
    216–18, 220–1; Oswald as warrior
    saint, 203, 206–7, 209–11, 212; Easter
    and Whitby, 224–6, 227–30, 231–5;
    Theodore and Hadrian, 236–40, 244–8,
    251–3, 255–7, 260, 262, 263–76;
    Nechtan, 278–9; contacts with Albinus,
    179, 275; and Ceolfrith, 278, 279;
    Ecclesiastical History of the English
    People, 6, 55, 60, 180, 192, 193, 212,
    218, 234, 263, 278, 296, 297; aims
    and presuppositions, 75, 204, 218,
    249, 297; flawed datings, 168; influence
    on German missions, 297; Lives of
    Cuthbert, 265–6; Letter to Egbert of
    York, 297; History of the Abbots, 220, 256

Bellerophon, on Hinton St Mary
    pavement, 16, 19, at Lullingstone
    villa, 17, 21

Benedict, St, 257; Life of, 152; Rule of,
    introduced by Wilfrid, 242; role in
    Biscop's Rule, 257

Benedict I, pope, 164

Benjamin, 131

Benty Grange, 69

Berchan, 154

Berhtgils (Boniface), bishop of East
    Anglia, 230

Berhtwald, archbishop of Canterbury,
    and Wilfrid, 288–9

Berhtwald, nephew of Aethelred of Mercia,
    aids Wilfrid, 257

Berino, St, Book of, 285

Berkshire, 63

Bernicia, Anglo-Saxon kingdom, 249;
    origins, 126–7, 190, 196 and attacks by
    Urien, 129–30; beats British and Dál
    Riata, 123, 131–2, 181; conquers Deira,
    123, 131; taken over by Deiran dynasty,
    133, 191; expulsion of heirs, 191, 201–2;
    breakdown of unity, 201, restoration
    under Oswald, 202–3, 207; army, 203;
    renewed breakdown, 208; recovery
    under Oswiu, 212–13; separatism,
    213–14, countermeasures, 214, and
    Synod of Whitby, 225; monastic
    foundations, 214, 216; royal fortress see
    Bamburgh; royal centre see Yeavering;
    see also Eata, Ida, Northumbria

Bertha, queen of Kent, orphan princess, 167; link to St Radegund, 167; marriage conditions, 167–8,190; role in initiation of mission, 168, 298; sister, St Martin and dedication of cemetery church, 39, 167; and Gregory, 177

Berwick, 268

Bethell, Denis, 2

Betti, 215

Beverley, 273

Bewcastle cross, 294–6

Bible, sophisticated knowledge, at Hinton St Mary, 19; in Constantius, 46; Patrick's use of Latin Bible, 143, 144; Gregory's understanding of, 175; Theodore's teaching of, 270; Syriac vernacular translations, 275; linking of British genealogy to, 282; Higham and knowledge of, in *Historia*, 283; Bede's commentaries on, 296; Old Latin version, 49, 291, 298; *see* Acts of the Apostles, Chronicles, Decalogue, Exodus, Ezra, Genesis, Gospel, Isaiah, Job, John, Joshua, Judges, Kings, Mark, Matthew, Prophets, Psalms, Revelation, I Samuel, Septuagint; *see also* New Testament, Old Testament, Scripture

Biddle, Martin, 7

Bidford-on-Avon, 69

Bifrons, 68

Birdoswald (Banna), 51; taken over by post-Roman chieftain, 106

Birinus, and Dorchester-on-Thames, 208, links to Merovingian kings, 217, and Honorius, 217–18; bishop to Cynegils, 208, 218

Birr, Irish monastery, 281

Biscop, Benedict (Biscop Baducing), nobleman, 265, 275; travels to Rome, 221; tonsured at Lérins 238; commanded by Vitalian to return to Rome, 238; abbot at Canterbury, 255; travel, 255; founds Monkwearmouth, 255; building and equipping of Monkwearmouth and Jarrow, 256; contacts with Cenwalh, 255; contacts with Ecgfrith, 255–6; contrast to Wilfrid, 255; book-buying and Cosmographers, 288

Bisi, bishop of East Anglia, 245, 247

Bivatisus, 90

Blacklow Hill, 193

Bladbean, 63

Blair, John, 193, 299

boars, in grave goods, 67, 69

Boisil, 264. 265

Boniface, archdeacon of Rome, 222

Boniface, bishop *see* Berhtgils

Boniface, St (Wynfrith), personality, 299; monastery of Exeter, 100; miracle at Geismar, 63; archbishop of Mainz, 300; martyrdom, 300; missionary books, 300

Boniface V, pope, 190, 195

Boon, George, 24

Bosa, monk of Whitby, bishop at York, 250; expulsion from York, 263

Bosham, monastery, 221, 258

Bothelm, 242

Boudicca, 3

Bourges, 36

Bourton-on-the-Water, 27

Bowen, Emrys, 91

Bradford-on-Avon, 25

Bradwell-on-Sea, 217

Brean Down, 38, 40

Brecon, 89

Brega, 261

Britannia, symbolic figure, cured by Germanus, 47; 'island of', 252

Britannia Prima *see under* Provincia

Britannia Secunda *see under* Provincia

British, Britons, *under Romans*, conquest and administration, 3, 11; Romanised elite, 3; martyrs, 5–11; Church of, 11–13, 16–31, 37–43; effects of Anglo-Saxon invasions, 52–73, and Gildas, 73–8, 80–2; *post Roman*, ch.3 *passim*, and phase of independence, 44–52; conversions of Anglo-Saxons, 75–6; indigenous saints and evangelists, 82–116, 119–23 (*and see* Cornwall, Dumbarton, Gododdin, Men of the North, Wales); relations with Patrick, 49–51, 135–9, 141–2, 143; influences of, in Ireland, 146, 148–9; Pictish isolation and slow evangelisation, 158–62, *see also* 277–80; *under Anglo-Saxon domination*, political and military alliances, 201, 203, 208, 215; failures in war, 132–3; Bede's judgement, 276; attempts at Christian unity, 176, 179–81; consecration of Chad, 229; and origins of Columban calculation of Easter, 226; tenacity and conservatism in liturgy, 226, 284; threat to, of Oswiu's policy, 232; acceptance of Roman Easter and Elbodus, 284; hopes

of military revival under Merfyn
Frych, 282–4; monasticism and Gospel
books, 284–5, 287; witness of Oswald
miracle, 210; flight of child healed by
Wilfrid, 243; see also Aetius,
Caedualla, Pechthelm, Tertullian,
Virgno the Briton

Brittany, Breton, refuge for British
Christians, 81, its bishops, 81, term
merzer in, 83; see Faustus; St Samson's
settlement, 95–6, and St Paul Aurelian,
95, their Lives, 93, 95; Breton,
develops from Brittonic, 97; and list
of Cornish saints, 100; and influence
of Theodore on, 273; and Arthur
legends, 273, 283

Brittonic, 161; relationship to: Old English,
57, to Grade I Latin, 79; Patrick's
mother tongue, 49; not used for Welsh
epitaphs, 87; break up into Celtic
vernaculars, 97, 160; merther from, 83;
Uinniau, name from, 108; meaning of
Rheged, 127; spoken in Ireland, 148,
development of Pictish from, 158;
derivation of both from, 161; and
formation of place-names, 160;
and Dinoot, 180

Brocmail, 150
Broíchán, 157, 158
Bronze age, 67; barrows, 89
Brown, Michelle, 291
Bruide (Bridei) mac Derile, king of Picts,
261; contacts with Adomnán, 161;
achievements, 279

Bruide (Bridei) mac Maelchon, Pictish
king, 114, 115; challenged by Columba,
119, 157–8

Brunhild, Merovingian widow of
King Sigeberht, 170; supports
English mission, 165; letter of
protection for Augustine, 169; and
Gregory, 177

Brutus, 282
Brycheiniog, British kingdom, 89–90
Bryn y Beddau, 89
Buchan, 161
Buckland, 68
Buckquoy, 121
Bueno, St, legendary Life, 93; defiance
of lay power and burial at Clynnog, 93
Burgh, 106
Burghead, 116
Burgundy, 165, 168, 170

Burrian, 121
Burrow Head, 104–5
Bushe-Fox, J.P., 39
Bute, 92, 93
Byzantium, Byzantine, lands in Egypt,
Palestine, 58; contacts with Cornwall,
98; style of image of Christ, 170;
bowls, Sutton Hoo: bowls from, 187,
workmanship on spoon from, 187–8;
gift to Edwin, 190; persecution of
Pope Martin I, 222; and Hadrian's
mission, 237; doctrinal controversies,
236, and Theodore, 238; Greek
pronunciation, 272; emperors and
Monotheletism, 251

Caananites, 284
Cadafael, king of Gwynedd, 215
Cadbury Castle, 116; see South
Cadbury
Cadfan (Catumanus), king of Gwynedd,
87–8, 285
Caedmon, 205, 299
Caedualla, Anglo-Saxon warrior, 259,
260–1, 262
Cadwallon, king of Gwynedd, 93; kills
Edwin, ravages Northumbria, 199, 201,
203; eliminates Osric and Eanfrith, 201,
203; Bede's judgement, 199; effects on
Northumbrian history, 207; defeat and
death, 203.
Caerleon, legionary fortress, 9–10; martyrs
of, 9–10, 82, 83; martyrium, 83, see
Mount St Alban
Caernarvon, Mithraism attacked, 36;
Caernarvonshire, 90
Caerwent, agape at, 24, 83
Caithness, 162
Caldey Island (Ynys Byr), 93, 95
Caledonii, Pictish alliance, 48
Calpornius, 49, 51
Cambridge, 174; Cambridgeshire, 63, 69,
70, 71, 72
Camel river, 94
Camelton, 70
Campanian sacramentary, 275;
saints, 275
Cana, 28
Candida Casa (White Church), 107–8,
110; see Whithorn
Candidus, 165, 168
Cannington, cemetery, 84, 102; infant
burials, 29

Canterbury, 190; Romano-British churches in, 39, 170, 171; Christian items, 21, 39, 41; amphitheatre, 198; lack of epigraphy at, 84; St Martin's church, 39, 108, 167, 170, 182, and Liudhard's medalet, 167; Aethelberht's town, 171; Augustine's entry, 170; endowment and churches, 169–71; British Christians in, 167, *see also* Sixtus, St; proximity to pagan sites, 177–8; Redwald's baptism in, 185; Chad's journey to, for consecration, 229; archbishopric of, and Augustine, 170, 179, 180–1; jurisdiction of, and British, 174, 176, 181, 284; and Felix the Burgundian, 217, 218; Gregory's plan to transfer to London, 179, 195, 253; lack of influence in later seventh century, 218; search for valid candidate, 231, 233, 236, *and see* Wighard; revival of authority under archbishop Theodore, ch. 7 *passim, see esp.* 234, 238, 276; archbishops *see* Augustine, Berhtwald, Deusdedit, Honorius, Justus, Laurentius, Mellitus, Theodore of Tarsus; monastery: foundation and dedication, 182, oral evidence from, for Bede, 180, 181, 244; and scourging of Laurentius, 189; as burial place, 182; abbots *see* Albinus, Biscop, Hadrian, Peter; school of, 270–6; *and see* Theodore of Tarsus, Hadrian

Cantwaraburh, 171
Capel Anelog, 90
Capel Bronwen, 90
Caracalla, emperor, 9
Carantus stone, 109
Carausius, emperor, 9
Cardigan Bay, 88
Carlisle, 51, 127, 268
Carrawburgh: mithraeum, 14, attacked, 14, 36; Coventina's well, 35
Carthage, 4, 5
Carver, Martin, 115
Cassian, St John, 45, 92, 95, 153
Cassington, 67
Cassiodorus, 291, 296
Castelldwryan, 88
Castellum Guinnion, battle, 283
Catalaunian Plains, battle, 52
Cathach, 290
Catlow, 241
Catreath *see* Catterick
Catstane, 109

Catterick, 21, 195, 200; battle, 124–7
Catumanus *see* Cadfan
Ceawlin, king of West Saxons, 183
Cedd, bishop of East Saxons, evangelist to Middle Angles and East Saxons, 215, 217; grant from Oethelwald, 220; prepares site at Lastingham, 220; chooses successor, 229
Cefn Hrfynydd, 90
Celestine, pope, 46, 134, 147
Céli Dé, 281
Celt, Celtic, 1, 2, 19, 32, 34, 36, 40, 62, 89, 91, 100, 113, 118, 153, 193, 196, 263, 274, 287, 291; river names, 57; burial practices, 29, 30; as description of church life in parts of post-Roman Britain, 82; and epitaphs, 87–8; style of hagiography, 93, 95; 'inter-Celtic' saints, 99; monastery settlement on Glastonbury Tor, 83, 103, Whithorn, 108; elements in Sutton Hoo burial, 186, 187, 188; religion of the defeated, 188; head cult, 7, 30; Oswald cult, 210; jewellery, 288, *and see* Sutton Hoo; Romano-Celtic, temple: at St Albans, 8, at Uley, 26
Cenberht, king of Wessex, 259
Cenél Conaill, 149, 156
Cenél Loairn, 163
Cenél nGabráin, 111
Centwine, king of Wessex, 257
Cenwalh, king of Wessex: expels Agilbert, 218; baptism at East Anglian court, 245; introduces Wilfrid to Alchfrith, 223; and Biscop, 255; stormy relations with bishops, 230; death, 255
Ceolfrith, St, abbot, 279, 288; prior to Biscop, then builds Jarrow, 256; writes Easter treatise to Nechtan 278, obtains *Codex Grandior*, 291; pandects, 291–2; takes *Codex Amiatinus* to Rome, 292; death at Langres, 292
Cerdic, 57
Ceredigion, 92
Ceretic, king of Dumbarton, 144
Ceretic, supposed king of Elmet, 204
Chad, abbot of Lastingham, 240, 245, 248, 250, bishop of York, 229; consecration, 229, appointment rejected by Wilfrid, 231; deposed by Theodore, returns to Lastingham, 239; consecrated bishop of Lichfield, 239; cult and death, 239; Gospels of, 285, *and see* Lichfield Gospels

Chadwick, Nora, 76
Chalcedon, Council of, 251
Charibert I of Paris, 166, 167
Charles-Edwards, Thomas, 21, 27, 43, 86, 89, 90, 101, 110, 144, 232, 271
Charon, 30
Chedworth, 21
Chelles, 172, 204, 205
Chertsey, Anglo-Saxon monastery, 247
Cheshire, 12
Chester, 24, 131, 181, 287
Chesterton, 22
Childebert, 168
Chilperic, 166
Chilterns, 259
Chimera, 16, 21
chi rho: origins, 13; villa sites, 16, 17, 19, 20, 21; found: on Phillack church, 101, at Poundbury mausoleum, 30, on lead tanks, 26, 27, on memorial stones, 87, 103, 104, 105, on communion vessels, 22, 23, on votive plaques, 23, on bowls, jar, pots, jug, 21, 24, 42, 83, on spoons, 42, in graves, 25, 101; Constantinian, 101, 104; rho cross, 21; chi formed by animal paws, 295; mistaken attribution, 21; missing on hanging bowls, 188
Christ, Jesus, 59; baptism, 28; sends apostles, 2; in Gildas, 9; scenes from Life in Augustine Gospels, 175; fasting imitated by Cedd, 220; in Mass vestments, on memorial stone, 90; and Petrine rock, 107; commemoration of Passion and Passover, 224, 266; Chalcedon definition, 251; chi rho, 13, 20, 103; crucifixion and Mithraism, 14; on stones on Tarbat peninsula, 116; on mosaic at Hinton St Mary, 16, 17, 19; named on strainer, 42; dedication of Canterbury cathedral, 171; Augustine's processional cross, 170; cross as sign of guardianship, 119; Patrick's vision, 142; Columba pilgrim for, 150; exile for, 221; and Marcellus, 10; and Paulinus, 194, 198; and Irish, 134, 140, 142, 147; Redwald's altar, 193; dedication of Britain to, and Oswiu, 231; Theodore and Wilfrid, 263; reluctance of Frisians to accept, 254; gifts to, on Franks casket, 293; Ruthwell cross, 294, 295; in St John's gospel, 297, *Chronographia*, 273, figure of Jonah, 277, St Andrew's sarcophagus and King David, 279, 280;

at Castellum Guinnion, 283; in Tertullian, 4; Christology, 273
Christianity in Roman Britain, 43
II Chronicles, 272
Cinnrigmonaid, 161
Cirencester, 12, 37, 81, 82
Claudian, 48
Claudius, emperor, 2, 84
Clocaenog, 89
Clofeshoh, Synod of, 245
Clonmacnoise, 153
Clovis II of Neustria, 172
Clyde, river, 123
Clynnog, 93, 285
Codex Amiatinus, 287, 292
Codex Grandior, 291
Codex Ragyndrudis, 300
Coeddi, St, 160
Coelian Hill, St Andrew on, Roman monastery, 168, 182
Coifi, 61, 192–4
Colchester, 11, 21, 25, 29, 31, 40, 41; Butt Road, 25, 31
Colchester House, 40, 41
Colcu, monk of Iona, 154
Coldingham, double monastery, 240, 249, 268
Colmán, bishop of Lindisfarne, 225, 227–8, 234, 265
Colonia Londiniensium, 11
Columba, St, 115, 121, 162, 163, 279, 281; origins and education, 149; journey to Iona, 113, 149–50, 151, 157; monastic life, 153, 154–6; journeys and mission, 153, 156–9, 160; and Easter, 223, 224, 225, 227, 229, 233, 234, 264, 265, 271, 279; and Atholl, 161; and Cathach, 290; and Ninian, in *Ecclesiastical History*, 108–9; and Cuthbert, 268–9; relations with Picts, 157–8; miracles, 153, 157–8, 159; rule, 152, 156; blessing of Áedan mac Gábráin, 156–7; Adomnán's Life, 19, 111, 114, 148, 202–3, 248, interpretation, 152–4, 155, 157; *Amra Choluimb Chille*, 153
Columbanus, St, 81, 217, 226
Conall mac Comgaill, king of Dál Riata, 150
Congresbury, 102
Connaught, 146, 234
Constans, emperor, 16
Constantine of Dumnonia, 77, 98
Constantine the Great, 13; issues Edict of Milan, 5, *see also*, 3, 4, 31, 80, 138;

summons Council of Arles, 11; Council of Nicaea, and decision on Easter, 223, 227; and Gildas, 73; and Oswald, 203; example to Aethelberht, 171, 176–7; roundel at Hinton St Mary, 16; Forum of, 272; *see also* Constantius Chlorus

Constantine III, emperor, 44, 52

Constantine IV, Byzantine emperor, 252

Constantine son of Fergus, of Dál Riata and Pictland, 280–1

Constantinian, 20, 28, 31, 35, 37, 101, 104

Constantinople, 253; church of St Ia in, 98; Golden Gate, 98; Forum, 272; and Theodore, 237, 273, 275

Constantius, priest and author, 46, 48

Constantius Chlorus, emperor, 8, 9

Contra collatorem, 134

Coquet Island, 268

Corbridge, 2

Cornwall, 77; political and economic situation, 78, 98, 100–1, 103, 111; lack of Romanisation, 81, 96; paganism, 94, 96; evangelisation, 96–102; saints, 83, 92, 93–7, 99–100; memorial stones, 87–8, 96–8, 119; place-names, 91, 99–102; monasteries, 94–5, 101; bishops from, 229; *and see* Tintagel

Coroticus, 137, 143–6

Cosmographers, 288

Coventina's Well *see* Carrawburgh

Covesea, Sculptor's Cave, 116

cowrie shells, 69–70

Craig Phadrig, Pictish fort, 188

Crantock, 101

Crawford, Barbara, 126

cremation, in East Anglia and East Midlands, 64; and animal sacrifices, 65; cinerary urns, 65–6; toilet implements, 65; Howard Williams's hypothesis, 65

cretem, 147

Crimea, 222

cross: on beakers, 23, on boar's nose, 69, on spoons, 187, on Byzantine bowls, 187; on quern, 113, on stone, 116, of gold foil, 183; equal armed, 209; on Pictish stones, 119–21, 278; role in Pictland generally, 119; used by: St Martin of Tours, 30, Columba, 119, Oswald, 203; made from fetters of Peter and Paul, 231; at Dupplin, 280–1

Cruithnechán, 149

Cuddesdon, 72

cú glas, 139

Cúl Dreimne, battle, 150

Cumbria, Cumbrian, 77, 123, 131, 133, 158, 160, 284, 294; Cumbric, 97

Cumméne, abbot of Iona, 161

Cummian, 226

Curghie, 105

Cuthbert, St, 263, 297, 299; origins and life at Melrose, 264; childhood cure, 266; guest master at Ripon, 265; expelled, 233, 265; returns to Melrose, 265; accepts Whitby decision, 265; prior at Lindisfarne, 264–5; withdraws to Farne, 266; becomes bishop, 267; contacts, with Picts, 267, 269, Anglo-Saxon elite, 268; achievement, 263, 269; death, 263–4; translation of body, 269, 290; personality, 266; cult, 269, 289; Bede's judgement, 265; Lives, 265 and biblical analogies, 263–4, 265–6, 269; and Lindisfarne Gospels, 289

Cwichelm, king of the Gewisse, 194–5

Cybele, 15

Cyneburh, daughter of Penda, 215

Cynegils, king of Wessex, 208, 213–14, 218

Cyprian, St, bishop of Carthage, 5, 143

Dagan, Irish bishop, 226

Dagobert II, 242, 253

Dallan Forgaill, author, 153

Dalmatia, epitaphs in, 86

Dál Riata, 114, 123, 279, 288, 290; origins and links to Antrim, 110–11; relationship to Dumbarton, 124; economy, 111; war fleet and rulers, 111, 113, *see also* Dunadd; warriors from, denounced by Patrick, 145; defeat at Degsastan, 132; and Christianity, 111, 113, 160; absence of Pictish symbols, 119; and Columba, 113, 150, 152, 156–7; Aidan, 206; martyrs of Eigg, 162, 163; refuge of Oswald and Oswiu, 159, 201–2; Christians from, and Oswald's victory, 203; relationships with Oswiu, 215, 232, 233; support for Aldfrith, 262; links to Northumbrian kings, 287; take-over of Pictland, 158, 280–1, 282; rulers *see* Áedan mac Gábráin, Conall mac Comgaill, Domnall Brec

Damian, bishop of Rochester, 230

Danes, 53; Denmark, and burial practices, 67

Daniel, 277
Darenth, river, 20
David, king, use of Goliath story, 230; on Pictish stones, 279–80; St Andrews sarcophagus, 280
David, St, of Wales (Aquaticus), legendary Life of, 91, 162; pre-eminence in South, 93; asceticism of Rule and Penitential, 92, not sustained in Rigyfarch's time, 287
Davies, Reuben, 91–2
Deben, river, 185
Decalogue, 16, 278
Decius, emperor, 5, 6, 10
Deer, Book of, 161
Degsastan, battle, 132
Deira, Anglo-Saxon kingdom, 132, 192, 195, 207, 249; siting, 190; warriors from, and creating of Bernicia, 126; slaves from, and Gregory, 164; conquest by Bernicia, 131; return of Deiran royal house, 133, 191, *and see* Aelle, Edwin, Oswine; reconquest by Bernicia, 201, 203, *and see* Oswald; separatism and tension, 209, 213–14, 216, 224–5, *and see* Oswine, Oethelwald, Alchfrith; and Synod of Whitby, 225–8, 234; underking of *see* Aelfwine; appointment of bishop for *see* Bosa
Demetae, 88
Denbighshire, 89
Dent, 241
Derry, near Louth, 156
Desert Fathers, 92, 154
Desiderius, 41
Deusdedit, archbishop of Canterbury, 229, 234, 236; and Wighard, 233
Devon, part of Dumnonia, 77; scantily Romanised, 81; memorial stones, 96; effects of infiltration and anglicisation of place-names, 100; British bishop from, 229
dia, 147
Dickinson, Tania, 67–8, 89
Digiwg, 93
Dinoot (Dunawd), abbot of Bangor-is-Coed, 180
Diocletian, emperor, 5, 6, 9, 15
Dionysiana, canon law collection, 222, 232
Dionysius Exiguus, 226, 247
Disciplina, 34
Diuma, 215
Docco, St, 83, 94
Dokkum, 300
Dol, bishop of, 95

dom, 293
dominicus, 148
domnach, 148
Domnall Brec, ruler of Dál Riata, 125
Don, river, 216
Doncaster, 199, 215, 251
Donegal, 149
Donnán, St, martyr of Eigg, 162–3
Dorchester-on-Thames, 28; bishopric, 208, 218; bishops: *see* Agilbert, Birinus
Dorset, 16, 19, 96, 102
Dover, 68
Dream of the Rood, The, 294–5
Driscoll, S.T., 278
Dronke, Peter, 143
Drostan, St, 161
Druim Alban, 114, 160
Druim Cett, conference of kings, 156
Drust, Pictish king, 279
Drycthelm, 298
Dubricius, St, 93
Dumbarton, British kingdom, 123–4, 125; wealth of rulers, 123; Rock as fortress, 123, see also Alt Clut; submission to Picts and Scandinavian conquest, 124; and Domnall Brec, 125; traditions of Old North, 124; effects on, of Nechtanesmere, 262; kings of: *see* Ceretic, Ryddarch ap Tudwal; Dumbartonshire, 123
Dumfries, 288, 293; Dumfriesshire, 108, 110
Dumnonia, 77, 99; lack of Romanisation, 96; memorial stones, 96–8; rulers of, and possible church endowment, 102; Romano-British Christianity, 102; chieftains, 101; succumbs to Anglo-Saxons, 100, 103
Dunadd, 113, 116, 288
Dunawd *see* Dinoot
Dunbar, 257
Dunfallandy, 277
Dunkeld, 161, 280
Dunstan, St, 1
Dunwich, 217, 247
Dupplin Cross, 121, 280
Durham, 114; county, 106
Durobrivae, 22–3
Durovernum (Canterbury), 39, 142
Durrow, 156, Book of, 290
Dursley, 26
Dyfed, 85, 88, 90, 92, 97
Dyfrig, St, 91

Eaba, Hwicce princess, 76, 258
Eadbald, king of Kent, 178, 189–90, 195, 207
Eadbert, bishop of Lindisfarne, 220, 264
Eadfrith, son of Edwin, 207
Eadfrith, bishop of Lindisfarne, 265, 289, 291
Eadhaed, bishop of Ripon, 250, 251
Eadric, 259
Eanflaed, queen of Northumbria, 194, 211, 214, 221, 224, 231
Eanfrith, son of Aethelfrith, 159, 201
Earconwald, bishop of London, 247–8
East Anglia, cremations in, 64, 102; Sutton Hoo, 185–8; royal house's connections to Sweden, 187; links with the Celtic world, 188; influence of court on Cenwalh, 218; Hild's links, 204–5; attacked by Penda, 214; kings: see Anna, Eorpwald, Redwald, Sigeberht; bishops: see Berhtgils, Bisi, Felix the Burgundian; splitting of bishopric by Theodore, 247; Fursey's monastery in, 217
Easter: and baptism, 24, 47; Easter money, 167; Easter Day in Edwin's life, 194,195, 214; Oswald's Easter feast, 206; Easter question and Bede, 108, 299; Ninian, 109; Adomnán's account of Columba, 153; Anglo-Saxon tables, 54; vigil and British Church, 284; origins of controversy, 222–4; role in Augustine's meeting with British, 179; Columban tradition, 226–7, 232; Columbanus, 226; and Northumbrian politics, 224–5; Synod of Whitby, 225–9, 244; reaction to, of Columban party, 228, 234, 242, 264, 265, 267, 269, 289; and search for archbishop, 231, 233; designs of Oswiu, 232; views of Theodore of Tarsus, 271; acceptance of Roman Easter by Irish churches, 225, 232, Picts, 278–9, British, 281; see also Bede, Wilfrid, Quartodecimans
Easter Kinnear, 114
East Lothian, 109, 160
Eastry, 178
Eata, abbot of Melrose, 223, 228, 250, 263, 265, 267
Ebroin, 238, 253
Eccles, 160
Ecgfrith, king of Northumbria, 240, 244, 256, 274, 287; hostage to Penda, 215; virginity of queen Aethelthryth, 249, 298; relationship with Biscop, 257;

endows Ripon abbey, 241–2, and attends dedication, 242; quarrels with Wilfrid, 248, 249; rejects papal decision, 255; imprisonment and release of Wilfrid, 255; relationship with Cuthbert, 267; conquers British lands, 241–2; defeat at Trent, 250; accepts wergild (blood price) settlement, 251; wins Two Rivers battle against Picts, 261; attacks Irish, 261, 262; killed at Nechtanesmere, 162, 261, 268; and see Iurminburh
Ecgric, 217
Edessa, 275
Edinburgh, 42, 12
Edwin, king of Northumbria, 201, 207, 214, 229, 298; origins, 131, 190; refugee with Redwald, 133, 190–1; takes kingdom, 133, 191; expels Bernician heirs, 191, 200; marries Aethelburh of Kent, 191; moves towards Christianity, 192–5, 212, baptised, 195; relationship to Paulinus, 191, 194–6, 199; conquers British lands, 191; imperium, 191, 208; persuades Eorpwald to baptism, 196; at Yeavering, 196–200; and Boniface V, 190, Honorius I, 195, and Lindsey, 196; supposed baptism in Rheged, 191; death, 199; effects, 218, 238; relics, 211, 212; name in Historia Brittonum, 212; and see Acha
Egbert, archbishop of York, 297
Egbert, king of Kent, 231, 233, 238
Egbert the Englishman, monk, 55, 254, 299
Egil, 293
eglos, 83, 99
Egypt, 58, 76, 136, Egyptian, 95
Eigg, 162–3
Elafius, 49
Elbodus, bishop of Bangor, accepts Roman Easter, 284
Elias, 142
Elijah, 242
Elisha, 94, 159, 242
Elmet, British kingdom, 131, 204
Ely, 240, 298
Emchath, 159
Eorcenberht, king of Kent, 214, 216, 222
Eormenric, king of Kent, 166, 167, 168
Eorpwald, king of East Anglia, 192, 196, 217
Eosterwine, abbot of Monkwearmouth, 256
Ergyng, 91

Ernan, 156
Esau, 263
Essex, Christian remains, in Roman period, 21, 24; East Saxons' kingdom and Aethelberht's ambitions, 182; king converted, 183; Prittlewell burial, 183; pagan reaction, 189, 193; baptism of king, 215; further mission, 217, 220; plague, 230, pagan reaction checked, 230, 258; appointment of bishop, 247; bishops: *see* Cedd, Earconwald, Mellitus, Wine; kings: *see* Saebbi, Saeberht, Sigeberht the Good, Sighere
Ethelburga, 247–8
Euric, 59
Europa, 21
Eusebius, 138
Eutychus of Troas, 242
Evagrius, 152
Exe, river, 78, 96, 102, 103
Exeter, 21, 100
Exodus, 143
Exuperius (bishop), 12
Ezra, 296; Book of, 297,

Faílbe, abbot of Iona, 165
Farne Islands, 264, 266–7, 269
Farnham, 260
Faunus, 35
Faustus, bishop of Riez, 82
Faversham, 70
Felix the Burgundian, 217, 218
Fergus, 280
Fergus Mor mac Eirc, 110
Fetternear, 161
Fib, 232
Fife, 114
Fifield Neville, 19, 43
Fin, Irish princess, 262
Fínán, bishop of Lindisfarne, 215, 217, 220, 232
Finglesham, 178
Finnian of Moville, St, 81, 108; teacher of Columba, 149; *and see* Uinniau, St
Firth of Forth, 207
Flamborough Head, 57
Flavia Caesariensis, 11
Flavian emperors, 3
Flawborough, 27
Fletcher, R.A., 261
Foclut, 113, 119
Fordhere, 194
Ford Laverstock, 71

Forsyth, Katherine, 114, 119, 121, 280
Forteviot, 280
Forth, river, 109, 159; Forth–Clyde isthmus, 47, 104
Fortriu, 114, 232, 261, 278
Forts of the Saxon Shore, 52; Bradwell-on-Sea, 217
Fortuna, 34
Fosite, 61
Foulden, 71
Fowey, 94
Frampton, 16–17, 19, 22
France, 59, 87, 226, 283; Francia, 166, 168, 253, 255, 273; Franks, Frankish *see* Gaul
Franks casket, 287, 292–4, 296
Friesland, 58, 254; Frisians, 53, 61, 211, 254
Frig, 62, 63
Frilford, 63
Fulda, 300
Fursey, 217, 218

Gaelic, 111, 114, 160, 163, 206, 213, 280, 281
Galerius, emperor, 5
Galilee, Lake, 46
Gallic Chronicle, 52
Galloway,104, 105, 108, 109, 127
Garden of Eden, 152
Garton Slack, 71
Gatcombe, 29
Gaul, Gaulish, 4, 9, 83, 163, 177, 200, 225, 237–8, 240, 246, 253, 287, 288, 292; *under Roman rule*, mission to Britain, 43; oversight, 22; aristocracy and St Martin, 37; and saint cult, 84; Celtic head cult, 118; conflicts, 44; *under Franks*, conquest, 56, 82; Palladius, 135; Patrick, 136, 137, 140; episcopate, 46, *see also* Germanus; influence on British and Cornish epitaphs, 86, 97–8; *relationship to Roman mission*, antecedents and conflicts, 165–6, 168; Kentish affinities, 171–2; Liudhard, 166–7; priests and interpreters, 169; consecration of St Augustine, 170; Old Testament regulations, 175; influence, on Eadbald, 189–90, Hild, 204–5, Sigeberht of East Anglia, 217, Wilfrid, 222–3, 228, 230, 242, 243; influence from, via Felix, 217, Birinus, 217, Agilbert, 218, Wine, 218; Easter question and Columbanus, 226; civilisation of papal patrimony, 165; fashion and Kentish aristocracy, 172, *and see* St Balthild; E-ware imported by

Dumbarton, 123; double monasteries, 204–5, 206; liturgy, 241; craftsmen used by Biscop, 255–6

Geake, Helen, 70

Geismar, 63

Gelhi, 285

Gelli Onen, 90

Genesis, 263

Geoffrey of Monmouth, 283

Geraint, 86

German *see* Anglo-Saxon

Germanus, St, origins, 46; pilgrimage to St Alban's shrine, 8, 47, relics and origins of Passion, 47; represses Pelagianism, 45–7, 134; sends Palladius to Ireland, 135; encounters Picts and Saxons, 47–8; returns to Britain, 49; Life, 45–7, 51

Germany, 48

Gewisse, 194

Gildas, 55, 90, 109, 145; life, education, residence, 6, 81–2; ignorance of Roman Britain, 74; on martyrs, 9–10, Alban, 6–8; evidence on Aetius, 52; on Mount Badon, 73–4; on evil British rulers, 77, 78, 88, 98, disappearance of indigenous paganism, 76–7; authority on monastic life, 81; correspondence with Finnian of Moville, 108; death, 74, 82; *De Excidio Britanniae*: sources, 6, 56, 73; use by Bede, 54, 75; Latin, 80; central theme, 54, 73–4; on Picts, 115; Anglo-Saxon interpolation, 74–5; quotation from, in *Historia Brittonum*, 129; Epistolary Fragments, 81, 148

Glamorgan, 82, 83, 90, 94, 101, 134, 135

Glasgow, 109–10

Glastonbury, 1–2, 92, 103

Glen, river, 199

Gloucester, 76, 81, 82; Gloucestershire, 26, 32, 36

Gododdin, British kingdom, 124–7, 207; *Y Gododdin*, 124–5, 128, 196

Golant, 94

Goliath, 280

Goodmanham (Godmundingham), 192–3

Gospel, 141, 174, 285, 291; in Patrick's thought, 138, to ends of earth, 140, preaching to all nations, 147; preaching of: by Gregory, 166, Ceolfrith, 292, Wilfrid, 222; Bede's response to Acts, 296; in Augustine, 181; and role of king, 213; Bede's translation of John, 297; Canterbury commentaries, 272; scenes

from: in Parker MS, 174–5, at Monkwearmouth, 256; synoptics, 227

Gospel Books, origins and evolution, 278, 288, 290, 294; and death of Boniface, 300; British valuing of, 284; of Hadrian, 275; Gaelic tradition of small gospels, 111; *see also* Berino, Chad, Durrow, Hereford, Lichfield, Lindisfarne, Parker, Ripon

Goth, 42

Govan, 124

Great Glen, 115

Green, J.R., 54

Gregory the Great, pope, 226, 292; origins, 166; and mission to England, 164–5, 166, 253; and Brunhild, 164; choice of missionaries, 168–9, requires Scriptural knowledge, 168, 237; mass baptisms, 171; sends more men and material, 174, 190; writes to: Aethelberht, 176–7, Bertha, 177; answers Augustine's queries, 175–6; attitude to British, 11, 174, 176, 180, 181; Gaulish bishops, 222–3; revises tactics, 61–2, 177–8, 193, 198; plans for episcopate, 179, 182, 229, 253; attitudes to: theft, 173, service, 212; biblical learning of, and Bede, 296; Easter vigil and British Church, 284; Whitby Life, 164, 195, 205; cult, 253; relics of, sent to Oswiu, 253; *Cura pastoralis*, 174; *Dialogues*, 152, 266; *Moralia in Job*, 165

Grierson, Philip, 187

Grove of Victory, Synod of, 74

Guilden Morden, 69

Gumeninga-hergae, 62

Gumenings, 63

Gwallwg, 129

Gwladys, St, 83

Gwynedd, British kingdom, and Maelgwn, 77; Cadfan, 87; Bivatisus, sacerdos, 90; Cadwallon, 93; Merfyn Frych, 284; and Caedualla, 199; Cadafael, 215; and traditions of Men of the North, 282; and *Historia Brittonum*, 130, 282

Hadrian, 273, 276, abbot of Nisida, diplomat, refuses archbishopric, 237; accompanies Theodore, 237–8, joins in visitation, 238–9; delay in Gaul, 238; abbot at Canterbury, 255, 270; scholarship, 270–1, 272, liturgy, 275; death, 275; Gospel book with

Neopolitan pericopes, 275; and Gospel text, 291

Hadrian, emperor, 2; Hadrianic period, 20

Hadrian's Wall, 2, 51, 127, 133, 215, 217; Christian presence on, 25, 35, 43, influence from, 78, 86, 104–6; churches, 39, 41; mithraea on, attacked, 36; and British kingdoms, 123

Halsall, G., 178

Hambledon, 29

Hampshire, 41, hanging bowls, 260

hanging bowls, origins and purpose, 188; at Sutton Hoo, 187; in illumination, 290

Härke, Heinrich, 68

Harlow, 32

Harrow Hill, 62

Harrow-on-the-Hill, 62

Hartlepool, 205

Hatfield, Synod of, 251, 253

Hatfield Chase, battle, 199, 211

Hawkes, Jane, 291

hearg, 62

Heavenfield, battle, 203, 209, 211

Hebrides, 156, 162

Helena, St, 272

Heligoland, 61

Helios, 142

Henderson, G. and I., 118, 120

Henig, Martin, 8–9, 17, 79

Henry II, king of England, 232

Hereford, diocese, 75; Herefordshire, 91; Gospels, 285

Hereric, 204

Hering, 132

Hertford, Synod of, 244, 246–7

Hesse-Thuringia, 63

Hewald brothers, martyrs, 299

Hexham, Heavenfield battle site, 202, 211; and Wilfrid, 211; abbey founded, 240, crypt founded, 240–1, library founded, 288; miracle at, 242; bishopric, 250, 263, 267; and Cuthbert, 267; Wilfrid's bequest, 289; bishops: see Acca, Eata

Hiddila, 259

Higham, N. J., 283

Hild, St, 250; origins and baptism, 204; and Chelles, 205; nun by river Wear, 205, abbess at Hartlepool, 205, abbess at Whitby, 205, 298; and Caedmon, 205; personality, 206; hostility to Wilfrid, 249

Hill, P., 108

Hilton of Cadboll, 116

Hinba, 154, 155, 156

Hingston Down, battle, 100

Hinton St Mary, villa pavement at, 16–19, 22, 42–3

Historia Brittonum, 126, 129, 191; author, 130; date and contents, 282–3; judgements on Anglo-Saxon kings, 212

Hlothere, king of Kent, 259

Hoddom, monastery, 110

Holborough, 68

Holme Pierrepoint, 41

Holy Cross convent, Poitiers, 167

Holywell Row, 71

Honorius, archbishop of Canterbury, consecrated at Lincoln, 196; and Felix the Burgundian, 217; consecrates Berhtgils, 230

Honorius I, pope, 195, 217

Honorius III, emperor, refuses aid to Britain, 44; condemnation of Pelagianism, 45, 47; ineffective in Ireland, 134

Hope-Taylor, Brian, 199

Horace, 35

Hos, 293

Housesteads: Mithraism at, 14; attacked, 36; church, 39; font, 25; post-Roman occupation, 106

Howlett, David, 143

Humber, 126, 183, 191, 196, 201, 207, 208, 215, 216, 232, 233, 238, 239, 244, 253

Huntingdonshire, 22

Hussa, 130, 132

Hwicce, 75, 179; king see Oshere; princess see Eaba

Hwitaern, 107

Hywel Dda, 91

Ia, St, 98

Iamcilla, 23

Icklingham, church and font, 25, 38; lead fonts, 27; pagan objects, 27; infant burials, 29; survival of Christian site, 37

Ida, founder of Bernician dynasty, 126, 131, 262

Idle, river, 132, 191

Ilchester, 30

Illtud, St, 83, 95

imperium, overlordship of Anglo-Saxon kingdoms, in Bede, 183, 190; *see under* Aelle, Ceawlin, Aethelberht, Redwald, Edwin, Oswald, Oswiu

Ine, king of Wessex, 1; laws of, 57

Innocentia, 23

Inverness, 114, 118, 157, 160, 188

Iona: size, 288; Columba's journey to, 149; and Conall mac Comgaill, 150; writing hut on, 155; crosses, 119; lack of oghams, 121; monks of, and sea, 155; monastic congregation of, 158, 160, *see also* 150–62; austere tradition of, 223; and conversion of Oswald, Oswiu, 159, 212; Oswald sends for mission, 203, 208, *and see* Aidan; and Oswald's northern campaigns, 207; Northumbrian kings' links to, 287; and Lindisfarne, 204; influence on Gospels, 289; and sulphide of arsenic, 113; influence on grave markers at Portmahomack, 115; Dupplin Cross and style of, 280–1; and Easter question, 224, 225, 226, 228, 232–4; and Melrose, 264; and Cuthbert, 265; and Nechtan, 279; and Aldfrith, 262; abbots: *see* Adomnán, Baíthéne, Columba, Faílbe, Ségéne, Virgno the Briton; Annals of, 161

Ioruerth, 89

Ireland, Irish, 161, 201; attacks on Britain, 48–51, 135; immigration, to Britain, 84, Dyfed, 88, Cornwall, 97, and formation of Dál Riata, 110, 111; and ogham origins, 85, in Dyfed, 85, 88, at Dunadd, 113, in Pictland, 85, 119, 121–3; paganism in, 50, 135, 141, 147, 159; Pelagian refuge, 134–5; mission to, of Palladius, 134–5, Patrick, 50–1, 135–48, and effects, 22, 146–7; danger to missionaries, 138–41, 144, 145; and Uinniau, 81, 108, 160, *see also* Finnian of Moville; influence of other British missionaries, 148–9, *see also* 208, 226; lack of Latin, 148; and *peregrinatio*, 147, 149–50, 156, 221, *and see* Fursey; Christian place-names in, 83, 91; and Cornish inter-Celtic saints, 99; sources for battle of Chester, 131; Columba, 149–50, 152–4, 156, slave girl, 157–8; and St Samson, 94 and cousin, 95; veneration of St David in, 92; and St Bueno, 93; monastic houses, 221, 264–5; missions: to Mercia, 215, to East Anglia, 176–7, 217; building at Lindisfarne, 220; Easter question, 224, 225, 226, 232, 234; tonsuring, 228–9; influence in Pictland, 160, 162, and Atholl, 160, *see also* Adomnán; asceticism and scholarship, 156, 223; way of life in a rural society, 299; in Western Isles, 162–3, and

possibly in Galloway, 107; influence on Oswald, 201, 203, and his cult, 211; training of Oswiu, 234, affair with princess, 262; effects of study in, on Agilbert, 218, Willibrord, 254; canon law collections, 222; withdrawal to, by Colmán, 228, and Mayo monastery, 234; Wilfrid's influence in, 243, and release of Dagobert, 242; tradition of generosity, 213; attitudes to warfare, 203, and effect on kings, 212; students of Theodore at Canterbury, 271, and penitential practice, 273–4; exclusion of wandering preachers at Hertford, 246; and Ecgfrith, 261, 267; prisoners' release, 262; traits in Cuthbert, 266; Sutton Hoo hanging bowl, 187, 188; emergence of Insular style, 290; Law of the Innocents, 281, 282; and Henry II of England, 232; churches, northern, 225, southern, 225

Irenaeus, 4

ires, 147

Irish Sea, 191

Iron Age, 29, 32, 62, 77; and Pictish symbols, 118

Irthing valley, 51

Isaac, 28, 156, 263

Isaiah, 228, 231, 233

Iserninus, 148

Isidore of Seville, 300

Isle of Man, 191; memorial stones, 104

Isle of Wight, 231, 249, 259, 260; *see* Wilfrid

Israel, 9, 73, 75, 136, 242, 280, 297; Israelites, 283, 296

Italy, 14, 84, 86, 168, 177, 217, 225, 226, 288, 291

Ithamar, bishop of Rochester, 236

Iurminburh, queen of Northumbria, influences Ecgfrith, 249, 298; infertility, 255, 262; and Wilfrid's reliquary, 255, 257, 262; illness, 257; relatives checking Wilfrid, 257, 298; with Cuthbert in Carlisle, 268; travels to York, 298

Jackson, Kenneth, 57

Jacob, 131, 156, 263

James the Deacon, 200, 224

Japheth, 282

Jarrow, monastery endowed by Ecgfrith, 256, Aldfrith, 288; development under Ceolfrith, 256; library, 288; and Bede, 220, 265, 296; dedication, 256

Jaruman, bishop, 230, 258
Jericho, 47
Jerome, St, 45, Life of Paul the Hermit,
    277; Vulgate, 284, 291
Jerusalem: True Cross at, 167; and
    St David, 92; and Lindisfarne, 264;
    Temple, 272, Roman assault on, 293;
    Jesus's lament over, 293
Job, 228, 256; Moralia in Job, 165
Jocelyn of Furness, 109–10
John, pope, and Wilfrid, 243
John, pope-elect, and Northern Irish
    Churches, 232
John, St, apostle, in Whitby debate, 225,
    227; Gospel translated by Bede, used by
    Cuthbert for healing, 297; and Lichfield
    Gospels, 285
John the arch-chanter, 252, 256
John the Baptist, St, 294
John of Beverley, St, 273
Jonah, 28, 277
Joseph, 263
Joseph of Arimathea, 1–2
Josephus, 293
Joshua, and Alleluia victory, 47; and
    Arthur, 283–4; Book of, 203
Judges, Book of, 283
Julian the Apostate, emperor, 13, 29, 35, 38
Julius, martyr, 9–10, 83
Jupiter, 17; Best and Greatest, 34
Justin Martyr, 14
Justinian, Byzantine emperor, 98
Justus, archbishop of Canterbury, 190, 196;
    as bishop of Rochester, 182, 226; to
    Gaul, 189
Jutes, 55
Jutland, 53

Keindrech, 'Fair of Face', 90
Kelvedon, 21
Kent, 163, 208; Christian presence in, in
    Roman Britain, 20–1, 25, 39; Anglo-
    Saxon grave goods in, 68, 68–9, 70; as
    basis for Christian mission, ch.5 passim,
    see esp. 160, 167, 168, 189, 190, and later
    weakness, 192, 230; wealth and Frankish
    links, 166, 183, 187; isolation as
    Christian power under Redwald, 192;
    Aethelburh's flight from, 200, 207; West
    Kent and its sense of independence, 182;
    'Kentings' and Roman law, 172; civil war
    in, 259; Cadualla grants land in, 260;
    diminishing political weight, 238; and

vernacular name for Canterbury, 171;
    kings of see Aethelberht, Eadbald,
    Eadric, Egbert, Eorcenberht, Eormenric,
    Hlothere
Kentigern, St (Mungo), 109–10
Killala, 136
Kilmorach, 118
Kings, Book of, 56
Kinrimonth (Cinnrigmonaid), abbot of,
    161; see St Andrews
Kintyre, 162
Kirby, J.P., 260
Kirkmadrine, 105; memorial stones at,
    105, 106, 109
Kirkton, 118
Kirkuk, 275
Knapdale, 163
Knight, Jeremy, 89
Koch, J.T., 125

Laisrán, 156, 161
Lammermuir Hills, 161
Lamyatt Beacon, 38, 40
'lan, 83, 99
Lanarkshire, 160
Landocco, 94
Langres, 292
Lankhills, cemetery, 41
Lapidge, Michael, 270, 271
Lastingham monastery, and Oethelwald,
    220; preparation of site, 220, 266; Cedd
    and Chad abbots, 220, 229, 239
Lateran Basilica, 171; Council, 237
Laterculus Malalianus, 273
Latinus, Latinus stone, 104–7
Laudabiliter, 232
Laurentius, archbishop of Canterbury,
    emissary to Rome, 174; scourging and
    Eadbald, 189; appeal to British, 226;
    death, 189, 226
Law of the Innocents (Lex Innocentium),
    281–2
lead tanks, for baptismal rites, 21–3
Leeds, 131, 204
Legio II Augusta, 9
Leinster, 50, 146, 149; Annals of, 162
Lennox, 123
Leo the Great, pope, 134
Leon, 10
Lérins, monastery, 46, 238
Leroux, 36
Letocetum (Wall), 76
Leutherius, bishop of West Saxons, 245

Leven, river, 123
Lewis, 162
Libya, 272
Lichfield: origins of bishopric, 216; bishops see Chad, Wynfrith, Seaxwulf; Lichfield Gospels, 285
Licinius, emperor, 5
Liddesdale, 109
Lilla, 194
limitanei, 106
Lincoln, 40, 84; possible bishop of, 11; St Paul in the Bail, 40; stone church, 196; Lincolnshire, 26, 68, 209; see Lindsey
Lindisfarne, 218, 230, 240, 250; allegedly besieged by Urien, 129–30; route to, from Iona, 161; founding of monastery, 204, church building and improvements, 220; receives Oswald's head, 208, 209, 210–11; Wilfrid, as youth at, 221, 264, in office, 263–4, 289; bishopric, 263; and Cuthbert, 263–7, 269, see Farne Islands; tradition of, 234, 235, 249, and Hild, 249; effects of Whitby on, 228, 234–5, 289; loan of Gospel text from Monkwearmouth-Jarrow, 291; bishops: see Aidan, Colmán, Cuthbert, Eadberht, Eadfrith, Fínán, Wilfrid
Lindisfarne Gospels, 285, 287; and Neopolitan pericopes, 275; purpose, 289; artistic blends, 289–90, 291; carpet pages, 291
Lindsey, Anglo-Saxon kingdom, 239, 250; monasteries in, 209, 248, 263; bishop of see Eadhaed
Litany of saints, 275
Little Spittles, 31
Little Wilbraham, 71
Liudhard, bishop, chaplain to Queen Bertha, 166–7, 171; likely death, 168
llan, 83
Llanbadarn, 92
Llandaff, Book of, 10, 91, 285; bishop of, 91
Llandeilo Fawr, 285
Llandewi Brefi, Synod of, 92
Llandough, 83, 94, 101
Llanerfyl, 88
Llangyfelach, 90
Llanllywenfel, 89
Llansadawrn, 90; see Saturninus
Llantrisant, 90
Llantwit Major, 82; and St Illtud, 83; and St Samson, 93, 95
llog, 83

Llyn peninsula, 90
Llywarch Hen, 128, 130
Loch Fleet, 118
Loch of Forfar, 261
Loch Lomond, 123
Loch Ness, 157, 158
locus, 83
Logierait, 160
London, 6, 24, 48; major port in Roman Britain, 2; chi rho on ingots from, 13; Mithraeum in, 14; Augurius, bishop and martyr, 10; Colchester House and possible cathedral, 40, 41; bishop of, at Council of Arles, 11; lack of small Christian remains in, 43; Anglo-Saxon cathedral, 182; role in Gregory's plans, 179; reversion to paganism, 189; bishopric, 230, 245, 247; conference at, and Theodore, 262; see Earconwald, Wine
Long Wittenham, 28
Lorcan, 93
Lorn, 163
Louth, 156
Lower Slaughter, pagan shrine, 36
Luke, St, portrait, 175; symbol, 285
Lullingstone, villa and house church, 20–1, 27, 38; Anglo-Saxon church, 21
Lundy Island, 96
Lupus, bishop of Troyes, 46
Lydney, temple of Nodens-Mars, 23, 32, 34; faulty dating, 35
Lyons, 4, 86, 222, 223

Maeatae, Pictish alliance, 48
Maelgwyn, ruler of Gwynedd, 77
Mael Ruba, 163
Magi, 42, 293
Magnentius, emperor, 30
Magonsaetan, 75–6, 179
Magundat, Anastasius, St, 275
Maiden Castle, 29
Mail, Shetland, 118
Mainz, 300
Malalas, John, *Chronographia*, 273
Malmesbury, 63, 260; see Aldhelm
Malton, 106
Man, Isle of, 104, 191
Manor Water, 109
Marcella, 45
Marcellus, centurion, 10
Mark, St, gospel, 19, 143–4, 175; symbol, 285
Market Rasen, 26

Mars, 17, 32

Martin I, pope, 222, 252

Martin of Tours, St, personality, 299; attacks paganism, 36–7; dedication to, of cemetery church, by Bertha, 39, 167, 170; in porticus of abbey, Canterbury, 182, of Whithorn church, 108; likeness to, of St Samson, 93; and John the arch-chanter, 252; Life of, by Sulpicius Severus, 12, 36–7, 152, 157; and Easter calculation by British Church, 226; influence on Cuthbert, 266

Mary the Virgin, St, 1, 256, 283, 295

Maserfelth, battle, 208–9, 214–15, 216

Matthew, St, gospel, 19, 150

Mauchteus, St, 148

Mavorrus, 105

Mawer, Frances, 41–3

Maxima Caesariensis, province, 11, 13

Mayo, Connaught, monastery, 234

Mayo, Co., 136

Meath, Co., 261

Meaux, 289

Mediterranean, 2, 251, literature and mythology, 19; Hadrianic busts from, 20; grave goods from, 67; imports, 78; memorial stones, 86, 87; and *refrigerium*, 98; amphorae, 106, 113; and Pictland, 278; written culture of, and Theodore, 244; exposure to, via Christianity, 287, 288, 300; and Wilfrid and Biscop, 255; in Lindisfarne Gospels, 289, 291; Ruthwell cross, 296; attractions of, to rulers, 298

Meigle, 277

Mellitus, 174, 175, 226; Gregory's letter, 177, 182, 193, 198; bishop of London, 182; expelled, 189; archbishop of Canterbury 190, 198

Melrose, monastery, 223, 228, 250, 264, 265; *see* Boisil, Cuthbert, Eata

Men of the North, 133, 282; *see* Old North

Mercia: pagan Mercians and expansion of kingdom, 76, 192, 214, 218, 230; fissile nature of kingdom, 215; battle of Winwaed, 215–16, consequences, 216, 239, 251; revival, 232; tension with Northumbria, 249; battle of Trent, 250–1, 261; loss of Lindsey, 239, 251; settlement of feud, 251; bishop's seat at Lichfield, 239; support for Wilfrid, 231, 257, 288, opposition, 257; reconciliation and Theodore, 262–3; Queen Osthryth

and Oswald's bones, 209; battle of river Idle, 191; bishops: *see* Chad, Jaruman, Wynfrith; kings: *see* Aethelred, Peada, Penda, Wulfhere; *see also* Penda

Mercury, 26, 28, 34

Merfyn Frych, ruler of Gwynedd, 130, 282, 284

Merovingian rulers: and Gregory the Great, 165; marriage of Bertha, 166–7; Liudhard, 167; marriage of Eadbald, 190; marriage of Edwin, 195; palace mayor delays Hadrian, 238; episcopate and attitude to Gregory, 222–3; pattern for Wilfrid, 222; vessels from, at Dunadd, 113; *see also* Balthild, Birinus, Brunhild, Chelles, Dagobert II, Franks, Gaul

merther, merthyr, merzer, 83, 99

Metheriana, St, graveyard of, 98

Middle Angles, 233

Middlesex, 62

Milan, Edict of, 5, 11; cathedral of St Tecla, 40

Mildenhall, 42

Milvian Bridge, 13

Minerva, 2, 30, 37

Minster Lovell, 71

Mithras, 14, 34; Mithraism, belief and adherents, 14–15, on Hadrian's Wall, 34; mithraea, damaged, 36; *see also* Caernarvon, Carrawburgh, Housesteads, Rudchester, Walbrook

Modranect, 62

Mommsen, T., 73

Monkwearmouth, monastery, 220, 255–6; abbots: *see* Ceolfrith, Eosterwine; Monkwearmouth-Jarrow, 291

Monmouth, 68

Monotheletism, 222, 236–7, 251–2

Montgomeryshire, 89

Moray Firth, 115, 116

Morgant, 129, 130

Morris, John, 6

Moses, 6, 42, 47, 143, 230–1, 241

Mote of Mark, 288

Mount Badon, battle, 73–4, 129, 283

Mount St Alban, 10

Mounth, 114

Moville, monastery, 108

Mrozek, S., 84

Mull of Kintyre, 111

Mungo, St *see* Kentigern

Mynyddog the Wealthy, 124

Mynyw/St Davids, 92
mystery cults, 13–14; *see* Atys, Bacchus, Cybele, Mithras

Naples, 237, Neapolitan pericopes, 275, 291
Nash-Williams, V.E., 89, 104; hypothesis on epitaphs, 86
Nathalon, St *see* Nechtan Ner
Nechtan, overking of Picts, 278–80
Nechtanesmere, battle, 114, 162, 261, 267, 268, 278
Nechtan Ner, St, 161
Neitano, 109
nemed, 140
Neptune, 17
Netherlands, 48, 300
Nettleton Shrubs, 40
Neuman de Vegvar, 295
Neustria, 172, 190, 205, 253
New Grange, 50
New Ireland (Atholl), 160
New Testament, 28, 42, 144, 224, 270, 272, 276, 278, 296
Nicaea, First Council of, 223, 227; Nicene creed, 252
Nidd, Synod of, 212
Nigg, 116, 277
Ninian, St, Nynia: and Whithorn, 107; mission in Scotland, and Bede's error, 108–9; lack of evidence for Pictish mission, 160; Ailred's Life, 108; *see also* Uinniau
Nisida, 237
Nithad, 293
Noah, 64, 282
Nodens, temple, 23; analysis, 32–3; Nodens-Mars, 32
Non, St, 99
Norfolk, 65, 71
North Africa, epitaphs in, 86; and Hadrian, 237
Northamptonshire, 31
North Channel, 111
North Connaught, 146
North Elmham, Anglo-Saxon diocese, 247
Northern Isles, 121
North Ronaldsay, 121
North Sea, 52–3
Northumbria, Anglo-Saxon kingdom: establishing unity, 131, and vicissitudes, 131, 159, 190, 199, 201, 233, 234, 238; external relations, 132, 181, 190, 196, 214, 232, 234, 241, 249, Rheged, 241 *see also* Bernicia, Deira; conflict with Mercia, 214, 249, 250–1; Nechtanesmere and effects of defeat, 114, 162, 261, 262, 276; relations with Picts, 162, 279, Nechtan's reconciliation, 278; slaves from and Gregory, 164, 201–2; conversion, 60, 201, and mission, 121, 161, 215, 216; Aidan, father of Christianity in, 228; paganism, 161, 190, 205; bishopric at Whithorn, 107; and Iona, 161, 208; Cedd missionary, 220; Chad bishop in, and deposition, 237; inner politics and Oswald cult, 211; and Biscop, 222, 255; and Wilfrid, 223, 224, 225, 229, 230, 242, 249–50, 255; Synod of Whitby and aftermath, 223–5, 228, 244, 299; and Cuthbert, 265–9; traditions from, and Bede, 60, 190, 207, 212; monastery at Hoddom, 110; fortress at Bamburgh, 116; Northumbrian renaissance, 235, 287–97; kings: *see* Aldfrith, Aethelfrith, Ecgfrith, Oswald, Oswiu; *see also* Aelfwine, Eadhaed, Peada, Penda
Nottinghamshire, 41

Oceanus, 17
Oengus, 280; *Martyrology*, 162
Oethelwald, son of Oswald, 214; supports Penda, 215; disappears, 216; grants land to Cedd, 220
Offa, king of Mercia, 211
Oftfor, bishop of Worcester, 275
Ogham script, 119; origins, 85; in Dyfed, 85, 88; in Cornwall, 97; in Dunadd, 113; in Pictland, 121–3, contrast to Ireland, 121; absence from Iona, 121; in Northern Isles, 121–3
Okasha, Elizabeth, 97
Old English Martyrology, 275
Old Irish, 113, 121
Old North, 123–4, 126–7, 284; *and see Y Gododdin*
Old Testament, 28, 64, 75, 93, 95, 175, 227, 230, 241, 270, 277
O'Loughlin, Thomas, 140
Olson, Lynette, 101
Origen, 4
Orkney, 48, 114, 118, 121
Ormazd, 14
Orosius, 73
Oshere, king of Hwicce, sub-king of Mercia, 257

Osred, heir to Aldfrith, 211
Osric, 201, 213
Osthryth, queen of Mercia, 209
Oswald, king of Northumbria, 216, 238, 262, 268, 287; exile and baptism in Dál Riata, 159, 201; sees vision, prays on battlefield, 203; kills Cadwallon, 203; inheritance, 207; sends to Iona, 161, 203–4, 208; relationship with Aidan, 204, 206, 228; and poor, 206, 300; marries Cynegils's daughter, 208, 213–14, 218; and mission in Wessex, 208; killed at Maserfelth, 208; dismemberment and cult, 208–9; miracles, 209–11; cult in Ireland, Selsey, Hexham, 211–12; and Offa, 211; significance of reign, 212, 221; nickname, 212; Bede's characterisation of, 233
Oswestry, 208
Oswine, ruler of Deira, 213–14, 216, 224, 233
Oswiu, king of Northumbria, 267, 268, 287; exile in Dál Riata, 159, 201; affair with Fin of Uí Neill, 262; marries Rhieinfellt, 132, 214; rescues Oswald's head, 208, and aids cult, 211, 234; marries Eanflaed, 214; has Oswine murdered, 214; expiation, 214, 220; aids mission, 215, 221; tribute to Penda, 215, kills him at Winwaed, 216, 234; endows monks, 216, benefits Whitby, 234; Mercian revolt, 216; dilemma re Easter, 224–5, solution, 227–8, effects, 228, 236, 265; choice of Chad for York, 229, 239, 250; and pope Vitalian, 231, 253, and hegemony in Britain, 231–3; expansion against Picts, 232–3, 261; achievements and Bede's judgement, 233–4; death, 233
Oundle, monastery, 288; endowment and founding, 231
Overkirkhope, 109
Owain, 131
Oxfordshire, 21, 28, 63, 67, 71, 72

Padstow, 94, 101
Paganism, Celtic and classical Roman in Roman Britain, ch. 1 passim; loss of Celtic shrines, 76; low-level survival, 32, in Cornwall, 94, Southern Scotland, 110; paganism: Irish, 50, 139–41, Pictish, 116, 120, 157–8, 163, Anglo-Saxon, 59–73, 169, 177–8, 183, 185–7, 192–3, 198–9, 230–1, 293, 301, on continent, 60–1, 67
Pagans in Roman Britain, 41

Palestine, 58
Palladius, 147, 148, 165; deacon of St Germanus, 46, 135; in Ireland, 134–5, possible aid to Patrick, 146
Pan, 35
Paris, bishop of, 238; Councils of, 95; king of, 166
Parker, Matthew, archbishop of Canterbury, 174; Gospels, 174–5
Passover, 224, 227
Pastor Hermas, 143
Paterninus, 89
Patrick, St, 90, 108, 163, 281, 299; origins and education, 49–50, 51, 143; enslavement, 49–51, 135; escape, 136; conversion, 135, 137, 142; mission to Ireland, 138–41, 142; relations with British churchmen, 137, 138–9, 141–2, 143; attitude to Empire, 80; legacy, 146–7; relations with Irish kings, 139–40, 142; relations with pagans, 139, 140–1, 147; relations with Gaul, 136, 137–8; his reading, 143; sin of his youth, 141; First Synod of, 147; Confessio, 22, 51, 135, 137, 139, 141, 143–6; Epistola contra Coroticum, 137, 143–6
Paul, St: and Patrick, 141, 147; and healing of Eutychus, 242; comparison to Wilfrid and Biscop, 222; and Dagan, 226; Sutton Hoo spoons, 187; dedication of Jarrow, 256; mission in Acts and Bede, 296; way of, and Oswiu, 231; feast day with Peter, and Leo the Great, 134; and dedication with Peter, of Canterbury monastery, 171, 182; birthplace and Theodore, 237
Paul Aurelian, St, 95–6
Paul the Hermit, 277
Paulinus, St, 61, 204, 224, 229, 236; chaplain to Aethelburh, 190; and Edwin, 191, 194, 195; consecration of Eanflaed, 194; missions: in Deira, and near Catterick, 195, at Yeavering, 196–9, in Lindsey, 196; baptisms in Trent, 196; builds church in Lincoln, 196, consecrates Honorius, 196; becomes bishop of Rochester, 200; stone cathedral at York, 240
Paulos, inscription, 187
Peada, king of north Mercia, 215; marriage and baptism, 215, 233; assassinated, 216
Peak District, 69
Pecthelm, bishop, 107, 108
pedilavium, 28

Peebles, Peebleshire, 109

Pelagius, 232; educated in Britain, 44;
doctrines, 44–5, author, 82; Pelagians,
Pelagianism, in Britain, 45, 46, 49;
condemned by Honorius, 45, 47;
attacked by Germanus, 45–7, and
St David, 92; and Ireland, 134

Pelagius II, pope, 166

Pembrokeshire, 59

Penda, king of Mercia, 214; kills Edwin,
199, 201; kills Eanfrith, 207; kills
Oswald, 208, 211; paganism and
domination, 208, 215–17; defeat by
Oswiu, 215–16, effects of, 234

Pennines, 127, 131

Pen Urien, poem, 128

peregrinatio see pilgrimage

Persian invasions, 237; Christian martyrs,
275

Perthshire, 114, 277

Peter, abbot of Canterbury monastery, 174

Peter, St, on plaster at Poundbury, 30; rock
and church at Whithorn, 107; church
dedications: by Nechtan, 279, at Ripon,
240, 242, at Monkwearmouth, 255, with
Paul at Canterbury, 171, 182; fetters, 231,
escape from, 257; scourges Laurentius,
189; baldness, 30, 228–9; and Whitby's
gates of heaven, 227; see of, 134, 221,
292; blessing of, 195; 'holy rule' of, 251;
name adopted by Caedualla, 260

Peterborough, 248

Petts, David, and lead tanks, 27, 28;
paganism, 31–2; memorial stones and
barrows, 89

Philip, St, 1

Phillack, 101

Physiologus, 293

Picts, Pictland, 55, 110, 123, 124, 126, 199,
215, 216, 233, 248, 250, 287, 290; origins,
47–8, 114; raiding, 47–8, 54, 145 (as
followers of Coroticus); fortress of
Burghead, 116; nomenclature, 47–8;
quality of horses, 114; paganism, 116,
118, 120; coming of Christianity, 158–62,
early Christian burials, 159; role of
Uinniau, 107, 108; Columba, 113, 152,
157, 159; Adomnán, 161; Eanfrith, 159,
201; memorial stones, 115–16, 118–23,
277–8, 281; symbols and cross, 119–21;
monasteries, 115; language, 158; oghams,
121; Latin usage, 121; place-names, 160,
161; hanging bowls, 188; isolation over

Columban Easter, 225, and Oswiu, 232;
Northumbrian pressure, 231–2; defeat at
Two Rivers, 261; victory at
Nechtanesmere, 261, 268, and effect of,
278; isolation eliminated by Nechtan,
278–9; representation at Birr assembly,
281; absorbed by Dál Riata, 114, 280–2;
loss of language, Church records, 280–1;
lost Chronicle, 114; relations with
Cuthbert, 267, 269, Aldfrith, 262; possible
presence on Eigg, 163; 'Pictish beast', 118

Piercebridge, 106

Pilgrimage, *peregrinatio*: of Germanus to
St Albans, 8, its shrine open, 49; and
martyria, 83; to Whithorn, 107, 109;
from Ireland to Northern Isles, 121;
codified in First Synod of St Patrick,
147; and Columba, 149–50, popularised,
156; Heavenfield site, 203, and Hexham
monks, 211; and Oswiu, 233; and *De
Locis Sanctis*, 262; and Wilfrid at
Lindisfarne, 264

Pionius of Smyrna, 5

Piro, abbot, 93, 95

Pliny, 70

podum, 83

Poitiers, 167

Pontardawe, 90

Pool, on Sanday, 118, 121

Popes *see* Agatho, Benedict I, Boniface V,
Celestine, Honorius I, John, John pope-
elect, Leo the Great, Martin I, Pelagius
II, Sixtus II, Vitalian

Porphyry column, 272

Portmahomack, monastery, 115

Potitus, 49

Poundbury, 19, 30, 42, 59, 84

Powys, 93, 191

Prittlewell, 122, 183

Prophets, 56

Prosper of Aquitaine, and Germanus, 46;
on Palladius, 134, barbarians, 134, 135;
Carmen de ingratis, 36, 45; *Contra
collatorem*, 134

Provinciae: Britannia Prima, 12; Britannia
Secunda, 11; Flavia Caesariensis, 11;
Maxima Caesariensis, 11, 13

Psalms: no.22 and Hinton St Mary
pavement, 17, 19; and Gildas, 56; on
Latinus stone, 105; nos 105, 146, and
Patrick, 144; and Donnán, 162; in Iona,
155; no.33, 155; no.45, and Columba,
157; in Aidan's entourage, 204; and

Wilfrid, 257; and Biscop, 257; in Lindisfarne and Farne, 263–4; in monasteries, 300

Publianus, 22

Putta, bishop of Rochester, 245

Quartodecimans, 227, 271

Quentovic, 253

Raasay, 119

Radbod, king of Frisians, 61, 62, 254

Radegund, St, 167

Rahtz, P.A., 103

Raphael, archangel, 266

Ravenna, 172

Redbridge, abbot of, 260

Red Sea, 6, 69

Redwald, king of East Anglia, kills Aethelfrith, 132, 159; *imperium*, 183, 185, 207; *ducatus*, 185; ineffectual baptism, 185; and polytheism, 185, 189, 193; and Edwin, 190–1; ship burial at Sutton Hoo, 185–8; effect on Christian mission, 189, 192

Redwald's queen, influence against Christianity, 185, 188, 298, for Edwin, 191, 298; the king's burial, 181, 298

refrigerium, 29

Renfrewshire, 108, 123, 160

Reuda, 110

Revelation, Book of, 20, 29, 136, 143

Rheged: geography and name, 127; resources, 127, 131; rulers, 128, 130, *and see* Urien, Rhun; weakened by Aethelfrith, 131; take-over by Oswiu, 132, 214; and Ecgfrith, 241–2, 294; Mote of Mark, 288

Rhieinfellt, princess of Rheged, 132, 214

Rhigyfarch, biographer of David, 92, 162, 287

Rhine, 44

Rhufawn, 126

Rhun, king of Rheged, 191

Rhydderch the Old, British king, 129

Rhynie, 118

Riata, 110

Ribble, river, 241

Ricbert, 196

Richborough, 25, 35, 39

Ricula, queen of East Saxons, 182

Riez, 82

Rimini, Council of (Ariminium), 12

Rinns, 105

Ripon monastery: founded by Alchfrith, 223; given to Wilfrid, 240; endowed by Ecgfrith, 132, 241; Eata and Cuthbert at, 265, withdrawal from, 265; Wilfrid as abbot of, 224, 231, appoints singing master, 240; use of stone, 240; crypt, 240–1; dedication, 241–2; regained by Wilfrid, 263; illuminated Gospels, 288; and Willibrord, 254, 299; Wilfrid confined at, 289; legacy, 289; bishopric, 250, 251; bishop: *see* Eadhaed

Risley Park, *lanx* at, 12

Riuallaun / Riuallon, king of Brycheiniog, 89–90

Rochester, dedication and foundation of bishopric, 182; *see* Damian, Ithamar, Justus, Paulinus, Putta, Tobias

Rockbourne, 41

Roman Britain: lack of knowledge of: in Gildas, 6, 9, Bede, 7; provinces, 11, 12, 13; Christian artefacts in, 22–4, 28–9, 30, 41–3; and origin of hanging bowls, 188, 290; lead tanks and fonts, 24–8; pagan cults and temples, 32–6, 37–8, mithraea, 14–15; churches, 7–8, 16, 20–1, 38–41; cemeteries, 29–32; funerary stones in, 84–5; imperial cult in, 3, 11, 34; martyrs, 4–11; Christian organisation, 11–12, 22; survival of term *ecclesia*, 160; effects of edict of toleration, 13, of Theodosius, 13; Christian villa owners, 15–21, and Llantwit Major, 82–3; Hadrian's Wall and Christians, 36, 39, 106; and Shepton Mallet, 103; assaults on, 47–50; invasions, 52–9, 74–5, 254; survival of rhetoric, 80–1; grammarians and ogham, 85; imitation of, by Welsh chieftains, 86–90; and Gregory the Great, 179

Romanus, chaplain to Eanflaed, 224

Rome, 6, 134, 163, 179, 187, 298; residence of Pelagius, 44; Germanus's study of law in, 46; and Ireland, 85; and memorial stones, 86–7; and Tintagel, 98; Uinniau's alleged journey to, 108; and Christian empire, 134; Gregory's origins, 166; slave market, 164, 253; Aurelian Walls, 171; Lateran Basilica, 171; and Augustine's entry into Canterbury, 170, and request for reinforcements, 174; and Aethelberht's law code, 172; communications with Canterbury, 175; dependence of English Church, 174; fashion, 171–2; and Sutton Hoo helmet and clasps, 186; monastic tradition, 218, 220; and James the Deacon, 200; Wighard's death at, 233, 236; and Biscop, 221, 238, 255, 256, 288; and Vitalian, 238; and Whitby, 225; orders from and Chad, 239; and Wilfrid, 241, 249, 253, 255, 256, 257; and Caedualla, 260; and Theodore, 237, 240, 244, 271, 275; and Ceolfrith, 292; in Bede's thought, 296; ancient Rome, 35; *see also* Easter

Romulus and Remus, 293

Roscarrock, Nicholas, 100

Rosetta Stone, 114

Ross and Cromarty, 277

Rosteece, 89

Rouen, 12, 22; and links to Wessex, 218; archbishop of *see* Victricius

Rowland, Jenny, 128

Ruallaun, 90; *see* Riuallaun

Rudchester, Mithraism at, 14; attacked, 36

ruminatio, 291

runes, 60, 68, 119, 172, 285, 293, 294, 295

Ruthwell cross, 287; site, 294, 295–6; comparison with Bewcastle, 294; comparison with Franks casket, 296; runes and *The Dream of the Rood*, 294, 295; links to Marian feasts, 295; and eucharist, 294, 295

Rydderch ap Tudwal, ruler of Dumbarton, 156

Saebbi, joint ruler of East Saxons, 230

Saeberht, king of East Saxons, 182; burial at Prittlewell, 183; his pagan sons, 188–9

St Albans (Verulamium), 6–9, 82, 84; temples, 8; churches, 7, 8, 41; Oysterfield Hill, 8; river Ver, 7; British enclave, 10

St Andrews (Kinrimonth), monastery, 161; sarcophagus, 279–80

St David's (Mynyw), 92

St Helens, Scilly Isles, 38

St Keverne, Cornwall, 101

St Kew, previously Landocco, 94, 101

St Martin, Canterbury, 39, 108, 167, 170; porticus to St Peter and Paul monastery, Canterbury, 182

St Neot, Cornwall, 101

St Pancras, Canterbury, 39

St Paul in the Bail, Lincoln, 40

St Tecla, Milan, 40

Sadawrn *see* Saturninus

Salyf ap Cynan, 93

Samson, Ross, 119

Samson, St, 287; monastic founder, 94; evangelist in Cornwall, 94–5; at Fowey, implored to stay as bishop, 96; bishop of Dol, Brittany, 95; compared to St Aurelian, 95–6; Life, 93, 95, 96

I Samuel, 280

Sanday, Orkney, 118

Sandwich, 178

Sant, king of Ceredigion, 92

San Vitale, Ravenna, 172

Saracens, 272

Satan, 60, 142

Saturninus (Sadawrn), 90–1

Saturus, 5

Saul, 131, 212

Saulos, inscription, 187

Saxneat, 64

Saxon, generic term for Germanic invaders, 48, 53; use by Constantius, 47–8, in Gallic Chronicle, 52; use by Bede, 55; use by Gildas, 54, 74; West Saxon dialect, 172; origins of Wine, 218

Scandinavia, 53, 64, 124, 187

Scilly Isles, 38

Scotland, 39, 47, 81, 88, 104, 108–9, 111, 119, 121, 123, 133, 155, 157, 160–2, 187, 284, 285

Scots, Scotti, 55; assault of, with Attacotti, 48, 50; breakdown of trade agreement, 50; God's punishment, 54; missionary work by, and Pictish stones, 119; effects of Degasatan, 132; Patrick's converts, 145; conquest of Picts, 158, 282; defeat of Edwin, 199; *see* Irish, Dál Riata

Scripture, 118; in Roman Britain: destruction of, by Diocletian, 5, representation on Hinton St Mary mosaic, 17, 19, Christian artefacts, 28, at Traprain Law, 42; in Ireland: Patrick's conversion, 135–6, 140, use of, 142–7; and Columba's journey to Iona, 150, 156; skill in understanding of, 153–5; use of Psalm 45, 157; in Pictland, study of, at Portmahomack, 115; representation, on monuments along Tarbat peninsula, 115–16, on memorial stones, 277–8, 280; in British Church, Gildas's use of Old Testament, 56, 73–5; and Vetus Latina, 284; derivation of early British in *Historia Brittonum*, 282; use of biblical numbers, 283; in Roman mission: stimulus of Second Coming in

Gregory's mind, 166, 176; role of
Scriptural proficiency, 168, 237;
relevance of Old Testament laws, 175;
Parker Gospels as missionary aid,
174–5; in Anglo-Saxon England: Aidan
and study of, 204, Caedmon, poetry and
teaching, 205, assimilation of Woden,
64, problems of interpretation in
debates on Easter, 224, 227, 228,
representation on Franks casket, 291,
294, inspiration from Moses's tabernacle
at Ripon, 241, study and Antiochene
exegesis, 270–3, 275, Bede's
commentaries on, and Ezra, and Greek
New Testament, 296, complexities of
interpretation and Lindisfarne Gospels,
291, Hebrew Scriptures and Patrick's
letters, 144, and Bede, 296,
interpretation on Bewcastle and
Ruthwell crosses, 294, 295; in
hagiography, parallels and analogies:
Germanus and Joshua, 47, Columba and
Garden of Eden, 152, David and Moses,
93, Wilfrid and Elisha and Elijah, 242,
Moses and Amalekites, 231, Cuthbert
and Tobit, 266, Samson and Elisha, 94,
Arthur and Joshua, 283, 284, Anglo-
Saxons and Children of Israel, 75;
versions: Vetus Latina, 49, 284, *Codex
Grandior*, 291, Septuagint, 270, 272,
Greek MS of Acts, 296, *Codex
Amiatinus*, 287, 292, Greek New
Testament, 270; *see also* Bible, Gospel
Books, New Testament, Old Testament
Sculptor's Cave, Covesea, 116
Ségéne, abbot of Iona, 152–3, 226
Selkirkshire, 109
Selsey, 211, 258
Senacus, 90
Senchus fer nAlban, 111
Senicianus, 22
Septimius Severus, emperor, 9, 47
Septuagint, 270, 272
Servan, St, 162
Severn, river, and Patrick's residence,
    51; post-Roman rulers, 77; and
    St Samson, 94
Severus, companion of St Germanus, 49
Shandwick, 116
Shepton Mallet, 103
Shetland, 118, 121
Shudy Camps, 70
Sidonius Apollinarius, 83

Sigeberht, king of East Anglia, 217; death
    in battle, 218
Sigeberht, Merovingian king, 165
Sigeberht the Good, king of East Saxons:
    baptism, 215, 233; supports Cedd, 217
Sigfrid, 256
Sighere, joint ruler of East Saxons, 193, 230
Silchester, 13; font, 25; supposed basilica,
    40, 41; Vyne ring at, 21
Silvanus, 35
Simeon of Durham, 114
Simon Magus, 229
Sixtus, St, British, 11, 176
Sixtus II, pope and martyr, 11, 176
Skye, 119, 157,159, 162, 163
Sleaford, 68
Slonk Hill, 193
Smith, Ian, 107
Smyrna, 5
Snape, 187
Soham, 63, 71
Sol Invictus, 16
Solway Firth, 104, 106, 110, 127
Solway-Tyne, 2
Somerset, 30, 38, 77, 81, 100
Southampton, 57
South Cadbury, 102
Southend, 183
South Shields, 39, 106
South Uist, 162
Spain, 9, 10, and Visigoths, 59; veneration
    of saints, 84; epitaphs, 86
Spong Hill, cremation cemetery, 65
stafolus, 198
Stancliffe, Clare, 297
Stephen of Alexandria, 273
Stephen of Ripon, 221, 227, 239, 243, 250,
    254, 255, 257, 258, 259, 288; author of
    Life of Wilfrid a saint suffering a series
    of trials by God, 231, 289, compares him
    to Moses, 231, 241, compares him to
    Elisha and Elijah, 242; conveys caustic
    tone at Whitby, 234; accuses Ecgfrith of
    bribing Theodore, 249; sees death of
    Aelfwine as God's judgement on
    Ecgfrith, 251; believes Theodore
    recommended Wilfrid for Canterbury,
    262
Stirling, 215
Stowting, 69
Stranraer, 127
Strathcarron, battle, 125
Strathclyde, 123, 125

Strathmartine, 118
Stretton-on-the-Fosse, 76
Suffolk, 25, 42, 185
Sulien, bishop of St David's, 92
Sulis, 37
Sul Minerva, 3, 37
Sulpicius Severus see Martin of Tours
Sussex, South Saxons: heathenism, 60;
    heathen sites, 62, 68, 76, 193; Irish
    monastery, 221, 258; Wilfrid: wrecked,
    230, escape, 231; mission, 249, 257–60;
    king see Aethelwalh, queen see Eaba; see
    also Caedualla
Sutherland, 162
Sutton Hoo, 185–8, 288, 290, 298; boar's
    head at, 69
Swale, river, 124, 195
Sweden, 155, 299
Swineshead, 63
Syagrius, bishop of Autun, 170
Syria, cloak from, at Suton Hoo, 187;
    churches of, and Theodore, 275

Tacitus, on first-century paganism, 60, 63
Tailtu, Synod at, 150
Taliesin, Book of, 127, 128
Talorcan, Pictish king, 215
Tara, king of, 150
Tarbat Ness, 115–16
Tarsus, 275
Tees, river, 124, 126, 190
Teilo, St, 285
Tertullian, 4; Adversus Judaeos, 4
Textus Roffensis, 172
Thacker, Alan, 243, 260
Thames, river, 6–7; castration clamp in, 15;
    Upper Thames Valley, 194
Thanet, 129, 163; and Aethelberht, 169
Theodebert II, king of Austrasia, 165
Theoderic, king of Burgundy, 165
Theodora, Byzantine empress, 172
Theodore of Tarsus, archbishop of
    Canterbury, 264, 267, 269; origins, 237;
    at Lateran Council, 149, 237; journey to
    England, 237–8; political experience,
    238; visitation, 238–9; deposes Chad,
    reinstates Wilfrid, 239, 242; appoints to
    bishoprics, 239–40, 247–8; summons
    Council of Hertford, 244–7; breaks
    up Wilfrid's diocese, 248–9, 250,
    see also 245–6; reconciles Ecgfrith and
    Aethelred, 251; summons synod at
    Hatfield, 251–3; claims as 'archbishop . . .

of Britain', 253; fosters cult of Gregory,
    253; in dispute with Wilfrid, 248, 249,
    250, 254; ill health, 259, 262, 270; makes
    peace with Wilfrid, 262–3, 288; school at
    Canterbury, 270–6; and Irish learning,
    271; scholarship, 270–3; Penitential,
    273–4, 301; liturgy, 275, and canon law,
    244–7; Syriac experience and confession,
    274, and vernacular, 275; Bede's
    judgement on, 248, 276
Theodosius, Count, 48
Theodosius, emperor, 13, 35, 45, 48, 166
Theodric, 129, 130
Thetford, 35, 38
Thomas, Charles, 21; baptismal tanks,
    27–8; memorial stones, 86–7, 88, 89–90,
    on Phillack, 101, St Kentigern/Mungo,
    110; Christianity in Roman Britain, 43
Thule, 48
Thunor, 63; mounds, 63, 169; god of
    lightning, 68
Thuringians, 53; see Hesse-Thuringia
Tiberius, emperor, 6
Tintagel, 116; Christian graveyard at, 78,
    98; trade, industry, ceremonial, and
    memories of Rome, 98; residence of
    kings of Dumnonia, 99; the Head at, 98
Tiree, 155, 156
Titus, emperor, 293
Titus Flavius Senilis, 32
Tiw, 62, 63, 69
Tobias, bishop of Rochester, 272, 275
Tobit, 266
Tonsure, 204, 222, 231, 269; Scriptural
    background, 228; Irish and Petrine,
    228–9; and Theodore of Tarsus, 237–8;
    Nechtan, 279; as means of forcing out
    claimants in Pictland, 279
Tours, 252; diocese, 36
Toynbee, Jocelyn, 26
Traprain Law, 42
Tre Fontane, Cilician monastery, 237
Trent, river, 196, 250; battle, 261
Troy, 56, Trojan, 282
Troyes, 46
Trumhere, abbot, 214
túath, túatha, 111, 139, 140
Tubman, Harriet, 51
Tuda, bishop of Northumbria, 228, 229
Turin, 5
Turner, Sam, 101
Tweeddale, 109
Two Rivers, battle, 261

Twrog, St, 285
Tyesmere, 63
Tywyn, 97

Uí Neill, and Dál Riata, 110–11, 157;
    Columba, 149, his prayers for, 150;
    commissioning of *Amra* poem, 153;
    succession of Aldfrith, 262
Uinniau, St, evangelist in south-west
    Scotland, 81,108; lack of evidence for
    Pictish mission, 160; mission to Ireland
    see Finnian of Moville, St, *also* Ninian
Uley, Iron Age shrines, 26; temple to
    Mercury, 26, 32; possible church at, 26,
    40, 41; casket with Scriptural scenes, 28,
    40; infant burials, 29; last years, 34
Ulster, 50, 146; *see Annals of*
Ur, 150
Urien, king of Reghed, attacks both British
    and Anglo-Saxons, 127–30, 132, 214;
    betrayal and death, 129; mourning
    poems, 128; effects of reign, 130, 133;
    see Pen Urien, Rhieinfellt

Valerian, emperor, 5,6,10
values, 272
Vendel graves, 187
Ventidius, 105
Ver, river, 7
Verulamium *see* St Albans
Vetus Latina, 284
Victoricius, 137
Victorinus, 32
Victorius of Aquitaine, 226, 232
Victricius, archbishop of Rouen, 12, 22
Vienne, 255
Vikings, 58, 116, 124, 191, 198, 280, 285
Vindolanda, 39, 106
Virgil, 35, 80; *Aeneid*, 56
Virgno the Briton, abbot of Iona, 154, 156
Visigoths, king of, 59; princess Brunhild
    from, 165; law code of, 172
Vitalian, pope, character, 236,
    correspondence with Oswiu and
    Northumbrian hegemony, 231–2, 236,
    237; fosters cult of Gregory the Great,
    253; searches for archbishop, 237–8; on
    Roman Easter, 244
Vivarium, 291
Viventia, 23
Viventius, British bishop, 105
Vollrath, Hannah, 54
Vortigern, 55, 77, 129–30, 282

Vortimer, 129, 130
Vortipor, 88
Votadini, 42, 124
Votecorigas, 88
Votepor (Voteporix), ogham, Votecorigas,
    memorial stone of, 88; *see also* Vortipor
Vulgate, 50, 148, 270, 272, 283, 284, 291
Vyne ring, 21

Walbrook, 14–15
Wales, 90, 104, 158; tyrants in, 77;
    memorial stones, 85–92, contrasts to
    stones in Scotland, 120, contrasts to
    stones in Cornwall, 96, contrasts to
    stones in North Britain, 103; common
    interest in ancestors, 119; origins of St
    Samson in, 93–4; flow of missionising to
    Cornwall, 96, 103; British Church in,
    282; and Arthur legend, 282–4; Welsh
    term *llan*, 83; development of Welsh
    language, 79, 98, 160; absence from
    memorial stones, 87, *see also* Brittonic;
    transmission of literary sources for
    North British kingdoms, 123; *see also*
    Gododdin, Pen Urien; origin of MSS of
    Synod of Grove of Victory, 71, *Historia
    Brittonum* and Gwynedd, 130; and
    sources for battle of Chester, 131;
    monasteries, 82–3, 92–3, 95, 131, 287;
    origin of Lichfield Gospels, 285; for
    Church in Monmouthshire and
    Glamorgan *see* St Illtud; Welsh speakers
    in Pembrokeshire, 59
Walesby, baptismal tank, 26
Wall *see* Letocetum
Wantsum, river, 169
Ward, Benedicta, 265
Wareham, 96; Christian memorial
    stones, 102–3
Warwickshire, 69, 193
Water of May, 280
Water Newton (Durobrivae), church plate
    at, 22–3; votives, 27, 38
Watling Street, 6
Watton, 273
Watts, Dorothy, 43; on *pedilavium*, 28,
    pagan revival, 35, churches, 41;
    *Christians and Pagans in Roman
    Britain*, 41
wealas, 57
Wear, river, 205, 255
Wenlock, 75
Went, river, 216

weoh, 62

wergild, under Ine, 57, Aethelberht, 173, Theodore, 274

Wessex, West Saxons: bulwark for Oswald against Penda, 208; and Oswine, 213–14; infiltrates Dumnonia, 100, 103; and Hingston Down, 100; and Augustine's meeting with British, 179; and origins of *Anglo-Saxon Chronicle*, 54; dialect, 172; and policy of Wulfhere, 258; laws of: *see* Ine; kings: *see* Alfred, Cenberht, Centwine, Cenwalh, Cynegils, Ine; bishopric of Aldhelm in, 103, vacancy, 230, *and see* Dorchester-on-Thames, Winchester; bishops: *see* Agilbert, Birinus, Leutherius, Wine; *see also* Gewisse

West Africa, 186

Wester Ross, 162

Western Isles, 119, 121

Western Sea, in Patrick's mind, 136, 137, 140, 146

Weyland the Smith, 293

Wheeler, Sir Mortimer and Lady, 35

Whitby, 115, 237; double monastery, 205; training ground, 234, for bishops, 205, 298; and Caedmon, 205; receives Edwin's body, 211; and Wilfrid, 249–50; character of Synod, 244, proceedings, 225–9, implications for Oswiu, 231–3, his skill at, 234, results in Northumbria, 234–5, 299; and choice of Wighard, 236; and Lindisfarne, 264, 289, Cuthbert, 269, Iona, 228, 232, 233, 234, 281; Life of Gregory from, 164–5, 205, 253

White Valley, battle, 127

Whithorn, 88, 106–8, 110; memorial stone at, 104, 106, 109

Wickford, 21

wig, 62

Wighard, candidate archbishop, 233, 236

Wigtonshire, 104, 162

Wilfrid, St, 131, 208, 267, 292, 298, 300; early life, 221–2; influence of Rome, archdeacon Boniface, 222, 241; and Merovingian episcopacy, 222–3, 230, 243, 245; loyalty to St Andrew, 222, 299; contacts with: Eanflaed, 211, 222, Eorcenberht, 222, Biscop, 222, Alchfrith, 222, 223, 224, Agilbert, 223, 224, Aethelthryth, 240, 249, Dagobert II, 242–3, Wulfhere, 248; speaks at Whitby in Roman cause, 225–6, 227, 234;

associates Easter issue with faith and heresy, 227, 232; bishop of Northumbria, 228; consecration at Compiègne, 228, 230; vanquishes pagans on Sussex coast, 230–1; abbot of Ripon, 231; building at York, Ripon, Hexham, 240–2; dedication feast, Ripon, 241–2; reinstatement at York, 239; diocese broken up by Theodore, 248–50; quarrels with Ecgfrith, 249, 255, 257, Iurminburh, 249; imprisonment, 257; appeals to papacy, 253–5; exiles and mission to Frisians, 254, 289, and in Sussex, 257–61; reconciled to Theodore, 262–3; regains bishopric at York, 263; abbot at Lindisfarne, 263–4 and effects, 263, 288–9; quarrels with Aldfrith, 288, and Berhtwald, 289; death and will, 289; miracles, 242, 243; liturgy and Gospel book, 240, 242; personality and asceticism, 223, 242–3, and preaching, 258; Bede's treatment of, 249; Life of *see* Stephen of Ripon

William the Conqueror, 84

William of Malmesbury, 1

Williams, Howard, 65

Williams, Hugh, 13

Willibrord, St, 61; and relic of Oswald, 211; at Ripon, 254; and Egbert the Englishman, 254, 299; Frisian mission, 254; Calendar of, 275

Wiltshire, 40, 71

Winchester: bishopric created by Cenwalh, 218, 230, *and see* Wine; and Theodore, 240; Lankhills cemetery, 41,

Wine, bishop of Winchester, origins, 218; appointment by Cenwalh, 218; consecrates Chad, 229; leaves Winchester, 230; buys bishopric of London, 245; death, 247

Winifred, St, 93

Winwaed, river, battle of, 216, 232

Witham, 24, 37

Woden, 62; and pagan farmers, 63; mounds, 63; in Anglo-Saxon kingship, 64; on Finglesham buckle, 178; Sutton Hoo helmet, 186; and Penda, 208

Worcester, 76, 81; diocese, 75, bishop *see* Oftfor; Worcestershire, 63, 257

Wormald, Patrick, 281

Wroxeter, 76, 83

Wulfhere, king of Mercia 216; revives fortunes of Mercia, 232, 250–1; baptism

and marriage, 216; aids Christianity, 216, among East Saxons, 230; as godfather to Aethelwalh, 258; and Wilfrid, 231, 239, 248; death, 249
Wynfrith *see* Boniface,
Wynfrith, bishop of Lichfield, 240, 245, 248
wyrm figures, on funerary urns, 67

Yeadon, river, 241
Yeavering, 132; name and background, 196; layout, 196, 198; mission and baptisms, 198–9; Yeavering Bell, 196
Y chromosomes, 58
Ymme, second wife of Eadbald, 190
Yr Hen Ogledd (the Old North), 123
Ynyre Gwent, 93
Ynys Byr *see* Caldey Island

York, 192, 251, 268; Romano-British bishop, 11; baptism of Edwin, 195, and burial of head at, 211; *see also* Aelfwine; Edwin's church, 195, restored by Wilfrid, 240; bishopric, archbishopric and Gregory's plans, 179, ignored by Theodore, 253; plea for, by Edwin, 195; and Oswiu's desires, 233; position at sought for Chad, 229, 231; Wilfrid and conflict, 242, 249–50, 253, 254–5, 263, 264; bishops, archbishops *see* Bosa, Egbert, Paulinus, Theodore of Tarsus
Yorke, Barbara, 132
Yorkshire, 71, 106, 124, 190, 192, 220; origins of Deira, 126

Zacchaeus, 28